MW00359220

The Story of Joseph
in Spanish
Golden Age Drama

The Story of Joseph in Spanish Golden Age Drama

Selected, Translated, and Introduced
by Michael McGaha

Lewisburg
Bucknell University Press
London: Associated University Presses

© 1998 by Associated University Presses, Inc.

All rights reserved. Authorization to photocopy items for internal or personal use, or the internal or personal use of specific clients, is granted by the copyright owner, provided that a base fee of $10.00, plus eight cents per page, per copy is paid directly to the Copyright Clearance Center, 222 Rosewood Dr., Danvers, Massachusetts 01923. [0-8387-5380-9/98 $10.00 + 8¢ pp, pc.]

Associated University Presses
440 Forsgate Drive
Cranbury, NJ 08512

Associated University Presses
16 Barter Street
London WC1A 2AH, England

Associated University Presses
P.O. Box 338, Port Credit
Mississauga, Ontario
Canada L5G 4L8

The paper used in this publication meets the requirements
of the American National Standard for Permanence of Paper
for Printed Library Materials Z39.48-1984.

Library of Congress Cataloging-in-Publication Data

The Story of Joseph in Spanish Golden Age drama / selected, translated and introduced by Michael McGaha.
    p.   cm.
    Includes bibliographical references and index.
    Contents: The Josephine tragedy / Miguel de Carvajal — Joseph's wedding / anonymous — The trials of Jacob, or, Sometimes dreams come true / Lope de Vega — Sometimes dreams come true / Pedro Calderón de la Barca — Joseph's scepter / Sor Juana Inés de la Cruz — Harassed but happy / Isaac de Matatia Aboab — Appendix : Speculum historiale / Vincent of Beauvais.
    ISBN 0-8387-5380-9 (alk. paper)
    1. Spanish drama—Classical period, 1500–1700. 2. Joseph (Son of Jacob)—Drama. I. McGaha, Michael D., 1941– .
PQ6221.S76   1998
862'.3080351—dc21   97-36306
                                                                              CIP

PRINTED IN THE UNITED STATES OF AMERICA

To my dear son,
John Mycue McGaha

יְשִׂמְךָ אֱלֹהִים כְּאֶפְרַיִם וְכִמְנַשֶּׁה

Contents

Preface

Few stories in the Hebrew Bible lend themselves as readily to dramatization as that of Joseph and his brothers (Genesis 37–50). The great themes it embodies—sibling rivalry resulting in betrayal, revenge, and ultimate reconciliation; the triumph of honor and chastity over sexual temptation; and the Cinderella-like rise of a man of humble origins to the enviable position of royal favorite in one of the mightiest empires the world has ever known—were among the favorite subjects of Spanish Golden Age playwrights and their audiences. It is therefore not at all surprising that a number of sixteenth- and seventeenth-century Spanish playwrights—like their counterparts in England, Holland, and Germany[1]—turned to that story for inspiration.

In addition to the biblical story, however, Spanish playwrights could draw upon a rich tradition of retellings of the Joseph story penned during the Middle Ages by Jewish, Christian, and Muslim Spaniards. In a previous book, *Coat of Many Cultures: The Story of Joseph in Spanish Literature, 1200–1492,*[2] I have translated and commented on seven of those versions: (1) the translation and commentary written by Rabbi Moses Arragel of Guadalajara in collaboration with the Franciscan Fray Arias de Encina for Don Luis de Guzmán, grand master of the Order of Calatrava, and now known as the *Biblia de Alba* (1422–33); (2) the anonymous Hebrew epic *Sefer ha-Yashar* (Book of heroes), probably written by a Spanish Jew during the second half of the twelfth century; (3) an anonymous Muslim romance called *The Story of Yusuf, Son of Ya'qub,* dating from the late fifteenth or early sixteenth century; two anonymous narrative poems imitating those written by Catholic monks such as Gonzalo de Berceo on the lives of the saints—(4) the Muslim *Ḥadith* of Yusuf (c. 1250–1400) and (5) the Jewish *Poema de Yosef* (c. 1350); (6) the approximately sixty chapters King Alfonso X the Learned of Castile devoted to the story of Joseph in his *General Estoria*

9

(begun 1272); and (7) a Valencian version in poetic prose written by Joan
Roiç de Corella before 1486. Each of these ethnic and religious groups
developed new interpretations of the story dictated by the historical circumstances of a particular time and place, yet each was influenced by the
versions created by the others. Ultimately, this grudging collaboration produced a uniquely "multicultural" version of the story.

The present volume includes six different dramatic versions of the story
written during the century and a half from about 1535 to 1685—that is,
from the earliest attempts at full-length drama to the end of the classical
period, which is usually dated as 1681, the year of Calderón de la Barca's
death. Three of the plays are full-length dramas, while the remaining three
are one-act *autos sacramentales.* Comparison of these six "variations on a
theme" enhances our understanding of the gradual evolution of both the
auto and the *comedia* genres during the Golden Age.

What is perhaps most interesting and surprising about these six plays is
the extremely varied interpretations and emphases given by the authors to
what is in essence a single story.

The earliest Spanish drama on the story of Joseph, Miguel de Carvajal's
Josephine Tragedy, draws heavily on Muslim tradition in its lengthy and
elaborate treatment of the episode of Joseph's temptation by Potiphar's wife,
which the Bible quickly and succinctly recounts in a mere fifteen verses in
Genesis 39. Other passages in the play demonstrate the author's familiarity
with some of the Jewish accretions to the story contained in the *Sefer ha-
Yashar* and the *Poema de Yosef.* All of this material, however, is subordi-
nated to the treatment of Joseph's story as prefiguring the passion of Christ.
Nevertheless, what is most intriguing about the play is the (apparently New
Christian) author's extremely ambivalent attitude toward his Jewish char-
acters.

The anonymous play *Joseph's Wedding* is based principally on Vincent
of Beauvais's thirteenth-century Latin reworking of the anonymous first-
century Greek (Jewish) romance *Joseph and Aseneth.* However, the author
seems to have known Carvajal's *Josephine Tragedy* as well, since he adopts
the name Zenobia that Carvajal had given to Potiphar's wife. *Joseph's Wedding* is a sort of "morality play" meant to inculcate the virtues incumbent
upon a good wife.

By the time Lope de Vega wrote his *Trials of Jacob* (1620–30), Carvajal's
Josephine Tragedy, which had been condemned by the Inquisition in 1559,
seems to have been forgotten in Spain, though it continued to circulate in
Sephardic Jewish communities elsewhere. Lope's play follows the biblical
story fairly closely. What is unique about this play is that it presents the
whole story from the viewpoint of Joseph's aged father Jacob, as the title

suggests. Interestingly, a bizarre bit of Jewish folklore finds its way into Lope's play, and will reappear thereafter in all the later Spanish dramatic versions. This is the fifth-century Midrash Genesis Rabbah's commentary on Gen. 42:1 ("And Jacob saw that there was food in Egypt . . ."). Troubled by the fact that the biblical text could not literally have been accurate (if Jacob was in Canaan, how could he have *seen* that there was food in Egypt?), the midrash stated "that there was a river that went from Egypt to Canaan, and Joseph, sensing that his brothers and father were looking for bread, sent straw with ears of grain, and they reached Canaan. When Jacob saw them, he said: 'By this I see that there is food in Egypt,' and that is why the text said: 'Jacob saw that there was food in Egypt.'"[3]

Calderón's *auto* entitled *Sometimes Dreams Come True* may have been partly inspired by *Joseph's Wedding*, since it too emphasizes Joseph's love for Asenath (now identified with the allegorical character Chastity) and the circumstances surrounding their marriage. A more direct source of inspiration, however, was Antonio Mira de Amescua's *Happiest Captivity, and Joseph's Dreams (El más feliz cautiverio, y los sueños de Josef)*, a play I have chosen not to include in this anthology because of its poor quality. It appears to have been hastily dashed off for a low-budget performance, and its main claim to fame is the fact that it served as Calderón's principal model for his far superior *auto*. Calderón took the title of his play from the subtitle of Lope's *The Trials of Jacob*. *Sometimes Dreams Come True* is the single most successful allegorical treatment of the story in Spanish drama. Calderón manages to relate practically every event in the life of Joseph to the life of Christ and to the institution of the Eucharist.

Calderón's *auto* in turn served as the major inspiration for the Mexican nun Sor Juana Inés de la Cruz's *auto* entitled *Joseph's Scepter*. Sor Juana's interpretation of the story is at times wildly far-fetched: among other things, she sees it as foreshadowing the conversion of the Mexican Indians to Catholicism. The most remarkable thing about her *auto* is that she presents the story from the viewpoint of Lucifer. The fact that the play consists for the most part of dialogue between Lucifer and his minions, rather than action, undermines its dramatic effectiveness but does make for interesting reading.

The final play in the volume, *Harassed But Happy*, by the Sephardic playwright Isaac Aboab of Amsterdam, while hardly a dramatic masterpiece, shows great originality in its treatment of the plot and is the only version in Spanish to present the story of Joseph principally in a comic vein. Aboab's major source of inspiration was Carvajal's *Tragedia Josephina*, so with this last play we come full circle. Aboab's play has never before been published.

I have translated all of these plays not only for silent reading but also for potential performance, constantly bearing in mind the actor's need for a text that can be easily and clearly pronounced and the audience's need for a text that can be readily followed when heard.

Acknowledgments

I am very grateful to Professor David M. Gitlitz, who has given me much encouragement and moral support as I worked on this project, has read the entire manuscript with great care, and has given me several excellent suggestions for its improvement. Professor Thomas A. O'Connor has also given me many helpful comments. My colleague and friend Dr. María Donapetry has often assisted me in translating very difficult passages from the Spanish. Jaime Fernández, S.J., helped me decipher a garbled Latin quotation in Carvajal's *Tragedia Josephina*. I owe a particular debt of gratitude to Wyatt Benner, my copyeditor at Associated University Presses, for remedying many stylistic infelicities in my original text.

Dr. Kenneth Brown called my attention to Aboab's play on the life of Joseph and has given me much information about Aboab; Professor Harm den Boer has sent me additional materials on Aboab. Dr. Isaac Benabu of the Hebrew University of Jerusalem helped me obtain a microfilm of Aboab's play. Dr. A. Rosenberg of the Ets Haim Library in Amsterdam kindly gave me permission to use the manuscript of the play. Professors Vern Williamsen and F. William Forbes have provided me information about Antonio Mira de Amescua's play *El más feliz cautiverio y los sueños de Josef.*

My wife Agnes has lovingly encouraged me throughout my work on this book. Finally, the students who have participated in three seminars on the subject of this book that I have taught at Pomona College have given me many new and valuable insights into these texts. Some of them are acknowledged by name in the following pages.

The Story of Joseph
in Spanish
Golden Age Drama

1

Miguel de Carvajal:
The Josephine Tragedy

In 1264 Pope Urban IV ordered that throughout the Catholic world the first Thursday after Trinity Sunday[1] be celebrated as the Feast of Corpus Christi in honor of the Real Presence of Christ in the Eucharist. Processions in which the Host was borne through the streets for the adoration of the faithful eventually became the most prominent feature of that holiday (such processions are documented in Spain as early as 1418), and by the mid-fifteenth century it had become customary to perform short religious skits or plays as part of the celebrations. By the 1490s floats (known as *carros* or "carts") were being used both in the processions and as stages for performance of the plays.[2] During the sixteenth century, as such performances were increasingly displaced by secular Renaissance spectacles in other countries in Western Europe, they became ever more popular and important in Spain, where they developed from mere pageants, with little or no dialogue, into a distinct dramatic genre known as the *auto sacramental* (sacramental act). As time went on, performance of the *autos* came to be funded by the municipal corporations, and the towns and cities in Spain engaged in heated rivalry to attract the best theater companies and stage the most elaborate plays.

Miguel de Carvajal's *Josephine Tragedy (Tragedia Josephina)* belongs to a transitional period before the *auto* had become standardized as a one-act allegorical play. The *Josephine Tragedy* was first performed on Corpus Christi day in Plasencia, a small cathedral town in the region of southwestern Spain near the Portuguese border known as Extremadura, sometime in the 1530s. Theater was then just beginning to emerge as a form of popular entertainment in Spain and was still dominated by the church. The best models of drama available for the intellectuals who were beginning to write theater were the Latin comedies of Plautus and Terence and the tragedies of Seneca. Naturally, since Carvajal's intention was to write a serious play, he followed the example of Seneca. In fact the use of the word *Tragedy* in the title probably meant only that this was to be a full-length (i.e., five-act) play on a serious theme. Dramatic terminology in Spanish was still in its infancy; hence Carvajal uses the word *parte* to designate what would later be known as an act (Spanish, *acto* or *jornada,* the latter term reflecting the notion that the events portrayed in an act should be limited to the time frame of a "day" or twenty-four hours), and *acto* for what we would call a scene. Following the example of Seneca, Carvajal wrote his play in five acts, each preceded by a prologue and concluding with a Chorus that summed up the act's moral.

The distribution of the plot material in the play is very uneven, as might be expected of an amateur playwright and one who was writing in the absence of a dramatic tradition. Carvajal begins the play in a very leisurely way, dwelling at length on the scenes when Joseph's brothers plot to do him harm, and devoting a great deal of space to Jacob's protracted lament over his son. Part 1 is approximately twice the length of part 2, and four times the length of parts 3 and 5. Part 2 contains the episode with Potiphar's wife and Joseph's interpretation of the dreams of the Cupbearer and Baker in jail. As the prologue notes, the play's tone changes from tragic to comic in part 3—the axis and center of the play—which portrays Joseph's interpretation of Pharaoh's dreams and his apotheosis as viceroy. At this point Carvajal seems to have become aware that the play was getting much too long, and the action thereafter proceeds at a much more rapid pace. The final part, in particular, is almost ridiculously short. Jacob receives the news that Joseph is alive, sets out for Egypt, arrives there almost immediately, has his interview with Pharaoh, and dies. Nothing is said about Joseph's administration of Egypt during the years of famine or about his marriage, though there is a very brief reference to his two sons.

The *Josephine Tragedy* appears to have been very popular; four editions (1535, 1540, 1545, and 1546) of it were published in rapid succession. However, the Inquisition's condemnation of the play in the Valdés *Index* of 1559 virtually doomed both it and its author to oblivion. Only a single copy of the play, in the edition published in Seville in 1545, is known to have survived in Spain, in a private collection. The play was rediscovered in 1852, and the first modern edition was published in Spain in 1870. I have based my translation on Joseph Gillet's critical edition of 1932.[3] Miguel Romera Navarro considered the *Josephine Tragedy* "the best religious play of the sixteenth century."[4] Melveena McKendrick has recently described it as "distinguished," noting that it is "unique in that it is a five-act play on a

religious theme written for public performance and shows all the uncon-
cern for unity of time and place of the popular religious drama."[5] In the
introduction to his edition of the play, Gillet has claimed for it the merit of
introducing—in the person of Putiphar's[6] wife Zenobia[7]—the first well-
developed female character in Spanish literature after *Celestina*. "Passion,"
Gillet writes, "had already spoken in the *Celestina,* the passion of young
love, still almost inarticulate; but nowhere in modern Europe had it risen to
such fullness of power and to such nearly tragic dignity" (p. lvi).

In an important article published in 1972, David Gitlitz argued that the
entire play is an allegory of Christ's passion. Gitlitz states that "it is possible that Carvajal was one of those *conversos* who, energetically rejecting
their past, adopted the anti-Semitism of the old-Christians, for the *Tragedia
Josephina* on the whole presents the Jews unfavorably. Nevertheless, it is
evident that whether or not Carvajal was a *converso,* his drama deliberately
concerns itself with the *converso* world through constant linguistic and allegorical references. Aside from its considerable merit and its recognized
place in literary history, the *Tragedia Josephina* deserves consideration as
an example of the studied juxtaposition of several worlds: the characters
are at once Joseph and his brothers, Jesus and the Jews responsible for his
crucifixion, and the old- and new-Christians of the world of Carvajal."[8]

Thus far, no one has been able to produce decisive proof that Carvajal
was in fact a *converso*. There is, however, considerable circumstantial evidence. Plasencia, his hometown, had been an important center of Jewish
life in Spain up to the time of the expulsion. In the spring of 1483, when the
illustrious Isaac Abravanel and his family fled Portugal to escape persecution at the hands of King João II, the first place they went was Plasencia.[9]
Don Isaac went on to become a close advisor and financier to Ferdinand
and Isabella, but his wealthy and influential nephews, Jacob and Joseph—
Joseph was also his son-in-law—settled in Plasencia, remaining there until
the expulsion. Joseph Abravanel served for a time as Queen Isabella's personal business agent.[10] One can't help wondering whether Miguel de
Carvajal was related to Luis Carvajal, who would later be governor of Nuevo
León, Mexico, and whose nephew, known as Luis Carvajal the younger,
would be burned at the stake for Judaizing on 8 December 1596, together
with his mother and three of his sisters.[11] David Gitlitz has discovered that
an investigation carried out by the Inquisition of Toledo in 1636 revealed
that most of the ancestors of a certain Ana María de Almaraz, a native of
Plasencia, were indeed *conversos*. Gitlitz has argued that it is very likely
that Almaraz's great-grandparents, Juan de Valencia and Juana Núñez de
Almaraz, were also ancestors of Miguel de Carvajal's mother, Isabel de
Almaraz, and of his wife, Teresa Núñez de Almaraz.[12] Additionally, the

Josephine Tragedy contains considerable material based on traditional Jewish folklore and perhaps drawn from sources such as the *Sefer ha-Yashar* and the *Poema de Yosef*.[13] It seems unlikely that an Old Christian would have been familiar with that material.

If Carvajal was indeed a *converso*, the choice of the story of Joseph from the Hebrew Bible as the theme for his Corpus Christi play must have been rather daring, especially in the 1530s. That decade, during which the Inquisition drastically intensified its scrutiny of all intellectual activity in the Peninsula, was a very somber time for humanists like Carvajal. In December 1533, Rodrigo Manrique, son of the inquisitor general, wrote to Luis Vives from Paris: "You are quite right: our homeland is a land of envy and pride, and you might well add: of barbarism. In fact it is constantly becoming more obvious that no one can cultivate literature in even a mediocre way in Spain without immediately being accused of a multitude of heresies, errors, and Jewish perversions."[14]

In the play's dedication, Carvajal reveals an acute awareness of the danger to which he was exposing himself by publishing this work. He expresses the hope that the patronage of the marquis of Astorga will protect him from the attacks of the ignorant or the "dangerous waves and battering of slanderers." His defense of the intellectual life, and of the value of literature, in his profoundly anti-intellectual society is especially poignant. He is well aware that it would be more prudent simply to keep his mouth shut and live a life of self-indulgence, like so many of his contemporaries, but such a course of action seems to him unworthy of a human being. He feels compelled to point out that his love of learning is not motivated by "idle curiosity," but that the cultivation of literature and the fine arts truly can contribute to the betterment of humanity. The prologue to part 1 sadly reveals Carvajal's sense that he was preaching in the wilderness—"even a town square full of people," he points out—"can sometimes be a wilderness," or casting his pearls before swine. He begins with the first line of a lofty introduction in Latin, but quickly realizes that writing it is pointless, since no one will understand it anyway. He then proceeds to mock his audience with a series of gratuitously obscene insults in German, Italian, and French. He concludes the prologue by averring that his purpose is "not to harm anyone but rather to please all, at least the wise and the good," but bitterly adds that "since these are about as numerous as white crows, it's more likely that we've sown our seed on sand and won't please anybody. . . ."

What literary analogue could better illustrate the harm done by envy to the Spanish Jews and their descendants, the *conversos*, than the story of Joseph and his brothers? Envy personified is the first character to speak in the *Josephine Tragedy* as she staggers onstage, dazzled by the virtue and prosperity of Jacob and his sons: "There's some great virtue out there, or something wonderful is happening to people. I've looked all around, but the only one I see prospering is Jacob." She immediately decides to turn Jacob's sons against each other: "[T]hey'll gnaw at each other till they finally do something so bad that Abraham's great house will be utterly destroyed." As is well known, Christians have interpreted the suffering of Jews throughout the ages as divine punishment for their rejection and crucifixion of Jesus. Envy's words here suggest that the Jewish "original sin," so to speak, was instead the crime of selling Joseph into slavery. Perhaps when he wrote these words, Carvajal had in mind the moving composition known as *'Eleh 'ezkerah* (These things I will remember) recited as part of the Yom Kippur liturgy. *'Eleh 'ezkerah* recounts how the Roman Emperor Hadrian, "searching our Torah for an excuse, yea, for a sword to slay us, found this law among our ordinances: 'And he that steals a man, and sells him, shall surely be put to death.' Elated, he summoned ten great sages of our Torah and put to them this question: 'What is the law if a man is found stealing his brother, one of the children of Israel, and makes merchandise of him and sells him?' And the sages instantly replied: 'That thief shall die.' And the despot said, 'They are your ancestors who sold their brother Joseph to the Ishmaelites. If they were living, I would pronounce sentence against them as you have spoken, but now you must bear your fathers' sin.'"[15] Envy's reference to Jacob's sons gnawing at each other probably refers to the fierce persecutions of the Jews of Spain by their former brethren who had converted to Christianity.

Surely the mere act of introducing Jewish characters onstage must have been controversial in the Spain of the 1530s. It appears that the character called Faraute who spoke the prologue wore a distinctively Jewish costume, and he refers to the uproar that that caused among the audience in the following words: "I think you know me, for it looks like some of you are thrilled, while others are upset. What could the reason be? Ha, ha, ha! Okay, I get it. Just listen, ladies and gentlemen, what an intelligent group! A lot of people are griping because Jews and their costumes always seem to butt into these affairs. And I have to admit they have a point, because all those black gabardines couldn't possibly be healthy in this summer heat. Nevertheless, I can't help suspecting that it takes one to know one." As Gillet explains, the original Spanish contains a "clumsy pun on *capirotadas* = *Jews with 'capirotes'* . . . and *capirotada* = *aderezo hecho con hierbas, huevos, ajos, y otros adherentes* ('condiment made with herbs, eggs, garlic, and other ingredients')."[16] However, as David Gitlitz has rightly observed, "he does not attempt to show the relation between the proverb about garlic[17] and the pun. It would seem that Faraute is saying that many people in the audience know about these Jewish hats . . . because they have personal experience in the matter of Jewish hats. . . . It is understandable how a *converso* audience might be 'alborotado' ('upset') watching an Old Testament play."[18] One of my students, Martin Isaac, has astutely commented that this sort of taunting of the *conversos* in the audience, which occurs in the prologues to parts 2, 4, and 5, was intended to stimulate the audience to hate the play, and thereby love themselves.

I cannot agree with Gitlitz that the *Josephine Tragedy* "on the whole presents Jews unfavorably." In my opinion quite the contrary is the case. It is certainly true that the play contains anti-Semitic slurs. Putiphar's lusty wife, when falsely accusing Joseph of rape, refers to him as a "Jewboy" and tells her husband that this is just the sort of behavior one might expect from a "circumcised little Jew . . . with that sort of background," but the audience of course knows that she is lying, and that the circumcised Jew Joseph is in fact a paragon of chastity. Likewise, we can hardly fail to sense the author's pride in his Jewish heritage when Joseph, unjustly imprisoned, tells Pharaoh's cupbearer: "Thank God, I am a Hebrew from Canaan, a direct descendant of Abraham and an enemy of paganism."

Perhaps the most memorable scene in the play is Jacob's long lament over the presumed death of his son Joseph. In the depths of its despair, unrelieved by any reference to a possible afterlife, the *planctus Jacob* recalls Pleberio's famous lament after the suicide of Melibea at the end of *La Celestina*. Both are poignant expressions of the *converso*'s anguish over the cruelty and meaninglessness of life in a society where merit counts for nothing, where one is doomed at birth to suffer for circumstances over which one had no control.

The play concludes with Jacob's holy death, and after paying lip service to the eternal reward stored up for the righteous, the Chorus advises: "As long as we are able, let's follow Jacob's holy footsteps, for even the most admired lives lead to the coffin." As if the admonition to follow Jacob's "holy footsteps" were not sufficiently shocking to a *converso* audience in the Plasencia of the 1530s, the Chorus adds a very unchristian statement of preference for life here on earth—"Death is most precious to the good and the saintly, and it fills the wicked with fear and torment. Still, I wish I could live forever to serve God, for life is truly glorious!"—only to conclude with the singing (significantly, *in Latin*) of the following paraphrase of Ps. 115:17–18: "Non mortui laudabunt te domine, sed nos qui vivimus in aeternam" [The dead do not praise you, O Lord, but we, the living, {will praise you} forever], embodying the Jewish concept that speculation about the afterlife is fruitless and that God is better served by living righteously here and now so as to transform the world into an earthly paradise.

It is hardly surprising that the Inquisition condemned the *Josephine Tragedy* and many other early Spanish plays of its ilk.[19] The chilling influence of such condemnations ensured that the prolific dramatic literature that developed in Spain later in that century, and in the following one, would avoid such dangerous themes and be much more conformist. The *Josephine Tragedy* is therefore a window to a lost world. It gives us a rare opportunity to hear a different voice, the voice of a Spanish theater that might have been—a theater teaching lessons of justice and tolerance for diversity— that would soon be forever silenced.

The original text of the *Josephine Tragedy* is written in a verse form known as *redondilla doble*—octosyllabic verses rhyming *abba; acca*. The first four acts end with *villancicos* of varying construction. The play's verse closely approximates the rhythm of normal Spanish prose; indeed, it is often indistinguishable from prose. Since it seemed to me impossible to achieve such naturalness in English verse, I have translated the play in prose, with the exceptions of Envy's invocation (which is sung) and the *villancicos*. The original text contains hardly any stage directions. I have added such directions as seemed useful, enclosing them in square brackets.

Dedication
To the Illustrious Don Alvar Pérez Osorio, Marquis of Astorga

Some friends of mine have often nagged me, illustrious sir, to collect some or most of my works and to publish them in a volume. I suspected that they felt sorry for the poor dears, who had been lured away from their father's house and were not behaving in the way they had been brought up; they were running the risk that daughters usually face in the prime of their youth. However, I thought that job would be about like trying to gather up the leaves the Sibyl tossed to the wind when she was swept up and carried away by the divine madness as she answered questions in the temple of a hundred doors.[20] Nevertheless, several considerations have now persuaded me to undertake the present task: first of all, the importance of honoring you in this way; secondly, the usefulness and benefit it would offer our kingdoms; and, finally, the realization that a man is not born for himself alone, but in part for himself, in part for his family, in part for his friends, and in part for his homeland.

After studying philosophy, I turned to the Sacred Scriptures and took in

hand the story of Joseph, son of Jacob, king of Canaan. I found it a most
excellent and precious model, and of the loftiest doctrine to be found anywhere. Having given this quite a bit of thought, I decided that it would be
very worthwhile to translate it into our vulgar Castilian tongue, and rework
it in a style that would be pleasing to all—so that the simple might enjoy
the story's surpassing sweetness, and the learned might raise their intellects to contemplate and understand it better. I was reassured by the knowledge that even if the new translation were somewhat flawed (as is usually
the case), your sponsorship would make it appear better than it was; so that
the ignorant would refrain from gnawing on it with their canine teeth, and
the learned would thank God that I had chosen so sure a patron as yourself.
Hence, I feel so sheltered from the dangerous waves and battering of slanderers that, with so strong a rudder as yourself, I think it will make it safely
to port. This is so true that I'm even inspired to attempt higher things (if
higher things there be). Knowing your lordship's eloquence and humanity,
magnanimity and magnificence—as well as all the other virtues pertaining
to the art of chivalry—is what emboldens me to brave such high seas and
deep gulfs, without being dashed upon Scylla or Charybis.[21]

Since my main purpose, illustrious sir, has been to honor you, and not
to go through life in silence like the beasts whom nature has made inclined
to obey the sensuality and appetite of their belly,[22] I wanted to leave behind
something crafted by these hands, in the hope that with your protection and
patronage, I need not be ashamed to publish it—not that I expect or deserve to win fame or glory thereby, but, as I said, to distinguish myself from
the brute beasts. For this reason my heart is often unable to hold back its
tears when I see so many brilliant minds well suited to produce such sweet
and excellent fruits that would greatly benefit human life; but—woe is me!—
they are mired in so many different sorts of vice that they are not mindful
of literature, nor (what is worse) of God and His saints. Oh, happy ages
when men so hated to waste time that even emperors, after managing and
governing their republics, let no day or night go by without writing speeches,
or poetry, or other intellectually lofty things, by means of which they made
up for many of their vices, as is shown by Julius Caesar, Nero, Germanicus,
Marcus Aurelius, and the host of others whom Gaius Suetonius[23] tells us
about! In those days not only did people not waste good minds or books,
they even dug up those that were buried in obscurity!

Mind you, I'm not saying this to praise idle curiosity and vain and excessive diligence. For it won't do you much good to burn the midnight oil
reading the divine Plato's *Republic* if the republic of your own soul is divided and rebellious and used to dirty, ugly thoughts. It won't do you much
good to read the philosopher Plutarch's *Lives* if you waste your time criti-

cizing others' lives, while your own is incorrigible and out of control. It won't do you much good to ransack the books of the Wisdom of Solomon if you lack the wisdom to control yourself and fend off vice, for it is written that "knowledge will not enter the malevolent soul."[24] It won't do you much good to read the books *De anima* if you have no soul, nor those of the *City of God* unless you have the desire and will to dwell there. How little good it will do you to plow through the Plinys and Senecas, nor to ransack the eloquence of orators, the truth of historians, the sweetness and profundity of theologians, the consolation of physicians, the security of the imperial laws—if all the while enormous, insatiable vices are firmly lodged in your soul, and it is incapable of receiving instruction or good doctrine!

However, all of this *will* do you good if you have good desires and increase them, and make them loftier and purer. Then if you turn to literature, you will learn how to deal with your friends and with prosperous or adverse fortune. Therefore, whenever I think about how much we owe those who first invented writing—whether, illustrious sir, it was the sons of Adam, as Josephus recounts in the first book of the *Antiquities of the Jews*, where he tells how, after they had found the secret of heavenly things, in order that they might pass such excellent information on to later generations, they made two columns such as the Greeks call obelisks, one of brick and the other of stone, which Josephus says endured in Syria down to his time, and on them wrote the secrets they had attained; or it was the Egyptians, for they take credit for being the first who invented it; or the Assyrians, for they too swear and affirm that it first appeared among them—I hold and affirm that it is a debt we can never repay. For by dedicating oneself to literature and the fine arts, the soul receives salvation, and the body authority, and life receives chastity and the lovely adornment of fame, and honor, and excellent virtues.

I shall not be more verbose nor bothersome to Your Lordship, for you have as little need of my praise as my work has great need of your favor. May Our Lord increase your life as Your Lordship deserves and we all desire. Vale.

PROLOGUE AND ARGUMENT[25]

Quanquan ad sacre solemnitatis ornamentum, [26]*etc.*

What pretty poppycock! Pray excuse me; I'd really forgotten that you're all such scholars that not one of you knows Latin. Too bad! I guess I'll just have to stick to plain English, but I wouldn't want you to think I'm not a linguist. You'd prefer German? All right then: "Das dich Gotts Leyden schend' Stinkert danke, gut lieber Herr schlief ich Landsmann."[27] Or, as the Italian bandits say: "Pota di Santa Nulla, farò dirò [chec]ché bisogna fin[o] al canchero che ti venga il mala della cantina ancora."[28] And when it comes to drinking, there's nobody like the French: "Par le saint Dieu, allez-vous en, mon ami, baille-ça du bon vin."[29] There's no need to render for you the gurgling of Burgundy and Champagne,[30] for that's a language we all understand well enough.

Anyhow, ladies and gentlemen, I am the Prologist, and for the moment represent the author who usually organizes the performance of scenes from sacred history for you here in this town. I think you know me, for it looks like some of you are thrilled, while others are upset. What could the reason be? Ha, ha, ha! Okay, I get it. Just listen, ladies and gentlemen, what an intelligent group! A lot of people are griping because Jews and their costumes always seem to butt into these affairs. And I have to admit they have a point, because all those black gabardines couldn't possibly be healthy in this summer heat. Nevertheless, I can't help suspecting that it takes one to know one!

Be that as it may, the author has really knocked himself out to please you this time. He ransacked everything from *Amadís de Gaula*[31] to the *Quest for the Holy Grail*[32] to find some harmless subject for today's play, but he found nothing there but horrible killings, weapons, camps, uprisings, fights, blows, and so many people run through with swords that it gives me the runs just to think about it! So for today's play the author has gone back to his forte, and for this holy feast of Corpus Christi has taken from sacred history a tragedy called *Josephine.*

The subject is how ten brothers, sons of Jacob, king of Canaan, out of envy want to kill their brother Joseph, but are persuaded by their brother Reuben to cast him into a well instead, and at last they sell him to the Egyptians. His father at length laments him as dead, and that's where part 1 ends. I'll be seeing you again before part 2. It is a story that allegorically contains the reason for today's holy feast, so listen to it attentively and keep quiet, for the author's purpose is to adorn the holy feast and not to harm anyone but rather to please all, at least the wise and good. But since those are about as numerous as white crows, it's more likely that we've sown our seed on sand and won't please anybody, for even a town square full of people can sometimes be a wilderness. I hope that's not the case with you today. In any case, may you, my lord, accept our service.

End of the Prologue.

PART 1

Characters.

Envy	Asher	Reuben	Putiphar
Judah	Zebulun	Jacob	Zenobia
Levi	Naphtali	Joseph	Benjamin
Dan	Gad	Shepherd	Chorus
Simeon	Issachar	Merchants	

ACT 1

[Envy comes out in front of the curtain as if emerging from darkness, shielding her eyes against the sunlight. Before she begins speaking she removes from her mouth a human heart she has been gnawing on. She is an ugly old woman, livid in color, with snakes instead of hair.][33]

ENVY. This unusual brightness is dazzling me, but I think there must be some other reason for my blindness. There's some great virtue out there, or something wonderful is happening to people. I've looked all around, but the only one I see prospering is Jacob. How happy Jacob is! What a big shot in Canaan! So many fine sons, and he never even thinks about me. Well, I'll just try my hand at spreading a little envy among those brothers, and if I don't mess up, his joy will soon go up in smoke!

Jacob is holy, his sons are young, and Joseph is virtuous, so they think nothing bad can happen to them. But I mainly attack the good, and my wickedness is aimed at those who are happiest. Little do these Jews know about such things. You can see by their smugness that they haven't had to deal with me yet. But I'll stir them up with my rage! That will teach them a thing or two.

Now I'll just go over there where they're all together in their hut, and I'll sow such discord that they'll die of envy, and they'll gnaw at each other till they finally do something so bad that Abraham's great house will be utterly destroyed.

She invokes [Lucifer] by singing:

Oh Lucifer, you spawned me
in Pride's polluted womb:

Come, parents, help me doom
these Jews. Do not disown me!
Come here with haste unholy.
I'll whisper in their ears
and fill them with such fears,
they'll do my bidding boldly.

They think that they're secure,
but today begin their woes;
just now from hell arose
four Furies all impure:
of pleasures ever fewer,
of pain a heavy dose.
Damn all the prosperous,
their joy we will soon cure!

To hell I must return,
but I'll leave my helpers here.
This place I sorely fear;
my friends are those who burn.
These idiots will soon learn
that their goodness can't defend
those whom Envy would offend,
for their happiness I spurn!

*[Exit Envy. The curtain rises. Judah, Levi, Dan, Simeon, Asher, Zebulun,
Naphtali, Simeon, Gad, Issachar, and Reuben are on stage. The scene is
a field where they are watching over their sheep.]*

JUDAH. Brothers, I think it must be noon, for the sun is at its highest point in
   the sky. Since we're all here together, let's sit down and eat, for we've
   been working hard.
LEVI. Well said, Judah. Brothers, there's nothing to stop us, for all the sheep
   are grazing very safely on these plains. Come on, Dan, hurry up!
DAN. Yes indeed, let's rest a while, for that will refresh us.
SIMEON. That's a very good idea. Let's have a good, big lunch. And since it
   was God's[34] will to bring us all together here, I want to talk to you about
   something that's been bothering me. It torments me more than hunger,
   and if we don't do something about it, we'll all look like fools. I hope to
   God I'm wrong, but you'll soon see if this isn't very bad news for us.
ASHER. Let's hear our brother out. I'm sure his advice will do us good, for

he's a very prudent and wise man; and if he's worried about something, there's bound to be a good reason.

ZEBULUN. Shh! My brothers, pay attention, and don't interrupt. Let's hear what Simeon has to say, because it's obvious he's upset.

NAPHTALI. It's lunchtime anyway, so we might as well find out what's up.

SIMEON. Since you're all in agreement, I'll get right to the point. I'd just like to know what you think of our brother Joseph.

JUDAH. Am I ever glad you asked! God bless you for that! That kid is too big for his breeches.

GAD. It's really hurts my feelings that our father pampers Joseph so much and forgets all about the rest of us.

ISSACHAR. Damn it, I can't stand it! It makes me sick to see how he loves Joseph more than us. There's nothing he'd rather do than hang around with Joseph, and every time he opens his mouth, it's "Joseph this," or "Joseph that."

LEVI. It's so unfair that Joseph's the only one he likes. He thinks everything Joseph does is just hunky-dory.

DAN. He gets such a kick out of Joseph's cute little tricks that the time just seems to fly when he's with him.

JUDAH. Yes, he thinks of nothing but Joseph. Joseph is his only comfort.

GAD. He's just turned into a silly old fool!

ASHER. The worst part is that he loves the kid so much, he asks his advice about everything.

ZEBULUN. What a disgusting way to throw away his love!

LEVI. He sure picked the worst one of us to love.

JUDAH. By God, you've hit the nail right on the head! Jacob really doesn't give a damn about the rest of us anymore.

ISSACHAR. Just remember what I said when he sent us out here.

JUDAH. Yes, it seemed like he just wanted to get us out of his sight.

REUBEN. Hold on a minute! Don't you think maybe he just likes Joseph because he's little and cute and clever, and because he's the child of his old age? It's only natural for him to enjoy having a kid like him around.

GAD. But don't you see how bad this is for us? He's a nasty little tattletale, and he's constantly telling our father lies about us, so that he despises us and treats us like strangers.

DAN. The old man believes everything he says. You'd think he was just a dumb kid himself!

JUDAH. I can't take it anymore.

SIMEON. Surely you all remember what a horrible crime he just recently accused us of.

DAN. I'm glad you mentioned that, Simeon. It still makes my blood boil!

LEVI. How dare that little pip-squeak accuse us!

JUDAH. If we don't do something about this, we'll never live it down!

NAPHTALI. As for me, I think it's shameful and wicked. This time we really need to get smart and use all our brainpower.

ASHER. Now he claims he dreamed we were all harvesting the wheat and binding our sheaves, and his sheaf stood up above all of ours.

LEVI. I still don't get it.

JUDAH. He also saw the sun and moon and eleven very beautiful stars bowing down to him and prostrating themselves at his feet.

GAD. So tell us, what does it mean?

JUDAH. That his father, mother, and brothers have all become his slaves.

LEVI. No way! We have to fight for our freedom.

JUDAH. I swear to God, I'll die before I'll be his slave!

GAD. So what are we going to do about it? Does anyone want to fight him?

SIMEON. He thinks he'll be our boss? I say he's dead meat!

LEVI. He's as good as dead already.

ASHER. Come closer, Simeon. We're stronger than he is. It looks like there's nothing for it but to kill him.

DAN. I swear to God, I'd massacre all Judea before I'd let him get away with this scheme!

NAPHTALI. This time he's met his match!

JUDAH. We all know it's a sin to bow down to anyone but God.

ASHER. I'd kill anyone who tried to lord it over me and be my master, even if he were my older brother. We can't let our children be enslaved!

ZEBULUN. I'm with you. We'll do what we have to do, and let the chips fall where they may.

GAD. Hold on, what's this we're planning?

JUDAH. To kill him so that we can live. We'll bury him and get on with our lives.

LEVI. That's what we all want, but tell me how we can do it?

JUDAH. It's only right that one should die to save us all.[35]

ASHER. We'll keep the kid's dreams from coming true, but we've got to act fast.

NAPHTALI. Yes, we'd better do it as soon as he comes.

ZEBULUN. There's no time to lose.

ISSACHAR. We all agree that he must die. Let's all stay together, and we'll find a way to do it.

JUDAH. Since I'm older and smarter, let me plan it.

DAN. If he has any sense, he'll give us a wide berth from now on.

REUBEN. Brothers, I've been paying close attention to everything you've said, but I have to disagree with what you're planning. Please don't even think about it! What you're planning to do is just plain crazy. Don't you think those dreams Joseph has had are revelations from God?

SIMEON. Yes, that's what worries us the most.

REUBEN. You're nuts if you think anyone can stop what God has decreed. Don't you realize that our God is so mighty that no power can change His judgments? Don't slaughter this innocent lamb whose meekness is a sign of things to come.[36] If God has ordained that Joseph shall command, what good can it do to envy him? Surely great good will come to all of us from his power and prosperity; so what on earth has given you these crazy ideas?

LEVI. If I can just get my hands on him, I'll give him a good whack on the back of his neck, and you'll see how he falls down! After that, he can dream about being king all he likes, for the only destiny God has in mind for him is that he obey us.

REUBEN. I can see how you may have a hard time understanding God's mysterious plan, but you know very well that He has commanded you not to kill a living soul, much less your own brother, who has done nothing wrong. In fact he's so wise and so good that he's the very image of God. What constant obedience! What a virtuous life! Don't even think such a thing, for it is diabolical wickedness! Just look at how innocent and sinless he is. He's the very picture of purity, faithfulness, and prudence painted with God's own brush!

SIMEON. Oh, shut up! He's nothing but a selfish, spoiled, stuck-up, mean little liar. If I get hold of him, I'll tear his eyes out!

ASHER. Forgot about those sheaves! I have some sticks I'd gladly bend in his direction!

JUDAH. Never mind that! My big knife will give him something to remember me by!

GAD. It warms my heart to hear you say that. But I want to be the one to finish him off.

REUBEN. My brothers, please don't be so cruel. God will reject you for this.

ZEBULUN. Just cut it out, quit trying to defend him. When I'm finished with him, you won't recognize him.

REUBEN. If the fear of your Lord God won't stop you, just think of how I feel. Think of the suffering and pain you'll cause our father. You're signing his death warrant. You'll ruin his health with this dreadful deed. How can you be so ungrateful? You're nailing the lid on his coffin with your brutal behavior. Oh my brothers, take pity on his old age! See what a just and saintly, chaste, patient, and good man he is. He's never harmed a soul. You should tremble at the thought that what you're doing is the same as if you were throwing dirt in his grave. You'll all be dressed in mourning before you know it! Think of the anxiety and distress you are causing the Jewish people. Think of the honor of the house of Abraham. Think of how your relatives and friends will feel. Think about how they'll condemn you. Remember that this child is the only consolation of his old age, and it's wrong to kill him for such trivial reasons. If you shed this just man's blood, you'll be sorry. Your deed will be known, and there is a God Who will condemn you. Don't think nobody will know just because you're in the middle of the wilderness. If you won't listen to me, your eldest brother, just think how you're angering your Maker. Jacob's life depends on this child. Seeing him is his only joy. He loves him dearly because he's never caused him any aggravation. He is the love of his life and the light of his eyes. Think of the pain you'll cause his mother Rachel. Yes, I know she's dead—but aren't you afraid to offend the dead and aggrieve the living at the same time? Why so much rage and carnage against an innocent lamb?

JUDAH. He brought it on himself with his evil tongue. Don't try to argue for him. He must be punished. One way or another, we have to teach him a lesson. We'll just see what good his dreams and gossip and mischief will do the spoiled brat now!

LEVI. I'm going to sharpen my cutlass!

ZEBULUN. Yes, you certainly don't want to cut him with a dull knife![37]

LEVI. I swear to God, you must be joking!

GAD. Reuben, don't waste any more of our time. He's been tried and found guilty. You can't appeal his sentence now.

JUDAH. Joseph should be making his peace with God, because as soon as he gets here, he's a dead man. Since our minds are made up, let's get on with our lunch.

REUBEN. [Aside:] Oh, pestilential Envy, mother of all vices! You drive men out of their minds! There has never been, and never will be, a wickedness such as this—not even Cain's slaughter of his own brother! Envy, your only delight is in sowing rancor, discord, anger. Everyone knows you for what you are, and you'll always be friendless for the wrong you do.

Let's eat then, and may it please God to change your mind about killing your brother.

LEVI. Pass the food over here, Zebulun. We're all hungry.

ASHER. Okay, Zebulun, you've done a good job of dividing up the food so far. Now see if there's anything left in the bag.

ZEBULUN. There's calaboose—I mean calabash—but this is not the best time to bring it up.

NAPHTALI. You're right about that, by God!

ASHER. Let's all get good and drunk.

GAD. I'm for that!

JUDAH. Reuben should drink first, since he's the eldest brother.

DAN. At least he can join us in that.

LEVI. Careful there, don't spill that innocent wine![38]

SIMEON. Now that *would* be a crime!

ASHER. Everyone's had enough to drink.

ISSACHAR. Everyone but Naphtali.

NAPHTALI. I do believe this wine's time has come.

ISSACHAR. Nah, it's still just a baby, but it *is* a little spoiled.

DAN. Slow down there! Is there any left?

ASHER. What we're about to drink, I think, will do us no harm at all.

SIMEON. Well, now that we've rested, gentlemen, let's leave the sheepfold and have a look at the flocks.

GAD. Good idea.

JUDAH. As for what we've just discussed, I want all of you to be on the alert.

[The curtain falls. Envy appears again in front of the curtain.]

ENVY. Oh Envy, what great things you have accomplished with your wiles! No one could help admiring you today! From this breast of mine have slithered out sins, rage, suspicions. I know their every weak point, and I've played this one exactly right. Out of envy they've agreed to kill an innocent man. Has anyone ever seen such a great sin? The eldest one tried to interfere, but it won't do him any good. Forget him, for the deed is already branded on their hearts. Just what my heart desires! If I can just carry it off, this will be a fight to remember! Poor Jews, your downfall will be greater than your rise, and it serves you right! I must hurry back to hell to take them the good news. There's no need for secrecy now, for their minds are so set on doing the deed that there's no way it can fail.

ACT 2

[Jacob's home in Canaan. When the curtain rises, Jacob and Joseph are on stage. Joseph is a blond. He is wearing an elegant white smock trimmed with lace over a loincloth.]

JACOB. My son, I'm very worried and distressed, because it's been a long time since I've heard where your brothers are. I think they must be somewhere in Shechem or Hebron. Go check up on them for me; I'm sure they're just wasting their time.

JOSEPH. Oh, my dear, merciful father! It's very cruel of me not to have visited them. I shall do as you say and go to see my brothers and the flocks right away, without a moment's delay.

JACOB. Oh, my son! You're just dying to leave me here all alone. Come back soon if you want to find me alive. Remember that you're my staff and my only comfort. Your departure makes me nervous. Be careful where you go!

JOSEPH. Father, don't get upset about my being away. I'll come right back.

JACOB. Oh, Fortune, my enemy! Son, I don't know what to say, I've been through so much misfortune. Your leaving is like my own funeral, and I can't help being choked up. Be sure and take your bag with you. Now give me a hug! Oh, my son and companion, I'll suffer while you're gone!

JOSEPH. My lord and father, please bless me with your own hands.

JACOB. May God bless you and your brothers. I'm overcome with grief to see my joy going away.

[Exit Joseph.]

How excitedly he sets out! He's so clever and polite! No one has ever had such a virtuous, chaste, pleasant, obedient, and smart son.

[Exit Jacob. Joseph reenters from stage right.]

JOSEPH. I think this is the way that leads to the valley of Hebron. No, I must be mistaken. But wait; this *is* the way I'm supposed to go. I'm so confused! If only I were a clairvoyant! But here's a path that will lead me the right way. God will just have to guide me through all these mountains and plains. I sure don't want to miss my brothers, nor to wear myself out before I get there. But even if it took a thousand days, it would be well worth it to get to see them! Now I feel really good and rested! I feel ready for whatever happens, as if it were my destiny! God be praised, for this is a great blessing!

[Enter a shepherd.]

SHEPHERD. Where are you going on this holiday? You look like you're lost.

JOSEPH. Brother, God must have sent you so I could ask you which one of these is the road.

SHEPHERD. Where are you trying to get to?

JOSEPH. The valley of Hebron.

SHEPHERD. *[Aside:]* Alas, poor ill-fated boy!

Over there, next to that glen is a very well-worn path. When you leave the path, veer to the right, and then just keep on right beside that there hill, and I'll be durned if you're not there before you know it.

JOSEPH. Is there a path all the way, or could I get lost?

SHEPHERD. No, I think you'll be okay, as long as you keep your wits about you. But tell me, what are you doing way out here in the boonies, where there's nothing but mountains and empty plains?

JOSEPH. Looking for my brothers. Maybe you've seen them around here.

SHEPHERD. Well, who are they, and where have they been?

JOSEPH. They are Jacob's sons, and they've been herding their flocks around here.

SHEPHERD. Ha, ha, ha! I sure as heck do remember! They're out there in Shechem. Just go like I told you, and you'll get there in no time.

JOSEPH. Well, I'd better be on my way. It's getting late.

SHEPHERD. You betcha, kid. Godspeed!

[Exit the shepherd.]

JOSEPH. And God be with you and protect you from all evil. Boy, the sun is hot on this hill! I think I'll put on my hat to shield me from it. Honestly, it seems like the further I go, the longer this road gets. Well, hang in there, kid! As soon as I get there, I'm going to hug every single one of them, starting with Reuben. Then I'll hug Benjamin, then Naphtali, Dan, Gad, and Zebulun, and Issachar, and Asher, and Levi too, right on down to Judah and Simeon. Are we ever going to have fun! I can't even find words to say how happy I'll be! I'll give them good news of our father, and we'll all have tons of things to talk about. I hear something.

[A faint sound of dogs barking and sheep baaing in the distance.]

Is it bells? No, it must be the dogs barking. How could that be? Have they left the sheep-fold? It sounds different now? Is it them? Yes, there they are! This is the valley of Shechem, and over there I see Judah and Reuben and Levi and Simeon.

[Enter the brothers.]

SIMEON. Hey, brothers! Here comes the dreamer! Don't anybody chicken out! Let's beat him within an inch of his life! I'd like to give him a good whack on the back of his neck.

JUDAH. Well, now's the time to do it. Here comes the little nut!

ZEBULUN. *[To Joseph:]* Come on, you little rascal! You'll not get away from us!

REUBEN. *[Holding out his arms, tries to protect Joseph from his brothers.]* Stop, brothers, don't kill him! It would be a horrible crime!

GAD. Hey, what are you guys waiting for?

JUDAH. Get out of the way, Reuben!

REUBEN. What do you think you're doing? You still want to slaughter that innocent lamb? He's your own brother! It'll kill your father! He's only seventeen. He's a nice, smart kid. Please don't try to do such a horrible thing! Don't be stupid! How can you play such a trick on your father? Aren't you ashamed to act like this? Don't you know this boy is the light of Jacob's eyes? How can you kill him like this in cold blood? When Jacob finds out, he'll scratch his face and tear out his beard! Just imagine how he'll feel. You know how he loves Joseph. If the kid has done you any harm, remember he's just a boy. Is killing him going to make you feel like big tough guys? Wouldn't it be more manly to forgive him?

JUDAH. Can you believe he's still defending him?

ASHER. I say the dirty little bastard deserves to suffer, since he's done nothing but cause us trouble!

GAD. *[Gesturing toward his crotch.]* Now we'll see if his sheaf stands more erect than the rest, or if it droops down to the ground where the ants can eat it.

LEVI. Let's kill the little smart-ass who thought he could boss us around!

DAN. And what's a whole lot worse, he thought we'd bow down to him!

JUDAH. That's it. He's a fine one, isn't he? *[Draws a knife and holds it at Joseph's throat.]*

ZEBULUN. Don't cut off his head! Move back a little!

REUBEN. So you've made up your minds to kill the apple of your father's eye. If you kill him, poor old Jacob's life is over too.

Before you kill him, listen to what I have to say; I think you'll be glad you did. There's a big well near here, and that's the cleanest way to kill him. Throw him in the well, and he'll starve to death. At least we won't have his blood on our hands.

JUDAH. I think Reuben's got the right idea!

LEVI. Me too! That's a much worse way to die than we had planned.

REUBEN. All right! Let's get going then. I've got some rope here.

GAD. *[Hurriedly starts tying the rope around Joseph's neck.]* Okay, the quicker we get him into that deep, dark well, the better!

NAPHTALI. Watch what you're doing! You need to tie a good tight knot. Here, I'll hold the boy for you.

GAD. Okay, that ought to do it! Come here, kid! You guys, hold him on that side; and the rest of you, on this side.

NAPHTALI. Now push him this way; but hold on tight to the rope.

REUBEN. Not so fast, he's choking! Cut him a little more slack.

LEVI. Hold on! Before we put him in the well, let's take off his shirt. Maybe it will be of some use to us. Anyhow, he's always bragging about it.

JUDAH. I swear to God, that's not a bad idea. *[Judah removes Joseph's shirt, leaving him dressed in a loincloth.]* But don't think you'll get it! It's staying with me.

JOSEPH. Oh, brothers, is this how you repay me for coming to visit you? I only wanted to love you, so why are you hurting me?

ZEBULUN. Your sweet talk will get you nowhere. *[To Gad:]* Here, you hold on to the rope.

JOSEPH. Oh brothers, may God forgive you! Oh, my good father Jacob! I know you meant no harm, but you should have known better than to send me to my brothers. *[They push him into the well.]*

GAD. Wow! He hit the bottom really hard!

LEVI. It does my heart good to see him down there!

REUBEN. *[Aside:]* What great wickedness! These people are nothing but animals! How could they throw an innocent child down there where he'll soon die? Let's see. Is there any way I can get him out of there?

Brothers, you've done what you wanted to, and I hope you're satisfied. But now you'd better beat it before anyone suspects you. *[Points to stage right.]* Go that way. I'll go look for some good pasture where we can take the sheep, and I'll be back here tomorrow.

[Aside:] Once they're out of here, I'll come back and pull the kid out.

[Exit Reuben stage left.]

DAN. Brothers, it would be better to pull the boy up and finish him off so he won't suffer so much.

JUDAH. I have a better idea. I see some travelers approaching through that glen. I think they must be merchants taking goods from Arabia to Egypt. Why don't we see what they'll give us for him? It would be better than killing him; and besides, I could use the money. I'd sure rather have it than Joseph. What do you think?

SIMEON. A brilliant idea, I swear to God!

ZEBULUN. Yes, let's do it. Let those merchants carry him off with the other stuff they're taking to sell. It looks like balm and perfume and other expensive stuff. If he dies once he's in a foreign kingdom, it'll be less dangerous for us.

LEVI. I'll sure be happy to take their money! It's about time we had a little cash.

NAPHTALI. What a terrific idea! Let's turn him over to those Ishmaelites. They'll sell him in some godforsaken country, and we'll never have to see him again.

GAD. Even if we wanted to, it would be impossible!

ZEBULUN. Okay, what are we waiting for?

GAD. We'll pull him up. You go and call the merchants.

[Exit Zebulun.]

How shall we do it?

ASHER. I can't figure out how to get him out.

DAN. Here, the end of the rope is just within reach.

SIMEON. Grab it and pull, and we'll all help you.

DAN. He's so heavy, I think he must be dead. Issachar, grab him!

[They pull him out, and move towards stage left.]

JUDAH. Hurrah, at last he's out! You dreamed of being a king, but now you're going to Egypt; and if you know what's good for you, you'll keep your eyes open there!

[Enter Zebulun from stage right with the merchants.]

ZEBULUN.[39] Where are you gentlemen going?

MERCHANT. Brothers, we're on our way to Egypt.

ZEBULUN. Stop a minute. I won't make you late. I have a message for you: Would you be interested in buying an outstanding slave from us at a very good price?

MERCHANT. What do you think? Buying and selling is how we make our living.

ZEBULUN. Well then, just follow me.

MERCHANT. Is it far?

ZEBULUN. No, you can see him from here.

[They begin to move across the stage toward Joseph and the other brothers.]

DAN. *[Punching Joseph.]* He may have dreamed about stars before, but we'll make him see stars in the broad daylight!

ASHER. Cut it out, what are we doing? The merchants are coming, and they won't stop for long. We'd better make a deal with them quickly.

JOSEPH. Oh, brothers. I can't believe you've come to hate me so! What are you going to do with me now?

JUDAH. We're going to sell you as a slave.

JOSEPH. That's awful! How can you treat me like this? Please take me home, or else just go ahead and kill me! By the God of Abraham, the God of Israel, by our dear father, I beg you: don't do this to me! If you sell me, I'll be taken away by people who speak a barbarous language. They'll soon finish me off, and you will be held responsible. They are foreigners from an ugly, monstrous country with a vile, disgusting religion![40] They're worse than animals! Don't you know that they do things that are weird and unthinkable? Surely you're not as angry with me as all that!

JUDAH. You're wasting your breath. We've made up our minds. You might as well get your stuff together, because they'll be here any minute.

JOSEPH. May God forgive you!

MERCHANT. Brothers, as we were passing by, this messenger came and told us you have a slave you'd like to sell. If that's the case, let's not waste any time. Just tell us what you're asking for him. If your price is reasonable and we like the merchandise, we'll make you glad you did business with us.

JUDAH. We're already glad, for we can see very well that you are honorable men, and we want to make you a very good deal.

MERCHANT. That's very kind of you. We'll be happy to pay you a fair price.

JUDAH. Well, here he is then.

SIMEON. Let's see your money.

JUDAH. I swear to God, the boy has no vices. He's a good servant, and he seems very bright to me.

ASHER. That's right, he's absolutely trustworthy.

MERCHANT. Okay, we get the message. Just tell us how much you want for him.

JUDAH. Give us thirty pieces of silver, and he's all yours.[41]

MERCHANT. Let's be on our way, friends. At that price we're not interested.

JUDAH. Don't try to bargain with us! You know he's worth an arm and a leg. Just take it or leave it.

MERCHANT. I'll give you twenty, and that's it.

JUDAH. Are you kidding? His hide alone is worth more than that!

MERCHANT. You're sure you won't sell him for twenty?

JUDAH. I swear to God, I wouldn't even take twenty-five!

MERCHANT. Is that so? Well, I'm offering you twenty-five.

JUDAH. Forget it! I might as well give him away!

LEVI. Give us the thirty and take him. Otherwise, we'll change our mind about selling him.

SIMEON. *[Aside:]* Boy, these people drive a hard bargain!
 You know the price is right. Why waste any more time?

MERCHANT. Twenty-five, and not a penny more! That's already more than he's worth. Is it a deal?

JUDAH. Not on your life! He's a very good servant, and he cost me more than that.

MERCHANT. Spare me! Anyone could see that he's not even broken in. What's the kid's name?

JOSEPH. Joseph, for my misfortune.

JUDAH. And, by God, a very loyal slave he is! Can't you see how quick and healthy he is, and how he jumps to your command?

LEVI. You won't find his equal in Yola, Mandinga, or Guinea!

JUDAH. I swear to God he's worth double what we're asking!

MERCHANT. There, there, my good man!

JUDAH. Give us thirty. You won't find his match!

MERCHANT. All right then. Thirty it is. Everything about him seems to be in order; but first you must promise me that I can trust him.

JUDAH. I swear to God he's as trustworthy a slave as you'll ever find. He doesn't drink, and he won't run away.

MERCHANT. Very well then. It's a deal.

LEVI. And a very good deal it is!

DAN. Let's give him to them.

ASHER. I swear to God, I won't allow it, unless they pay the customs duties.

JUDAH. No, we can't go back on our word. What do you say, brothers?

ZEBULUN. Let them have him, even though he's worth more; and may God reward us for this generosity.

MERCHANT. We only want to do what's right. Hold your hand still; take a good look at my money. Are you satisfied? Then stay here, and don't follow us.

JUDAH. Yes, sir. Go with God, and may He bless you!

[The merchants leave with Joseph.]

ZEBULUN. There he goes, the little creep! At last we're rid of him!

NAPHTALI. And we did it all on the up and up.

LEVI. They must have thought he was really cute, 'cause they wanted him bad.

DAN. Well, he's as bad as they come.

GAD. Good riddance!

SIMEON. They sure thought they got a bargain! What do you bet they'll live to regret it?

ISSACHAR. Well, at least maybe they'll cure him of those dreams of his.

ASHER. What a lot of nonsense he talked!

SIMEON. They'll soon fix that.

[Exeunt the brothers to stage left. Joseph and the merchants enter from stage right.]

JOSEPH. Oh, Jacob, my honored father! I feel terrible when I think how you'll worry. Oh, dear land of Canaan where I was born and grew up! Oh, my dear brothers, why have you banished me?

MERCHANT. Just keep it up, and I'll give you something to whine about, you little bastard! Let's get a move on! What are you staring at?

JOSEPH. Oh, sir! I just realized that this field is Ephrath, and that's the grave where Rachel, my mother, is buried. May I please see it? Could we just rest here for a while? *[Without waiting for an answer, he goes over to the grave.]* Hail, oh grave, more kind than cruel, since you spared my mother Rachel this bitterness! Oh, hard stone, soften, so that my cries can penetrate you! Oh Mother, pity my pain and my great misfortune! You were lucky not to have seen your son thrown into a well and then sold as a slave. It would have broken your heart to see your child suffer like that! Mother, Mother: look down on the child whom you carried in your womb! Take me with you! If I could fit into your womb, surely there's room for me in your grave! That's the only thing that could free me from this agony. Tell me, Mother: Why did you bother to bear such an unlucky son? I would have been much better off if I had died at birth. Mother, why don't you answer my sad cries? You seem to be hiding from me, which only increases my sadness. Oh, cruel tomb: be not so strong! Before I die, let me see my mother Rachel! Open to me now, for my life is more bitter than gall! Oh, Mother: Why doesn't my senseless affliction cause you pain? Your heart may well break now! Don't leave me like this? Hear my lamentation!

[He sings:] Super flumina Babylonis, illic sedimus et flevimus: cum recordaremur Sion.[42]

If there be any feeling left in your bones, pity me, for my life of luxury is over. Just as if I were a wicked traitor, they've sold me as a slave.

MERCHANT. You, mourner, finish up. We can't waste any more time.

JOSEPH. Farewell, Mother!

ACT 3

[Egypt. The street in front of Putiphar's house. Enter the merchants. Putiphar appears at an upstairs window.]

PUTIPHAR. Where are you off to, gentlemen?

MERCHANT. Sir, we're out to make an honest living.

PUTIPHAR. Indeed. But tell me, what good things have you brought from the East?

MERCHANT. A lot of things. This slave, for one.

PUTIPHAR. Well, what do you know! I'll buy him from you if I like his looks.

MERCHANT. He's a very expensive lad! My partners here can tell you how much he cost us.

MERCHANT 2. Over forty pieces of silver.

MERCHANT. I swear upon my wife's head!

PUTIPHAR. Well, if my wife agrees, we'll you pay you well for him. Hey there, wife!

ZENOBIA. *[Offstage:]* What do you want, my lord?

PUTIPHAR. Would you like to have this slave?

ZENOBIA. *[She looks out the window.]* Yes, buy him. We need one.

PUTIPHAR. *[To the merchants:]* Bring him on up. I'll wait for you here.

MERCHANT. Get your money ready if it's not too much trouble. *[To Joseph:]*

I hate to leave you here as a slave, but you know that money is the only
thing that really matters to me. Anyway, it's nothing to cry about, for
I've just sold you to King Pharaoh's majordomo.

JOSEPH. Out of the frying pan, and into the fire! What an insult—for one
man to sell my body to another! Oh, my God and Creator! How can You
bear to see Abraham's great-grandson in chains?

*[The merchants take Joseph in the house through a door at center stage.
Enter Reuben. The scene is now back where the brothers cast Joseph
into the well.]*

REUBEN. Now that my brothers have gone, I can take Joseph out of the well,
and at the same time free them from the sin they've fallen into. But
they'd better not be hiding! They are so envious, they'd kill us both! No,
the coast is clear. Have you ever seen such insane behavior or such a
disgusting deed? But this time luck is with me, for it's a very dark night.
They threw him in there naked, just to be even more cruel, so I don't
know what I'll use to pull him up. Ah, I'll just reach this branch down to
him and pull him out with it. Hey, Joseph! Grab hold of this! Where are
you, kid? Oh, no! How horrible! He doesn't answer. He must be dead.
Tell me, my brother: Where are you? He must not be here. Those wicked
men must have killed him. I don't know what to do! Oh, where have you
gone, Joseph; what's become of you? If I hadn't gone away, you wouldn't
be dead. Oh, why was I ever born? Damn my sinful carelessness! I
should have died, wretch that I am, and not you, an innocent child so
loved by your father and your people! Judah, Levi, Simeon, where are
you? What are you doing?

JUDAH. *[Offstage:]* Who's that crying out with such pain?

[Enter Judah and the other brothers.]

Brother, what do you want?

REUBEN. Please set my mind at ease. Tell me: Have you killed our brother?
Where have you put him?

LEVI. Calm down, and wipe those tears from your eyes.

REUBEN. Don't play any tricks on me, or I'll do something crazy!

SIMEON. Reuben, brother, come to your senses! Joseph is safe and sound,
and that's the truth.

JUDAH. Since you were so worried about him, we pulled him out of the well
and sold him as a slave to some merchants from Egypt. We decided that
was a lot better, because that way he wouldn't die in the well. But don't
worry, we drove a hard bargain!

REUBEN. Unbelievable! Who ever heard of such a thing? And just how much
did you decide his life was worth?

JUDAH. These thirty pieces of silver.

REUBEN. And you call that a deal, eh?

JUDAH. Cut it out! You'll get your fair share, just like everyone else.

REUBEN. I wouldn't dirty my hands with that money! How could you sell a just man's blood? You'll pay for this! Are there no limits to the power of greed? But what are we going to do now? How are we going to keep our father from finding out about this?

LEVI. I've got that all figured out. Just leave it to me; I'll take care of every-thing. First, we'll kill a goat. Then we'll take that shirt we took off of Joseph and dip it in the blood, and I'll tell our father that we found it like that next to a path. He'll think some wild animal killed him.

DAN. That's a good idea if I ever heard one!

ASHER. Okay, somebody get a goat.

GAD. I've already got one right here.

LEVI. I'll cut its throat then.[43] You see how I was right? Now dip the shirt in the blood. I swear to God, anyone who saw that would be sure he'd been eaten up!

NAPHTALI. Okay, that's enough!

SIMEON. We don't want too much blood on it.

DAN. Let the blood flow freely!

ZEBULUN. Stop, that's plenty!

LEVI. A pretty sight that is! Now let's go where our father is. Everything's going to be just fine.

REUBEN. All right then, let's go. May God sharpen your wits so you can break the news to the old man gently. Otherwise he'll just drop dead. Let me go first. I'll do the talking and prepare the way for you.

ACT 4

[Jacob's house in Canaan. Enter Jacob].

JACOB. I see my sons coming. What a happy group! I can't find words to express my joy! They took so long, I was worried to death about them. Now I can breathe easy again. They are my only comfort in my old age.
[Enter the brothers.]

REUBEN. Father, may God bring you happiness and preserve your good-ness!

JACOB. And I pray that He protect you wonderful young people! But I can see my prayer is already answered, for He has brought you here. Oh, sons, I was dying to see you! What kept you so long?

LEVI. Father, we had a change of plans. We discovered that the pasture was much better in Shechem than in Hebron, so we took the flocks there. That's what took so long, but now we've come to see you.

JACOB. But tell me, where is Joseph? Is he on his way here, or did you leave him with the sheep?

LEVI. What are you talking about? Joseph wasn't there with us.

JACOB. Oh, my God! I sent him there to see how you were doing.

JUDAH. Levi's telling you the truth.

JACOB. Almighty King of Heaven, what a horrible situation! Who ever heard of such a thing? My son is wandering lost in the mountains with no one to take pity on him!

SIMEON. Father, if he had gone to our lodge, he would surely have run into us. There's no way he could have missed us, even if he tried.

JACOB. Oh, how blind I was! How foolish of me to send a mere child into the wilderness like that!

LEVI. Tell us what he was wearing, if you remember.

JACOB. He was wearing a white smock over his tunic.

LEVI. Oh, no! If it's the one we found covered with blood by the side of the road, we'll all soon be wearing black! If that's the one, some monster caught him, and he's surely dead.

ASHER. My gut tells me that it has to be him.

DAN. Oh, what a terrible loss for all the family!

JACOB. Don't say that! Don't give me such painful news!

Here begins the lament of Jacob
who weeps for his son Joseph,
thinking he was eaten by beasts
or torn apart.

Jacob's lament:

Let me see that shirt. Yes, it is his. Oh, my dear son, can this be your blood? Why did I live to see this day? What a disaster! Oh, Fortune! What can you do to me now? *To the beast:* Oh, wicked, cruel dog to eat my son like that! Didn't you see how cute he was? How could you sink your teeth into such a precious jewel? You're a cursed, wicked monster! Still, I half adore you, for you have my treasure buried in your belly. I'd even forgive you if you'd kill me now so that I could join my beloved son.

LEVI. How swiftly suffering overcomes us! As soon as I saw that shirt, such sadness came over me that I thought I would die. Oh, excellent brother!

We'll go back and look for you again. Oh, what a mistake to send that innocent child by himself!

JACOB. How could I have imagined that an animal would seize my son and tear him to pieces? It's unthinkable! How you must have cried out for your father and your loved ones! I should tear myself apart with my own teeth! *He tears his cloak.* These are no longer my clothes. How could I wear such things when I am mourning such a loss! My sons, help me grieve for my loneliness, for very soon I'll be leaving you. From now on my only bed or chair will be the bare ground,[44] since God has turned against us. I feel His sharp dagger right here at my heart! The good times are gone forever, so let my house fall into ruins! Cover this old man with sackcloth, put ashes on his head. The older I get, the more I suffer!

REUBEN. Oh father whom the whole world admires, stop tearing your hair, for what's happened is part of God's mysterious plan. How can you complain of His deed? You're insulting God, and He may turn His fury against us. We know you're suffering, but remember that it is in great suffering that a great heart is revealed. What good will all this weeping do you?

JACOB. There can be no consolation for such a fresh and terrible blow. My life is just a living death. Oh, Jacob, no one has ever suffered like this before! How can your heart bear it? Heavens, bear witness to my complaints! Sun, moon, and stars, what have I done to deserve this? Oh men, can you believe this is happening? Pity me now, my friends! *To the earth:* Oh, earth, why didn't you open to prevent this tragedy? And you, elements: I blame you for not swallowing up that monster! I blame the Almighty, Who should have struck him with lightning. I can't help believing that today I've been touched by the Lord's hand. Oh, Creator of humankind, where is Your justice? Why don't You come down from heaven to avenge such wickedness?

GAD. Sir, you go too far in your grief! Remember, you still have many sons, even if they can't compare with him.

ISSACHAR. Yes, you've carried on long enough! If we were all to die right in front of you, what more could you do or say? Control yourself! Praise God before He does something even worse to you. In disasters like this one must show prudence and acknowledge that it is Divine Providence. Weeping won't change anything, so what's the point of all these tears and sighs?

JACOB. I'd have been much better off if I had been stillborn!

ZEBULUN. What's the matter with you? What happened to your wisdom, your moderation, your discretion, your goodness, your dignity?

JACOB. Nothing matters anymore. From now on, my days will be nothing but travail and anguish. My words might as well be as futile as everything else in my life.

NAPHTALI. Father, you used to be stronger than everyone else. You have to make an effort to put an end to this grief.

ASHER. I always thought our honored father had such a great soul that even if he lost everything he owned, and all his children, and even a hundred others, he would still suffer in serenity and silence. Now he's behaving just the opposite. How could such a wise man let himself be so affected by misfortune?

DAN. Haven't you always heard that it's the wisest men who make the biggest mistakes?

JACOB. Let the world never forget this! May my infinite pain be known to all! He was just a child, like a little blossom that the slightest wind could blow away! A lovely flower in the morning that is already faded by afternoon.

ASHER. Why have you lost the crown of patience, father dear? If God willed that a lioness should devour your beloved sons, you should give Him thanks for at least sparing you and your property.

BENJAMIN. Father, I'm the youngest of all, and I beg you for my sake to be comforted by my love. You've always loved God and rejoiced in Him. Praise Him now, for you know that He always does what is best.

JACOB. Oh Lord, why did You decide to be so cruel to man? You made him of flesh, nerves, skin, and bones—of such fragile materials that he was always subject to pain. Man is really nothing but dust, hardly better than the animals, and as if that weren't bad enough, you made him take a wife so that he could multiply this wretched human race. How much better it would have been not to have been born to see such sorrow as I have seen! To see a child like a flower, the loveliest You ever made, indeed Your masterpiece, die like a dog. You've given me a life sentence, for there can be no more comfort or pleasure for me now.

LEVI. You really must control your anger. What God has done is all part of His mysterious plan.

BENJAMIN. You know very well that life is just an endless struggle, full of pain, that it begins bitterly and ends even worse. Just as birds are born to fly, man comes into the world to suffer. Stop that crying right now! It's stupid and undignified. What's happened to you is certainly terrible; but don't you know that lots of people have lost sons, and no amount of weeping ever brought a single one of them back?

JACOB. Misery may love company, but other people's pain is no comfort to me, my son, because my pain is so much greater than theirs, and I have so much more reason to grieve. This pain just keeps goading me ever closer to the grave.

DAN. You're right that our little brother was very truthful, and he had good advice to offer for such a young person.

JACOB. Talking about him does no good. The only thing I want to do now is scratch my face.

GAD. Oh, father, don't be like that. This endless weeping seems more like madness than grief. No one has ever seen anything like it!

JACOB. Sons, leave me. I'd like to have a private conversation with God about this.

[Exeunt the brothers, except for Levi and Simeon, who remain at stage left, almost in the wings.]

Oh my God, where were you? When did my Guiding Light grow dark? Where were your angels? Couldn't they defend you from that animal? Where were the stars? Why didn't they fall from heaven? What were the sun and moon doing that they didn't prevent your death? And the sea full of fish, the land full of cattle—why didn't they help him? Where was the day, since it didn't show me so much pain and wickedness? Why did the night cover up such gruesome deeds? Where was Your greatness? How could you let a weak man like me suffer so? Where was Your strength? For all strength comes from You. I beg You just this once, oh my God, tell me what I have done to deserve this. I'll accept Your judgment. Such a pure youth that He was the very image of You! Why couldn't You kill this old man instead? My body is worn out anyway. It would have been a mercy for You to put me out of my misery. But a seventeen-year-old boy, yet so mature in goodness?

To Rachel: Oh, Rachel, how lucky you were to die when you did! How could your woman's heart bear for the boy you carried to end up in the dragon's mouth?—the boy you loved so much, your comfort and my pet!

JUDAH. Oh father, I feel so sorry for you that I wish to God this were the day of my own funeral. I'd rather see my own babes in arms torn apart than see you so sad!

JACOB. *To death:* Oh death, why do you snatch those who want you least, and you won't even look at those who are dying for you? Fortune, why do you demolish virtuous beginnings and give long life to vicious extremes?

LEVI. I really don't know how to comfort you, father. My heart aches to think that the flower of humankind has withered. Oh Joseph, little brother—but greatest of all in virtue!

JACOB. If he had died some other way, I would have given him such a burial that at least that would have been some comfort to me. But like this! Oh God! I don't even know where he is. Sons, take me to that beast. It was savage enough to kill my child, but I'm sure that innocent lamb must have tamed it by now. My son buried there in his body will make him listen to me if I find him. I may be old and frail in body, but my heart would give me the strength to kill that beast. Oh my sons, let me do this before I die!

SIMEON. Don't you think you've wept enough? Joseph wasn't immortal, you know. What you're doing now is worse than what happened to him. God gave him, and God has taken him away. Joseph couldn't help dying; but you used to be a strong and tough-minded man, and you've let yourself become a whimpering coward.

JACOB. Give me that shirt so that I can stain my gray hair with his blood. Have you ever heard anything so awful? How could wild animals have taken my son's life? Oh tears, flow freely from my eyes! No joy could compete with my sorrow! If only I could have seen his broken body and watched him die in my arms, I wouldn't feel so bad! But, oh God, not like this! Oh my God, if only I could argue with You face to face! How could You allow an animal to eat such a heavenly child? If I can't move heaven with my laments, I'll go down to hell and end my days weeping with the damned and piling evil upon evil. My sons, these terrible feelings cannot bear the light of day! Take me to a dark room where my torment can increase!

[Exeunt. The curtain falls, and Envy comes out in front of the curtain.]

ENVY. Well, what do you think now? Have I done a good job or what? Did you get a good look at how the brothers fixed that high and mighty dreamer? And what about the old man's grief? Can you believe how much he cried? He'll soon be in his grave. Everything will be destroyed before its time.

Here begins the Chorus,
which consists of three maidens:

MAIDEN 1. Sisters, have you ever seen anyone so cruelly betrayed, or such diabolical envy, or so terrible a crime as this? Ten brothers sold their innocent younger brother, and at the same time killed their father and damned their own souls.

MAIDEN 2. That's how Envy is. She even lays hands on herself and is most cruel to those who are closest to her. She hates goodness so much that as soon as she sees a virtuous person, she can't wait to see him rot in his coffin.

MAIDEN 3. She's just like a lightning bolt. She strikes whatever is highest. She can't stand for others to be happy; she just wants them to suffer. Just look at what she did to that poor old father! Let's comfort him with a cheerful song.

[They sing:]
Villancico.

Grief must be borne. It won't go soon,
but time will surely heal all wounds.
Only be prudent and wait a while;
before you know it, you will smile.
If patience your cares won't beguile,
use self-control. You'll change your tune,
for time will surely heal all wounds.

PART 2

PROLOGUE

I thought that lament of Jacob's would never be over! I guess that explains why all his descendants are such crybabies. In part 2, ladies and gentlemen, you'll see Joseph sold again as a slave in Egypt; and you'll see how his mistress tries her best to seduce him (of course, we all know women never really do such things!). Then you'll see how she falsely accused him, and he was put in jail. This is a really juicy and fun part; it contains some fine love scenes and sweet talk. I doubt if there's any need to insist that you pay attention, for this lady's polished and elegant style and way of speaking will suffice to keep you alert even if you have been erect for a good while. Too bad it's only a play!

In this second part, ladies and gentlemen, I call your attention to Joseph's patience, virtue, and intelligence—and that of his mistress as well. Since the author is a bit clumsy and crude, and knows little of love, he begs your pardon if this part is not hot enough to get everybody's blood circulating. As for me, I'm sure all of you—no matter how frigid you may be—will feel the heat today. The author did his best to find experienced and knowledgeable people who could provide the instruction he needed, but all he found was a couple of worn-out whores. *[Zenobia sticks her head out through the curtain with an indignant expression on her face.]* Well, you have to take what you can get. I'd better get out of here, because that woman is bursting at the seams to get on stage, and I'm sure she's annoyed by my delays.

ARGUMENT

Zenobia, Putiphar's wife, inflamed with love for Joseph, flirts with him. He cleverly pretends not to notice. Putiphar gets up and, on Joseph's advice, goes to King Pharaoh's house. Zenobia offers Joseph every freedom; he refuses so as not to soil his chastity. Putiphar returns. She puts him off by pretending to be sick. Joseph is affronted by her obscene solicitation. They struggle, and Joseph leaves his cape in her hands. The lady cries out and sends for Putiphar. Joseph is thrown in jail with evildoers, and there he interprets certain dreams.

Characters:

Zenobia	Servants	Pages	Cupbearer	Jailer
Joseph	Putiphar	Chorus	Baker	Prologist

ACT 1

[Zenobia's bedroom in Putiphar's house. It is early in the morning. When the curtain rises, Zenobia is sitting up in bed. Joseph soon arrives in answer to her call.]

ZENOBIA. Boys, boys!

JOSEPH. Yes, ma'am. What can I do for you?

ZENOBIA. Oh, dear! I can't remember what it was I wanted. Anyhow, just stay here.

JOSEPH. Ma'am, it's already past the time for my master Putiphar to get up to go to the king's house. I need to go right away to arrange for the meal to be prepared for great King Pharaoh. Please make my excuses to my master so that he won't be angry with me.

ZENOBIA. My dear boy, what's the point of all these lies and tricks? Don't treat me like this; you're frightening me. You argue with everything I say, and I don't understand why you're constantly aiming your arrows at my heart. Now then, you hateful dog, tell me why you're hurting me like this. Why do you run away every time we're alone together, and why are you always making excuses to get away from me? Why? Answer me! Can't you see I got up early because I have something to say to you?

JOSEPH. Yes, ma'am. Go ahead and say it then. I'll be happy to do whatever you say.

ZENOBIA. You little bastard, you know very well what I mean, but you're trying to play dumb!

JOSEPH. *[Buttoning his jacket.]* Begging your pardon, ma'am, I have to go to the king's house now.

ZENOBIA: Button up good! You look just like a rich man! *[Exit Joseph.]* You bastard, why don't you understand my secret pain? He's out of here faster than an arrow! I don't know what to think. Is this just a silly infatuation? Oh, I'm all choked up! What am I going to do? This is going from bad to worse. Now I can't help believing in the god of love, and I know that he can be meek and bold, and I know he's just a boy, and he's blind. But I'm not about to worship him, because he makes no sense at all. I was happy till he came along, and now he's got me all upset! How could I let this happen? I am a high-class lady, and my husband is crazy about me. How could I let myself be attracted to a kid who's a foreigner and my slave to boot? I can't believe it! A mere teenager, who treats my gods and me so hatefully! I've got to stop thinking about him! This is so embarrassing! If anyone in the king's house found out, I'd never have a moment's peace. A fine example I'd be giving the other court ladies. What would they say? That if it was good enough for me, surely it was okay for any of them to get involved in hanky-panky with their servants too.

Damn it, why do I have such bad luck? Every time I see that boy, it seems like his radiance clears away all the clouds. A thousand times I've thought that the gods must have painted that face. He's so gorgeous, so handsome, so perfectly proportioned! And what a sweet tongue, and what wise things he says! And that hair! There's no purer gold in Arabia! He's just a divine masterpiece. Those teeth are like crystal! And those scarlet lips! The most beautiful women pale by comparison with him.

So what if I've sinned! Who can resist love? And no one could blame me for desiring such a jewel, even if I am a married woman. Although he's a slave, I've heard that he was born in the House of Israel. He didn't respond to my hints, but he's still wet behind the ears. Still, even a block of wood catches fire if you hold it close to the flame long enough. This love is consuming me, and the more I bottle it up, the hotter it burns. I'm just going to have to spell it out for him clearly, calling a spade a spade. But I can't help being afraid of that great God of Abraham, whom Joseph worships so zealously and loves. I'll convert! I'll offer Him sacrifices, for these Egyptian gods of mine seem pretty weak.

Oh, I don't know what to do! Should I speak to him or forget him?

Should I yell at him? Seek his pity? I know he doesn't like me, and that's the worst part! But I am burning with love for him that I don't know how to satisfy. What a mess I'm in! No pain could be worse than the one that's devouring me! Everything seems to be governed by rational laws except love. Where did this overpowering passion come from?

To love: Oh, dangerous love! What a state you've got me into. One minute I'm terrified, then hope dawns anew, only to be dashed again. I don't have a moment's peace. Love for me has meant nothing but anxiety and suffering. I'm so unhappy! Why must I suffer like this?

So what am I going to do? If I rape him and they find out, I'll certainly be put to death. But if I give him up, I know I'll die of longing. Which shall I choose? My mind is made up. As soon as he comes back, I'll speak to him. Little by little, I'll tell him what to do. If the little devil tries to get out of it, I'll just have to get physical. Yes, that's definitely the way to go. The kid is bashful, and he's never been in love before. What does he know? If anybody catches me or my husband shows up suddenly, I'll just say he raped me. I'm sure Putiphar will fall for that. That is, I hope the devil's not deceiving me, for if Putiphar ever found out what was really going on, I'd be in a pickle! He has the worst temper of any man alive! If he ever heard about this, there'd be the devil to pay! I don't know what to do. I just can't win for losing!

I have to be strong. This vile female sex is so weak that I almost gave up for a minute there. I think I hear voices. It must be Putiphar. I guess he finally got up.

ACT 2

[Enter Putiphar.]

PUTIPHAR. Good morning, wife! How come you didn't call me? I should have been at the palace by now, because his majesty will be wanting his food.

ZENOBIA: There was no need, sir.

PUTIPHAR. Why not, my queen?

ZENOBIA. Because that loyal servant of yours was up bright and early and hurried over to his majesty's house to make sure everything was ready.

PUTIPHAR. That's good. But what's the matter then? I'm sure I heard you muttering to yourself, and you sounded really upset.

ZENOBIA. On the contrary, I was just thanking the gods for letting you get some rest and live such an easy life for a change.

PUTIPHAR. Yes, the boy's a wonder! And have you noticed how handsome he is?

ZENOBIA. He's just perfect in every way. You've never had such a slave before.

PUTIPHAR. You know what I think? Ever since he came, my life has gotten better. We've both stayed healthy, and we get richer every day. He's a good kid, and good-looking too.

ZENOBIA. Don't forget he's just a little Jew. Hush, I think he's coming.

ACT 3

[Enter Joseph. He is now wearing a cape.]

JOSEPH. Sir, I'm happy to report that I left his majesty at the table happily eating his breakfast.

PUTIPHAR. Well, I'd better be off, then. Son, you're a lifesaver. Stay here, and look after my house and my wife. I know you love me, and I love you too. From now on I'm treating you as my eldest son.

JOSEPH. Oh sir! May God give you long life and give me the strength to repay such a favor!

[Exit Putiphar.]

ZENOBIA. The other servants have all gone out. What's on your mind, Joseph?

JOSEPH. What's on my mind? My only wish is to do your bidding.

ZENOBIA. You're a sly fox! Do you know I could make you happy?

JOSEPH. My happiness and my destiny are in the hands of God.

ZENOBIA. You can do better than that. Pay attention to what I'm saying, and answer me properly. Oh, I'll never find another like you! Please don't say things like that anymore. Don't be bashful. Don't you know you're not a boy anymore, you're a full-grown man? Can't you see how I've used my influence to make your master love you?

JOSEPH. That's because he knows you're a good wife, which is more important than anything I've ever done for him.

ZENOBIA. Well, I've told him lots of good things about you—and all true too!

JOSEPH. May God reward you!

ZENOBIA. Oh, cut it out! Come closer. Tell me if you have any brothers or sisters.

JOSEPH. Thank God, I have eleven brothers and one sister.

ZENOBIA. If she's as good-looking as you—and I'm sure she must be—she won't have any trouble marrying a rich man.

JOSEPH. Ma'am, where we come from goodness is considered a better dowry than beauty.

ZENOBIA. That's a good one! Come closer, you nasty boy! I want to know if you're in love, for I can see the hunger in your eyes. There's something I'd like to know. If a very beautiful woman took you to a hideaway, and tried to force you to make love to her, what would you do? Would you defend yourself or would you let her go ahead?

JOSEPH. I can't believe any woman would be so shameless as to do something like that. Anyhow, you can't scare me, because no woman would be strong enough to make me do that.

ZENOBIA. *[Aside:]* This is not working; I don't like this one bit. How rudely he answered me!

What if I asked you to do it right now?

JOSEPH. You'd be sorry! But I'm sure you're just teasing me.

ZENOBIA. Come closer, snuggle up! *[Joseph sits down beside her on the bed.]* How could you think such a thing? *[She tries to put her arms around him, but he resists.]* Damn it, don't try to get away from me! Just hug me nice and tight. Don't I deserve it? Why won't you just give what I've asked for so nicely? Why are you such an ingrate? Why do you let me suffer like this?

JOSEPH. I can't do it.

ZENOBIA. You're crazy! Just why can't you do it?

JOSEPH. I can't wrong someone who's been so kind to me. I am indebted to Putiphar, and I won't do something so wicked. Kill me if you like, but I will not soil his honor or his bed.

ZENOBIA. Stop staring at the ground and look at me! Do you know how much I'm worth? Do you know what I can do to you?

JOSEPH. I'm better off just looking at the ground, for that's where we'll all end up sooner or later.

ZENOBIA. Give me a break! Don't be such a scaredy-cat! Enjoy my beauty, and I'll give you your freedom. I've got it right here in this finger!

JOSEPH. I'll never offend my God or Putiphar that way. I'd rather die a thousand deaths.

ZENOBIA. Well, you're not getting away from me. Whether you like it or not . . .

JOSEPH. Ma'am, my master is coming. You'd better get out of here.

ZENOBIA. Oh, he would choose just this minute to show up! He's such a killjoy! I'm going for now, but don't think this is over. I'll get you!

[Exit Zenobia. Joseph quickly gets out of her bed.]

JOSEPH. Oh, dear me! What am I going to do in this awful situation? Great God of Israel, help me! I don't know.

It was bad enough when my brothers tried to kill me, and threw me in that well, and sold me to these foreigners, but this is ten times worse! I'm afraid this mistress of mine will finally be my downfall. No, no, I will not sin! Virtue must triumph in the end! I'd rather be in my coffin than make my God angry. I know this is going to get me in a lot of trouble, but there's nothing I can do but stand up for what I believe. I'd rather die pure than enjoy her beauty and commit a sin, for I know that all the joys of this life taste sweet at first but turn bitter at the end.

Act 4

[Enter Putiphar.]

PUTIPHAR. My servant Joseph, where is your mistress?

JOSEPH. She just now went to your room. I think she was on her way to the living room.

PUTIPHAR. Please look for her, and if she's there, ask her to come here. On second thought, never mind. I'm going there myself anyway.

[Zenobia appears in the doorway.]

JOSEPH. Oh, here she is now, sir.

PUTIPHAR. Wife, I just rushed over here to tell you to fix your face and put on your best clothes and jewelry. As soon as you can get ready, I'll take you to the palace, where they're having a wonderful party where you can relax and have a good time. All the ladies are going. There's never been a party like this before, and I doubt we'll ever see its like again. Come on, we're wasting time! The decorations are fabulous, and you won't believe the entertainment! I've never seen so much gourmet food, or so many good-looking people! Come on; Joseph will keep an eye on things here while we're out.

ZENOBIA. Oh, sir, if only I could go! I feel so bad, I think I must be dying!

PUTIPHAR. What's the matter, darling? *[He puts his hand under her chin and raises her face toward him.]* Let me see your face.

ZENOBIA. *[Aside:]* Damn this sinful desire!

I hardly know what to tell you, I feel so weak.

PUTIPHAR. Well, tell me. I'm worried about you.

ZENOBIA. *[She gets into bed.]* While you were out, I think I must have had a heart attack. The pain was unbearable! Otherwise, I'd like nothing better than to go to the party with you.

PUTIPHAR. I really wish you could see this party! But I certainly don't want
you to die. You stay home then, and Joseph will nurse you, and comfort
you, and make sure you have anything your heart desires.

[Exit Putiphar.]

ZENOBIA. Off you go! What a stupid jerk he is, rushing over here like that,
all excited about some dumb party! He gave me quite a scare, though! I
hope he never comes back, damn him!

Zenobia addresses Joseph: Baby, why are you such an ingrate? Why
do you keep playing hard to get? What's the good of making me suffer
like this? Don't you see how silly it is for you not to enjoy my beauty?
No one can see us now. Take me. I'm your mistress; don't despise me
like this. Treat me like a Moor! Come here, you big dumb stud! Just
think of me as your equal. I'll even be your maid, if you like that better!
Hurry up, damn it! Before somebody catches us, come on in and help
yourself. You can have anything you want. I'm all yours.

JOSEPH. It's not my place, ma'am.

ZENOBIA. This has got to be the worst thing that's ever happened!

JOSEPH. I know it's painful, ma'am, but you just have to control yourself.

ZENOBIA. Spare me your advice, my dear. I'm a consenting adult. Just give
me what I'm entitled to.

JOSEPH. What could I give you?

ZENOBIA. Your heart, my dear. You needn't blush. If I could be this bold for
your sake, surely you can too. You're not dumb. You must know that
things like this happen all the time. It's just part of life. You know what
I mean. I'm not ugly. Don't make me beg.

JOSEPH. What you're asking me to do is ugly, even if you're not. You can
hack me to pieces, but I won't give you what you want.

ZENOBIA. Can't you see how I'm shaking? Don't you see these tears? Have
you no pity?

JOSEPH. I will not commit such an outrage against my blood, my master, or
my God, for He knows everything.

ZENOBIA. Oh, yes you will, you bastard—or else I'll kill you with my own
hands; or I'll tell my husband you raped me, and he'll fix you so you
won't ever trouble a woman again. You're not the only one who can play
hardball. Get the picture, smarty-pants? Come here now, and love me
like an animal! Just keep on coming till I'm too exhausted to be mad!

[Joseph approaches her bed.]

JOSEPH. Ma'am, I really sympathize with you, and I'm very sorry I can't
help you out.

ZENOBIA. That will get you nowhere. We've talked enough. Just do it now!

JOSEPH. You know I can't.

ZENOBIA. Just hold still then, and kiss me, baby! *[She embraces and kisses him, while he struggles.]*

JOSEPH. Oh, my God and Creator, I call You to witness this!

ZENOBIA. I'm not too proud to rape you, if that's what you want. *[She tries to get on top of Joseph. They wrestle fiercely and at length. Both have their clothes half torn off. At last Joseph pulls himself free and runs away. She clings to his cape, which tears off and remains in her hands.]*

Go ahead then, run away. It won't do you any good, for this garment of yours is your death warrant.

Help, help! Oh, the pain! Pages, pages!

[A page comes running in.]

PAGE. What is it, ma'am?

ZENOBIA. Run straight to Pharaoh's house, and tell my husband to come home at once.

[He leaves.]

I'll see that you suffer more than anyone who's ever been born!

Alas, poor womenfolk! Every Tom, Dick, and Harry thinks he can have his way with you, but you're the one who always gets blamed. Oh, who am I kidding! Just embrace me, and I'll forget all about it. You won't? Well, then you'll have to die! Where did you get your nerve? What have I ever done to encourage you to attack me this way? Oh, come here, baby, I can't hate you! You don't like me? Then you'll feel death's cold embrace before this day is over. Oh, what is keeping Putiphar! I want him here right now so he can punish that bastard! Oh, husband: How could you have trusted that man? How dare he rape a modest married lady?

[Enter Putiphar.]

PUTIPHAR. Why did you need me here so fast? What's all the yelling and screaming?

ZENOBIA. Sir, just look at my veil. See how my clothes are torn, and my body is bruised! Look at my teeth all bloodied by that bastard servant of yours named Joseph, the worst of the worst!

PUTIPHAR. Oh, my darling, what a disaster!

ZENOBIA. As soon as that dog saw that the other servants had gone out, he thought I was sleeping, and he climbed in my bed and tried to rape me, but I screamed like a crazy woman.

PUTIPHAR. How horrible! Who would ever have thought such a thing?

ZENOBIA. He ran away, but he left this cape behind as evidence of his wickedness. Punish this ugly deed if you don't want me to die.

PUTIPHAR. I never dreamed that something like this would even cross his mind, he's always been such a well-behaved lad.

ZENOBIA. I don't want to hear it! You should have known that blood will out. He and his whole family are nothing but circumcised little Jews.

PUTIPHAR. It's all so strange! I would have thought he was too intelligent to try something like that.

ZENOBIA. With that sort of background what could you expect? Even the Jews didn't want him. That's how he got here in the first place.

PUTIPHAR. So all his loyalty to me was just an act! Oh gods, where are you? How can you permit such wickedness? Is there no more honesty and loyalty left in the world? How can you trust anyone, even your own brother? Anyone would have said Joseph was a person without vices, someone who wouldn't have known how to misbehave if he wanted to—and all the time he was this vicious rapist whom you wouldn't trust with your worst enemy. But I swear by holy Anubis[45] to give him the punishment he deserves. *[Calls out to his servants:]* Hey, boys! Fetch me that little bastard at once, and take him straight to jail, where he belongs. *[They go offstage and return with Joseph in chains.]* No, don't take the little bastard! Come here, you horny little dog, so I can take those chains off you! *[Joseph starts to move toward him.]* I loved you so much, I wanted to make you a master instead of a slave! And you hurt me like this! Take the criminal away, double his chains! *[Exeunt servants with Joseph.]*

[To Zenobia:] Don't cry, darling. Don't let this upset you anymore. When he's chained up in the dungeon, he'll pay for what he did to you.

ZENOBIA. Ay, ay, ay!

PUTIPHAR. What's the matter now? I'm afraid Joseph will be the death of you yet. You are really the last word in female virtue!

ACT 5

[Pharaoh's jail. A jailer is sitting at a table. Putiphar's servants arrive with Joseph.]

SERVANT. Jailer, what are you doing? Take this prisoner and put a heavy chain on him, and lock him up tight with the other criminals who are jailed here for their crimes. And make sure you don't let anyone see him!

JAILER. Don't worry, men, I know how to do my job. I can see that he must have committed some horrible crime.

SERVANT. He's very sneaky. You'd better take extra precautions with him.

[Exeunt servants.]

JAILER. Buddy, since you've had the bad luck to end up here in jail, I'll take good care of you. Boy, are you good-looking! Anyone could tell by looking at you that you don't belong here. Well, try not to be blue about it. You can have a good time here too if you know how. It's against the rules, but I just can't stand to lock you up. Just make yourself at home, and feel free to roam around the jail as much as you like and enjoy yourself as much as you can. I can tell you're a really good guy. You must be exhausted. Take a load off your feet. *[Joseph sits down at a table, and the jailer hands him a plate full of food.]* Here, have a bite to eat. Just ask me if there's anything I can do for you.

JOSEPH. Jailer, I don't know how I can ever repay your kindness, but I want you to know I'm very grateful.

[Enter the Cupbearer.]

JAILER. I can tell you're a classy guy. I'd like you to meet the king's cupbearer. I'm sure you two will have a lot in common.

JOSEPH. This seems more like sweet freedom than jail.

CUPBEARER. Welcome to jail, amigo. Too bad we have to meet under such circumstances. But what brings you here?

JOSEPH. My sins. It's God's will, and since that's what He wants, there's nothing to do but bless Him and praise Him. This is what I got for doing the right thing.

CUPBEARER. Well, it's really nice to have a young guy here.

JOSEPH. May God preserve you, and get you out of this jail!

CUPBEARER. The same to you! I can tell by the way you talk that you're not Egyptian.

JOSEPH. That's right. Thank God, I am a Hebrew from Canaan, a direct descendant of Abraham and an enemy of paganism.

CUPBEARER. Since you Jews are so intelligent and learned, and know more than anyone else, please do me a favor. I've had a dream that's got me really upset. Tell me what it means.

The Cupbearer's dream.

I dreamed I saw three grapevines, and there was one cluster of grapes that looked good enough to pick and squeeze into the king's cup. Like a good servant, I offered that juice to the king with the usual ceremonies, and he drank it with pleasure. My friend, can you interpret this for me?

JOSEPH. Certainly, brother, I'll be glad to tell you what it means. In three days you will be released from prison and will go back to serving the king in your former post. So you can forget all about your sadness and pain, for soon you'll be happily getting out of jail.

CUPBEARER. I feel certain what you've told me is true. Oh, what wonderful news! And to think that I had such a dream while locked up in jail! This is not an earthly matter. It comes from God.

JOSEPH. Praise God, you're right. So you might as well sit down and have a good dinner. But please, when you get out, remember me; for you know that I've done nothing to deserve being put in prison.

CUPBEARER. Of course, I'll do that and even more for you. I can never repay you for what you've done for me. You're a great man and a great soul, and you are to be praised for your knowledge and goodness. You deserve to be prosperous. I'll certainly remember you. *[Enter the Baker and another prisoner.]* But right now I want to tell these friends of mine who are also prisoners here. Brothers, in case you haven't met this prisoner you see here, you really ought to, for he is the most prudent, most wise, most excellent lad you could ever hope to see. I had a dream that had me all upset and worried, and he interpreted it for me. I think he knows everything.

BAKER. Well, I've also had a dream that's caused me a lot of anguish. Since you say he possesses occult knowledge, maybe he can interpret it for me.

JOSEPH. Tell me, friend, and with God's help, I'll do what you've asked.

BAKER. Then tell me the meaning of what I dreamed last night. I haven't had a moment's peace since then.

The Baker's dream.

I dreamed that I had three baskets stacked on my head. Two of them were full of bread, and the third one was overflowing with all kinds of rich and rare foods fit for the king's table. Just then some birds flew over and carried off all the food.

JOSEPH. Brother, what you've told me is strange and sad. I'm afraid you won't be pleased with its meaning.

BAKER. Well anyhow, don't keep in suspense, since you have the answer.

JOSEPH. Friend, I wish I had something better to interpret for you. I really hate to be the bearer of such bad tidings, but I'd better just tell it straight, for that's the way it is. The two baskets you dreamed about mean that you have only two more days to live. The third one means that on the third day you will be crucified, and for your crimes the birds will eat your flesh. Please forgive me. I wish it were not so, but I can only tell you the truth.

[The curtain falls. Enter the Chorus, consisting of three maidens.]

MAIDEN 1. The things Love can do! That was some wrestling match! She really put his virtue to the test, but he came through it with his purity and faithfulness intact. Do you think that anybody nowadays could resist her charms?

MAIDEN 2. Life is really unfair! First his brothers hate him, then his mistress loves him—but, regardless, they all try to kill him. How horrible of that woman to falsely accuse the man she loved just because she fell for him!

MAIDEN 3. I feel sorry for Joseph, but you can't blame that poor, weak woman. You obviously know nothing about love! It knows no master and harms its followers most. God protect us from its wrath!

[They sing:]
Villancico.

Love is something you cannot trust;
give up your heart, and suffer you must.
Love begins with sweetness and light,
you think it's unalloyed delight,
but then it hits you with all its might.
Your honor and life will soon bite the dust,
give up your heart and suffer you must.

PART 3

PROLOGUE

Ladies and gentlemen, I come before you both embarrassed and very upset. Embarrassed by the behavior of the actors and the audience. Upset by seeing some of you upset, or rather angry. You've no business getting angry at me, for I have performed in the Roman Colosseum before the pope and cardinals; and in Bologna and in Augsburg before the emperor;[46] before the great King of Romans[47] in Bohemia; and in London before the king of England; and in Paris before the king of France; and in Naples before the viceroy and princes; and in Constantinople and Cairo before the Grand Turk;[48] and not least, before the great Sophy, emperor of Russia;[49] and in Lisbon before the king of Portugal; and in the field before the marquis of Gasto[50]—and those illustrious audiences have always listened to me with pleasure and the utmost attention for six long hours. You guys, on the other hand, seem all too ready to attack and decapitate a saint! Well, I'm putting you on notice that these days there are no saints worth decapitating.

Now comes part 3, which you'll find is shorter and more enjoyable than

62   MIGUEL DE CARVAJAL

the previous ones. Here, ladies and gentlemen, you will at last see Joseph's
dreams come true, and you'll see his father and brothers show up before
him, first scared, then happy, and finally sharing in his glory.

I know the sun is really hot out there this afternoon. The author has used
every trick in the book to keep you so caught up in his play that you won't
feel the heat; but maybe, like a cheap awning, he's stretched himself too
thin. Just bear in mind that he's not asking for jewels or money. All he
wants is for you to lend him your ears for a while. Surely that's not too
much to ask. Just take it easy, and if you're hot, give each other a good
blow; and remember that the blacksmith behind his forge is a lot hotter
than you are. Be patient. It's not easy to shorten something that took a lot of
years to happen, like this story. Pay attention then, for it's sweeter than a
honeycomb. See you later!

ARGUMENT

Pharaoh, king of Egypt, disturbed by some dreams he had, sends for his
sages and fortune-tellers to interpret them for him. When they don't succeed, the king hears from his cupbearer about how when he was in prison
Joseph, Putiphar's slave, had interpreted some other dreams for him and a
baker of his, and the interpretations had turned out to be true. The king
reprimands him for not thinking of Joseph sooner, and has Joseph taken
out of jail and brought before him. Joseph admirably interprets the king's
dreams and offers him a plan for dealing with the great famine that is to
come. Satisfied with his interpretation and impressed with him, Pharaoh
makes Joseph governor of Egypt, puts him in charge of all the wheat, and
orders his people to do everything Joseph tells them and to acclaim him as
Savior of Egypt and Knower of Secrets. Having been appointed governor,
Joseph very intelligently makes arrangements so that there will be no shortage of bread during the coming seven years of famine.

Characters:

Pharaoh	Cupbearer	Framech	Crier
Canopeus, chamberlain	Zarahan	Joseph	Chorus

ACT 1

*[Pharaoh's bedroom. Pharaoh is in bed, and his chamberlain
Canopeus is standing beside him.]*

PHARAOH. Am I glad to see the sunlight! What a night I've been through! Just tossing and turning all night long! What could that dream possibly mean?

CANOPEUS. God save you, sire. Begging your pardon, I couldn't sleep a wink either because of the noise your majesty was making.

PHARAOH. I was very upset about some dreams I had. You know I think it's silly to pay attention to dreams; but these dreams had such a consistent pattern to them that I couldn't help thinking they might be some sort of revelation from God. I want to consult my sages and fortune-tellers. If dreams ever have a meaning, I feel sure these do. Canopeus, go find Framech and Zarahan wherever they are, and tell them to come here at once.

[Exit Canopeus. Enter the Cupbearer, who serves Pharaoh his juice.]

CUPBEARER. Sire, I couldn't help overhearing what you said about your dreams, and I felt just like hanging myself. What an ingrate I've been! Damn my thoughtlessness!

PHARAOH. What are you so distressed about? Have you offended me in some way?

CUPBEARER. Not at all, sire. I was just remembering how, when one of your bakers and I were in prison by your command a while ago, I made friends with Joseph, Putiphar's servant, a Canaanite by birth, who had been falsely accused. That baker and I each had a dream, and our friend interpreted them for us exactly right. He told the other man that they would hang him on the third day; and he told me that I would be released right away. And sure enough, they hanged the baker shortly after that, and I was brought back to Your Majesty's house. I promised my friend the diviner that I would do what I could to win his freedom and help him out, and I honestly forgot all about him.

PHARAOH. Your thoughtlessness is really unforgivable. But anyhow, go to the prison right now and bring me that praiseworthy young man at once.

CUPBEARER. Oh sire, I assure you his wisdom is admirable. I promise you, if he's still alive, there's no one who can speak better than he.

[Exit Cupbearer. Enter Zarahan and Framech.]

ZARAHAN. Canopeus summoned us. What does Your Excellency desire?

PHARAOH. Oh, I'm glad you're here. Yes, since you're so learned, I'd like you to interpret a couple of dreams I've had about the future, which I suspect were sent to me by Divine Providence. And I'll tell you, these dreams are so bizarre that I think some very weird things are in store for us.

FRAMECH. May the immortal gods protect your majesty from adversity and deliver you from all evil! We are experts in predicting the future. Our science has nothing to do with the interpretation of dreams, which is just a vain superstition. We analyze the behavior of animals and other natural phenomena, and then we draw our conclusions. For example, if the earth were to shake now, or if there were a battle between the sun and the moon . . . if this river dried up, or if an animal bellowed unnaturally, we could tell you what that meant right away. But interpreting dreams is nothing but trickery and fraud. If there's any truth in it, nobody has found it so far.

[Enter the Cupbearer, followed by Joseph. Joseph has grown a long beard.]

CUPBEARER. Sire, here is that poor boy Joseph that I was praising before. He's been in jail all this time.

[Joseph kneels before Pharaoh.]

PHARAOH. I'm so glad you've come! Get up, my boy, and touch me with your hand, because I can tell you're full of grace. Tell me, my friend, how long have you been in prison?

JOSEPH. This beard is a good indication, for I've grown it in prison.

PHARAOH. Well, that's all behind you now. I implore you by your God to interpret two dreams I've had that have troubled me greatly. I've already consulted my sages, but they can't do it, so you're my only hope.

JOSEPH. Tell me about it. I hope that God will prosper you, and will give me the grace to serve you as I wish.

Dreams.

PHARAOH. I dreamed that on a hill beside the Nile seven cows were grazing. They were so fat their skin was practically bursting. Then came seven lean ones, and they were so hungry, they ate up the first seven and still weren't satisfied. Then I dreamed of seven ears tightly packed with wheat, and seven other empty ones that consumed the full ones. I think this must mean something important, yet I find it very puzzling. If you understand its meaning, please explain it to me.

JOSEPH. All knowledge comes from God. He has shown me that the cows and the ears of wheat mean the same thing. Seven years are coming during which Egypt will have an enormous abundance of bread, more than you could ever desire. But after that will come seven years so extraordinarily sterile that they will consume all that abundance. Pardon my boldness, Your Majesty, but you really should begin storing up for the future. As God is my witness, I assure you that what I have told you will certainly happen.

PHARAOH. You've given me quite a shock! It looks like my work is cut out for me. Gentlemen, what do you think? What knowledge! What divine skill! His words and gestures and his brilliant mind all suggest that our immortal gods are speaking through him. Brother, since you are so close to your God and so knowledgeable, tell me what we can do to keep such a disaster from befalling us.

JOSEPH. Only God can take away that sterility. But He has given you the chance to save yourselves by taking advantage of the time of abundance. What Your Majesty should do is find a very intelligent and reliable man, someone you can trust, to administer during the seven years of abundance. He will arrange for one-fifth of all the wheat harvested during that time to be collected and stored up. That will provide for you during the famine you dreamed about.

FRAMECH. An excellent idea! I can't think of anything better.

PHARAOH. I really like your spirit and your way of speaking. But where could we find such a man? There's no question that you're the only one who could do this properly.

FRAMECH. By the immortal gods, in all my years of reading and studying I've never come across anything like this! How divinely he speaks! What knowledge! What intelligence! He seems destined for a fate more than human. Zarahan, what do you think?

ZARAHAN. I have no doubt that he has the most penetrating mind that has ever been, or ever will be.

FRAMECH. Oh, gods! And what skill at solving the most vexing problems!

PHARAOH. It's settled then. I order you, I beg you, and I ask you to take on this task, since the gods have endowed you with such recondite knowledge.

JOSEPH. It's quite a job for a lowly slave, but if that is what you command, it must be God's will.

CUPBEARER. Most Serene Lord, I can attest that there's no one better qualified in the world.

PHARAOH. He is worthy of great honor. Since he has agreed to do as I've asked, he will be my closest friend and the greatest man in my kingdoms. Chamberlain, bring him a choice robe right away. Joseph, sit down here next to me as my brother and partner. You will be my treasurer and governor, and all my kingdom will have to answer to you. I order it proclaimed throughout Egypt that your every command shall be obeyed without delay. Take this chain of mine and this ring too as a sign that everyone must bow when you pass by. In Egypt and its kingdom you shall have the title of "Savior of the Peoples," because you managed to interpret secrets that my sages could not penetrate, as all present have witnessed.

JOSEPH. May the great God of Israel prosper your majesty, and give me the ability to serve both you and Him.

PHARAOH. Everybody, go with him. Canopeus, bring my sedan chair, and have Joseph carried in it to my headquarters immediately. Prepare a palace for him just as if he were a member of the royal family, the same as you would do for me. My friend, why don't you get some rest now. *[Exit Canopeus. He returns immediately with other servants bearing the royal sedan chair.]*

JOSEPH. Sire, your wish is my command.

PHARAOH. Go with him, don't delay!

[Joseph gets into the sedan chair.]

CANOPEUS. Gentlemen, help me carry his grace. Let his royal trumpeters announce the Savior's coming, and you footmen, march before us. *He reads a proclamation:* The great King Pharaoh commands that all bow down before Joseph, governor of Egypt and its kingdom. He further commands that this gentleman be titled "Savior of Egypt and Knower of All Secrets."

JOSEPH. Since God has exalted us, and it is my duty to serve His Highness, I order a proclamation made throughout the state that no one should sow or store up grain without first registering with me, and without my written permission. Very severe penalties, such as prison, death, and the other usual punishments shall be given to violators. You shall also proclaim that whoever is in need should come to my house, and you will provide them with bread. And because the Nile is such a long, deep river, as a symbol of the abundance of this royal house, let every man empty straw into the Nile to symbolize that I have enough room in my granaries to store up bread for everyone.

The Chorus begins.

MAIDEN 1. What a glorious triumph! Virtue is rewarded! It has survived that insane envy, near death in the well, slavery, the threat of that illicit love, and prison; and now at last you see it exalted to the heights.

MAIDEN 2. Life is full of rude shocks. What fluctuations, what drastic changes it brings! Now we see the lowly exalted, and the high and mighty cast down. I think the moral of all this is that when virtue survives all temptations, there's always a happy ending.

MAIDEN 3. What brilliant judgments! Did you see how that dreamer Joseph has become a great lord? His brothers hate him so much and are so insane that they'd like to tear out their own eyes. How vain it is to resist God's will!

[They sing:]
Villancico.
When faced with Heaven, human power
can only cower, can only cower.
He is our Maker, we can but surrender
our lives to His will.
As his humble servants, we know we must render
obeisance, His orders fulfill.
Let no one imagine his own puny will
can challenge God's power.

End of Part Three.

PART 4

PROLOGUE

I'm happy to see that you were all glad part 3 was so short—just as short as the first two were long. Still, I can't help suspecting that you must all be starving by now. Too bad! You'll just have to wait for the seven years of plenty.

As I'm sure you've noticed, ladies and gentlemen, the author has worked hard to cover all of that stuff as quickly as possible in order to get to what he knows you really want, which are these last parts we're coming to now. You'll soon see how far they exceed the rest in excellence, art, and pleasure. Here you won't see any more sackcloth, mourning, and laments, but only pleasure, gladness, and rejoicing; although, when you're dealing with Jews, there's bound to be some discontent, since they're such a quarrelsome bunch of troublemakers, who always want to see just how far they can go. You'd better pay close attention during this journey from Canaan to Egypt, because if you'll just keep your mouths shut, we plan to get through it in the wink of an eye.

ARGUMENT

Jacob, seeing how the famine was taking such a toll in Canaan, sends his sons to Egypt for bread. There Joseph, Pharaoh's governor, controlled the sales of bread. When the brothers get to Egypt, Joseph recognizes them. He gives them a good scare by accusing them of being spies. Then he orders that they be given bread. When he hears them mention Benjamin, he decides to hold Simeon hostage until they bring Benjamin to him. Jacob at first refuses this request but finally yields to his sons' pleading. They take him before Joseph, and he orders that they be given more bread. In order to find out whether they dislike Benjamin as they did him, he orders a golden cup put in the young man's sack. When his men discover the cup, they arrest all the brothers as thieves and bring them before the governor, who insults and mistreats them until at last he reveals himself to them, at which they rejoice greatly. Joseph sends for his father. When his father and relatives arrive, Pharaoh is pleased to give them homes and lands in Goshen. Jacob lives in Egypt for seventeen years.

Characters:

Naphtali	Porter	Levi	Jacob	Steward
Simeon	Judah	Issachar	Joseph	Captain
Dan	Zebulun	Reuben	Pharaoh	Soldiers
Gad	Asher	Benjamin	Chorus	Prologist

ACT 1

[The set is a cutaway view of Joseph's palace. The street outside is at stage right. We can see some of the facade, an anteroom (the anteroom contains a staircase leading to an upstairs landing with a window overlooking the street), where a porter stands guard, Joseph's receiving room, and a small private chamber behind his throne. Joseph is sitting on the throne with servants flanking him. Enter Naphtali, Simeon, Dan, Gad, Judah, Zebulun, Asher, Levi, Issachar, and Reuben.]

NAPHTALI. Nothing could be more wearisome than traveling.
SIMEON. It's bad, all right, but hunger is a lot worse! Thank God, at last we've reached Egypt.
DAN. This fine palace must be the Savior's house.
GAD. I hear people inside. Let's knock. *[Gad knocks, and a porter answers the door.]*
PORTER. Who is it? What do you want?
JUDAH. Please take us to the Savior. We've heard proclamations that bread is distributed to everyone here. We've come all the way from Canaan, and we'll be happy to pay for it.
PORTER. Just wait outside, and I'll inform the governor. *[The Porter goes back inside to consult Joseph.]*

ZEBULUN. This wretched famine will be the ruin of us yet! As if we hadn't suffered enough, now we're in this foreign country and have to put up with snotty porters.

[The Porter returns.]

PORTER. Come on in, you foreigners. His lordship is waiting.

REUBEN. God save Your Excellency, Great Lord Governor, and give you long life, and make you prosper!

[The brothers enter, and are brought before Joseph.]

JOSEPH. Who are you, gentlemen, and where are you from?

REUBEN. We are Your Lordship's servants, and have just arrived here.

JOSEPH. You look nervous. I think you must be spies.

LEVI. Sir, please let me explain . . .

JOSEPH. *[To his servants:]* See how they're sweating? I'll bet they're spies, and they've come to see how we're surviving in this country.

SIMEON. God forbid that any of us should ever be a spy! Please let me explain to Your Lordship. We are direct descendants of Abraham, and we have come from Canaan, where the famine is raging fiercely. All ten of us are sons of Jacob. There were twelve of us, but God took one some time ago, and the youngest stayed home with our father to comfort him in his old age. It was our father who sent us here for bread.

JOSEPH. I'm not impressed. Criminals always have excellent alibis. But it won't do you any good. I can spot a criminal face anytime, and I know for a fact that you came here planning to do us harm. I'll give you the punishment you deserve. Anyone could tell from your clothes that you're lying, and that you've come here as scouts. You're not related at all; you're just a band of thieves who have joined together to come here and rob us. I'll bet you come from many different regions, and you thought you'd fool us! There's no family resemblance among you at all. It's easy to see that you're from a faraway land. But I'd really like to know how an ordinary man could have ten sons like you. A king would be thrilled to have such handsome offspring!

Reuben's speech.

REUBEN. Great Lord, I beg Your Excellency to hear what I have to say. With all due reverence, when we heard of your compassion, your virtue, and your generosity, we made bold to come before you. I can certainly understand how seeing so many young men together might make you suspicious, but please don't think we are spies nor that we have come to do any harm. It was your goodness that encouraged us to come to Egypt. This famine has lasted so long that it has left our country desolate. When we heard that here they give bread to foreigners as well as natives, we decided to come; and that's all there is to it. Necessity, the mother of invention, brought us here and showed us the way. Our only reason for coming was to ensure our survival and that of our children. We have no desire to harm your king nor his kingdom. We're not that sort of people; after all, we too are of royal blood.

We are all members of the same family, sons of Jacob, a good Hebrew and Canaanite man, although we have four different mothers. There were twelve of us in all, but one named Joseph died, and we mourned greatly for him. The youngest one, a lad named Benjamin, has stayed with our poor old father to comfort him in his old age. He enjoys having a young boy around. If you don't believe what I've said, please send someone to our land to investigate, and you'll find out that we're no spies, but rather just some poor Canaanites who mean you no harm.

JOSEPH. I still say you're liars, and you won't get out of here unless you bring me that other brother. Let one of you go for him right away, and I'll keep the others in prison until he returns. I've never seen such wickedness! Hey, guards! Take these men to jail! On second thought, I think I'll just keep this one. *[Points to Simeon.]* Tie him up well. The rest of you, go home with your wheat, and if you bring the other one back, I promise to set this one free and give you the food you need. Now get out of here before I change my mind!

REUBEN. Sir, we will do as you say, though God knows you've misjudged us.

JOSEPH. *[Aside:]* Servants, give those foreigners their wheat, and when they're not looking, put their money in their sacks.

[The brothers go out into the street.]

LEVI. How just is the wrath that we've suffered today! God is punishing us now for the hatred we harbored toward our brother.

REUBEN. Why wouldn't you listen to me when you made up your minds to get rid of him? Now we've had to leave Simeon here in jail. Surely Jacob has suffered enough. How can we tell him he's lost another son? This time it will surely kill him! He's not strong enough to go through that sort of grief again. Oh wretched mortals who desire a long life, what's the point if you have to spend it in pain and anguish? How will that poor old man react to this news? What will he do?

JUDAH. There's nothing to do but go on. The animals just keep moving. Somehow I feel that, God willing, everything will turn out for the best.

[Exeunt the brothers.]

JOSEPH. I'm so glad to know that my father and brothers are all alive and well! Blessed be God, who willed that this should happen. Now I can forget all the suffering I endured; but I still want to scare them a little more, so that afterward their joy will be even greater.

ACT 2

[Jacob's house in Canaan. Jacob and Benjamin are on stage when the curtain rises.]

JACOB. I think I hear a noise. It must be my sons. Yes, I'm sure they must be coming now.
   [Enter Reuben, Levi, Gad, Asher, Zebulun, Judah, and Dan.]
REUBEN. Oh, father dear! God save you and keep you!
JACOB. Welcome home, sons! Blessed be God for bringing you back to me. Tell me what happened. I want to hear all about it. I've been so worried about you, but now you can tell me that everything is all right.
LEVI. Father, they gave us all the bread our beasts could carry, and we've brought it here. But we do have some bad news too. We had to leave your son Simeon in jail there until we take them Benjamin.
JACOB. Holy God, what are you saying? You left my son in jail? How can I bear to hear this? Has anyone ever suffered like me?
GAD. Listen, listen, father.
JACOB. No, go away! Don't tell me any more!
ASHER. Oh, father, stop your crying and listen to what I have to say. There is a governor in Egypt who is over all the land, and he personally distributes all the bread that's stored up there. He is the one who has taken our brother prisoner, because he's afraid of a war. When he saw so many of us young men together, he thought we must be spies. He was very suspicious, and he demanded that we tell him all about our ancestry. Simeon did so in order to oblige him; and when he found out that we were eleven brothers, and the youngest one was here with you, he arrested him to find out whether what he had heard was just slander.[51] He intends to hold Simeon until we bring him Benjamin. He impressed me as a God-fearing man who will keep his promise to us.
JACOB. Who would have thought such suffering could still be in store for me? Oh, what a life full of woe! And you tried to keep this from me! I'd rather die of hunger than see anything happen to my son Benjamin. He is all I have left. Please don't ask me for him. Don't even think about it. No matter how much you nag me, I won't give in.
ZEBULUN. I beg you, honored father, don't do this to us. How could someone as good as you allow this to happen? You know that Simeon is being

held hostage and is suffering in jail. We only left him there because we trusted in your virtue. It would be wrong for us to go back there without Benjamin, because Simeon has sacrificed himself for the good of our children and relatives.

JACOB. Don't talk to me about it! You might as well just offer me a coffin.

JUDAH. Jacob, father, I must say what I think. The governor swore that if we appeared before him again without Benjamin, he would have us all tortured and killed. There's no way we can go back there and buy the food we need unless you give us Benjamin. We promised to bring him, and we have to keep our promise.

[While this conversation is going on, Dan is dragging some of the sacks of wheat onstage. Then he begins untying the sacks.]

ZEBULUN. Father, you must realize that our women and children will soon consume all the bread we've brought, and there's no place else where we can get more. It would be a grave mistake not to provide for the coming famine. This is what it comes down to: if we go back to Egypt without Benjamin, we'll be condemned as spies and executed; and if we stay here, they'll kill Simeon, and we'll all starve; and we'll have lost our good name to boot.

DAN. Listen, what is the meaning of this? All the money we paid the steward for the grain is in our sacks.

JACOB. No wonder he suspected you! Now I'm sure he must have killed Simeon.

REUBEN. Father, don't be afraid to give us Benjamin. I will be his guarantor. If any harm—no matter how slight—befalls him, you can kill these two sons of mine. Please don't put off giving him to us; for the longer you delay, the more you put our family honor in jeopardy.

JACOB. You boys are some comfort to your father! I've already lost Joseph, and now I suspect another of my sons is dead. Aren't you ashamed to take this boy off to an early grave? You just want to take him because you know he's my favorite and my only comfort. Don't do this to me, sons. It will be the death of me!

JUDAH. Sir, you can see how terrible the famine is. If you refuse to give us Benjamin, you're sentencing us all to death. Give him to me. I'll take full responsibility, and you can be sure I'll bring him back to you as you wish. Our children may starve to death at any moment. Why torment them like this when you don't have to! I think it's worse than if you just poisoned them all. If I don't return to you with Benjamin, consider me a murderer, the worst that ever lived, and I will suffer the consequences.

JACOB. What a cruel dilemma! I can't bear to see my children starve! But if I give them Benjamin, I'll die alone. Oh, do what you want! At least

death will put me out of my misery. But please take good care of him.
Oh, God! I beg You to watch over him. First let me hug him; I may not
ever see him again. *[Jacob embraces Benjamin.]*

Take a lot of the best fruits of this land and give them to that governor as presents: there's plenty of honey, sweet gum, and almonds. Take
money to pay for your purchases, as well as the money that was put
back in your sacks.

REUBEN. We will do as you say, and we'll get started right now.

JUDAH. Everything is in readiness.

JACOB. May God prosper this journey, which is causing me so much pain
and grief!

BENJAMIN. Father, may He comfort you and keep you from worrying.

NAPHTALI. Let's get going! The caravan has already left, and we'll have to
catch up with it.

JUDAH. Benjamin, you go next to me so that no one will bother you.

[Exeunt the brothers.]

ACT 3

*[Joseph's palace; as in part 4, scene 1. Joseph is sitting on his
throne, as before, with his steward beside him. Enter the brothers.]*

PORTER. *[Looks out an upstairs window.]* Who's there? Oh, yes, it must be
Simeon's brothers. They certainly didn't waste any time.

REUBEN. Behave yourselves, brothers. The porter can see us.

LEVI. May God prosper you!

PORTER. And may He make your prosperity increase! *[The Porter goes down-
stairs and whispers in the steward's ear.]*

STEWARD. Sir, those Hebrews from Canaan who took bread from here a
while ago are back.

JOSEPH. Put them up in a very nice room, and see that their feet are washed.
Then invite them to dinner. Treat them very well, for they deserve it.
Hurry up! My reputation is at stake.

*[The Steward brings the brothers into the anteroom, closing the door
that separates it from Joseph's reception room.]*

STEWARD. My lord has ordered me to bring you in here. Make yourselves at
home. He'll be here soon, and he wants you to stay for dinner.

JUDAH. Brothers, I don't like this one bit. I think he intends to have *us* for
dinner! He's going to make us pay back that money we found in our
sacks.

ASHER. If that's all it is, we should just tell him what happened.

JUDAH. Sir, we want you to know that when we emptied out the wheat, we found all the money we had paid you for it. We've brought it back here with us, as well as more money for the bread we need to buy now.

DAN. We don't know how this could have happened, but we hope you realize we had nothing to do with it.

STEWARD. Don't worry about it. I still have all the money you paid me. It must have been your God who put that money in your sacks. *[Enter Simeon.]* And here is your beloved brother, who has been languishing in jail.

REUBEN. Oh, Brother, we've missed you so much! Let me give you a hug! I thought sure you were dead.

LEVI. Could we please see His Lordship the Governor?

STEWARD. Yes, you may go right on in. He's not busy now.

[He opens the door, and the brothers enter and stand before Joseph's throne, offering him gifts.]

REUBEN. Sir, your servant Jacob sends Your Lordship his greetings and this gift of some products that grow there: honey, sweet gum, resin, turpentine, and fine wax. Please accept it with his compliments. *[Pushes Benjamin forward.]* He is also pleased to send you his beloved son Benjamin.

JOSEPH. I'm very grateful for your kindness. And since I see that you told me the truth, I'll withdraw the charges against you. I'm glad to hear your father is alive. So this is Benjamin, my brother—I mean, *your* brother! He seems a little bashful. I'm so happy to hear the news you've brought me today!

JUDAH. Canaan is doing fine, except that everyone is worried about Simeon.

JOSEPH. *[Overcome with emotion, he goes into the inner chamber behind the throne.]* How I've longed to hear that news! What an incomparable pleasure! What a miracle! I can't help crying for joy. My suffering is over, and my joy is complete. How handsome Benjamin is! He's the spitting image of my father. God bless you, brother! I've never been so happy in my life! *[He comes back out to his brothers.]* Well, let's have something to eat and take it easy for a while. I know it's forbidden for Egyptians to eat with Jews because of their vices, but I'm going to break that rule today. *[Aside:]* I want to find out how they feel about Benjamin. I wonder if they hate him the way they did me? *[He summons the Steward to follow him back into the inner chamber.]* Steward, come here. Take a rich cup, and secretly put it in the youngest brother's bag. Take all the money they gave you and put it back in their sacks. Then tell them they can go.

STEWARD. Sir, they're still resting. They were very tired.

JOSEPH. Then find my captain and tell him to come here right away.

[The Steward leaves and returns at once with the Captain. Meanwhile, servants have spoken to the brothers, and they go out the front door.]

CAPTAIN. *[Aside:]* Damn it! With all the officers he has, why the hell does he always send for me?

What does Your Lordship command, My Lord Governor? If there is anything you need done today, you can rest assured I am only too eager to do it for you.

JOSEPH. Captain, I'd like you to keep an eye on those Hebrews from Canaan. When they leave, go after them. Act like you're enraged, and roughly search all their baggage. When you find one of my cups, arrest the man whose bag it's in and bring him back here as a thief.

STEWARD. I've done as you commanded. They just left, full of gratitude to you.

JOSEPH. I've told the captain what I want done.

STEWARD. Well, he'd better get a move on, for they're long gone by now.

JOSEPH. Mind you, I don't want any bloodshed!

ACT 4

[On the road from Egypt to Canaan. Enter the brothers, pursued immediately by the Captain and soldiers.]

CAPTAIN. Halt there, you damn Jews!

REUBEN. You don't have to be rude.

CAPTAIN. That's how we treat liars and thieves around here.

SIMEON. Stop, everybody! Can't you see how upset he is?

LEVI. Gentlemen, won't you tell us what this is all about?

SOLDIER. Where the hell are your asses?

GAD. You just can't wait to kiss them, huh?

CAPTAIN. *[Brandishing a sword.]* Just watch out, you dirty Jews, or I'll give you what you've got coming!

SIMEON. Is that so? Just a little while ago we were honored and favored and invited to dinner; so why are you insulting us now?

CAPTAIN. You filthy bastards! Give me the golden cup you stole from the governor right now, or I'll hang the lot of you!

REUBEN. I can't believe this is happening!

CAPTAIN. No more stalling! Give it up, or I'll cut you into such little pieces the ants can carry them off!

SIMEON. Brother, don't talk back to him. Let them search as much as they
    like, for they won't find anything.
JUDAH. Nothing but a few good kicks where the sun never shines!
SOLDIER. Untie those sacks. We'll soon find out who the thief is!
[They begin to open the sacks, and the soldiers examine their contents.]
CAPTAIN. They're all thieves, as far as I'm concerned.
ISSACHAR. Just watch who you're calling a thief!
CAPTAIN. Get out of my way! I'm not about to fight with a dog like you!
ZEBULUN. You don't scare us! Go right ahead and search all our baggage! If
    you find anything, you're more than welcome to kill all of us.
CAPTAIN. Is that a promise? There's nothing I'd like better than to hack all of
    you to bits!
SOLDIER. *[Pointing to Benjamin.]* This is the only one left to search. He
    must be the one then, damn it! Tie him up well, and let's get going!
    We'll take him back to the scene of the crime, and punish him there.
    Hey, you guys! Don't try resisting arrest! Line up by twos! Get a move
    on! We'll give you a punishment you won't soon forget! You pass your-
    selves off as honest men, but you're nothing but common thieves! You're
    just a bunch of loan sharks and swindlers! You'll be sorry!
*[The soldiers roughly line the brothers up and make them march in front
of them.]*
REUBEN. What terrible persecution the Lord has sent us! Today we are
    touched by His hand. It was our own sins that brought this upon us, and
    now we're being led away to life imprisonment.
LEVI. Zebulun, let's fight them! It's better to die fighting!
ZEBULUN. You're right! Why should we put up with this when we've done
    nothing wrong?
JUDAH. Let's kill them all and set fire to the town!
REUBEN. First say a quick prayer, and then aim for their hearts!

ACT 5

*[Joseph's palace, as before. Joseph is sitting on his throne. The
brothers appear in the street outside, fighting with the soldiers. The
soldiers at last subdue them, and one of the soldiers goes inside
and bows before Joseph.]*

JOSEPH. I heard a loud noise. Who is causing this disturbance?
SOLDIER. Sir, it's those Jews whom you honored so much. They stole the
    golden cup from your table. *[The soldiers push the brothers into the*

room and force them into a kneeling position before Joseph.] We found it in this boy's sack.

JOSEPH. Well, that's gratitude for you! This is how you behave after bragging about your ancestry? You claim to be descendants of Abraham and sons of Jacob! Sure you are! About as much as I am, and that's a fact. In punishment of this crime this boy will be my slave henceforth.

REUBEN. Sir, we'll all be your slaves.

JOSEPH. No, just the guilty one. I don't need so many slaves. What exquisite politeness! Is this how you do things in Judea? Well, I must say I'm not impressed.

JUDAH. Please listen to us, Your Lordship.

JOSEPH. What more is there for me to hear? I've never seen such villainy.

Judah's speech.

JUDAH. I beg you to listen kindly and dispassionately to what I have to say, for that's the way one ought to judge. There's no way we can deny something that's been clearly proven, but this is an opportunity for you to show your sublime virtue. At the same time we can't believe this young lad would have committed such a theft. We didn't put that money in our bags either, so we suspect that somebody who was envious of your kindness to us is trying to frame us. It's only natural that people should envy foreigners, but it was your kindness that provoked that envy. And if Benjamin did steal that cup—which I don't believe—surely you realize that crime requires criminal intent. What sort of criminal intent could there be in a lad of such a tender age? To tell you the truth, his father was afraid something like this might happen, and that's why he didn't want to let us bring him, and we had to plead with him to get him to agree. Benjamin is all he has left in his old age. We pledged our own children as guarantors for Benjamin's safety, and we assured our father that he could count on your word and your kindness. So if you don't intend to pardon him or give him back to us, you might as well just kill us all now, for there's no way we can go back home. If we went back without him, Jacob would surely drop dead of grief. He's already very frail, and depressed, and old. He hasn't been the same since our brother Joseph died. Ever since we lost his virtue, we've had nothing but bad luck and worries. And if none of what I've said so far convinces you, and you insist that the crime was really so terrible, then I can only beg you for clemency, which you've never denied anyone.

REUBEN. *[Aside:]* Oh, Joseph! How fortunate you were that death saved you from my sad fate! You're the only one of us who has been spared this bitterness. If you had lived, the pain would have killed you! Oh, Jacob! You must be worried sick by this delay! This time your patience will run out, and the pain and anguish will finally kill you! What bad luck you've had! You've never had a moment's peace in your whole life.

JUDAH. Sir, isn't the most important thing that this crime be punished? Please release this child so that his father won't suffer, and punish me in his place. If you need to keep one of us as a slave, there's no one better qualified than I, for I really like to be of service. Here I am, ready to do your every command. Please do us this great kindness! We all beg you here prostrate on the floor, for the sake of our ancestors, for your friend Pharaoh, for your own nobility, don't deny our petition! Let your virtue and perfection put an end to our weeping.

JOSEPH. Isn't it enough that I've agreed to let him be my slave instead of executing him?

ALL. Mercy!

JOSEPH. *[To the soldiers:]* Go outside, and clear the hallway.

[All go out except Joseph and the brothers.]

I can't take it any longer! I am your brother, Joseph! Get up, give me your hand. Yes, I'm that dreamer. Don't be afraid! Don't worry because of the way you treated me. It wasn't really your wickedness, it was God in heaven who made you do it. Stop, stop crying! Get up off the floor! Oh, my brothers, you don't know how I've missed you. Come and hug me!

[They begin to stand up but are hesitant to approach him.]

JUDAH. Lord, we recognize you now, but we're so ashamed of the wrongs we did you that we dare not look you in the face.

JOSEPH. Let's forget about the past. I don't intend to think about it anymore. If I gave you a hard time, it was just to make this moment even happier. I was really glad to see how you treated your little brother. You behaved just like noblemen! What I did was just to test you and find out if you loved each other. Now all of you, come and hug me. You too, little Benjamin!

[All come and hug Joseph.]

LEVI. Here we are, sir. Do with us as you will.

JOSEPH. I want you to go back home and get my father, whom I've missed so much, and come back here with your cattle and your households to live. The famine is going to last five more years, and you'll be much better off here.

REUBEN. We shouldn't keep the old man anxiously waiting any longer than necessary. But how will he ever believe such joyous news?

JOSEPH. Take him this stole I'm wearing as a sign, and I'll have my men fill up each of your sacks to the top. *[Gives Reuben the stole.]*
REUBEN. We really should be off to take Jacob the good news.
[Dan goes out through the front door and offstage.]
JOSEPH. I wish you were already back here with him. I just hope this good news reaches him before he dies! Don't stop for anything on the way! Get there as fast as you can! I know that Pharaoh will be delighted to hear about this. *[Joseph goes offstage through the inner chamber, and returns immediately, accompanied by his chamberlain.]*
    Chamberlain, you know what to do. Give them everything they need. The king commands that they be given his camels all loaded up right away. Oh, Benjamin! You have my mother Rachel's face. Brother, take this little jewel. *[Gives him a ring from his own finger.]* I have plenty of gold for the rest of you. Before you leave, I want to hug every one of you. God protect you! Hurry back here, for I have wonderful things to give you. You'll all come here with your families to live.
[Dan returns.]
DAN. The camels are loaded.
REUBEN. Sir, God keep you!
JOSEPH. May He guide you. Travel carefully!
[The brothers go out to the street. Joseph goes up the stairs and waves to them from the window.]
SIMEON. Who would ever have thought such things could happen? Oh, Divine Judgment! Our wickedness is revealed, and his dreams have come true.
REUBEN. What do you think of that? If our brother weren't so meek and kind and easygoing, there's no telling what he might have done to us!
LEVI. Thank God, we needn't worry about that now. We should just keep our eyes on the road, and praise God for His goodness to us.
[They sing:]
Laudate Dominum, omnes gentes: laudate eum, omnes populi. Quoniam confirmata est super nos misericordia eius, et veritas Domini manet in aeternum. Gloria Patri, et Filio, et Spiritui Sancto. Sicut erat in principio, et nunc, et semper, et in saecula saeculorum. Amen.[52]

Chorus.

MAIDEN 1. Sisters, what do you think of Joseph the dreamer now? Isn't it wonderful how he figured out the king's secrets, and brought such comfort to his aged father? Oh, Rachel! You were a fortunate mother to have such a son!

MAIDEN 2. How ashamed those brothers must have been to find themselves in the hands of the one they had sold as a slave! How fathomless are the secrets of human weakness, and how God in His greatness has provided for all!

MAIDEN 3. Just look at how his nobility enabled him to rise to the top! His meekness must also have helped, and his fortitude ensured his triumph. Now let wickedness be crushed and goodness triumph, as God has revealed the truth to all.

[They sing:]
Villancico.

In honor of this joyous day
let us rejoice and be of good cheer,
for God has seen fit to visit us here.

Let the misfortunes of the past
nevermore be brought to mind.
This triumph of a heavenly kind
has remedied our woes at last.
Henceforth our duty and our task
is to thank our God so dear
for giving us this day of cheer.

PART 5

PROLOGUE

I can hardly believe such a big crowd has managed to keep so quiet during that last part. I guess that just shows how much you enjoy seeing Jewish people and their way of dressing.

Well, it's late now, and the day is declining, although the sun is not hot—all the more reason not to talk too much, especially with such polite and patient people as yourselves, and so fond of novelties. The author doesn't want to displease you or wear you out today, for he thinks that for many years to come, you'll do what he's asked you to do today—that is, lend him your ears. Therefore, on his behalf, I beg you not to complain that we're going on too long, for a story of this quality deserves to be treated at length. Nothing's left now but the last part, and even if we wanted to lengthen it, the actors are too tired. Still, it is no less polished, excellent, and dazzling than the rest, and before you know it, it'll be over!

ARGUMENT

When Jacob hears his sons come home rejoicing, it is a great comfort to him, especially when he hears the amazing news that they have hastened there to give him news about Joseph. Words can hardly describe his pleasure or theirs. As a reward for Joseph's goodness, Pharaoh orders large tracts of land given to his father Jacob for them to live in, and also for their cattle. Jacob dies after living in Egypt seventeen years. Joseph spends enormous sums of money on his burial, which takes place in Hebron. Jacob lived 147 years in no less honor and dignity than his forefathers.

Characters:

        Jacob   His sons   Pharaoh

ACT 1

[Jacob's house in Canaan. Jacob is onstage when the curtain rises. His sons' voices are heard still singing "Laudate Dominum," and they enter immediately afterwards.]

JACOB. What music and singing is this I hear? It sounds like my sons. Yes, it's definitely them! Heaven help me, what a comfort, and what a relief! Oh, sons, God bless you! What is it that you're so happy about? Tell me right now!

REUBEN. Father, your days of grief and sadness are over! We bring you wonderful news!

JACOB. Let me share your joy then, since I've shared your pain!

SIMEON. What wonders! What a triumph!

ASHER. Oh father, we just can't find words to tell you!

JACOB. Come on, son, out with it!

LEVI. Our brother for whom you have grieved so much is alive and well.

JACOB. Almighty God in heaven!

REUBEN. I left him safe and sound. What's more, he's lord over all Egypt and its land; so there's no need for you ever to weep again, Father.

JACOB. Sons, I don't know whether to believe what you're saying. You've never brought me anything but bad news before; and now how can I believe such joy? Even if it's true, I don't know what to do. All my senses are so full of my unspeakable sorrows of the past that there's just no place to put a joy like this.

REUBEN. Stop grieving, and believe what I say, for I saw it with my own eyes.

JACOB. Are you sure it wasn't a hallucination, or some sort of mass hysteria? Such outrageously wonderful news seems like the raving of a madman.

ZEBULUN. Father, why do you persist in doubting when there's no reason to do so? Cheer up, and enjoy this good fortune.

NAPHTALI. How can you not be happy now?

ASHER. Oh, blessed be the day when at last you have no reason to be sad!

GAD. And you have still another reason to celebrate. That great King Pharaoh and Joseph, his viceroy, have summoned you, and they've sent you camels so that you can go and see them.

ASHER. And wagons and presents! Joseph himself sends you this stole to show you that his dreams have come true. Just as he dreamed, even you will have to bow down to him as Savior of the Peoples.

DAN. He wants you to bring all your cattle, and your sons, grandsons, wives, relatives, and servants.

JACOB. This must be a dream! You're making it all up! Who ever heard of such sublime triumphs? This wonderful news makes me want to leave right away.

JUDAH. It's all true. And you're right, we're just wasting our time here.

JACOB. Oh, my son! How have you been? Is it possible you're alive? I've never been this happy before. Help me take off this sackcloth. I need to get dressed for a party. This calls for a big, long celebration! Sons, wives, hurry up! Let's get going!

[Exeunt stage left; after a brief pause, all reenter, but this time with some women and children as well, in a confused mass from stage right.]

My sons, always remember to praise the Lord, for you know that He is just, and He will comfort you. It is through His holy favor that we have received this great blessing.

REUBEN. Not so fast, everybody! Calm down! We need to travel in an orderly manner.

JACOB. Oh, my dear sons! Thank you for bringing me the good news! Tell me, Reuben, are we getting close?

REUBEN. We'll be there soon. As soon as we get over those hills you see to the south, you can consider your troubles over.

JACOB. My sons, you must be tired from all this traveling. Just let me know if you want to stop and rest. Otherwise, I won't stop as long as I have breath in my body!

[Exeunt. The scene changes to Joseph's palace, as before. Offstage shouts of "Hurrah! Long live Jacob!," etc. Enter Jacob and his sons.]

JUDAH. Father, they can see you coming from your son's palace. Can't you hear them shouting for joy?

[Joseph comes out of the palace.]

JACOB. Oh, my beloved son! Oh, light my eyes have longed for! Blessed be the day that I begat you!

JOSEPH. Oh, my father and my lord! Oh, my glory and joy! No one has ever been so fortunate as I! What have I have ever done to deserve such bliss? Now I would gladly go blind, for I'll never again see a sight to match this one!

JACOB. I can't believe I've been granted this comfort! Oh, son! I'll never tire of looking at your face! There's nothing else for me to desire in my life, since the light of my eyes is shining right here!

JOSEPH. Now, brothers and sisters, nephews, nieces, friends: my glory and my highest honor is just seeing you!

JACOB. Son, you've cured me of all my ills and taken away my sadness!

JOSEPH. Let's go see the king. He's very eager to see you.

ACT 2

[Pharaoh's throne room. Joseph leads his family in before Pharaoh, who is sitting on his throne.]

PHARAOH. Joseph, my special friend, tell me: Who are these people? I can see that you're entertaining them royally.

JOSEPH. God save and prosper you! This man you see before you is my father. The others are my brothers and relatives, with their children and other members of our family. They have all come with their cattle and baggage to offer you homage. That is their sole intention.

PHARAOH. I'm delighted to see you so happy! I welcome all of you here. Joseph, even if I gave you my kingdom, it wouldn't suffice to repay you for your services to me. Ask your family where they would like to live here, and what they would like to do, and if you're agreeable, give them anything they want.

JOSEPH. All they want is to be shepherds and to live together.

PHARAOH. Oh, saintly, honored father! You must be very old.

JACOB. Yes, sire, that's true.

PHARAOH. Just how old are you anyway? I have to confess, I was shocked to see you here.

JACOB. I have now lived in this world for 130 years; but that's less than any of my forefathers lived.

PHARAOH. Oh, what a well-spent life, and what a great mystery! I am very glad that you have come to Egypt, blessed father. Your sufferings are over now. It is a great and sovereign gift of the gods to have preserved you to see this day. Please be so kind as to give me your blessing.

JACOB. May the great God of Abraham and Isaac bless your goodness and all your works, and give you His comfort.

PHARAOH. Your words have given me great comfort. I am certain that your coming to live in my kingdom was part of God's mysterious plan. Joseph, make sure you give them fine homes and excellent lands, both for themselves and their cattle. Now why don't you all go and get some rest? Don't think of this as a foreign land; consider yourselves at home. Here you'll find everything you want, and may the gods make you prosper!

JACOB. And may they preserve you!

ACT 3

[Joseph's palace. Jacob is lying in bed surrounded by his sons.]

JACOB. God bless you all, my sons!

JOSEPH. Father, you are about to die.

JACOB. Yes, son, my time has come. Our pathetic human life is short-lived, and goes by too quickly!

JOSEPH. What a sad day this is!

JACOB. Oh, my beloved sons, I command you to make every effort to carry out my will, and thereby you will please God. Love His holy peace, and that will comfort me. Now gather round me, my sons. I want to see you one last time, for I am dying, since that is God's will. I command you to divide my property lovingly, and give Ephraim and Manasseh some of the best part. Then I want you to take my body to Canaan and bury me in the valley of Hebron. I can't go on. My body is racked with pain, and death is overtaking me! God bless you all!

The Chorus begins.

MAIDEN 1. Sisters, old Jacob died a victorious death. His memory will be an inspiration to all. I think the moral of this story is to serve God continually, for that is the way to heaven.

MAIDEN 2. Virtue is the greatest thing a man can possess in this life, for it is the means to eternal happiness. As long as we are able, let's follow

Jacob's holy footsteps, for even the most-admired lives lead to the coffin.

MAIDEN 3. Death is most precious to the good and the saintly, and it fills the wicked with fear and torment. Still, I wish I could live forever to serve God, for life is truly glorious!

[They sing:]

Non mortui laudabunt te, Domine, sed nos qui vivimus in aeternum.[53]

Deo gratias.[54]

Here ends, illustrious sir, the tragedy called *Josephine,* which is dedicated to Your Lordship's honor. I beg Your Lordship to accept it as a service. If it didn't turn out as well as I wished, at least the desire was not lacking. So I send it to you, polished and chiseled—though not with so sharp a chisel as I would have liked—but I've done the best I could. It's not full of ill-considered quests and vain battles, but rather it is a garden full of beautiful and fragrant flowers, where Your Lordship can amuse himself by gathering a bouquet.

Ito bonis auibus.[55]

Laus Deo, pax viuis,
et requiem defunctis.[56]

2

Anonymous:
Joseph's Wedding

The Greek romance known as *Joseph and Aseneth* is believed to have been written by a Jew of Alexandria around the year 100 C.E. As a member of that large and prosperous Jewish community which often found itself hard-pressed to defend its traditions against the competition of the prestigious Hellenistic culture surrounding it, the author was particularly concerned with the dangers of assimilation and intermarriage. His primary motive in writing the romance seems to have been an attempt to explain how Joseph—"the model of chastity, piety, and statesmanship"[1]—could have married a non-Jew who was furthermore the daughter of a pagan priest. The romance answers this question by postulating that Aseneth must have converted to Judaism and undergone a period of purification before her marriage to Joseph. Drawing on the conventions of Hellenistic romance, it portrays Aseneth as "an utterly conceited heroine who is swept off her feet by a handsome male and then thrown into the blackest despair[,] from which she disentangles herself by self-abasement and supernatural assistance."[2] There has been speculation that the various stages of Aseneth's conversion—especially fasting, change of name, and participation in a symbolic meal—may reflect conversion rituals adopted by first-century Alexandrian Jews under the influence of the Greek mystery religions, but thus far no concrete evidence has been found to prove this.

Joseph and Aseneth seems to have had little if any influence on later Jewish elaborations of the legend of Joseph. However, it was very popular and much imitated (e.g., in lives of the saints) in the Greek, Syrian, Armenian, Ethiopic, and Russian churches. Marc Philonenko has argued that *Joseph and Aseneth* was probably a primary source for the many Muslim legends of Yusuf and Zulaikha. He points out in particular that the Muslim stories may have borrowed from the Greek romance the emphasis on Joseph and Zulaikha's striking beauty and the portrayal of Zulaikha as an idol-worshiper converted by her love for Joseph to the worship of the true God.[3] The romance first became popular in Europe when Vincent of Beauvais (c. 1190–c.1264) included a Latin abridgment of it in book 1 of his very influential compendium of world history entitled *Speculum Historiale.* As Burchard has pointed out, this condensation was "often separately copied and found its way into numerous other compilations, both handwritten and printed, in Latin, Czech, Dutch, English, French, German, Polish, Russian, and Scandinavian, including Icelandic, down to the eighteenth century."[4] Sometime in the second half of the sixteenth century, an anonymous Spanish playwright used Vincent of Beauvais's version of *Joseph and Aseneth* as the basis for an *auto sacramental* entitled *Joseph's Wedding (Los desposorios de Joseph).* Since there is no modern English translation of the *Speculum Historiale,* I have included my own translation in an appendix to this book.

The Spanish *auto* has survived in a sixteenth-century manuscript[5] acquired by Madrid's Biblioteca Nacional in 1844. The manuscript contains ninety-six short plays, all anonymous except for an *auto* on the story of Cain and Abel attributed to Jaime Ferruz. Another of the plays, *Naval and Abigail,* has been identified as composed by Lope de Rueda (died c. 1565) for performance at the Corpus Christi celebration in Seville in 1559. Eduardo González Pedroso published sixteen of the plays from this manuscript, including *Joseph's Wedding,* in volume 58 of the *Biblioteca de Autores Españoles* in 1865.[6] The entire contents of the manuscript were published in 1901 in a much more carefully prepared edition by Léo Rouanet under the title *Colección de autos, farsas y coloquios del siglo XVI.*[7] I have based my translation of the play on this edition. Rouanet argues that most of the plays in the manuscript date from about 1550 to 1575.

Unlike most of the other plays in the manuscript, which Melveena McKendrick has described as "for the most part static discussion with little movement or conflict,"[8] *Joseph's Wedding* is a lively and fast-paced play with considerable dramatic interest. The author closely follows Vincent of Beauvais's version of *Joseph and Asseneth,* borrowing some speeches almost verbatim. His principal innovation is the introduction of comic relief through the character of the Fool *(bobo)*; however, the use of the *bobo* had become a standard convention of the *auto* by the latter part of the sixteenth century. The play's comic scenes are somewhat crude and intrusive, and detract from its overall seriousness. The entire play, including the prologue (or *loa*) is written in a verse form known as the *quintilla:* five octosyllabic

lines rhyming ABBAB. Since, however, the Spanish verse is fairly unob-
trusive and is really rhymed prose rather than poetry in the modern sense, I
have translated it in prose.

At the time when *Joseph's Wedding* was written, the custom of dedicating the *autos* performed on Corpus Christi principally to celebrating the
mystery of the Eucharist had not yet been uniformly adopted. Any short,
didactic play on a religious subject was considered appropriate. Arguably,
there is some slight reference to the Eucharist in *Joseph's Wedding* in the
scene where the angel offers Senec the "bread of life" to eat, but the play is
obviously not centered around the theme of the Eucharist. As the prologue
suggests, the play's didacticism seems principally concerned with the sacrament of marriage, and it contains some additional teaching on the behavior proper to young, unmarried women. It seems clear, however, that the
auto's principal purpose was simply to entertain, albeit in an edifying or at
least harmless manner.

According to J. Sánchez Arjona, *Joseph's Wedding* was performed in
Seville in 1575.[9] The noted director Alonso Riquelme performed it in Madrid
in 1608. He submitted the following instructions for building the sets to the
City of Madrid:

> For the *auto* of *Joseph's Wedding:* the half-cart[10] should be a Palace with
> a drawing room and an altar with some idols; the Palace should be as rich
> as possible, and if the chapel containing the altar I have mentioned can be
> in the middle of four drawing rooms, it will be better.
>
> The other half-cart should have a "heaven" above the house with a
> pulley by means of which a character can descend from it and return to it.
> If it is painted on the outside, it should be Pharaoh's cart with Joseph in it
> dressed as a king. There should be a table with a device enabling the
> plates on it to disappear from view.[11]

Rouanet comments:

> Here the setting of our *auto* is perfectly indicated in a few lines. On one
> side, Putiphar's palace, "as rich as possible," surmounted by a functional
> gallery, with four facades if possible, where one sees the altar with the
> idols and to which Senec will go up whenever the action requires. On the
> other side, the young woman's room, surmounted by a "heaven" whence
> the angel can descend. The scene takes place at first on the ground floor
> of the palace (verses 61–152). Then, Senec speaks from the upper gallery
> (153–58). She comes down the stairs while the *fool* recites verses 159–
> 63. The dialogue continues on the ground floor until Joseph's arrival is
> announced. At that moment (verse 204), Senec withdraws into the wings,

while Putiphar and Zenobia go out to meet the viceroy. At verse 236 Senec reappears on her balcony. Then she comes back down to the lower floor (286–331), only to reappear in the gallery (386–415). The actress probably took advantage of verses 416–30, said by the *fool,* to move onto the second cart. This change of place was necessitated by the device that allowed the angel to descend from heaven and go back up. Nowadays, we would insert an intermission between verses 430 and 431. Such a division would be all the more appropriate, since the last part of the *auto* takes place seven days after the first part (526–35). Still, if one adheres to the letter of the text, the actress could disappear for a moment in the wings (v. 531) and come back bearing the honey. That is what must have taken place, either in the beginning or in towns where the machinery offered fewer resources than in Madrid. The angel disappeared after pronouncing verse 580. With verse 596 the action moved once again to the first cart, in the palace, where it remained up to the end.[12]

One can easily imagine that a holiday crowd would have found *Joseph's Wedding* highly entertaining. The combination of comic relief with lofty rhetoric, fairly elaborate staging, and reinforcement of conservative morality—what would nowadays be termed "family values"—must have been quite satisfying. The *auto* is short enough to hold the interest of spectactors crowded into the town square under a hot afternoon sun without taxing their patience or their intellects. The role of Senec, the only character in the play who undergoes any real development, would have offered a fine opportunity for a good actress to demonstrate her talent.

Characters:

Butifar	Joseph
Zenobia	An angel
A fool[13]	A secretary
Senec[14]	King Pharaoh
A courier	A drummer

PROLOGUE

Exalted, magnificent, noble clergy; elite audience: the fact that I'm standing here before you is surely ample proof of my boldness. This occasion calls for two things, but they're both tricky and require the greatest prudence. Alas, my feeble intelligence is just as deficient in the ability to ponder your immeasurable worth as your merits are beyond all praise. Although

Cicero himself would drown if he tried to fathom the sea of your goodness, love will keep my flimsy craft afloat, for my good intentions and longing to please will safely patch the most gaping holes my ignorance can puncture. I dare not even begin to praise you, since no praise of mine could ever encompass your infinite virtue; silence then is the better part of valor. That takes care of one of my two obligations.

The other is to beg you in your kindness graciously to heed what we have to tell you. Before your very eyes you will witness the celebrated marriage of that renowned Joseph who was governor of Egypt. God Himself arranged his marriage by divine intervention, which should be an example and a remedy for anyone who is a Christian and travels along that path. You will observe how pleased God is by a perfect life, and how well He rewards a person with whom He is satisfied. There are a thousand things worth noting about this marriage, so you'll need to concentrate and pay close attention. But you'll soon see what a delightful play it is, and it's so clear that it needs no further explanation. May Joseph's virtue make up for any faults the actor may commit!

Enter Butifar and Zenobia, his wife.

BUTIFAR. The gods in their goodness, through no merits of my own, have shown me favor and raised me to a high estate. They have made me high priest of the great city of Heliopolis, one of the greatest titles and highest-ranking positions in all Egypt. What more could I ask? There is only one other thing I want, Zenobia, my dear: to arrange a good marriage for our only daughter and sole heir. If the gods would be so gracious as to give my daughter the husband she deserves, my happiness would be complete.

ZENOBIA. My lord Butifar, if we want to marry our daughter, I'm sure we'll be able to make a good match for her. The problem is that I can't think of any man who deserves her. Nature has endowed her with so much wisdom and virtue, and not only is she very rich, she's your daughter, which is something to be proud of. But above all, she is a chaste virgin, has had a very sheltered and religious upbringing, and has never shown the slightest interest in boys.

BUTIFAR. You're right about that! No one could claim she's ever flirted or done anything that might harm her reputation. Even if they wanted to gossip about her, they couldn't get away with it, for we've made sure she never had a chance to do anything like that. She's not like the girls nowadays, who think of nothing but parties and fun and boyfriends.

They spend so much time strolling up and down the street that some of them are practically streetwalkers!

ZENOBIA. It's true that maidens these days are not as innocent as they used to be.

BUTIFAR. Maidens! Even the word sounds quaint. These days it seems they can't get rid of their maidenhead fast enough. Real maidens are shrinking violets and stay-at-homes, always blushing and stammering, not like these party girls who like nothing better than to show off their gift of gab. Never trust a woman who loves the sound of her own voice. Since they insist on playing with fire, is it any wonder that they often get burned?

[Enter a Fool.]

FOOL. Yo, boss! What's up?

BUTIFAR. Watch your tongue, you idiot!

FOOL. I'll bet you can't guess why I'm here.

BUTIFAR. Some of your usual nonsense, no doubt.

FOOL. Damn, you got it! I came to tell you there's company coming; and what could be stupider than having company? They can all go to hell, I say! They just come here to mooch off us anyway. Am I right, ma'am? I'll tell 'em to go to a hotel.

BUTIFAR. Who is it, you ass?

FOOL. Oh, it's just that dreamer Joseph. Of course now he's become a real big shot because of that wheat business. Can you believe it? They're even calling him "the Savior."

BUTIFAR. And what's it to you? Is he already here, or is he on his way?

FOOL. They said he was somewhere near the Broom Bush Valley, so he'll be here pretty soon.

BUTIFAR. I'm so glad he's coming! Okay, you idiot, run upstairs and call my dear daughter, and tell her I want to talk to her.

FOOL. *[Yells:]* Yo, Senec! Hey, boss lady! Get on down here, girl!

SENEC. *[Comes out on an upstairs landing or gallery.]* Who's the ass that's yelling?

FOOL. Me . . . I mean, your dad. I mean, okay, he may be an ass, but he's the one who wants you.

SENEC. I asked who was yelling.

FOOL. Oh, in that case, I don't like to brag, but I have to say it was me. And just what do you mean by "ass"? No ass can bray as loud as me. I could even get a job as town crier, if I do say so myself.

[Senec comes down the stairs, but can't get into the room, because the Fool is in her way.]

SENEC. Dummy, will you get out of my way!

BUTIFAR. Move aside, stupid!

SENEC. What does Your Holiness want?

BUTIFAR. Daughter, I wanted to tell you that Joseph, the Strong Man of God, is coming to town today and is going to be staying here with us. It's a very big honor! Yesterday he sent me a message that he wanted to stay here in my own home. I thought I should tell you, daughter, that he is God's chosen one, holy, just, and blessed, and the king has appointed him viceroy of Egypt on account of his infinite worth. I've given it a lot of thought, and for your sake, if he's willing, I'd like to offer him your hand in marriage. He would be a worthy consort for you.

SENEC. I can't believe it! You think a foreign slave is my equal? What a crazy idea! The only husband I want is the king's son. He's the one I intend to marry.

FOOL. Hey, you're my kind of girl! Don't let them push you around! He'd be a better match for me—and even that would be pushing it. If that's the best you can do, just forget it! What more can I say?

[Enter a courier.]

COURIER. Sir, I've come to inform you that Joseph is here.

BUTIFAR. Let's go out to welcome him. Come, Zenobia my dear, let's go out and show him a warm welcome. Daughter, get upstairs!

[Exit Senec.]

FOOL. Okay, let's all get a move on!

[Joseph appears in the doorway.]

BUTIFAR. *[Bowing to Joseph.]* I bow before your goodness and supreme excellence, offering you the respect your majesty and presence so richly deserve.

JOSEPH. *[Bowing to Butifar.]* And as your humble servant, I render you the homage due to your great honor and holy office.

ZENOBIA. Though all unworthy, I beg you, sir, henceforth to consider me your servant.

JOSEPH. Nay, madam, it is I who must serve you.

FOOL. Don't forget me! Just think of me as your brother and count on me to help you out in any way I can.

BUTIFAR. Must you butt into everything?

FOOL. *[To Joseph:]* Let's just shake hands. I'm sure we're going to be friends.

BUTIFAR. Come inside, Your Excellency, and rest a while. *[To the Fool:]* Chamberlain, run and get some water and towels to wash his feet. *[Exit the Fool.]* Sit down, Your Excellency.

JOSEPH. You sit down first, Your Lordship; and you sit down too, my lady.

BUTIFAR. We'll all three sit down together.

[They sit down on three chairs.] The Fool returns and washes Joseph's feet. Senec appears at an upstairs window and watches.

SENEC. I'm very sorry to have insulted such a man. When people are angry, they always speak out of turn like unruly beasts. Behold, the Sun itself has come down to us in his triumphal chariot from heaven on high! Joseph is indeed the son of God, but I was unaware. What man could beget beauty such as this? What woman could conceive him, or what womb could enfold such brightness in its cloister?

JOSEPH. Who is that woman at the window? Have her leave the house at once, for they're always bothering people.

BUTIFAR. Sir, that is my daughter, who despises all men. She is such a chaste virgin that no man has ever laid eyes on her until this moment. If you wouldn't mind, I'd like her to come down and greet you.

JOSEPH. If she really hates all men, I'll be glad to talk to her. I'll love her as a brother. Call her. I'm delighted by that hatred of men, which is a sure sign of chastity.

BUTIFAR. I'll bring her right away.

ZENOBIA. I'll go with you.

[They go upstairs and come down with Senec between them.]

JOSEPH. If she is such a modest virgin, she won't annoy me. There's nothing that pains me more than loose women.

BUTIFAR. Greet your excellent brother, who is so chaste and modest that he despises all other women. Since your purity and withdrawal from the world have led you to despise men, you two have that great virtue in common.

SENEC. God save you, blessed man of God on high!

JOSEPH. God bless you and give you life, since all life in heaven and earth proceeds from Him!

BUTIFAR. Come, my dear, and offer Joseph the kiss of peace.

JOSEPH. No, no, not that! Don't come any closer! Forgive me, but that would be unlawful. He who honors the Living God tastes the bread of blessing and the chalice of incorruption with his own lips. Those lips must never touch a foreign woman, for their mouths are used to kissing vain, deaf, mute idols, and eating the bread from their tables. Such a woman must not so much as touch my garment!

FOOL. Saints preserve us! If you'll excuse me for saying so, Sir Joseph is sure a cold fish! How could anyone refuse such a nice kiss? I sure wouldn't. Look how sad you've made the poor girl. That's some way to repay her friendliness! You've hurt her feelings, and now she can't stop crying. Come on, go over and whisper some sweet nothing in her ear.

JOSEPH. Don't argue with me. I know that I'm right. *[To Senec:]* My dear girl, may the God of my fathers bless and comfort you.

SENEC. And may He comfort you too as a reward for the comfort and joy you have given me with that holy blessing.

FOOL. That's the spirit! Well, I certainly did a good job of getting those two together!

BUTIFAR. It's time for dinner, sir. You, my dear daughter, go on back up to your chapel.

SENEC. Excellent man of God, I kiss your hands and feet in parting.

JOSEPH. And I humbly return the favor.

[She goes upstairs.]

FOOL. Likewise, I'm sure!

BUTIFAR. Come sit down, Your Excellency. *[To the Fool:]:* Bring us some food! *[To Joseph:]* I feel very fortunate indeed and overjoyed at the high honor Your Excellency has shown me today. I am truly delighted that you have chosen to honor my humble abode with your presence.

JOSEPH. And I appreciate your hospitality.

BUTIFAR. There's nothing left for me to say except that my joy would be complete if you would grant my humble request and stay here and relax with us today.

JOSEPH. I assure you that nothing would make me happier. However, my job requires that I leave right away, and it's very important to the kingdom. I have to visit two or three other towns, and then I'll come back and make an inspection of yours. I give you my word, sir, that I'll be back here in eight days. I'm really sorry to eat and run, and I hope you'll forgive me.

BUTIFAR. Forgive? You are too kind, dear sir! I gladly accept your offer and look forward to seeing Your Excellency again eight days hence.

JOSEPH. Well, you'll have to excuse me now. I really must be on my way, but I promise to come back soon. Please let me know if I can be of any assistance to Your Holiness.

BUTIFAR. No, no, it is I who should serve you!

FOOL. Enough, already! Let the poor guy go. The sooner he goes, the sooner he'll come back. He'll be back soon; he wouldn't lie to us.

ZENOBIA. God save Your Lordship!

JOSEPH. And may it please God, my lady, to grant you prosperity and happiness.

[Exit Joseph through the street door. Butifar, Zenobia, and the Fool go inside the house. Senec then appears upstairs at a window.]

SENEC. I'm so depressed! That perfect man rejected me because I am a heretic and worship vain idols. Now that I think about it, he's right. These idols I worship are no powerful gods. They're just man-made objects of wood, silver, and gold. They're deaf, they have no feelings, and I was wrong to worship them. I've just been wasting my precious time honoring them, but I've learned my lesson now. I'll throw them down from this high window. I must also repent for the wrong I've done. I don't care how I look from now on! Let all my dainty dishes be fed to the dogs! Give me mourning clothes. I'll stay in my room and put ashes on my head. I'll do penance for honoring those idols, and when Joseph comes back, I'll ask His Excellency what God I ought to worship.

She throws the idols out the window. Enter the Fool.

FOOL. I saw something shiny fall out of the window of that tower. I hope it's something to eat! Maybe it's some yummy candy. *[He sees the idols on the ground.]* Hold on! What's this? Look here! I've found myself a treasure! What a darling little saint! This one is gold, and this one is silver. All of a sudden, I'm rich and respectable. I think I'll run for city council. Next year I'll try for magistrate. Before you know it, I'll be His Honor the Mayor. I may even buy my own herd of pigs, or become a loan shark.

[Exit the Fool. Senec reappears at the window. She is veiled and dressed in sackcloth, and her arms are smeared with ashes.]

SENEC. Yesterday made seven days, and today's the eighth, the day when my Joseph, the joy of my life, promised to return. Yes, he's coming today unless my anxiousness made me count wrong, or Fortune has conspired to disappoint me. Today I'll prove that my love for you is more than passion, more than love itself, for it's cloaked in suffering. This is no yen for earthly joy. This is far more than just love. My very soul is aflame with fire from heaven. This was no dart from Cupid. It's clear that Joseph must be a reflection of the Supreme God, since he has smitten me so excessively. And since this inner fire that's consuming me renders me guiltless, please come now, my lord, if my love pleases you. And if you hate me for my former wickedness and awkward stumbling on the path of grace, surely you can't help being pleased by how I've changed. Come then, and reward my hope as it deserves. But alas, poor sinner that I am, it's not yet dawn, and I wish he were already here. *[She kneels.]* Yes, I want him, yes, I beg and plead that he may come!

Enter an Angel.

ANGEL. Senec, holy virgin, arise if you will.

SENEC. Here I am. Tell me, who are you?

ANGEL. Look at me, Senec. Get up, and listen well to what I have to say. I am a prince of the house of the great God of Sion. Take comfort, and listen well to what God has decreed. Take off those ugly clothes and that rough belt. Shake off the ashes of sadness, and wash your face at once with living water. I must speak to you and honor you. Don't cover your face, for you are an honorable virgin. Take off that veil, and rejoice like an immaculate rose. Today your name is written in the Book of Life, never to be erased, for He Who gives life has exalted you. From now on you will surely eat bread of incorruption, and you will drink from the holy chalice. You will be anointed with blessed oil and chrism. You will be Joseph's wife. From now on your excellent name will be Refuge of the People because of your holy penitence. That penitence, like a true daughter of the divine essence, interceded with Him that He might take pity on you.

SENEC. My lord, tell me your blessed name.

ANGEL. Child, my name is written with the finger of God in His infinite register. It is a book of marvels; what it contains is infallible, but it is not right for men to inquire about such things nor is it possible to recount them.

SENEC. If your loving servant has won favor, please grant me yet another grace and sit down upon this bed where no man has ever sat so that I may bring you something to eat.

ANGEL. Set the table quickly.

SENEC. *[Sets the table.]* Eat, Excellent Lord.

ANGEL. You must bring a honeycomb.

SENEC. I'm sorry, but I don't have one.

ANGEL. Go into your pantry and you will find delicious honey.

[She goes inside and returns with the honey.]

SENEC. I swear, sir, I did not have this precious food before. Your word is powerful.

ANGEL. You were blessed because you left your gods and forswore their worship and believed my word and did penance. All who serve my God and do penance will be likewise blessed, for they too will taste the sweet honeycombs of heaven. This is the honeycomb made by the bees of heaven from the divine distillation of the consecrated liquor of celestial roses. This is what the angels eat, and he who eats of this will never die. Eat this, Asenec, for it is given you in graces. Today God gives you His bread of life. With His chrism you are anointed and in His holy oil you are redeemed. Your beauty is renewed. Your flesh and bones will never grow old, and you will never die. You will remain forever young. Your loveliness will not diminish nor will your beauty fade, for God on high will preserve you.

SENEC. Sir, I have seven maidens here who keep me company. I beg you to be so kind as to give them your blessing.

ANGEL. May God in heaven bless them that they may be seven pillars of wondrous cities of refuge and comfort. Clear the table now.

[Exit the Angel. Senec kneels.]

SENEC. Oh, seraphic man! Oh, resplendent man! Prostrate before you, sir, I humbly beg your pardon for having spoken boldly to you. Pardon my rudeness! I wish I could have served you better. Don't forget me, though my faults have made you disappear. Accept my unworthiness in your high dignity, for I tell you truthfully that if I failed to serve you as I ought, it was unintentional.

Enter the Courier.

COURIER. Is anyone at home? I've come to announce that the Strong Man of God is here.

SENEC. What's that?

COURIER. He's dismounted.

SENEC. Can it be true?

COURIER. Can't you see?

SENEC. Oh, joyous day!

[Enter Butifar, accompanied by his secretary.]

BUTIFAR. I was honored when he promised to come back, and I'm even more honored now that he has done so.

[Enter Joseph.]

JOSEPH. And I, sir, am happy to be at your service.

SENEC. Welcome, Your Excellency! This is the happiest day of my life. Words cannot express how happy I am to see you!

JOSEPH. God save you, my lady.

SENEC. Father, there's something I need to discuss with you, for God commands me to speak, but I also need to ask your permission before doing so. Modesty demands that I keep silent, as virgins ought to do, but the pain I feel is stronger than my obedient nature, and God compels me to speak.

BUTIFAR. Daughter, I'm only too happy to grant you the permission you request. Go ahead and say what's on your mind.

SENEC. Strong Man of God, don't try to tell me that what I'm asking for is vile. Trembling with embarrassment, I ask you for God's sake not to deny me what God requires me to ask. An angel of God came to me and granted me a great favor, telling me that you, sir, will marry me today and will be my refuge, my stronghold, and my help. God has done this for me because I renounced my former gods, and drew near to your God. Please accept this, for my faith deserves it.

JOSEPH. Since this has been decreed by revelation, I shall joyfully accept you in holy union as my wife and consort.

BUTIFAR. What a happy turn of events! Blessed be the day that I begat you, my daughter, since it is now our high privilege to give you such a husband!

JOSEPH. In order to make it official we must notify our King Pharaoh and ask him to come and perform the marriage. Let a messenger be sent to him at once. I'm sure he'll be pleased. He's not far away, so ask him to leave right away and come here swiftly.

BUTIFAR. Secretary, on your way!

JOSEPH. And be sure to tell the king all about how I decided to get married.

SECRETARY. Sir, I'll leave at once.

BUTIFAR. I think he'll be overjoyed to hear this news. My son and lord, let's go inside to eat and rest.

JOSEPH. Your wish is my command.

BUTIFAR. Let's go then, for words cannot express my pleasure.

[All go inside. Enter the Fool.]

FOOL. Has she ever changed her tune! One minute it's "Drop dead, loser!" and before you know it, she's crooning, "Give me a kiss, baby!" Now she likes him better than any other guy in town. This marriage business is just like the lottery. Some people get the winners, and others are stuck with sinners.

Enter the Courier, blowing a trumpet.

Hear, hear! Don't you hear that? What's all the racket about? Good Lord, it's the courier. Am I glad to see you! You certainly made good time. Is the king coming?

COURIER. Yes, indeed. He'll be here any minute. Where is His Holiness?

[Enter Butifar.]

BUTIFAR. Here I am. How did it go?

COURIER. Sir, His Majesty was overjoyed to grant your request. He sent me here to tell you he's coming, and he left right after I did.

BUTIFAR. What's that? He'll be here soon?

COURIER. That's right. He and his retinue left right after I did.

BUTIFAR. Spread the news through the city immediately. Summon all the nobility, and let there be music and singing and fireworks, dancing and all kinds of celebration. Let this old gray head rejoice at this supreme happiness. Ring all the bells, have everyone come here!

A drummer enters, plays a drum roll, and unrolls and reads the following proclamation:

DRUMMER. His Holiness Butifar, Revered High Priest, issues the following proclamation: "Let all inhabitants of this city—knights, hidalgos, squires, goodmen, farmers, taxpayers and those who are exempt, religious brotherhoods, confraternities, guilds and tradesmen—celebrate this festive day with music, rejoicing, trumpets, and drums. Let them bring out their banners and give a proper welcome to our king Pharaoh."

[More trumpet blasts and drumrolls. Enter a large crowd carrying banners from the left, and the King from the right. At the same time Joseph enters from inside the house.]

BUTIFAR. We offer you our warmest welcome, Your Majesty.

KING. And I am very pleased to see you.

JOSEPH. May God in His goodness prosper your estate, my lord! I apologize for my boldness in inviting you here so abruptly. I hope my plan does not displease you.

BUTIFAR. If your majesty has any reason to oppose this wedding, please don't hesitate to say so, for you know we are all your obedient and humble servants.

KING. Nothing could make me happier than for Joseph, whom I regard as my own son, to marry your daughter Asenec. *[To Senec:]* Come here, my dear child. I give you Joseph as your lawful wedded husband. My precious Joseph, it gives me great joy to give you Asenec as your consort. *[The King places crowns on Joseph's and Senec's heads.]* Accept these crowns, which I place on your heads with great love, to signify the high honor and incomparable value of your persons.

JOSEPH. *[Kneels before the King.]* Mighty King, may God repay you for this supreme favor!

KING. Get up, Joseph, for I want to give you a demonstration of my love. Starting today, I proclaim a seven-day holiday. Let all the shops close down, for everyone is invited to my royal banquets. Whoever comes up with the best entertainment during the celebration will be richly rewarded, and there'll be plenty of prizes for the runners-up. I want the whole town lit up at my expense, and I'll also sponsor a lavish fireworks display, and we'll have all kinds of fun. Strike up the music! Let me hear those clarinets!

3

Lope de Vega:
The Trials of Jacob; or,
Sometimes Dreams Come True

The most prolific playwright the world has ever known, Lope de Vega is considered the father of Spain's national theater. When he began writing plays, theater in Spain consisted of short, one-act comic skits heavily influenced by the Italian commedia dell'arte and performed by a few itinerant troupes; attempts at tragedy in the classical manner written by intellectual courtiers; *autos* (like *Joseph's Wedding*) written to be performed as part of the celebration of Corpus Christi, Christmas, and Easter; and pageants, usually based on classical mythology, performed in conjunction with major court celebrations such as royal weddings. During a career spanning over fifty years, Lope created a dramatic formula that was to endure with few changes until well into the eighteenth century. That formula, outlined in his *New Art of Writing Plays* (1609), consisted of a three-act play mixing tragedy and comedy, written in a variety of native Spanish and Italianate verse forms that alternated constantly to suit the tone of a particular scene, and usually dealing with the themes of love and honor. The new type of play Lope developed was enormously popular, appealing both to educated and unlettered audiences, and formed the basis for a thriving commercial theater. Lope himself was hard-pressed to meet the voracious demands of his public. Ten years before his death, he claimed to have written over a thousand plays, some of them in twenty-four hours! That was certainly an exaggeration, but modern scholars believe he may in fact have written as many as eight hundred; over four hundred have survived, and many others are known to have been lost. Besides his prodigious dramatic output, he wrote several long epic poems in the Italian Renaissance manner, a pastoral novel, a Byzantine novel, a collection of novellas, a volume of literary criticism, and much occasional poetry.

Like his contemporary Shakespeare, Lope rarely invented the plots of his plays. Instead, he adapted materials from history, legend, mythology, previous literature, lives of the saints, and the Bible. *The Trials of Jacob (Los trabajos de Jacob)*, first published in *Part XX* of his collected plays (1635), is thought to have been written between 1620 and 1630.[1] It was conceived as a sequel to his *Rape of Dinah (El robo de Dina,* 1615–22) and was to have formed a trilogy with a final play on the Exodus from Egypt, which appears never to have been written. The text of the play that has come down to us is unusually short; it has only 2,238 verses, as opposed to an average of about 3,000 for Lope's plays. Critics have therefore speculated that the extant version may be one that had been edited for performance. My translation is based on the edition published by Marcelino Menéndez y Pelayo in volume 3 of Lope's *Obras* (Madrid: Real Academia Española, 1893).

The play consists mainly of a fast-paced, straightforward adaptation of the text of Genesis 37–50. As was his custom, Lope adds a subplot of his own invention recounting the rustic shepherd Bato's love for the shepherdess Lida, who in turn loves Benjamin. The subplot provides comic relief by contrasting the loves of these plebeian characters, expressed in stylized rustic language, with the unrequited love of the noble Nicela (the name Lope gives Putiphar's wife) for Joseph. Benjamin's chaste rejection of Lida mirrors his brother Joseph's rejection of Nicela. Bato is the standard comic character *(gracioso)* of Lopesque comedy—motivated by lust, hunger, and, cowardice—and thus a suitable foil to his noble, idealistic master Benjamin. Except for the subplot, the play contains few departures from the biblical text. In act 2 Jacob refers to the midrash according to which Joseph cast straw and ears of grain into the river so that they might be borne to Canaan and so inform his family that food was available in Egypt. A scene in the same act in which Nicela waits for the viceroy Joseph to pass by in state may be derived from a Muslim source. Chapter 25 of *The Story of Yusuf, Son of Ya'qub* [2] similarly describes Zalikha as often waiting at a crossroads for Yusuf to pass by. A brief scene in act 2 in which Joseph is called upon to judge the case of a man who had killed his older brother out of envy emphasizes Joseph's wisdom and compassion, and is no doubt of Lope's own invention. Nicela's reconciliation with Joseph, and his intervention with Pharaoh to secure Putiphar's promotion, bring the story full circle, further emphasize Joseph's noble character, parallel his reconciliation with his brothers, and enhance the sense of harmony with which the play ends. Lope's play contains only a single Christian reference—Issachar's allusion in act 3 to the three youths who visited Abraham as symbolizing the Trinity. There is one very odd departure from the biblical text. Lope's play attributes to Issachar Judah's famous speech in defense of Benjamin. One of my students, Brian Lottman, has observed that, in spite of his importance in other versions of the story, Judah in fact does not appear in this play at all (only six of Jacob's twelve sons—Reuben, Issachar, Simeon, Joseph, Naphtali, and Benjamin—are characters in the play). This is no doubt due to the fact that the cast already includes more than twenty-five characters (though the same actors probably covered more than one of the minor roles in performance), and to have enlarged it further would have exceeded the possibilities of most Spanish theater companies of the time, which usually employed between sixteen and twenty actors. It was Judah's idea to sell Joseph, but since that scene is omitted from the play, there was no need to include him. Lope's decision to exclude Judah can be explained by his identification in Christian interpretations of the story with Judas Iscariot, the disciple who betrayed Jesus.

The play is carefully structured to maintain audience interest. Lope begins the play in medias res with a conversation between Joseph and Nicela, which provides a natural opportunity for Joseph to explain why his brothers envied him and how he came to be sold into slavery. Nicela's attempt to seduce Joseph quickly follows. The episode is handled with remarkable decorum; Miguel de Carvajal had presented the seduction scene in far more graphic, erotic detail in his *Josephine Tragedy,* but the Inquisitional censors in Lope's time would surely not have tolerated such a scene in a religious play. Each of the play's three acts also has a tripartite structure. Lope constantly alternates between episodes in Joseph's story and Jacob's reaction to those events, thus providing a continuous balance between the fast-moving action and pauses for tender lyricism and philosophical reflection. Act 1 begins in Egypt, moves to Canaan for the deeply moving scene in which Benjamin attempts to console his father, and returns to Egypt to conclude with Joseph's triumphant appointment as viceroy. Act 2 begins in Canaan, as Jacob decides to send his sons to Egypt to buy wheat, then depicts Joseph's initial encounter with his brothers in Egypt, and concludes in Canaan, when they return home and inform Jacob that they must take Benjamin back to Egypt with them. Act 3 opens in Egypt, as Joseph hears of his brothers' return, portrays his arrest of Benjamin as a thief and his reconciliation with his brothers, then moves to Canaan, where the brothers bring the happy news of Joseph's survival and success to their father, and concludes with Jacob's reunion with Joseph in Egypt.

Lope's *Trials of Jacob* is unique among the adaptations of the Joseph story collected in this volume in that it focuses not so much on Joseph himself as on the sufferings of his father Jacob. As its title indicates, Jacob is the play's real protagonist. Lope obviously felt a strong sense of identification with the patriarch. The Bible records that Jacob's two wives (Leah and Rachel) and two concubines (Bilhah and Zilpah) bore him twelve sons and one daughter. Lope is known to have fathered fourteen children by two wives (Isabel de Urbina [died 1595] and Juana de Guardo [died 1613] and two of his mistresses (Micaela de Luján [died 1607?] and Marta de Nevares). Like Jacob, he seems genuinely to have been in love with one of his wives, while his other marriage was one of convenience. By the time he wrote *The Trials of Jacob,* he had lost both of his wives and one of his mistresses, and only four of his fourteen children—Marcela, Lope Félix, Feliciana, and Antonia Clara—were still living. The death of his beloved six-year-old son Carlos in 1612 had been particularly traumatic for Lope; after the death of his wife Juana the following year, he had turned for solace to religion and had been ordained a priest in 1614. A passionate love affair with Marta de Nevares had restored his zest for life in 1616, but in the early 1620s Marta lost her eyesight, and around 1626 went insane; she would die at the age of forty-two in 1632. Lope was also saddened by separation from his daughter Marcela, who entered a cloistered convent in 1622. Thus, in the 1620s, as he wearily entered the sixth decade of his life, he too felt bereft of most of his family, was miserable in his personal life, and looked back with nostalgia to the days when he had been young, strong, and in love. He must have felt, like the Jacob in his play, that "throughout [his] life things turned out for the worst." Once again he turned to religion for comfort, worshiping daily at the church of Our Lady of Atocha, frequently visiting the sick in Madrid's hospitals, and writing religious poetry, such as *Divine Triumphs* (1625) and his epic on the life of Mary Queen of Scots, *The Tragic Crown* (1627).

The Trials of Jacob is probably the most skillful dramatization of the story of Joseph written in Spain. It is a good indication of why Lope's theater became so sensationally popular. Lope employed no fewer than nine different verse forms (*redondillas, quintillas, décimas, romance, octavas, soneto, lira, canción,* and six-syllable assonant verse) in this play. Over 65 percent of the play is in either *romance* or *redondillas,* which closely approximate the rhythms of normal Spanish prose. I have translated those passages in prose. Much of the remainder, however, is in more intrusive verse forms and is highly lyrical; I have therefore translated those parts of the play in verse.

Characters:

Bato, a peasant	Joseph	Musicians
Lida, a peasant woman	Putiphar	King Pharaoh

Jacob, an old man	Asiris, cupbearer	An angel
Reuben	Soldiers	Thebanus
Issachar	Naphtali	Two wise men
Simeon	Phoenicia	Elius
Nicela	Lisenus	Isacius
Delpha	Benjamin	Servius

ACT 1

Enter Nicela and Joseph.

JOSEPH. Though working for you has sweetened my slavery, I still can't understand why you want to hear a slave's sad tale of woe.

NICELA. It's always a pleasure to hear other people's stories. Besides, all women are curious, and hearing you will entertain me.

JOSEPH. Since you ask me, I will recount those painful memories.

NICELA. Yes, Joseph, do tell me your story.

JOSEPH. All right then, Nicela, listen.

NICELA. Let's hear it.

JOSEPH. After the rape of Dinah,[3] the great Jacob, my father, came to Horeb to see my grandfather Isaac in the green valley of Mamre, Abraham's land. He had already lost the beauteous Rachel, who had died with great pain in giving birth to Benjamin; she was his beloved mother and mine. Isaac was then 180 years old, and Esau came from Seir with his mighty captains to bury him. I had just grown to manhood, and I began to go out into the countryside with my brothers so that they might teach me the shepherd's trade. Daily I watched the rosy dawn emerge over the mountains amidst pearly white and blue iridescences. My childish thoughts were occupied only in contemplating the age-old winds and watching the skies revolve on their celestial hinges, now ushering in a new day, now taking out the old, without ever exceeding their proper limits. I saw the countryside rejoice as the sun entered the sign of Aries,[4] and watched it fill up with ears of grain as it gilded the sign of Virgo.[5] I noted the grazing of the sheep and how the lambs begin to dance as the sun drops low in the sky, the savagery of jealous bulls, and how that of men, even when not jealous, exceeds that of the animals. Sometimes, Nicela, I considered my brothers' loathsome vices and reported them to my father. This important duty made them dislike me, though fraternal correction is not the same thing as gossip, when there is an evil that should be remedied. Jacob loved me well, not for any qualities of my own, but because he had fathered me in his venerable old age. He himself made me a tunic, both to serve as my garment and to honor me. This only increased their envy, which has always been like a moth in woolen garments. One day I told them a dream, though I might as well have kept it to myself; but that was the will of heaven. I have paid for it, as heaven knows. "I dreamt," I told them, "that one day, as we were binding up our sheaves, my fertile one stood up among all the others, and as it stood like that, your sheaves sought to bow down to the ground to adore it." They replied: "Will you perchance be our king? For such words show that you want to subject us and exalt yourself." Then I dreamed another dream, and I told it to them one afternoon: "I saw eleven stars adore me, as if I were the sun and moon." Jacob scolded me for that, saying: "By calling yourself the Sun, do you presume that your brothers and I must adore you?" Now envy could no longer be camouflaged nor contained; for after all, it was envy that made men mortal. A few days after that, my father sent me to Shechem to visit my ten brothers in the fields. I left the valley of Hebron, and since I didn't find them in Shechem, I went on to Dothan, where I found myself amid bay trees and willows. They saw me coming from afar and conspired to murder me, and once I was dead, to throw me in a well that was among some brambles. "Let's see," they all said, "whether his dreams will do him any good now." But Reuben answered them, hoping to free me: "Brothers, let us not kill him. We would do better to cast him alive into the well rather than commit so infamous a crime." I got there; and hardly had I greeted them, Nicela, when they stripped me of my tunic. They cast me into that well, which many sterile years had finally dried up. Then they sat down nearby to eat. You should not be shocked to hear that envy, once avenged, can eat, rest, and take its ease. As thus they sat on carpets of flowery enamel, dining on their envy and guzzling its blood, they saw some Ishmaelite merchants coming through the countryside—they recognized them by their clothing—with camels and baggage, for they were bringing perfumes from Gilead and elsewhere to sell in Egypt. To prevent them from killing me, Judah advised my brothers to sell me to them for twenty pieces of silver. They then sold me to your husband, as you already know.

NICELA. What an amazing story!

JOSEPH. Dreadful, you mean.

NICELA. What terrible pain that must have caused your father!

JOSEPH. It must have been just like a poisoned arrow that pierced his heart the moment he heard the news; or else it must have been a heroic test of his nobility.

NICELA. Why didn't your good looks make them take pity on you, my dear
Joseph?

JOSEPH. *Aside:* Now she's starting up with her insane desire again.

NICELA. If I had been there when they sold you, I'd have given a thousand
lives for you, or they would have had to kill me before they could offend
you.

JOSEPH. Only a woman of your nobility would show such honor to a slave.

NICELA. *Aside:* I can't believe he doesn't see that I'm in love with him! His
intelligence is superhuman. I have seen its divine effects in several admirable instances that have occurred in my house. And, as for the
soldiers whom my husband captains . . .

JOSEPH. I think I've stayed here too long, and it looks bad for a slave to
spend so much time in conversation, madam. What would you have me
do?

NICELA. Listen.

JOSEPH. This is no time for talking.

NICELA. But I want to give you your orders.

JOSEPH. If you intend to order me to stay here, you can do that later, when I
return. I am on my way somewhere else now.

Exit Joseph.

NICELA.   Vain thought, what do you want
            from a slave? What's your desire?
            How can you thus aspire,
            to something so repugnant?
            As his humble suppliant,
            to beg is quite insane,
            if you go on in this vein
            Joseph my lord will be;
            this love will transform me
            to slave from chatelaine.

To the sound of drumbeats, enter Putiphar, Nicela's husband,
accompanied by soldiers.

PUTIPHAR. The parade was a great success!

SERVIUS. And the king was delighted to see your troops pass in review.

PUTIPHAR. Indeed, it was dazzling, though it went on rather long.

SERVIUS. My lady is here.

PUTIPHAR. My dear Nicela!

NICELA. My lord, my love, hearing such good news is music to my ears! Did
the king honor you?

PUTIPHAR. My love, seeing you happy means more to me than the highest
honors.

NICELA. My dear, I'll go prepare a place where you can rest.

Exit Nicela.

PUTIPHAR. I can find no rest but in you. *[To the soldiers:]* Gather up those banners, and go to take your turns at standing guard.

Exeunt the soldiers. Enter Joseph and Thebanus.

THEBANUS. It was a splendid review!

JOSEPH. I didn't see it.

THEBANUS. Go on up to him. What are you waiting for?

JOSEPH. *[Kneels before Putiphar.]* Great Lord, let me kiss your feet.

PUTIPHAR. Oh, Joseph! Oh, my beloved Joseph!

JOSEPH. I was your slave before, but your kindness enslaves me even more.

PUTIPHAR. Arise, get up from there.

JOSEPH. May heaven raise you to such a height that all whom earth today esteems may look up to you in awe.

PUTIPHAR. Joseph, my friend, I have no other servant whom I esteem like you. I think you are just and saintly, and that God is with you. Since everything has gone well for me since you've been in my house, as you have increased my possessions, you've increased my love as well. You oversee my household staff, and I wish you could also have command over my banners, captains, and soldiers.

JOSEPH. No words could express how much I am obliged to you; the only appropriate response is for my mouth to touch the ground where your feet tread. I am your slave a thousand times over.

SERVIUS. Sir, the king has sent for you.

PUTIPHAR. I haven't even had time to rest or take off my armor, and already the king is sending for me?

JOSEPH. Do as he asks, Great Lord, for one who serves with love can hope for a good reward.

PUTIPHAR. Tell him I'm coming. Farewell, Joseph. Govern this house as its master while I'm away.

JOSEPH. May holy heaven keep you.

PUTIPHAR. May it preserve us both.

Exeunt Putiphar and Servius.

JOSEPH.   Oh, King of heaven immense,
                 who with your holy hands delivered me
                 from the envious offense
                 of my barbarous brothers' perfidy:
                 your mercy I magnify;
                 no longer slave but master here am I.
                 And ere his golden head
                 the haughty sun shall raise above these hills,

resplendent light to spread,
crowning the whole expanse of rocks and rills,
hands humbly joined in prayer,
will give you souls, the stars' absence to repair.
Nor will the shady night
extend her mask o'er that broad face,
disguising day so bright,
which the last rays of sunset do efface,
ere my breast offers you
as sacrifice a broken heart so true.
Enter Nicela.

NICELA. Joseph!

JOSEPH. My lady!

NICELA. What are you doing? Or perhaps I might better ask, considering how your love has tortured me: Joseph, what are you trying to undo? You just go about your duties, serving your unjust master instead of me; and meanwhile you're making me lose what little sense I had.

JOSEPH. What are you saying, my lady? I don't understand you.

NICELA. I have made up my mind. Leave me now, honor, for when love ceases to fear, it deems you worthless.

JOSEPH. She's dizzy. So what I've suspected all along has really turned out to be true; but my just loyalty will vanquish her desire, and my firm faith, her fickleness.

NICELA. Where has your master gone?

JOSEPH. The king sent for him.

NICELA. Joseph, now is your chance to satisfy my love.

JOSEPH. It is not love but madness that drives you to pester me.

NICELA. And what is it that drives you to kill me? Remember, I am a woman, and I have told you what's on my mind.

JOSEPH. God help me!

NICELA. You should thank your lucky stars, you fortunate slave, for I have despised a generous man for the sake of your good looks; his shining armor, which could give pure light to the sun, his plumes, worthy to crown its golden locks, all his adornments and the honor in which he's held—I have come here prepared to give all that up for you. Love me well, and you will have rich gifts beyond imagining. Now you give orders to servants, but then you will command their masters, for you will be the lord, and I, the slave of your love. If I can rightly be called your master's heart and soul, you will now be lord over your lady, and hence, over your master's soul. What have I ever done to you, Joseph, that you torment me so? You were wrong to stare at me; I didn't stare at you. I am beside myself! Give me back my own being! You have taken it from me, you have killed me; I now accuse you of that theft, and I'll see that you're properly punished, for the only thing worse than stealing is murder. Besides that, you Hebrews must be sorcerers, for anyone who can engender this kind of desire is more than a sorcerer. But to bewitch me like this, and then refuse to love me—has a greater crime ever been seen or heard of?

JOSEPH. Say no more, for I think that even listening to this is an offense against your honor. How dare I let you talk like this? My lady, I see two things against you, and against me too, that defend me from you, and can even defend you from your desire: the power of the Most High God in Whom I believe, for it is immense, and this offense would therefore be equally immense; and the power of your honor and your husband, for love has no defense against offended honor. He has entrusted his house to me, his honor, his keys, his property. Would it be right for me so ungratefully to offend him? Forget this vain obsession, and to prevent further problems, stop looking at me with amorous eyes, for love whimsically exaggerates whatever it chooses to look at. Just think how handsome he looks when he comes here in all his armor—so elegant, so impressive in all his martial finery. Then think of my low estate—a poor, humble, ragged slave. No, I'd rather die than give you what you want! Your love is disgusting, and I am right to resist.

He tries to leave.

NICELA. Stop, stop! Hold on, wait a minute! *[She seizes him by the cloak.]*

JOSEPH. Let go of my cloak!

NICELA. You monster, let go of my soul!

JOSEPH. It is God's will that I abhor your love.

NICELA. You dog! So you'll continue to treat me so ungratefully?

JOSEPH. I tell you, it is impossible for me to offend my master.

NICELA. I am a woman.

JOSEPH. Yes, you're a woman, man's worst enemy.

NICELA. I will not let you go.

JOSEPH. Then I'll leave my cape with you as a token of my loyalty to Putiphar. You can take revenge on it, or maybe it will cover up your vices. Yes, take your woman's revenge on that cape, just as the bull vents its rage on the cape for the man that got away.

Exit Joseph, leaving his cape in her hand. Enter Putiphar and the soldiers.

PUTIPHAR. What's going on here?

NICELA. Can't you see? That slave whom you adored has tried to rape me, and has left me his cape.

PUTIPHAR. What are you saying, Nicela?

NICELA. I am telling you that for a long time now this vile Hebrew slave, whom you love and trust so well, has been trying to seduce me. I suffered in silence, because I feared your just anger. Now you've seen it; this is what's going on.

PUTIPHAR. Soldiers, servants, people! Come here, my captains and guards!

ALL. Sir!

PUTIPHAR. Where is Joseph?

DELIUS. Didn't he just leave this room?

NICELA. Yes, he just left here, for since his master was with the king, he saw his chance to commit such a vile act of treason. He tried to rape me, woe is me! When I defended myself, he left his cape here, as you have seen.

SERVIUS. Pardon me, sir, if a soldier of your guard dares speak so boldly to you. This is all your fault.

PUTIPHAR. Arrest him.

SERVIUS. *[Aside:]* This will put an end to the favoritism he has shown Joseph, and to my envy of him.

Exeunt the soldiers.

PUTIPHAR. How dare he behave so boldly? How could a slave in a foreign land, a man I bought to tend the horses of my house, dare to attack his mistress!

The soldiers bring Joseph out in shackles.

DELIUS. Get a move on, you dog!

JOSEPH. Why do you treat an innocent man like this?

PUTIPHAR. You dog! Cursed be the confidence I had in you! I can see that your brothers and relatives had a good reason for selling you back there in your own land! Take him to jail at once. Handcuff him and put guards around him. Let him die a vile death by hanging. His foul neck doesn't deserve to sully an Egyptian sword.

Exit Putiphar.

JOSEPH. My lady, your . . .

NICELA. Shut up, you dog! This is how ingrates pay the debt they owe their masters.

JOSEPH. You are a frightful woman; but, provided that my innocence survive, I'll gladly die of your revenge.

They take him away to prison. Exit Nicela. Enter Bato and Lida.

LIDA. How dare you say such things to me?

BATO. You act as if this were the passion of some horse or donkey. Am I not a man with a nose, and eyes, and a forehead?

LIDA. You are indeed; but they don't say things like you've told me to other women.

BATO. Just what have I said anyway? Is that all you're upset about? Is it some miracle for me to tell you that I've got the hots for you? If this morning I had told my lady Dinah, the sister of my masters, what I've just told you, I'd understand if she answered me indignantly. But you?

LIDA. I would follow her example and defend my chastity.

BATO. But I am your equal.

LIDA. Yes, you are my equal, but I don't love you, so it would be very unequal of me to encourage you.

BATO. What saints you all pretend to be when you are not in love! But once a woman falls in love, no matter how stuck-up she may be, she may try to play coy by acting serious and smart-alecky, but she'll end up gladly bearing more saddles than any ass!

LIDA. Just for saying that, Bato, I'll never be yours so long as I live.

BATO. Okay, then, lying Lida, here's a curse I've concocted especially for you: God grant that you love another with the following cruel conditions: may you always work a lot but have very little to eat; may your husband deny you the pleasures of marriage; may your stew stick to the pot, and may he pelt you with many sticks!

LIDA. Listen, don't get so close, for my master, Jacob, is coming.

BATO. Oh, what a stupid love has any man who trusts in you womenfolk!

Enter Jacob, a venerable old man, and Reuben and Issachar,
dressed as Hebrews.

JACOB.   Pray, do not comfort me;
            these eyes are now beyond all consolation,
            by death's anxiety
            now veiled by pain and tears and sore vexation.
            The loss that I regret
            is too great for me ever to forget.
            Indeed, the woeful tale
            of Joseph, while I live, will yet remain.
            His memory I bewail,
            and when I think of him I am in pain,
            Surely 'twould be wrong
            for eyes and lips this grief not to prolong.

REUBEN.   Jacob, my father dear,
            of what avail is all this memory?
            You should forget, 'tis clear,
            that sad and lamentable history.

	My own dire grief is spent: Joseph is dead, my garments I have rent.
JACOB.	As soon as I laid eyes, dear Reuben, on this field, I thought again of Joseph's sad demise.
ISSACHAR.	Father, I'd better comprehend your pain as beyond all compare if Joseph were an only child so rare; but since God did you bless with eleven other sons, it is a sin to mourn with such excess.
JACOB.	No, Issachar, there is no error in my mourning; it is right. Of all my sons, Joseph was my delight. I was already old when lovely Rachel bore him unto me. How beauteous to behold was Rachel! Worthy indeed was she of fourteen years I served for her in cruelty and tears.
REUBEN.	That's true, but you have still another son by Rachel, handsome Benjamin, who Joseph's place can fill. How lovely are his eyes, his hair, his skin; his speech, how fair; and he can hunt and slay the fiercest bear.
JACOB.	Is there a shepherd here?
ISSACHAR.	Here's Bato. He's awaiting your command, our lord and father dear.
JACOB.	Leave now your flocks to graze upon this land. To Benjamin now go, and bring him to Jacob who loves him so.
BATO.	I'm off!

[Exit Bato.]

JACOB.	May God on high, who let me live on earth so many years, grant that he dry my tears.
ISSACHAR.	Lida's here too.
LIDA.	And I too cry.
JACOB.	Is my daughter Dinah well?
LIDA.	She is inclined in solitude to dwell;

from men she'd hide,
as if she bore some guilt for the wicked act
of that lad full of pride,
by whom she was well loved and ill attacked.

Enter Bato and Benjamin, dressed as a very handsome shepherd lad,
with a sash around his waist and a bow and arrows.

BATO.   There beside that rill,
oh Benjamin, your father sits and weeps;
that brook he'll fill
with tears, as Joseph's memory he keeps.

BENJAMIN.   Who else is there?

BATO.   Issachar and Reuben.

BENJAMIN.   I declare,
my father I'll embrace.
For his sake all my sport I would forgo.
Dear father!

JACOB.   'Tis the face
of Rachel.

BENJAMIN.   Let me hug you.

JACOB.   Now I know,
as I behold your charms,
my heart complains of these too-feeble arms.
Where were you, my boy,
as lovely as the sun at dawn's first light
when the dew brings joy
as with its pearls the grass it does bedight?
Those pearls aren't real,
but nonetheless, our eyes long them to steal.
I dreamt of love,
and now I see you, with your bow so taut,
come down here from above;
and yet to flatter you I have not thought.
That beast I fear
that slew dear Joseph. Would that he were here!

BENJAMIN.   Oh, father, I would fain
possess the heaven-sent ability
to console your pain;
for then so very fortunate I'd be,
your grief forestalled,
not Benjamin, but Comfort, I'd be called.
Rachel gave me the name

               of Son of Sorrow, for I caused her death,
               and therefore I blame
               myself for stealing my own mother's breath.
               What comfort can I give,
               since with this name of Sorrow I must live?

JACOB.   Sometimes in September
               we see a brilliant red carnation bloom,
               and like a glowing ember,
               defend itself against the winter's gloom,
               and that late flower
               brings great joy to the owner of the bower;
               thus you were born, my son,
               to bring relief from all my many woes
               like a bloom when summer's done,
               in my bleak September, at life's close.
               You brought me joy profuse,
               especially when that garden I did lose.
               Come now, please do,
               for by this brook I heartily desire
               to have a talk with you.

BENJAMIN. If I'm the ember of your love's last fire,
               I'll warm your heart
               as memories of Rachel I impart.

Exeunt. Enter King Pharaoh, his cupbearer Asiris, and two wise men,
Elius and Isacius.

PHARAOH. If you can't explain this for me, what good is all your learning?

ELIUS. Sire, such secret things are beyond my ken. There are so many different kinds of dreams that their interpreters disagree about what to make of them. If this is an animal dream, it may well merely be a product of your own thoughts.

ISACIUS. Heaven reveals certain things to the dreamer, Unvanquished Lord, by means of his dream.

PHARAOH. You are both ignorant. You are in charge of the school of Egypt? You're the ones who read the course of the heavens and the planets? A fine pair of Hermes Trismegistuses[6] you two are!

ASIRIS. Heavens, I've just remembered that lad Joseph, who told me so many things that came true when I was in jail! I humbly bow before you. Pardon my forgetfulness.

PHARAOH. What are you talking about?

ASIRIS. I might have served you better, were it not that I have the memory of a palace servant, who remembers only himself. When you ordered me and the man who was in charge of your bread arrested, a Hebrew lad was in the same jail because of an unjust accusation. The warden placed us in his charge, for he was very fond of him on account of his great virtue. Both of us prisoners had dreams one night, just when dawn was blotting out the stars. We told him our two dreams, and he interpreted them so accurately, sire, that there was not the slightest discrepancy. I dreamed I saw a grapevine with three branches which all at once sprouted blossoms and grapes, thus making it very beautiful. I held your cup in my hand, and squeezed the grapes into it, and gave you that juice to drink.

PHARAOH. Well then, how did he interpret your dream?

ASIRIS. "The three branches are three days," he said with divine knowledge, "after which the king will summon you, and once again you will offer him his cup at table, as you formerly did. When that happens, remember me, and ask him to take me out of this jail, for I am innocent; I've done no wrong." When the man who was in charge of your bread saw the lad's prudence, he said to him: "I dreamed that I was carrying three baskets on my head, full of flour and bread, and that all of a sudden birds flew down to eat them." He sadly answered him: "Three days from now the king will cut off your head and hang you on a gallows, where the birds will come to eat your flesh." You know very well how true his interpretations turned out to be!

PHARAOH. Indeed, you have been ungrateful. Go for him, and tell the warden that it is my command.

ASIRIS. Surely there was some reason why I forgot him.

Exit Asiris.

PHARAOH. Oh, fierce ingratitude that blinds the eyes, so they can't see the light of the good deeds done unto them! Earth has produced no animal so poisonous, not even the fierce Python[7] or the Lernaean serpent.[8] Royal palaces, once someone enters there, are like the river of forgetfulness. The wretch's humble plea, petitions, pleas for justice rarely succeed. The courtier seeks only his own advancement and is concerned only with his own profit.

Enter Joseph, in rags, Asiris, and a guard.

ASIRIS. Go on up to the king, he's waiting for you.

JOSEPH. *[Kneels before Pharaoh.]* Sire, Joseph, of Hebrew nationality, newly come from jail, embraces your unvanquished feet. Finding myself at your feet is surely heaven's reward for so much suffering.

PHARAOH. Arise. *[Aside:]* What a handsome and stately man!

Joseph, Asiris has told me that you are a man who has proven by experience that you can penetrate uncertain futures. I am troubled by a

dream. These so-called wise men of Egypt—a nation known throughout the world as mother of the sciences—can neither understand nor
interpret it.

JOSEPH. Then God will give you understanding.

PHARAOH. I dreamed that I was on the banks of a river, on whose shore I saw
seven fat cows grazing in the green grass. Then came another seven so
skinny that, even after they devoured the first seven, they were hardly
better off. The pain of seeing that awakened me. But then I fell asleep
again, and this time I saw seven lovely stalks with ears of grain; but
another seven that were sickly, black and withered, consumed the first
ones.

JOSEPH. Listen, sire, that you may know what God means to reveal to Pharaoh in this dream.

> The fat cows and the seven ears of grain
> mean seven years of plenty are in store;
> the withered ones that gave you so much pain
> are seven years unlike the ones before.
> By doubling your dreams, God would explain
> that they are true, and that you should therefore
> take action, being absolutely sure
> that this will happen, as those dreams ensure.
> Appoint a man of wisdom o'er your land
> to store up grain in all those plenteous years;
> once such preventive measures you have planned,
> you will be proof against all future fears.
> The providence of men who understand
> can make a vital difference, it appears.
> If grain for days of famine you reserve,
> your empire in your time you will preserve.

PHARAOH. Joseph, where could I find a man as brilliant as you? Since God
speaks through your mouth, inspiring you, you are as good as any sibyl,
and in your rare intelligence, you are an oracle of heaven, better than
Apollo himself. You are my chosen man, for you are prudent and sen-
sible; you know how to preside wisely and to give good counsel. During
the time of plenty, you will make provisions for all the ravages of the
sterile years to come. Bring him a tunic right now. Dress and adorn him.
From this day forward, Joseph is governor of Egypt. Bring my chariot,
that rich one that I use to show myself to the citizens on my birthday.
Let Joseph go out in triumph, and let all the people bow to my second in
command. Though his original name is a good one, and comes from his
fathers and his own land, I wish him to be called Savior of the World

from this day on. Savior, hold out your ring finger, for I shall put upon it the ring that bears my seal.

JOSEPH. Sir, you exalt your creature just as the light does; for while shedding light on others, it always retains its own first source of light. I am your slave.

PHARAOH. *[To his courtiers:]* What do you think? Isn't it a good idea to make the Savior of my kingdom my second in command?

ASIRIS. All of us, sire, gratefully kiss your feet.

ELIUS. Joseph is truly deserving of such a high office.

ISACIUS.   Spread laurels and flowers
             all over the ground,
             for fortunate Egypt
             her Savior has found.

                    Voices sing offstage:
             Spread laurels and flowers
             all over the ground,
             for fortunate Egypt
             her Savior has found.

*While they sing, Joseph parades around the stage with the king
at his side.*

JOSEPH.   Thou only art Savior,
             Who in heaven dost reign,
             Who for a poor slave
             dost a kingdom ordain.

*Flageolets or other musical instruments play. Exeunt with loud
applause, and thus ends act 1.*

ACT 2

Enter Bato and Lida, holding on to either end of a ribbon.

LIDA. Let go, you silly fool!

BATO. I don't understand why you are so mean to me.

LIDA. Is it mean of me to call you a fool?

BATO. What could be meaner? I don't think nature has formed any animal fiercer than you.

LIDA. It takes one to know one.

BATO. In that case, I wish heaven had made me a wise elephant, a lion, or a strong, frightening dragon, and given me their ferocity. Anything would be better then being a fool!

LIDA. Well, I think that's what you are.

BATO. I don't agree.

LIDA. What could be sillier than loving someone who hates you?

BATO. You're wrong, for that's a sign of real intelligence. Loving someone who loves us back is merely to act justly and sensibly.

LIDA. Do lovers obey?

BATO. Yes, indeed, for love is obedience.

LIDA. Then get out of here.

BATO. Calm down; I'm leaving. *[Aside:]* I'll hide behind these poplar trees.
He hides. Enter Benjamin, dressed as before.

BENJAMIN. You can run as much as you like, but I'll pursue you, though you fly on the wings of the wind.

LIDA. Come here, handsome Benjamin.

BENJAMIN. I'm chasing a wounded doe.

LIDA. Why not take me instead? I have surrendered to the carnation and jasmine in your face, the weapons of your great beauty. Why vainly chase the wind? Benjamin, give me that hand that nature made of snow to cool off the fire of your loveliness.

BENJAMIN. Lida, I wish you all the best, but you must let me go before that doe jumps into the river or somewhere I can't get to.
She grabs him.

LIDA. But you've already trapped my soul, dear ingrate.

BENJAMIN. Let go of me! Don't be a nuisance; for I know nothing of love.

LIDA. In that case, please just do me one favor.

BENJAMIN. What is it you want? Out with it!

LIDA. Just let me cut a few locks of that rich hair.

BENJAMIN. Lida, don't spread the word that I'm afraid of your witchcraft. Just stop pestering me. Farewell, Lida.
Exit Benjamin.

LIDA. I might as well be dead.
Enter Bato.

BATO. Me too, for we are equally unlucky. Now, ungrateful Lida, I understand why you've ignored me.

LIDA. You sneak! You were eavesdropping? I might as well be dead.

BATO. I'll tell the master.

LIDA. Bato! Bato!

BATO. There's nothing more to say. Either you'll love me, or I'll tell all about your love and your attempts at sorcery.

LIDA. I will love you.

BATO. Then cut my hair instead of Benjamin's if you really meant that as an act of love.

LIDA. All right.

BATO. Cut away. After all, you'd do the same thing to any little piglet back at home.

LIDA. The master's coming. I'll have to do it later.

Exeunt Bato and Lida. Enter Jacob, Reuben, Issachar, and Simeon.

JACOB. This is a cruel and sterile time. My family is perishing.

REUBEN. It's sad to live here in the country now. These dried up leaves bring no joy to the spirit.

ISSACHAR. It seems that earth has somehow offended heaven, which no longer maintains its own creation. The cattle can find no grass, and the wasted meadows compete in dreariness with the snow-clad mountains.

JACOB. My sons, everything has dried up so much that the only rivers to be seen are those that flow from our own eyes! The earth itself, desolated by this drought, seems to be opening a thousand mouths with which to complain to heaven. The cattle vainly low, and the rocks echo their bellowing. The little birds sadly return to their nests from the fields. Yet amidst all this woe, I've heard that there is plenty to eat all over Egypt. Go there, my sons, and buy some wheat. Please go, though I will miss you, for there seems to be plenty of food there. Even the rivers that flow here from there bring signs of that.[9]

REUBEN. Good Jacob, your trials always find such respite. But what else can we do, since the heavens are angry and the elements are in turmoil, full of a thousand evil omens? We hadn't dared suggest this to you, sir, for we didn't want you to suffer from our absence; but now that you yourself have thought of it, oh pious and prudent father, how shall we go about it?

JACOB. I'd rather not be party to your departure, but there's no alternative. Since this is so, hear me now, sons of Jacob: my soul was once divided into twelve parts, but now that Joseph is gone, you are eleven. Let the sons of Leah go—Reuben, Levi, Simeon and worthy Judah, Issachar and Zebulun; the sons of Bilhah, who waited on my Rachel, Dan and Naphtali; the sons of Zilpah, whom Leah gave me, Gad and Asher. Let only Benjamin remain with me, for he is all that I have left to remember how I loved my adored Rachel. He has been my consolation since I lost Joseph, the only breath of hope that has sustained my old age. Now go, my sons, and may God give you the blessing He promised to my grandfather Abraham and my father Isaac. Go, my sons, for if God's own voice assured me of a rich posterity, that must be true.

Exit Jacob.

NAPHTALI. He's sad to see us go.

ISSACHAR. Well, he's our father.

REUBEN. Let's get going, Issachar.

ISSACHAR. Have Bato summon Naphtali and the others.

Exeunt. Enter Nicela and Delpha.

DELPHA. They say the viceroy often comes this way.

NICELA. I'm not sure whether he's an angel who delights me or a devil who consumes me in his fire.

DELPHA. Do you love him that much?

NICELA. Today, just as on the first day that I saw him, my dreams of love are the soul that animates this body. My pain is only worsened by the knowledge that my former slave has risen to such greatness and such power. And when I think that Joseph's gotten married and has sons, my love turns into envious madness. Alas, two sons have been born to him, Ephraim and Manasseh.

DELPHA. It's hard to believe you still cling to those memories, when so much time has passed!

NICELA. I suffer more than ever, for when love is unfulfilled, it stubbornly gives life to desire.

DELPHA. He's coming. Get out of his way; come here.

NICELA. Alas, my slave! Who would believe I'd ever see him in such grandeur, only to become more envious!

Music plays. Enter Joseph, sitting in a triumphal chariot. Asiris and Putiphar walk on either side of him, and servants precede him, scattering flowers and branches on the ground.

JOSEPH.   As of today, the sun has run its course
six times, my friends, encircling the sky,
since I was raised to glory by the force
of that compassionate God who dwells on high;
For though the king may be the direct source
of my greatness, and I'd not deny
that I reflect his light just as the moon
reflects the sun, I owe him not this boon.
    For God moves all things in this world below,
though your wise men would call it destiny,
from Him comes life, He honor does bestow,
and He the center of all things must be.
God makes, preserves, and causes them to grow,
and He protects the humble, as we see.
He even creates kings, and all good things
derive from Him, and not from earthly kings.

PUTIPHAR.   Great Savior of the World, you've justified
that name that Pharaoh gave you. By your hand

you've saved the world. As viceroy you preside
o'er all, for without you this mighty land
would perish. As our savior we've relied
on you, and we are freed by your command
from hunger and oppression. Without you,
confusion in our land would reign anew.

JOSEPH.   When we get to the palace, please give ear
to all who humbly come to seek our aid
in their affliction, and I want it clear
that first attention to the poor be paid.
Of food, mankind's inheritance most dear,
an equal distribution must be made,
that all may be sustained in perfect peace.

PUTIPHAR. Oh Savior, heaven grant your life increase!

*The chariot turns around with musical accompaniment and leaves the
stage, accompanied by Asiris, Putiphar, and the servants, as before.
Nicela and Delpha remain on stage.*

DELPHA. What do you say now?

NICELA. I'm left speechless from beholding such grandeur.

DELPHA. What God Himself has raised up, He will defend. Envy cannot
endanger the favor he has won from the king.

NICELA. It infuriates me to see him hold such power and enjoy such favor.

Enter Putiphar.

PUTIPHAR. Nicela, what are you doing here?

NICELA. My lord!

PUTIPHAR. I'm surprised to find you at the palace gate.

NICELA. I've come here veiled amid the public throng, because I wanted to
look upon our slave.

PUTIPHAR. That's no way to talk. The king has commanded that all call him
Savior.

NICELA. You think I'd call him Savior?

PUTIPHAR. Is it not because of him that you're alive today?

NICELA. Don't flatter him; there's nothing to be gained by doing so.

Exit Nicela. Enter Joseph.

JOSEPH. General, give permission for anyone who wishes to come in.

PUTIPHAR. *(Kneels before Joseph.)* May heaven prosper your life, which
means as much to us as heaven itself!

JOSEPH. Get up, for I have not forgotten that you were once my master.

PUTIPHAR. Your grandeur is enhanced by your prudence and good sense; for
a man who can still recall his former humble lot after God has raised
him up has won the greatest of victories.

(Aside:) I can't believe that this man wronged me. I'm jealous of Nicela; she has surely offended me. He must have been innocent, for whenever a man who is dominated by vice becomes powerful, he does whatever he likes. Since it wasn't Joseph's fault, it must have been hers, and he brandished that cape to fend off her attack. The desire was all hers; she was the cruel bull, because if she hadn't charged him, he wouldn't have thrown that cape in her eyes.

Joseph sits down. Enter Reuben, Naphtali, Issachar, Simeon, and Bato.

SIMEON. Can that man be the Savior?

NAPHTALI. They said he was in here.

SIMEON. Well, go on up to him.

NAPHTALI. Do you think we can go up just like that?

REUBEN. How should we show him our respect?

BATO. I'm just a country hick, but even I know that you must kneel on the floor before him. Go on up.

All kneel before Joseph.

REUBEN. Oh, Savior of Egypt, at your great feet behold some poor Hebrew people who have come to buy the wheat that your prudence set aside for the present years, as we have been told. Please order, sir, that they give us whatever seems right to your grace, so that in these times we may have some help in our great need.

JOSEPH. *[Aside:]* Heavens! What's this I see? Heavens! Who could understand Your secrets? Oh, highest, supreme Compassion! Are these not my brothers?

REUBEN. Why is he so surprised? What is he thinking?

ISSACHAR. He has turned pale.

NAPHTALI. Men who govern tend to get distracted like that, just like men of letters.

JOSEPH. *[Severely:]* You guys, where do you come from?

BATO. He called them "guys"; that's a bad sign.

JOSEPH. *(More upset.)* Where have you come from, you guys?

BATO. Tell him: from Adam and Eve.

REUBEN. Sir, we have come here from the land of Canaan to buy wheat.

JOSEPH. *(Angrily:)* That's obviously a lie.

BATO. Didn't I tell you?

JOSEPH. You are certainly spies; your very clothing gives you away.

REUBEN. Spies, my lord! Please don't think our nobility is capable of such a treacherous thought. We were twelve brothers, sons of the same father, though by different mothers. Eleven of us have survived. The next to the youngest died, and the youngest has stayed behind with the old man to comfort him for the one who died. This is the truth, my lord.

JOSEPH. One is missing.

BATO. How angry his face looks!

JOSEPH. Tell me how he died.

REUBEN. It was on a holiday in the valley of Mamre when he was going to take water to the flocks. A fierce animal killed him.

JOSEPH. Fierce, my eye! Anyone could see that you've made all this up. You are spies, and you have come to see what walls, what gates, and what defenses Memphis has.

ISSACHAR. Sir, this is the truth.

JOSEPH. *(Gets up.)* As the king lives, you traitors, you will not get out of jail until the brother you say stayed back there to console your father comes here! Let the most diligent among you go for him, while the rest of you stay here in chains and shackles.

REUBEN. Sir . . .

JOSEPH. There's nothing more to say; the proof that you're telling the truth is that brother you've mentioned. If he comes, I'll know it's true; if not, you are lying. Captain!

PUTIPHAR. Sir!

JOSEPH. Chain these men up and put them in jail.

REUBEN. We are justly punished for our crime.

NAPHTALI. Yes, for the pure innocence of our brother cries out to heaven.

REUBEN. Didn't I tell you then that it was wrong?

SIMEON. Now this undeserved misfortune has befallen us because of what we did to him.

PUTIPHAR. Get going.

BATO. Captain, I'd just like to point out that I am not one of those men whom the viceroy condemned.

PUTIPHAR. Who are you, then?

BATO. I'm just the guy who takes care of their animals.

PUTIPHAR. Well, you'll have to take care of yourself now.

BATO. Poor Bato, who'd have thought you'd end up losing your skin in a foreign land!

Putiphar leads them away.

JOSEPH.   Oh, tears that fill my eyes,
              solicitous pity that love does engender,
              cease now to sympathize,
              or, like a dammed-up stream, fully surrender
              and, bursting, my heart sever,
              for wrath soon ends, but love goes on forever.

Enter Phoenicia and Lisenus.

LISENUS. He must die, Phoenicia!

PHOENICIA. It is not so, take pity!

JOSEPH. What's this about?

LISENUS. Great Lord, I beg Your Majesty for justice.

PHOENICIA. And I for pity, savior of us all.

JOSEPH. Are you her husband?

LISENUS. I am.

JOSEPH. Speak then.

LISENUS. I had two sons by Phoenicia.

PHOENICIA. They are both of our sons. Please hear me.

JOSEPH. Woman, even if the pain of childbirth makes you impatient, you must let the man speak first.

LISENUS. My younger son killed the older one out of envy. He has been arrested. I want him to die, but Phoenicia disagrees.

PHOENICIA. Sir, one is already dead. It would be terrible to kill both of them.

JOSEPH. You are right. I will order him removed from prison right away. May God punish him for the blood he shed.

PHOENICIA. May you live a thousand years, oh sovereign Savior of Egypt!

JOSEPH. This is exactly like what happened with Jacob's sons.

Exeunt Phoenicia and Lisenus. Enter Putiphar.

PUTIPHAR. Those Hebrews are in jail now.

JOSEPH. When they've been there for three days, set them free.

PUTIPHAR. You must have found out what mischief they are up to.

JOSEPH. A certain Joseph warned me about them. He was born in their homeland, and now he is in Egypt.

PUTIPHAR. Is this someone you know?

JOSEPH. Very well.

PUTIPHAR. I will set them free.

JOSEPH. Before they can leave the city, seize the one of them whose name is Simeon. It's important that he remain in jail till they return, for they must bring their other brother here. Give them wheat, but first put their money back in their sacks, and don't let them see what you're doing. Do you understand?

PUTIPHAR. Very well.

JOSEPH. Captain, I praise your loyalty. It is no easy thing to serve a man who was once your slave.

Exeunt Joseph and Putiphar. Enter Lida and Benjamin.

LIDA.   The worse that you treat me,
   the more my true love grows;
   such cruelty, everyone knows,
   only enhances beauty.
   Nature, God's deputy,

created hills, and men, and beasts, and human hearts,
but in spite of all her arts,
she cannot cause two hearts to beat as one,
nor soften them, though marble be undone
and broken into tender crystal parts.
      Oh, Benjamin, alas, who would have thought,
dear Seraph, such a thing could come to be!
I knew at last you'd be the death of me,
but that such loveliness could kill, imagined not.
Of love you'll not be taught
though your fair body swells in its springtime.
Now in your youthful prime,
why won't that frozen body yield,
since everywhere, in mountain or in field,
all things surrender to sweet love sublime?
      The lowest animals now seek to mate,
though without souls that in our bodies yearn;
even the palm tree to her mate does turn;
the little birds of love are heard to prate,
as in sweet songs their passions they express,
warbling of longing and great tenderness;
the little brooks unto the rivers go;
while you alone, oblivious to my woe,
you snake, objections to my love address.

BENJAMIN.   If I of love but knew,
my heart I would incline
to that for which you pine,
and cease offending you.
Your beauty then would do
to me as nature indicates is only just,
and yet insist I must
that I have never felt love's awesome power,
though bird, and beast, and plant or lovely flower
it conquers and entwines in burning lust.
      Love is an inclination
mysterious, that causes us to yearn,
a fire that in our very souls does burn
and fills our hearts with glad anticipation.
Its only inspiration,
dear Lida, is one's pleasure or desire.
My soul does not inspire

	me to seek such pleasure in your arms, for though my eyes do gaze upon your charms, my soul has not caught fire.
LIDA.	If you were really bright, you'd know that such disdain just causes love to gain more boldness and more might. But though you shrink in fright, and lukewarm would me spurn, these arms with fire do burn!

She tries to embrace him.

BENJAMIN.	Stop, fool!
LIDA.	Please don't mope.
BENJAMIN.	Here's Jacob.
LIDA.	Now no hope have I his warm embrace to earn.

Enter Jacob.

JACOB.	Absence is painful for love to endure, a torment to the soul beyond compare; when one is insecure, patience runs out, he is oppressed with care, for day and night, his mind is tortured by a memory unkind. I have good cause to fear. No comfort now my love can satisfy. My love's too great, 'tis clear; such love has caused my fears to multiply, tormenting me with fright.
BENJAMIN.	Dear father!
JACOB.	Benjamin so bright! I think you've understood how comfortless I am in so much pain.
BENJAMIN.	Indeed I have, for that pain surely would make even our land's mountains now complain, and with you they would weep, at sunset and when dawn disturbs their sleep. Surely my brothers will come home quite soon; add not unto your trials with such fear.
JACOB.	My fear is not for naught, 'tis my fortune: for Jacob's trials have always been severe.

  Indeed, I think I'm cursed;
  throughout my life things turned out for the worst.
BENJAMIN.   When you were young, you did not think that way,
  tending the flocks that to Laban did belong
  for many a night and day,
  as for my precious mother you did long,
  for Rachel loveliest
  of women, and of womankind most blessed.
JACOB. *(He cheers up.)*
    How could I now retell
  what I endured, content with all my woes!
  When one is young, all's well,
  that joy from our life's April surely flows.
  While waiting her to wed,
  for seven years old Laban's flocks I fed.
    I was a handsome boy,
  when, dressed up in my best, to her I'd go—
  for then I knew love's joy—
  but later on, your mother let me know
  (once we were man and wife)
  that jealous fears had stabbed her like a knife.
    Sometimes we boys would fight,
  and if some bully dared to look at her,
  honor would give me might,
  imagining that man she might prefer.
  Then that man I would press
  until my right to Rachel he'd confess.
    The wolves I did dismay;
  the fiercest lions trembled at my sight.
  Those shepherds then did say
  that I was the greatest of them all in might.
LIDA.   How well him you've distracted.
BENJAMIN. 'Tis on your own example I have acted.
       Enter Bato.
BATO. I've gotten ahead of the others so that I could be the bearer of good
 tidings, if this news can be considered good.
JACOB. Bato!
BATO. My lord!
JACOB. Don't even speak to me, for I know you'll just add some new misfor-
 tune to my trials. Are my sons coming?

BATO. They'll be right here.

JACOB. All of them?

BATO. The eldest of them are already here; you'd better save such questions for them.

Enter Reuben, Issachar, and Naphtali, sadly.

REUBEN. May heaven preserve you.

ISSACHAR. May heaven give you health.

NAPHTALI. Permit us to kiss your feet.

JACOB. I can tell by the expressions on your faces that you have not come with happiness.

REUBEN. Father, we arrived in great Memphis in Egypt, famous among the cities of the world and close to heaven, with its marble pyramids. Pharaoh has a viceroy, a man of notable qualities, who wields the scepter in his place, and whom he allows to be called Savior, for indeed he has saved the whole Egyptian kingdom in these dreadful times. As soon as we got there, we went to visit him. We bowed low to the ground before this handsome and severe dignitary. He asked us where we were from. I told him from this valley, along with other information that should have sufficed to allay his suspicions. He said that we were spies, but no matter how much we insisted that we were noblemen, twelve sons of a single father, and told him our whole story—how we are now eleven, since Joseph was slain by a wild beast that bathed his clothing in blood, and how Benjamin was back here—he refused to believe me unless we brought him Benjamin to prove we spoke the truth. He kept Simeon in jail there as a hostage, and we too spent three days there weighed down with heavy chains. Father, give us Benjamin—may heaven increase your days!—because there's no question of our returning to Egypt without him. Furthermore, we are distressed, because when we opened our bags of wheat, we found every bit of the money we had paid inside them. If this was a mistake, it's certainly an extraordinary one.

JACOB. Why do you wish me long life, since Jacob's trials increase with every passing moment, and they were already disproportionate to my age? You have left me without sons. As God knows, that beast you spoke of killed Joseph. Simeon is in jail, and now you would deprive me of my dear son Benjamin? I have already lost Joseph; I'll not be deprived of this living image of him. If that should happen, this white head would descend to the dark center of the earth dissolved in wretched tears.

REUBEN. Don't take it so hard, father. You have wept enough. If you go on like this, you'll end up blind. Give me Benjamin, sir, for if I don't take him there, no amount of gold will suffice to ransom my brother from jail. If I don't bring him back to you safe and sound, you have my permission to kill my own two sons. The famine is increasing here; and we must go back there to rescue Simeon.

JACOB. Why did you tell that man I had another son, since you didn't need to mention that unless he asked you?

NAPHTALI. May heaven abandon us, destroy our flocks and ruin our fields if we intended any harm by that! We were only trying to give him a proper answer to his questions.

JACOB. All right, then, sons, take him with you if there is no other way.

BENJAMIN. Don't cry. Those tears offend the courage that enabled you to wrestle with an angel. How could God fail to give what He has promised you? Before that could happen, the world would disappear and the heavens would be wiped out. You have seen God face to face. What are you afraid of? Who could possibly harm you now, when you defeated that divine giant?

JACOB. Your words are comforting, but you intend to leave me, so what comfort will I have then? Still, Benjamin, you must depart, and part of my soul goes with you.

BENJAMIN. I hope to embrace you soon in a happier time.

JACOB. My sons, may my blessing prosper all of you.

Exit Jacob, weeping.

ISSACHAR. Stay with him for a while. We have to go, but we don't have to leave quite yet.

REUBEN. As soon as everyone has had a chance to rest, we'll set out.

Exeunt. Bato and Lida stay behind.

BATO. Stay here!

LIDA. What nonsense!

BATO. Would you begrudge a measly hug even to a tiger, even if it were as black as those sunburned folks that dwell in Ethiopia?

LIDA. Bato, whatever gave you the idea that I'm obliged to hug you, since I don't love you?

BATO. You owe me that hug, not because you love me, but because I love you.

LIDA. All right then, Bato. Just so you won't call me rude for not being as loose as other women, come and get your hug.

BATO. May heaven keep you, Lida! You shouldn't fail in courtesy, for that's considered a defect even between lovers. Surely you've seen those fools who can't bring themselves to doff their hats even an inch above their heads. Or what about those others who get into arguments about how they should be addressed? As long as the other person's standing, they refuse to sit down. Besides being idiots, they're just asking for people to criticize them and publicize their vices.

LIDA. So what you want is for me to hug you with both my arms?

BATO. Well, since they're yours anyway, what could it hurt?

LIDA. Since I'm only half inclined, wouldn't one arm suffice?

BATO. So now you'd split your love between me and Benjamin? He loves
you. Who could doubt it? But I'll get revenge, for he'll not come back
here.

LIDA. What do you mean?

BATO. Just keep that hug. Some other fool may want to split the difference,
but as for me, I'm too stiff to do such splits.

Exit each one on opposite sides of the stage.

ACT 3

Enter Joseph and Putiphar.

JOSEPH. What? Have those Hebrews come back from the land of Canaan?

PUTIPHAR. They are full of ardent desire to kiss your feet.

JOSEPH. Has the youngest one come with them too?

PUTIPHAR. He has, and even though some of them are very good-looking,
they can't hold a candle to Benjamin—they say that is his name—for he
is handsome as the sun itself, and by comparison, they are the merest
shadows.

JOSEPH. So the lad has come at last!

PUTIPHAR. That seems to make you happy.

JOSEPH. You will soon know why.

PUTIPHAR. They didn't understand why you sent for the eleven of them.
They thought it must have been the money they found in their bags.
They gave it back to me, but I told them I didn't want it, and that you
were inviting them to dine. They were very excited about that.

JOSEPH. Summon them.

PUTIPHAR. They're just outside.

JOSEPH. Joseph, what more could you ask of merciful heaven now? Today I
shall ascend to Pharaoh's very throne. Yet this is no excess of pride, for
I do this only to fulfill the will of God. Though He has raised me high,
my own humility remains intact.

*A canopied throne atop a dais is on stage; Joseph ascends the steps and
sits down. Enter his brothers.*

ISSACHAR. *[Kneels before Joseph.]*

Behold, in humble reverence before you now,
as you sit on that royal throne whose gold

envies the laurels placed upon your brow,
crowned with an Idumaean splendor bold,
Oh Generous Viceroy, before you bow
ten Hebrew men from Mamre's vale so old,
come here to demonstrate to you, forsooth,
when they first spoke with you, they spoke the truth.
    Oh, Mighty One, if you could see the pain
of Jacob, their old father, you'd surrender.
From feeling pity you could not refrain,
for that old man, once strong, has now grown tender.
The promise we made you was not in vain,
for we our children unto him did render
to guarantee the safety of this youth.
Give us our brother, for we've told the truth.

JOSEPH. *[Aside:]* How can I keep up this front? How can I keep from showing my affection for my own flesh and blood? Oh, eyes, take pity on this
broken heart! Now you are full of tears. Weep, then, for no man alive
has ever suffered so much from love as I. No, I shall not cause them
more distress. The lad is so handsome that just looking at him suffices
to set my heart and eyes at peace. He is the very image of that beauty
for which Rachel was so famed. If my mother looked like that, it's no
wonder that my father served Laban so long for her. I will go down to
them.

                    He descends the steps.

BATO. The king is staring at you, Benjamin.

BENJAMIN. Since I first saw him, I have been distressed.

BATO. How so?

BENJAMIN. I can't exactly say. All I know is that my heart was moved within
me with a strange emotion.

JOSEPH. Hebrews!

REUBEN. Sire!

JOSEPH. Is your father well?

REUBEN. Yes, he is well, if he can go on living when lacking his very soul.

JOSEPH. Is this that brother you told me about?

REUBEN. It's he.

JOSEPH. Bring him here.

BENJAMIN. *(Kneels before him.)* Give me your feet, and let me kiss your
heroic hand.

JOSEPH. No, I would rather embrace you.

BENJAMIN. I am unworthy of your embrace.

JOSEPH. *[Aside:]* Oh, God! With what tight bonds You twist my heart! How can I keep from weeping? I'm trying my best to control myself, but I can't resist those tears. If I stay here, I'm lost. Captain!

PUTIPHAR. Sir!

JOSEPH. Is the table set? It must be time to eat.

PUTIPHAR. Yes, sir.

JOSEPH. Then tell them to go on in.

PUTIPHAR. All of you, come into the dining room.

REUBEN. He is showing us a signal favor.

NAPHTALI. You can see that he likes us by the way he has been acting.

BENJAMIN. Let's go in, Bato.

BATO. Benjamin, this won't end well. I tremble before every majesty. A good cheese seasoned with garlic in my hut tastes better to me than any Arabian phoenix the most powerful king enjoys.

BENJAMIN. What nonsense! You obviously have no taste.

BATO. What I say is that I've never heard of garlic poisoning anyone, great or small.

Exeunt.

JOSEPH. Listen, Captain.

PUTIPHAR. Sir!

JOSEPH. When they have finished eating, give them everything they need.

PUTIPHAR. What is the matter with you?

JOSEPH. This is pity, Captain, and love. I was moved by seeing people from my own land. Wasn't that Benjamin handsome?

PUTIPHAR. As handsome as any king.

JOSEPH. Listen.

PUTIPHAR. What would you have me do? I don't understand what's going on. If this is just pity and love, you seem awfully upset.

JOSEPH. Put their money back in their bags of wheat, but don't let them see what you're doing. This is my way of showing my fondness for my homeland. And put my precious cup in the youngest brother's bag.

PUTIPHAR. Surely there's more to this. He must have some reason for what he's doing.

JOSEPH. Later, I'll explain privately how you are to pursue them as thieves and arrest them.

PUTIPHAR. I shall do as you say, for I'm sure there is some mysterious explanation.

JOSEPH. I'm going to eat now.

PUTIPHAR. But sir, how can you punish and reward at the same time, conferring both honor and shame?

JOSEPH. You'll understand it later.

Exit Joseph.

PUTIPHAR. I am totally bewildered, for I can't figure out what mysterious reason there could be for all of this.

Exit Putiphar. Enter all the brothers.

REUBEN. That famous Savior is certainly kind!

SIMEON. Oh, yes, that was a lovely prison he put me in.

ISSACHAR. Look, we were all really sorry about that.

REUBEN. It hurt me to see how much my father Jacob suffered.

NAPHTALI. The poor old man couldn't stop crying over your absence; but things only got worse when I asked to bring Benjamin here, for he's the apple of his eye.

BATO. Thank the God of Israel that now he'll see you all together again, and loaded down with the wheat he needs.

REUBEN. When we tell him how the Savior treated us, even descending from his lofty throne to eat with ten uncouth farmers, that will prolong his life.

ISSACHAR. Yes, he is a generous man. Arresting Simeon on suspicion was just something he had to do because he's the viceroy. That high office requires not only that he govern but that he prevent any harm from coming to the kingdom.

REUBEN. What a great banquet he gave us!

BATO. The majordomo gave me plenty to eat too. By gosh, I've never seen so many chickens! Did you see those big monkeys on both sides that were storing up the nuts to eat at their leisure? Well, I stuffed my cheeks just like those monkeys. I wanted to be well stuffed before starting this trip, for it's sure to be long, and there won't be much to eat.

REUBEN. As long as you get plenty to eat, you'd gladly go from the Black Sea to the Red Sea.

BATO. So what? They say that all the pleasure in the world is nothing more or less than eating. The rich eat more, the poor eat less.

BENJAMIN. Who are those people coming toward us?

ISSACHAR. Judging by their clothes, I'd say they're the king's men.

REUBEN. They're coming after us . . .

BATO. But why? What for?

Enter Putiphar and Soldiers.

PUTIPHAR. Halt, traitors! Heraclius, intercept those others. Hold on, you dirty Hebrews!

REUBEN. Are you talking to us?

PUTIPHAR. That's right. How could you be so vile? After receiving such outrageous kindness from my lord the king in Memphis, who shows such favors to foreigners—why, he even came down from his royal throne and humbly ate with you as if he were your equal—you stole his cup.

REUBEN. We stole his cup? What are you saying?

PUTIPHAR. It's missing from his plate-room.

REUBEN. What greater proof of our loyalty could you ask for to temper this unjust rage? Didn't we give you back the money you had left in our bags?

PUTIPHAR. You were just trying to fool me, because you were afraid I'd punish you. Untie those sacks.

REUBEN. If you find any gold or silver in any of our bags, let the owner of that bag die.

PUTIPHAR. All of you, untie them one by one.

BATO. I'll untie Benjamin's, for I'm in charge of it.

REUBEN. Death is too light a punishment; we'll all be the slaves of that blessed prince of yours.

SOLDIERS. Here's the cup.

REUBEN. There?

SOLDIERS. The youngest one must have hidden it there.

REUBEN. You, Benjamin!

BENJAMIN. Why are you looking at me? May heaven destroy me if I've ever seen that cup before! I would not be unworthy of the blood of Abraham for all the precious cups that human greed has acquired since the day the world began.

PUTIPHAR. You knaves! You thought you'd get away with this? Arrest them.

REUBEN. Benjamin, I am rending my garments and my very breast.

PUTIPHAR. You are all thieves, I know what you're like now. Take them to the viceroy.

NAPHTALI. Oh, heavens!

BENJAMIN. Brothers, don't think that I have ruined your trip like this; I am falsely accused.

REUBEN. We know that you're an angel.

PUTIPHAR. Get a move on.

BENJAMIN. Merciful heavens, reveal the truth!

REUBEN. I trust that God will help us out.

BATO. Are we going back to Egypt?

SOLDIERS. Yes.

BATO. Poor Bato! My stomach's churning; I wish I hadn't eaten that last chicken.

Exeunt. Enter Pharaoh and Joseph.

PHARAOH.   When the sweet fruits of victory I reap,
             gladly shall I divide them all with you.

JOSEPH.   I'm grateful, sire.

PHARAOH.   Don't go, 'tis early yet to sleep.

JOSEPH.   It's better that you retain the revenue;
            only the land do I desire to keep.
            Unvanquished Mars, Bashan for peace will sue;
            they tremble at your sight.

PHARAOH.   I'd have no fear
            if this wartime were but a fertile year.
                  Soldiers are disinclined to go to war
            in times of famine. The desolate fields distract
            them; and there's precious little honor
            in a victory o'er men with hunger racked.
            I leave this place trusting in your valor,
            for you've redeemed and have preserved intact
            my realm. For saving us from that great risk,
            I'll raise your statue on an obelisk.

                              Exit Pharaoh.

JOSEPH.   Oh Sovereign King, on You have I relied!
            You loved my fathers, Abraham the bold,
            Isaac the pious, Jacob now grown old;
            and You have crushed my persecutors' pride.
                  'Tis by Your mighty hand I here preside:
            for thus do You defend the innocent,
            frustrating the malevolent intent
            of brothers who were bent on fratricide.
                  Your merciful arm has raised me to this state,
            exalting me unto the royal sphere,
            proof against all whom envy filled with hate,
                  for envy is a beast that has no peer.
            Only a mighty God like You could liberate
            a man like me from envy's mortal fear.

Enter Putiphar, the soldiers, and Joseph's brothers.

PUTIPHAR.   Come in, you knaves, for now 'tis death you'll face,
            not just the governor.

                  The brothers kneel before Joseph.

REUBEN.   Generous Savior,
            now we are at your mercy in this place.

SIMEON.   We've come with that poor lad who meant no malice,
            though on him has been found your golden chalice.

JOSEPH.   You're criminals, though now you humbly kneel.
            How could you be inclined
            to wrong me, when to you I've been so kind?
            Did you come here from Canaan just to steal?

	To do me harm you'd seek
	when I have honored you? You have some cheek!
REUBEN.	Sir, all we want—for it is only right—
	is to become your slaves;
	now brand us all as knaves,
	and mark us with that iron as dark as night;
	for when our faces bear that ugly brand,
	your justice all mankind will understand.
JOSEPH.	Heaven forbid! Indeed, the only slave
	I'd have is surely he
	who, as you all can see,
	has dared so horribly to misbehave.
	The rest of you are free now to return
	unto your father, who for you does yearn.

ISSACHAR. Oh, Sovereign Viceroy of this Illustrious Realm, Savior both in name and in heroic deeds; oh, Fortunate Prince, who, after heaven, deserves to be offered fragrant incense; you, whose name the Medes and Parthians, Syrians, and Armenians adore: we have come here from that Hebrew vale where Abraham once saw three youths—a divine figure of the holy Trinity, in essence one, a single immense God. Sir, we have come, I say, rapt in memories of better times, for these years have shaved the mountains back there, once covered with green grass, of all their hair and beards. April has brought not one flower to the meadow, not one stalk of grain to the fallow land, nor has heaven bathed them with a drop of rain. Our dear father advised us to come here. You asked us all about ourselves, whether our parents were living, and whether we had brethren or relatives; and we told you all we had was an aged father and a little brother, who was his only comfort. This lad here, and another who died a long time ago, were sons of a single mother, the apple of Jacob's eye. That lovely woman's name was Rachel, and I think her beauty was the least of her attributes. "Bring him," you said, "for I would like to see him to find out whether all you've said is true or false." I answered you: "I think that that's impossible, because if we take that child from him, the old man will die of pain." You then replied: "If I don't see him, you will not see my face again." Then we departed. Back in Canaan we found your servant Jacob. When he heard our story, he was lost in thought. "Today," he said, "I'll lose both sons I had by Rachel; if you take this one away, I won't even have his face to remember her by." Consider then, my lord: if we go back there now without his Benjamin, who is his heart and soul, what will become of us, since his

brother is already dead? I offered my father my two fine sons as secu-
rity; but I also solemnly swore to defend Benjamin as if he were my
own son. How can I now return without him? That saintly old man is
180 years old. His white hair hangs down upon his illustrious breast.
We all on bended knee now beg you, shedding tears, to spare his life.
ALL. Please, sir!
JOSEPH. I can't go on. Egyptians, leave the Hebrews here, but you depart.
SOLDIERS. What is this?
PUTIPHAR. I don't know.

                     Exeunt Putiphar and the soldiers.

JOSEPH.   Alas, my heart
        can bear no more of this. Tears, freely flow,
        without restraint. Now know
        that I am Joseph . . .
REUBEN.   How's that again?
JOSEPH.   . . . and that a merciful pain,
        for which there is on earth no antidote,
        has my soul in my throat,
        for surely today of love do I complain.
ISSACHAR.   What answer can we give?
JOSEPH.   I am your brother Joseph whom you sold.
        Come up to me, be not afraid but bold.
        I think that I shall die of so much pleasure,
        Fear not, for my joy is beyond all measure.
        If I should die, my last breath I'll employ
        to praise this pleasure so without alloy.
        If in the past my very strength of soul
        kept me alive, in sadness did console,
        it seems that now I'll die, instead, of joy.
BENJAMIN.   That weeping, Joseph dear,
        reveals your great soul even as you grieve.
JOSEPH.   Of so much suffering you now relieve
        me. What a joy to have you near!
        I am so glad to hear,
        oh Benjamin, the news that you've sustained
        our father dear, so pained,
        and helped him to survive.
        You've kept us all alive,
        for the life that he gave us you have maintained.
                He loved to gaze on Rachel every hour,

I see them both in you;
they say I am like unto
them, but you have our father's power.
Today is reborn the flower
once murdered by fratricidal Cain;
that mirror you regain
in which the old man dearly loved to gaze;
for such great age, a mirror beyond praise.
Benjamin, come to my arms again!

They embrace.

BENJAMIN.   My lord, my brothers one and all do now
mutely express their love, though in silence
so proper, one can hear no difference
between their voices as they humbly bow.
Your kindness, though, with boldness did endow
my tongue with eloquence, so that I speak
courageously and am no longer meek;
and all the more so, when in your embrace
that mirror that I'd lost you did replace,
and gave me of that former joy a peek.

          When I saw how your face mine did reflect,
I know not why, but in my heart I spied
a great love for you. I was satisfied
to see your face so handsome and perfect.
It spoke to me, but my poor intellect
the soul's saying could hardly comprehend:
the reason why my heart to you did bend
was that half of my soul in you did dwell,
and thus at last the other half saw well
its sundered state, and now at last could mend.

REUBEN.   Sweet brother—though indeed I hardly dare
call you my brother after what we did,
though I was not among the most livid
against you, for I sought your life to spare—

          forgive us now because of who you are,
and deign to look upon us with pity.
Please do not punish us, Your Majesty,
though the crimes that we committed have no par.

          Now we would go our father to inform
that he should come to see you and here dwell.

JOSEPH.   Before you leave, to show I love you well,
                a gesture of that love I would perform.
                    Come with me now, you all must kiss the hand
                of Egypt's king.

BATO.   Take no offense,
                oh, Your Magnificence,
                if a poor peasant dare before you stand.

JOSEPH.   Naphtali, is that you?

BATO.   No, I am little Bato, Mighty One.
                We used to have such fun
                when childish pastimes we two did pursue!

JOSEPH.   Seeing you gives me joy.

BATO.   I thought some vicious beast did you devour
                when by bad luck you fell into its power.

JOSEPH.   No, that was just a ploy.

Exeunt the brothers, genuflecting as they pass by Joseph. Benjamin and
Bato stay behind.

BENJAMIN. Bato, let's go and take this news to that old saint.

BATO. I'm afraid that joy will be too much for him.

BENJAMIN. Hurry up!

BATO. Since now you're going to be a great nobleman, will you give me Lida?

BENJAMIN. I never loved her.

BATO. Do you swear that on your life?

BENJAMIN. Upon my life! Please take her as your wife.

BATO. This time I'll get revenge. By golly, she'll have to beg me for it now,
but I still won't love her!

Exeunt. Enter Jacob.

JACOB.   Oh, Mighty Lord of Heaven,
                Master of earth's empire,
                Whose feet are kissed by every potentate;
                Who dwells in highest heaven,
                eternity's sapphire,
                Whose ageless life knows neither hour nor date:
                in my solitary state
                console this piteous breast,
                whose weakness all abject
                Your greatness did protect;
                at Bethel in Your glory was I dressed.
                Let now my trials plead
                for down to death my years now will me lead.

When Laban sought to slay
me, for his daughters two I took,
deceiving him as he did me deceive,
and Esau, in war array
all semblance of fraternal love forsook,
You rescued me and granted a reprieve.
As I prepared to leave
this life, my dear Dinah was raped,
and Joseph, torn by a beast, did cry.
Please do not let me die
ere Benjamin this danger has escaped.
May death amend
her ways, and my trials bring to a better end.

Enter Dinah in dancing costume, with shepherd-musicians
and Lida.

DINAH. We have to cheer him up in this sad time.

LIDA. You'll only make him sadder. I know what he's like.

DINAH. Father, you've wept long enough over our brothers' absence. We've
come to cheer you up.

JACOB. In such anxiety I can hardly find relief from care. Torn between love
and fear, my trials have brought my life to its sad end.

DINAH. Sir, rest from your worries for a while. Sit down and watch and
listen to our rude celebration. Your sons will come home soon.

JACOB. Dinah, I feel like I'm dying.

He sits down, and Dinah and Lida dance with two shepherds, while the
musicians sing.

MUSICIANS. The pretty mountain girl,
          the one with the lovely face,
          the glory of these woods—
          What?— and honor of this place;
          For in her mouth and teeth,
          unlike the other girls,
          in this little village
          she bears—What?— corals and pearls.
          That handsome shepherd Jacob
          hopes her he will deserve
          For her sake seven years—
          What?—Laban he would serve.
          But time is without meaning
          to a love so great,

for it can't keep a man—
What?—from longing for his mate.
Today they will be married
with pomp and circumstance,
right here where all these shepherds—
What?—perform their merry dance.
For a love so long,
Rachel, my love pure,
the years are all too short,
for life will not endure.

Offstage noise of camels and horses with bells, and voices crying out:
"Whoa, bring those horses to a halt!"

JACOB. Hold on! What noise is this?

LIDA. I see dromedaries and elephants, carts and coaches approaching through the willow trees.

JACOB. That couldn't be my sons, for they were bringing back the wheat in a humbler caravan.

Enter Bato and Reuben, running.

BATO. I'll be the first one there!

REUBEN. Slow down, you beast!

BATO. Just who are you calling a beast?

REUBEN. My lord and father, let me kiss your feet.

BATO. Joseph's alive! Tell him the rest of it.

JACOB. What's this, Reuben?

REUBEN. Sir, we went to Egypt . . .

BATO. Tell him that Joseph was the viceroy.

REUBEN. You animal! Will you just let me talk?

JACOB. What is Bato talking about, Reuben?

REUBEN. I don't know what to say, father. He's already told you that Joseph is alive.

JACOB. Joseph? My son?

DINAH. Slow down; for pleasure can take one's life as well as pain.

Enter Benjamin and the other brothers.

NAPHTALI. Let us kiss your feet.

JACOB. My sons, embrace me! Oh, my dear Benjamin!

BENJAMIN. Have you heard that Joseph is alive? Look, he has sent for you, and Pharaoh gave us all this gold and silver and these loads of rich gifts borne here by dromedaries and elephants.

JACOB. If my son Joseph is alive, my sons, now I can die.

REUBEN. Sir, he has sent for you, so that you can see him and talk with him, and go to live with him, for he wants to give us a whole valley where our family can dwell.

JACOB. Immense heaven, give me strength! Since my trials haven't killed me, don't let me die of this joy.

ISSACHAR. Joseph got lost and wandered into Egypt, and there his great virtues caused the king to exalt him to the throne.

JACOB. I am so overjoyed, I don't even want to know the explanation. Sons, leave me alone for a moment.

BATO. What's new, Lida?

LIDA. Just your usual nonsense.

BATO. Do you know that you're to be my wife? I'll get my revenge now.

LIDA. What? Do you mean to kick me? What other kind of revenge could you be thinking of?

Exit Lida.

REUBEN. Bato, bring the others in.

NAPHTALI. Bato!

BATO. Bato this! Bato that! Enough, already!

NAPHTALI. Take the animals to the stable.

BATO. As far as I'm concerned, they can all starve, the devil take them! This Lida would make of me a second Jacob, though cut of coarser cloth. If she thinks I'll wait so patiently for her, she has another think coming!

Exeunt. Jacob remains on stage alone.

JACOB.   Always, oh Lord of this land,
            throughout my life, You've been
            the Light by which I have seen;
            You have led me by the hand.
            Always from every brigand
            You have rescued me. Be blessed!
            My eyes must have some rest,
            but I shall talk to You while I'm asleep,
            tell me Your will for I would surely keep
            Your sovereign behest.
                 The Well of the Oath is here;
            and here I shall lie down
            ere I set out for that town
            where I'll see Joseph dear.
            My thought to You is clear:
            I'll not go unto Joseph without You;
            let us decide this thing between us two,
            for even the wisest man is surely wrong

when he attempts, headlong,
to take a step without his God so true.

He falls asleep. Music plays, and an angel descends in a cloud. The
cloud opens, and the angel emerges, resting his feet, or the throne on
which he is seated, on the rim of the well.

ANGEL. Jacob!

JACOB. Sovereign Lord, who are you?

ANGEL. The mighty God of your father. Go to Egypt. I will go with you,
Jacob, and I will also bring you back.

JACOB. Lord . . .

ANGEL. Fear not, for I will make you great among the nations.

As music plays, he returns to the cloud and ascends.

JACOB. I am Your servant.

He awakens.

Don't leave me, divine Lord! Please wait, sweet Lord! He's gone. What
is this that I've seen? God Himself has spoken to me. Now I will go to
Egypt. Oh, vale of Canaan, farewell! I'm off to see my Joseph. How
wrong I was to think that he was dead! He is my very life; since he
survived, I'm still alive.

Exit. Enter Nicela and Joseph.

NICELA. You must do me this one favor.

JOSEPH. It's strange to hear you talk like that, Nicela. Have you forgotten
that once I served you and was in your power?

NICELA. When I remember that, my lord, I feel guilty for the wrong that I
committed. My only excuse is love.

JOSEPH. Love is nothing but excuses.

NICELA. Only love could have been cruel enough to invent those charges
against you, and only a woman would be foolish enough to voice them.
I am so sorry; I beg you to forgive me, if there is any way to satisfy your
injured innocence. Yes, I was crazy to love you, but after all, I am only
a woman. Nevertheless, love is no reason to dishonor anyone or have
them put to death. My husband is Pharaoh's general. He has served you.

JOSEPH. And I, Nicela, have been your slave.

NICELA. Now all are your slaves.

JOSEPH. I am not one of those courtiers who let their power go to their heads.
Kings are men too. All states have their beginning, and their rise and
fall. The human condition is like a weathervane tossed by the wind.
Today I am, but I may cease to be. If that is so, and I should cease to be
tomorrow, what power would I have then? I shall do what I can to help
your husband. I'll put in a good word for him, both because he has
served me well, and because I am fond of him.

NICELA. Here comes the king.

JOSEPH. Go into the next room. I'll speak to him on behalf of your husband.

NICELA. Please don't remember that it was my love that put you in jail. Just think that if that hadn't happened, you would never have reached your present royal state. It was my treachery that raised you to the throne.

Enter the king. Joseph kneels, and the king helps him get back up.

PHARAOH. I have good reason to complain of you. Joseph, shouldn't you have told your king about this happy news?

JOSEPH. What news, sire?

PHARAOH. After your brothers returned to your land, and I gave them carts, gold, silver, and silk, my camels and elephants so that they could bring back your aged father—over 180 years old—in greater state, you didn't even bother to tell me that they'd arrived?

JOSEPH. You may think that was negligence, but I wanted to hear that news from your own lips, since you are the one who brought it all about. To celebrate this good fortune, I beg you to grant me a boon.

PHARAOH. But what more could I possibly give you?

JOSEPH. Sire, all rulers are obliged by love to seek the welfare of those whom they love.

PHARAOH. What do you want?

JOSEPH. That general who is Nicela's husband *[aside, to Nicela:]* (Come here and kiss his feet) . . .

Nicela kneels at the king's feet.

has served you well both in peace and in war. He was my master, as you know.

PHARAOH. Yes, Joseph, I know I am indebted to him. You hold the second rank after the king; let him be third in command. He will preside over my council.

NICELA. Nicela kisses your feet in gratitude for such kindness.

JOSEPH. Now, Unvanquished Prince, my father is coming here.

Jacob is carried onstage by four of his sons and followed by the others.

JACOB. Though my own feet won't support me, let me at least kiss those of your highness, and I shall see Joseph's face.

JOSEPH. Father!

JACOB. Now, Joseph, let me die, for my trials at last are over.

REUBEN. The third part of this play will tell you all the rest—the great tragicomedy of the exodus from Egypt—but here the poet put an end to *The Trials of Jacob*. Belardo[10] humbly kisses your feet.

4

Pedro Calderón de la Barca:
Sometimes Dreams Come True

Pedro Calderón de la Barca was born in Madrid in 1600. His mother died when he was ten years old, and his father, a minor member of the aristocracy and a court bureaucrat, died when Pedro was only fifteen. From Pedro's early childhood, his parents had decided that he should be a priest. Although he was educated for the priesthood at the Jesuit Colegio Imperial and the universities of Alcalá and Salamanca, he seems to have resisted accepting that vocation for many years, during which—according to Manuel Durán[1]—he was probably tormented by guilt feelings. After a restless youth, during which he served in several military campaigns, was involved in duels and other scandalous behavior, began his successful career as a playwright, and fathered an illegitimate child, he apparently suffered a severe psychological crisis in the 1640s—perhaps brought on or worsened by the deaths of his two brothers in 1642 and 1645—after which he was at last ordained a priest in 1650. Durán explains that "ultimately, the inner crisis in Calderón's life was resolved by an act of will, of renunciation: instincts and passions must be repressed and suppressed, only in this way can salvation be attained."[2] After that, as Gerald Brenan has observed,

> Thirty years of life were left to him. They were years of steady output. Every summer he produced two *autos* for the municipality of Madrid and wrote plays on mythological subjects for performance at one of the court theatres. Except for the time given to rehearsals, he seems to have lived in great retirement. For some years he was at Toledo, occupying a room at the Hermandad del Refugio, to which he was chaplain. Then he lived in Madrid in apartments which he filled with pictures, reliquaries, ivory crucifixes, gilt vases, polychrome statues—a whole museum of religious *objets d'art* which the painter Claudio Coello was given the task of valuing after

145

his death. Here he spent much of his time in reading. But it is a mistake to think of him as a scholarly man: the scope of Calderón's interests was very limited and his notions on history and geography wildly inaccurate. The subjects he studied in his retirement were those he needed for his plays—pagan mythology and theology.[3]

Calderón was Spain's leading playwright for almost fifty years, from the death of Lope de Vega in 1635 until his own death in 1681. During his long career, he wrote over one hundred plays, including one of the best known and most influential works of world drama, *Life Is a Dream (La vida es sueño)*. Nevertheless, some critics have argued that the more than seventy *autos sacramentales* he wrote constitute his greatest contribution to Spanish literature, and there is widespread agreement that Calderón was the supreme practitioner of that uniquely Spanish genre. The *autos* of the sixteenth century were for the most part awkward attempts to combine entertaining pageants—based on biblical stories, the lives of the saints, or folklore—with religious instruction of a relatively simple kind. As time went on, the *autos* came to concentrate increasingly on the dogma of the real presence of Christ in the Eucharist, then under attack by the Protestants—in other words, they evolved into a sort of hybrid genre combining elements found in the medieval mystery and miracle plays. The anonymous *auto* entitled *Joseph's Wedding* is a good example of how the genre had developed in the latter part of the sixteenth century. The obligatory reference to the Eucharist is provided by the angel's statement that God will send Senec the bread of life, which the angels eat, and "he who eats of this will never die," but it is not especially emphasized. One could interpret the Joseph of the *auto,* presented as the Strong Man of God who provides bread for the starving Egyptians, as foreshadowing Christ and his gift of the Eucharist, but there is no systematic attempt to encourage such an allegorical interpretation. Furthermore, like other *autos* of the period, *Joseph's Wedding* appeals to the lowest common denominator in the audience through the antics of the *bobo* or Fool.

Calderón transformed this rather awkward and tentative genre into a genuine art form capable of expressing subtle philosophical and theological concepts by means of poetic allegory. He had an extraordinary gift for relating the most diverse subject matters—ranging from biblical stories to pagan mythology—to the mystery of the Eucharist, which for him contained the central meaning of human life, "lost in a cosmic confusion until it encountered the light of the Eucharist, which illuminated and guided its intellect; or in other words, sinful man blindly surrendering to his passions until redeemed by the sacrifice of Christ, embodied in the eucharistic bread."[4]

Nowhere is this more evident than in his 1670 treatment of the story of Joseph, *Sometimes Dreams Come True (Sueños hay que verdad son),* which Ángel Valbuena Prat has singled out as one of Calderón's two most distinguished *autos* based on the Hebrew Bible.[5]

Calderón sees the story of Joseph as revolving around two major motifs—dreams and chastity—and he divides his *auto* into two symmetrical parts. It was Joseph's dreams that initially brought about his downfall. Chastity, his preeminent virtue, becomes his advocate before the throne of God, thus pointing to the moral lesson that "if a man practices a virtue, when he falls on hard times, she will defend him." The *auto* begins as the allegorical character Chastity, in the form of the lovely Aseneth, argues that since Dream has so damaged Joseph, it is up to him to set things aright. She further advises Dream: "If you realize that there is a double meaning in all that happens to him, you will see that hidden and covered up in all of this is a mystery, which in future ages, when the shadows have cleared away, will be Mystery of Mysteries, Miracle of Miracles, Wonder of All Wonders, and in conclusion, the light, truth, and life of the Sacrament Most High." Dream then induces the dreams of the cupbearer and baker, and of Pharaoh. Joseph's interpretation of those dreams results in his appointment as viceroy. Dream now argues that he has more than compensated Joseph for the harm he had done him, but in spite of his best efforts, he cannot see any "signs and glimpses of that high sacrament she mentioned, which will be the fulfillment of all that's happened." In the *auto*'s second half Chastity reveals the remainder of Joseph's story, carefully pointing out how everything in his life prefigures the life of Christ, and in particular, the institution of the Eucharist.

The alternation of scenes from the biblical story and interpretations and comments provided by Dream and Chastity also enables Calderón to accelerate the play's action; only the most dramatic scenes in the story are actually performed, while transitions are provided by the dialogues between Dream and Chastity. Nevertheless, the comments of the two allegorical characters, who form a sort of Greek chorus, are kept relatively brief and never overwhelm the *auto*'s fast-paced and interesting plot. The *auto* also makes effective use of visual symbolism, particularly in the scene where Joseph appears with his arms outstretched between the cupbearer and the baker, foreshadowing Christ's crucifixion between the two thieves. The action is so fast-paced that Calderón even jokes about it, in the comment of the comic character Bato: "This may be rushing things a bit, but what's the difference? It's in the script." This comment also reveals Calderón's self-conscious artistry. The use of such devices as flashback and what we would now term "voice-over narration" sometimes seems almost cinematic.

Calderón was certainly very familiar with Lope's *Trials of Jacob; Sometimes Dreams Come True* contains many textual parallels that suggest that Calderón consulted Lope's play while writing his *auto*. One particularly interesting one is the comparison of Potiphar's wife to a bull, and of Joseph to a bullfighter. Calderón of course borrowed the title of his *auto* from the subtitle of Lope's play, and he also adopted the character Bato (both the name and the general character traits) from that play. However, comic relief in Calderón's *auto* is kept to a bare minimum—just enough so that the least serious members of the audience wouldn't feel cheated. Calderón even manages to include some romantic interest and intrigue in the play, in the form of Joseph's love for Aseneth, and her chaste, if halfhearted, resistance. Perhaps he knew the *auto Joseph's Wedding;* it is intriguing to think that he might have attended the 1608 performance of the *auto* in Madrid as an eight-year-old child. Now an old man, he may have recalled the impression that performance made on him when he was called upon to write an *auto* for performance before the eight-year-old King Carlos II, and therefore have chosen the same subject for his own *auto*. However, the major source of inspiration for *Sometimes Dreams Come True* was Antonio Mira de Amescua's (died 1644) *The Happiest Captivity, and Joseph's Dreams (El más feliz cautiverio, y los sueños de Josef)*. Numerous passages in Calderón's *auto* paraphrase Mira's text, especially in the sections portraying the chaste love between Joseph and Aseneth, and Calderón even lifted a few lines verbatim from Mira's play. Nevertheless, comparison of the two texts reveals that, while the basic elements of the plot were already present in Mira's play, Calderón vastly improved upon the material he took from Mira, conferring greater psychological depth on his characters and transforming Mira's often rather crude and clumsy dialogue into some of the most exquisitely lyrical passages to be found in Spanish Golden Age drama.

Calderón's *auto* is further enhanced by the restrained but effective use of stage machinery, and by the introduction of several lyrical songs and a beautifully crafted sonnet. The latter, Joseph's "Oh, lovely lights in whom I see foretold . . . ," was recycled from the play *Mujer, llora y vencerás* (Woman, weep, and you will conquer), as Valbuena has pointed out,[6] but it is nonetheless appropriate in its new context.

The *auto* entitled *Sometimes Dreams Come True* is a splendidly unified work of art that gives poetic form to the biblical story of Joseph in order to teach both moral and dogmatic lessons. As Alexander Parker has observed: "All its parts [are] directed in a balanced order to the one end of conveying a certain meaning in a certain way. Form and content are equally important, but they are inseparable. Each has its significance in and through the other."[7] At the same time its poetry is ambivalent enough to encourage philosophical reflections about such things as the ultimate meaning of human life, and the relationship between life and dreams. It is so carefully and logically structured that the triumphant celebration of the eucharistic mystery in the concluding scene, a symmetrical mirror image of the cup-bearer's and baker's dreams at the beginning, seems absolutely inevitable.

The present translation is based on my critical edition of the *auto,* published jointly by the Universidad de Navarra and Edition Reichenberger (Kassel, Germany) in 1997 as part of a series of Calderón's complete *autos* under the general editorship of Ignacio Arellano and Ángel Cilveti. I have added a few new stage directions, which I have enclosed in brackets. The original *auto* is entirely in verse. I have translated it in prose, except for Joseph's sonnet and the passages intended to be sung.

PROLOGUE

Characters:

The Aster	Olympus
The Larkspur	Diana
The Carnation	The Violet
The Rose	The Sunflower
The Olive	The Narcissus
The Willow	The Laurel
The Stock	Musicians

Enter Diana bearing a shield on which is painted a garland of flowers with a D in the center. From the other side enter Olympus with a shield also decorated with a garland, with an O in the center.

DIANA. Olympus, king of the mountains!

OLYMPUS. Who calls me?

DIANA. One who desires your assistance in a lofty and glorious matter.

OLYMPUS. How can I refuse, since the letter on your shield tells me that you must be Diana, goddess of mountains and woods? As a mountain, I must obey you.

DIANA. So you've recognized me! Even if I hadn't summoned you, I would have known you were Olympus by that *O* on your shield which proclaims your fame. Listen carefully.

OLYMPUS. Speak, Diana.

DIANA. You could have just called me Ana,[8] since Ana means "grace,"[9] and grace is the queen of all gifts. Hence my name and majesty are included in that word; but we'd better not go into that. So much for majesty and name! Let him who wishes, understand. Now that we've established that, Olympus—whose eminence proclaims you king of mountains—I wanted to inform you that, by paying attention to the sun's course through the skies, I have noticed how the world grows sad when it departs, only to rejoice the next morning. Thus the Sun sets only to rise again the next day. This is a good example of how all of us mistakenly alternate between joy and sadness. I repeat that while this is the day when faith celebrates with joyful applause the rarest and most supreme accomplishment of that true Jupiter, whose greatness calls him God of Gods, it's also the day when the newborn Sun returns to earth, to add the joy of this feast day to other pleasures that have been, if not withdrawn, at least suspended for a while.[10] Therefore, since this happy new Sun today pursues its sphere, we must consider this with the affection, worship, and reverence that is its great monarchy's most sovereign right, in the praises of the church and the triumphs of true faith. As is my duty to this feast-day, and with fitting gratitude, I'd like to make a garland for his brow, to adorn his beauty and demonstrate my goodwill. For that reason, since I repeat that you are king of the mountains, I'll draw on you, secure that in your plants and flowers you will offer me a garland of different lovely shades. Newborn, in the gorgeous springtime of their youth, they'll serve my purpose perfectly. But let them explain how they'll join in friendly competition to offer worship. Theirs will be the triumph, but the offering is mine.

OLYMPUS. Your idea is so excellent that I can only hasten to reply. Let your voice inspire me that mine may carry more authority.

DIANA. Come from the crowned mountain!

OFFSTAGE CHORUS 1. Come from the crowned mountain!

OLYMPUS. Come from the flowery woods!

OFFSTAGE CHORUS 2. Come from the flowery woods!

DIANA. Hear me!

OLYMPUS. Pay me heed!

CHORUSES. Who's there, who summons us?

DIANA. Olympus.

OLYMPUS. Diana.

CHORUSES. What then is your command?

OLYMPUS. That, performing that trope which by poetic license . . . ,

DIANA. . . . when the irrational speaks, is called personification . . . ,

OLYMPUS. . . . you come to weave the flowery garland . . .

DIANA. . . . with which to crown the golden locks . . .

OLYMPUS. . . . of the Sun, who happily brings back the day.

DIANA. Let earth's Faith honor Heaven . . .

BOTH. . . . by lending joy to this celebration, and let the beautiful sight exceed even our holiday joy.

Enter the Choruses.[11]

DIANA, OLYMPUS, AND THE CHORUSES. *[They sing:]*[12]

> Come, come and celebrate!
> Come weave the flowery crown
> for the golden locks of the Sun
> who has brought the new day down.
> Let earth's faith honor heaven,
> and at this joyful sound
> let sight exceed even the feast day!

Enter, singing and dancing, all the flowers listed above, and musicians. Each flower wears a card with the initial letter of its name in the center of a garland, and carries bouquets of those flowers in its hands. [The cards corresponding to Willow and Laurel can be flipped over to reveal the letters E and G on their reverse side.]

NARCISSUS. Since the colorful troupe of flowers and plants has come at the urging of your sweet voices, let me be the first flower to offer my gift, with the *N* in my name, in honor of the Sun, though I don't know who he is; it is enough that you applaud him.

He presents a flower to Diana. All do likewise, one by one, and she pretends to weave them into a garland.

I am Narcissus, and none can go before me, for Nature's first perfection is beauty.

CARNATION. You're right, for though all are born at once, not all are born equal. Hence let the second gift be the one that fortune gives with the lovely royal purple of the carnation, which flower represents crowned majesty.

STOCK. Yet majesty, if not adorned with other generous traits, will be less lovable; so it should have pure gold in the gilded petals of stock.

SUNFLOWER. But that gold requires the further merit of being worked into a crown so that it may shine throughout the world. No flower can better signify its power than the sunflower. Like a well-wrought crown, it follows his gorgeous light through his estates, encircling the orb.

LAUREL. And so that everywhere he may attain victories, triumphs, and mighty deeds, let laurel add his green leaves to the garland.

LARKSPUR. Larkspur can attest to that, for I am the squire who helps the knight's foot into his spur.

OLIVE. Don't forget that peace makes a king just as heroic as war, for majesty sustains both justice and military might: one must rule that the other may conquer. Hence let the olive add triumphs of prudence to the judgments of valor.

WILLOW. That the world may chant his prowess in war and peace, the willow will take down its harps, which were left hanging on it.[13]

ROSE. At the sound of their strings, Solomon's song will intone the divine wonders of the waiting Spouse, represented by the tender age of this virgin rose.

VIOLET. And to love her and adore her, let violet express his love with purple passion.

ASTER. You have all done such a beautiful job of adorning the garland that I would lose all hope of competing with you if I didn't know that all your glories would be but fleeting pomp without my aid, and that none of you is so important to the common good of all as I am.

ALL. What flower are you?

ASTER. The aster.

ALL. What are you saying?

ASTER. It goes like this *sings:*

> As feasts and garlands are prepared,
> for the new Sun that's risen today
> to celebrate the Mystery
> that's worthy of the highest praise,
> when it comes to flowers, you all should know,
> Aster is greatest of them all.
> Narcissus brings beauty all aglow,
> Carnation, a royal purple gown,
> and Stock its glittering gold bestows,
> which the Sunflower works into a crown.
> Laurel gives victories in war,
> and Larkspur helps attire the knight,
> while Olive gives peace, which all adore,
> both justice and military might.
> Violet offers words of love
> with which to court Rose's winsome wife;
> but what's the good of all of those
> without the supreme gift of life?
> And life unending, immortelle,[14]
> Aster is held to symbolize.
> Thus among flowers, you all should know,
> Aster carries off the prize.

ALL. We must admit you're right!

ASTER. Then let all our voices gaily repeat in unison:

MUSICIANS AND ALL. *[They sing:]*

>When it comes to flowers, you all should know,
>Aster carries off the prize, etc.

As they sing and dance, Carnation, Aster, Rose, Larkspur, Olive, and Stock line up so that their cards spell the name CARLOS, while the other flowers and Diana and Olympus arrange their cards to spell out S, E, G, V, N, D, O.[15] *Diana removes a garland from hiding, as if she had been weaving it out of the flowers, and holds it over all of them.*

DIANA. Since the garland of flowers and plants is now complete, let's take it to its rightful owner.

OLYMPUS. Wait a minute! We still need to know who that owner is. Initially we were content to obey your command just because of who you are, but before we go marching off to throw ourselves at his feet, we'd like to know just who this new Sun is, who has come to replace the former one.

DIANA. I must point out that your hesitation is impertinent, if not downright foolish.

OLYMPUS. Why?

DIANA. Can't you read? The letters that compose this garland spell out his name, which one day will be written in the stars.

OLYMPUS. How's that?

DIANA. Just read it and you'll see.

OLYMPUS. Gladly.

DIANA. Be sure to include our letters. What do they spell?

OLYMPUS. Carlos Segundo.[16] Sire, let me kiss your feet! This will be the first time I've bowed down to kiss such heroic and lofty feet.

ALL. We all say the same thing!

DIANA. But we can't let our offering end with this acclamation. Today, in honor of the mystery he's celebrating, we'll provide dancing, music, and joyous entertainment for the occasion.

ALL. What else have you arranged?

DIANA. A play.

ALL. What is it called?

DIANA. *Sometimes Dreams Come True.*

ALL. And who's the author?

DIANA. He shrinks from your applause, but if the play is flawed, his obedience is perfect.

ALL. Where will you put it on?

DIANA. In Madrid, the court and sphere of his faith and religion.

ALL. In that case, we'll all go and help you.

OLYMPUS. And with such happy haste that right now we'll start rehearsing the prologue.

DIANA. Stop there, for there'll be no prologue.

ALL. Why not?

DIANA. A prologue serves to beg pardon for our many failings, but to do so would offend this audience, for we can surely count on the indulgence of so handsome a king, and such a pious queen, so many lovely ladies, the learned prudence of the royal council, such a great gathering of nobility, such brilliant commoners. Hence, we can skip the prologue and start right off with the dance!

ALL.: Here goes, then, and our joy offers praise in unison to the great Carlos Segundo!

[They sing and dance.]:
When it comes to flowers, you all should know,
Aster is greatest of them all.
Narcissus brings beauty all aglow,
Carnation, a royal purple gown,
and Stock its glittering gold bestows
which the Sunflower works into a crown.
Laurel gives victories in war,
and Larkspur helps attire the knight,
while Olive gives peace which all adore,
both justice and military might.
Violet offers words of love
with which to court Rose's winsome wife;
but what's the good of all of those
without the supreme gift of life?
And life unending, immortelle,
Aster is held to symbolize.
Thus among flowers, you all should know,
Aster carries off the prize.
[Exeunt.]

Characters:

Chastity	Naphtali
Aseneth	Manasseh[17]
Dream	Simeon

First Shade	Levi
Second Shade	Issachar
Cupbearer	Zebulun
Baker	Joseph
Jailer	Benjamin
Reuben	The King
Judah	Jacob
Gad	Faith
Asher	Bato
	Musicians

Enter Chastity as a lady, crowned with flowers, and Dream.

DREAM. Where are you taking me, oh lovely virtue? Among all the choirs of virtues that follow the law's Lamb, your curly locks alone are crowned with the curling petals of all the virgin roses, an indication that all gladly do homage to you. Where are you taking me, I repeat? In many sacred texts you are the hard-won laurel of victory, the trophy that those who triumph over themselves in the struggle with the senses at last attain. It seems offensive to your decorum for you, supreme ornament of virtues, to lead me to this place which is the center of all vices. This is the jail of Egypt, as anyone could see. Here dwell homicide and theft, fraud and adultery. How can this be, for you are Chastity, as both your appearance and your lofty name declare? You are the pinnacle of purity. You vanquish the body's rebellions, giving the soul victory; but this is the sink of vice, where the politic government of the republic casts its pernicious garbage, the ash heap of the age. How dare you then enter here? Don't you fear being sullied by the vapor of its breath? Furthermore, why have you taken on the appearance of Aseneth, lovely daughter of the priest of the Temple of Heliopolis, City of the Sun? She's like a sun herself! Please explain this strange behavior to me, for my intellect is in suspense until I hear your will.

CHASTITY. Vague fantasy, with your delirium you can quiet down the senses and hush their rude clamoring. When calm has introduced you to bring rest, you treacherously transform rest into risk. Fantastic apparition, as I have taken on the appearance of Aseneth to carry out a gloriously chaste enterprise, you took on the shape of Morpheus with that black face, that gloomy, pale, and rigid form. That answers your second question, for if you have dressed in shadows and I in lights, it was because to represent a concept, we must be veiled as Morpheus and Aseneth, for I am Chastity and you are Dream. As for your other question, concerning why a jail should be the field where our duel will take place, I will not answer it, although I could, until I've told you the reason I am angered by your unreason. But seeing it will be more effective than just hearing, so come with me. What do you hear?

Offstage sound of moans and chains being rattled.

DREAM. The same as you, I hear and see a noise of chains and a voice lamenting.

CHASTITY. Go over to the side, and listen to its fearful accent.

OFFSTAGE VOICE. Is anyone in the dungeon?

DREAM AND CHASTITY. Who goes there?

OFFSTAGE VOICE. A prisoner sent here by his master to serve as slave to all.

Enter the Cupbearer and the Baker in chains.

BOTH. His master sends a slave to serve us all?

CUPBEARER. Who can this wretch be—so wretched that, already a slave, he's sent to prison doubly captive, since slavery and imprisonment have doubled his chains?

BAKER. He must be quite a rascal, since his master would rather send him to jail than put up with him at home.

CUPBEARER. Must you always think the worst? Oh, heaven! Might he not be another poor wretch, who innocently suffers, as I suffer?

BAKER. I too am innocently punished, but that doesn't make me think that others must be guiltless.

CUPBEARER. Let's see who this prisoner can be.

Enter Joseph in chains. [He kneels before them.]

JOSEPH. One who, because he knows this womb is a sepulcher of the living, painfully content, considers it good fortune to be your slave.

CUPBEARER. Get up from there! What a good-looking boy, and what a good attitude!

BAKER. As our new "classmate," he should treat us to dinner.[18] Does he look like he's good for that?

JOSEPH. I was a wretched slave in my master's house, and I'm a wretched slave here, for I have come to serve. What could I possibly give you?

BAKER. You could give up that "cap and gown."

CUPBEARER. It's not right for you or anyone else to talk to him like that, for it's wrong to afflict the afflicted, especially someone as helpless as he.

BAKER. Next you'll feel sorry for him.

CUPBEARER. That's right. Good looks are the address Heaven writes on its letters of recommendation, to endear the bearer to those it wants to like him.

BAKER. That's too highfalutin for me. I'm not wasting my time listening to such goody-goody nonsense.

Exit the Baker.

CUPBEARER. I just can't help myself, especially since I've never seen a nicer-looking person in my life. Where are you from?

JOSEPH. I am a Hebrew.

CUPBEARER. What country are you from?

JOSEPH. Canaan.

CUPBEARER. And what's your name?

JOSEPH. Joseph.

CUPBEARER. That means "increase."

JOSEPH. The only thing I've seen increase is trouble.

CUPBEARER. What unfortunate events brought you to Egypt?

JOSEPH. My story is too sad! You really don't want to hear it. I'd better just suffer in silence.

CUPBEARER. I didn't mean to bring back bad memories. This is my cell. I was Pharaoh's cupbearer. The next cell over is my companion's. He was his baker. We were accused of a crime, but I hope we'll get out of here soon. I've taken the opportunity to tell you this so you'll know who we are and where we live, for there's a huge amount of work to be done in this jail, and you'd have a hard time finding your way back here without directions. Here you can make yourself at home. Now you'd better finish your tour. Since you've come here to serve, I wouldn't want to get you into trouble. You can count on me!

JOSEPH. Forgive me for not thanking you, sir. This is the first time I've ever had occasion to thank anyone, for I am so unfortunate that no one has ever done me a favor, so I've never really learned how to say thanks.

CUPBEARER. Go with God! *(Aside:)* Besides being handsome, that young man seems smart too. It breaks my heart to see him so unhappy!

Exit the Cupbearer.

JOSEPH. Heavens! If my loyal service failed to please a single master, how will I ever manage to please so many? Oh, if only my dreams had not aroused the envy that brought me to this state!

Exit Joseph.

CHASTITY. I could have wasted a lot of time recounting his suffering, but he's told you all about it in a moment. He's complaining of those dreams you gave him—the one where he saw the golden necks of his brothers' sheaves bend over, though no wind was blowing, as if obeying his; and, as if that weren't bad enough, you also made him dream he had the sun, moon, and stars at his feet. I'm not sure whether he was smart to tell them, for there is something mysterious about it; it wasn't just a mistake.

The point is that they despised him and insulted him by calling him "dreamer." Their envy kept increasing until brotherly love turned to hatred, and they threw him in a well. Not content with that, they sold him; and now he's sunk from slave to prisoner. You wonder why I care? I'll tell you: in all the world there is no one else who venerates me as he does. To preserve my purity and to avoid offending his master, attentive both to the demands of religion and loyalty, by running away, he overcame the sweetest siren, the most flattering snake, the most treacherous crocodile, the commonest of poisons, and the wildest hyena. He was deaf to her voice, mute to her pleading, unmoved by all her tears, and swift in his flight. But what good did it do him, since his cape was caught on the horns of that fierce monster? I'm sure you've heard it said that if a rock fell from heaven, it would be less wonderful for it to stop in midair than for a man to resist temptation. That being so, since you brought about his ruin, and I am to reward his victories, does it surprise you that I've brought you here to see how low your dreams have laid him? Since your dreams did the damage, now they can provide the remedy. I know very well that God is First Cause, and that we depend on Him, and without Him neither you nor I can do anything. However, I'm also aware that God wants us to use the means at our disposal, so as in our human way to testify to His immense love, power, and knowledge. Since the ephemeral cannot comprehend the eternal, it must be given some visible sign before a concept envisioned by our limited understanding can be put into practice. Therefore, our performance in this temporal theater will demonstrate that if a man practices a virtue, when he falls on hard times, she will defend him. God restores equity with exquisite justice, as Job could amply testify, for by the very same steps that he sank to the depths, he rose back up to the heights. That's why, since my intention is to restore him to his freedom, my choice of you as instrument was not in vain. I want to see whether, with Heaven's help and yours, I can accomplish the same thing: since dreams have done this damage, let them indemnify him. Wretched, poor, afflicted—he's no longer just a slave, but slave of many. Today I leave him in your hands. Defend him and me. I give this order not just because you should be horrified by his misery, nor that the world may see that the body's vile inclination is no match for the soul's noble virtue. It is rather because in this lad I've seen lights, glimpses, and signs of a greater matter, which must remain veiled in shadows until the appointed time. As you observe his actions from here, if you can see through the hatred of his brothers, his being sold as a slave, and his present status as a convict, you will understand that there's something supernatural about him. If you realize that there is a double meaning in all that happens to him, you will see that hidden and covered up in all of this is a mystery, which in future ages, when the shadows have cleared away, will be Mystery of Mysteries, Miracle of Miracles, Wonder of All Wonders, and in conclusion, the light, truth, and life of the Sacrament Most High.

Exit Chastity.

DREAM. Hold on there, wait! Not only have you left my intellect confused, absorbed, and in suspense—which is hardly surprising, since Dream has always been an obscure spasm of the intellect—but what's more, you've actually convinced me. And just when have I ever been known to listen to reason? But that's not really true, for God has revealed infinite secrets in dreams—to mention only one, the dream this boy's father had about a ladder that connected heaven and earth.[19] So if this request comes from a virtue, and I've let myself be convinced, surely God has ordered this. What then am I waiting for? I can only obey. *He sings:*

> Sleep now, ye mortals, sleep!
> For the great man and the small
> are equal when they're asleep.
> Ye mortals, in this prison
> of the world you lie in chains,
> condemned to drag your shackles,
> dragged 'round by errors vain.[20]
> Sleep, sleep now to the sound
> of my enchanting lay.
> Life's quiet harmonies
> have vanished with the day.
> Sleep, sleep I say, but seek not
> merely the body's rest;
> pay heed to Heaven's message
> to you in shades addressed.
> Come hither, you ideas
> in fantastic shapes transformed,
> men's joys, like living pictures,
> and sorrows to perform.
> For God has heard the prayer
> of a virtue, and has employed
> a dream that it might repair
> all that a dream destroyed.

Enter the Cupbearer and the Baker. [They join Dream in the refrain.]

Sleep now, ye mortals, sleep!
For the great man and the small
are equal when they're asleep.

Exit Dream.

CUPBEARER. Why am I feeling so sluggish?

BAKER. I'm so sleepy, I feel as if he had treated us to that dinner after all.

CUPBEARER. How can I shake this drowsiness?

BAKER. The same as me: take a nap.

CUPBEARER. At this hour?

BAKER. It's the same as with eating. The clock strikes dinnertime when I'm not hungry, so why should I wait for it to strike when I am hungry? Stupid! Eat when you're hungry, sleep when you're sleepy. Are our guts clockwork?

CUPBEARER. Stop your jabbering. Still, I'm going to have to lie down in spite of myself.

BAKER. And I'll gladly do so, for when I'm sleeping, I can't tell whether I'm in prison or a free man. It's just like that song says:

To the sound of offstage singing, two hinged platforms at either side of the stage move toward the center to reveal two Shades.

Sleep now, ye mortals, sleep!
For the great man and the small
are equal when they're asleep.

They lie down on opposite sides of the stage: the Cupbearer on the cart containing the hinged platform on which will appear the Shade under a vine; and the Baker beneath the one that will bring out the Shade with birds and baskets of bread; as the two hinged platforms open from the wings to meet in the center, the Shades sing as follows:

SHADE 1.　　Bread, kneaded with the dew
　　　　　　that fell from heaven,[21] when at beauteous dawn,
　　　　　　a fluffy cloud conveyed
　　　　　　light, shadow, and good sustenance to all.[22]

SHADE 2.　　This hearty, generous wine
　　　　　　came from a fine cluster of grapes
　　　　　　when the desert's scarcity
　　　　　　to fertile Promised Land gave way.

SHADE 1.　　With God's divine consent
　　　　　　it was given to mankind,
　　　　　　but woe to the man whose bread
　　　　　　vile birds scatter to the wind!

SHADE 2.　　With God's divine consent
　　　　　　I give it to that lucky man

in grace for whom I press the grape,
for to save and preserve him is God's plan.
SHADE 1. From vile nocturnal birds
I cannot it defend!
SHADE 2. This fruit cannot be spoiled
by hail or winter's wind!
SHADE 1. Woe to the man who abhors it!
SHADE 2. Happy is he who adores it!
SHADE 1. It's Bread of Death to him who eats in sin.
SHADE 2. But if in grace, it is Wine from Heaven.
BOTH. Sleep now, ye mortals, sleep!
For the great man and the small
are equal as long as they sleep.
They awaken, terrified.
BAKER. Go away, you horrible, cursed Shade!
CUPBEARER. Don't go, you sweet and lovely apparition!
BAKER. I'll run away from you . . .
CUPBEARER. I'll follow you . . .
BAKER. . . . until you're out of sight.
CUPBEARER. . . . until I catch up with you.
Enter Joseph.
JOSEPH. What's this? Why are you two frightened, distressed, and upset?
I've come here to serve you, and I'm anxious to know what's going on.
BAKER. Don't be surprised . . . ,
CUPBEARER. Don't be afraid . . . ,
BAKER. . . . for something painful . . .
CUPBEARER. . . . for such a pleasure . . .
BAKER. . . . hurts even in a dream.
CUPBEARER. . . . even in a dream goes by too quickly.
JOSEPH. If you'll give me leave to inquire, I'm really curious to hear about
it.
CUPBEARER. Though I know one should pay no attention to dreams, this one
was so vivid, I'm obliged to appreciate it more than other dreams.
BAKER. I could say the same thing. And just to get rid of it, I'll tell it to you.
Listen carefully. Since our fantasy in dreams always represents whatever we deal with most during the day, it was natural—since, after all,
I'm a baker—for me to dream that I had arranged to have bread baked
for the king. I was carrying three baskets of this white and tasty bread;
and as I was on my way to serve it at the royal table, I saw some flocks
of vile, nocturnal birds dive down at it. They carried off so much that
my joy quickly turned to sorrow, for they ate big chunks of it and tore it

all to pieces, so that not even crumbs were left—or if they were, they were so tiny that the wind carried them away. Thus the pleasure I took in doing my job was first fouled by birds and then blown away by the wind.

CUPBEARER. My fantasy was likewise marked by the signs of my trade, for I dreamed that in a pleasant meadow I saw a lovely grapevine. Its tendrils were full of leaves and sweet and excellent fruit—each grape was like a ruby, and each cluster was like amber. I dreamed that two clusters hung from the topmost branch. I picked one of them and squeezed white liquor from it with one hand, and not a drop of that precious liquid went to waste, for in the other hand I held a golden goblet. Thus I gathered it all up and saved it.

JOSEPH. Oh, Heaven help me! What a difference between one dream and the other! Such a waste of bread, and so much wine preserved! On the one hand ruin, and on the other, increase! Both dreams are surely glimpses of some divine mystery, some high sacrament, but at present they're so veiled that I think I'm seeing life and death in wine and bread.

CUPBEARER. How is it that after hearing us, you seem to have fallen mute, absorbed, and in a trance, without giving any reply?

JOSEPH. When I listen to both of you, I'm confused about what I should do. I know a lot about dreams, for they have cost me dearly. I'm trying to make up my mind whether I should keep quiet about what I should say, or say what I should keep quiet about.

CUPBEARER AND BAKER. When in doubt, it's better to speak than keep quiet.

JOSEPH. But what if it causes pain?

BAKER. For that very reason.

JOSEPH. And what if it brings pleasure?

CUPBEARER. For that very reason.

BAKER. So that the one whose dream means pain can take precautions against it.

CUPBEARER. And it would be cruel to hide the other one's pleasure.

JOSEPH. For my part, even though I'd prefer . . .

CUPBEARER AND BAKER. Speak!

JOSEPH. . . . not to give pleasure so as not to give pain, there is a higher reason. You've decided you want me to speak?

CUPBEARER AND BAKER. Yes!

JOSEPH. Your dreams are almost alike. There is bread, which is life, and is death. There is wine, which is death, and is life. Your dreams mean that you [to the Cupbearer:]will go free, while you [to the Baker:] will be convicted. You will soon return to your post; and you will soon be put to death.

BAKER. I would be very worried by such an interpretation if I didn't imagine that you're just trying to get revenge because I teased you.

CUPBEARER. That's the right attitude. Pay no attention to the bad interpretation; you can see that I'm not excited about the good one.

BAKER. Not so fast! Just because I said I don't believe his prediction, that doesn't mean I'm not going to punish him for lying to me.

CUPBEARER. You'll have to fight me first!

BAKER. I'm ready!

JOSEPH. Between the two of them, I'll surely die!

They start fighting, but Joseph gets between them with his arms outstretched, keeping them apart, with one man at the end of each of his arms, as they look at him in amazement.

BOTH. What is this?

BAKER. Who stopped me?

CUPBEARER. Who has blinded me with this new light?

JOSEPH. I find myself between you in the shape of a cross, which quells your anger, and this foreshadows a second mystery. On my right hand is he who will live, and on my left is he who must die.[23]

The Baker tries to attack Joseph again.

BAKER. Well, no one can stop me from killing a vile slave!

Enter the Jailer.

JAILER. You shouldn't try to kill someone, since you're about to die yourself. Your sentence has come down as the law and justice require. You are convicted of your crime, and the king has sentenced you to death.

BAKER. Heavens, what am I hearing?

JAILER. *[To the Cupbearer:]* You, however, were found innocent and have been cleared of all suspicion. You are restored to the king's favor, and will once again have the honor of serving him his cup. *[To the Baker:]* You may as well resign yourself to your fate. I'm covering your face with this black gauze as a sign that you are sentenced to death.

He puts a black veil over the Baker's face.

BAKER. Oh, woe is me, for I must pay for my crime!

CUPBEARER. Oh, lucky me, to have lived to see this day!

JAILER. *[To the Baker:]* You come with me; *[to the Cupbearer:]* and as for you, you may leave whenever you like. The door is open for you.

[Exeunt the Jailer and Baker.]

CUPBEARER. *[To Joseph:]* Come, let me give you a hug, for I owe the good news of this joy to you. You were the first one to tell me about it.

JOSEPH. If you want to repay me, there's one thing you can do.

CUPBEARER. What's that?

JOSEPH. Remember me; and since you are going to serve the king, tell him of my sad plight. You know how painful it is for an innocent man to be imprisoned, so take pity on me for God's sake. I have been greatly wronged, for the only crime I've committed was to refuse to commit a crime.

CUPBEARER. I'm sorry to leave you here. Don't thank me—for I don't yet deserve your thanks—but I give you my word and my promise that I will defend you. Let's shake hands on it.

JOSEPH. You give me your word, your promise, and your handshake?

CUPBEARER. Yes, I do.

JOSEPH. Then I accept.

Exit the Cupbearer.

JOSEPH.   Oh, lovely lights in whom I see foretold
                in elegant calligraphy, obscure designs,
                the measure of my woe in endless lines,
                vast page on which my sufferings unfold:
                which one of you, shining up there in the cold,
                has caused the sorrow for which my soul repines?
                Which one of you unequal heavenly signs
                must bear the blame for my distress untold?
                I think it must be you, who twinkle there
                almost bereft of light, poor excuse for a star,
                so hear me out. Here's what I have for you:
                it's no complaint, but something far more rare—
                my gratitude my good fortune you'll not mar:
                what isn't there, you hardly can undo!

My only consolation in so much sorrow is that I have nothing left to lose. I seem to be a magnet for misfortune. Yet my cup of sorrow is not really full; there's one more pain that lies in wait for me, and that is the news that my misfortune has caused my father's death. I've never heard from him; but I can't imagine how my brothers could have persuaded him that there was any reason to sell me as a slave. But of course they must not have told him at all, for such treachery is always sneaky. Yet even if they've hidden what they did, my father will have died from missing me. Oh, aged father! Woe is me! For who could doubt that this sorrow must have been the last straw? You loved me tenderly because I was Rachel's son, and her beauty cost you so dear. I know you cannot hear me, father, but even so, I beg you to let Benjamin make up for my absence. He looks even more like his beautiful mother than I do. Since you have him there to mirror the loveliness of your late wife, who lies buried in Bethlehem's fertile field, please don't grieve for me! And you,

Benjamin, comfort him. Treat him with lovingkindness, for old age is rejuvenated by the presence of children. But, alas, this prayer must be in vain, for I can't help thinking he has died of grief because I'm not there. My brothers surely told him that I ran away; that's the simplest explanation for my absence; and they'll have told him they don't know what happened to me. Let heaven hear my cry! Perhaps one of its pure virtues will feel sorry for me—not that I deserve it, but out of unalloyed pity—and tell me how they covered up their treason, and what he did; and thus free me from this nagging doubt.

Enter Chastity, crossing the stage in front of him.

CHASTITY. I am that virtue. Your prayer is reasonable, for a doubt like that will always produce confused phantasms until it is resolved. It's only natural. Judge for yourself. Maybe you'll even see what it is you're judging.

Exit Chastity.

JOSEPH. Come back! Don't go! I want to speak to you! Oh, heavens, I must be mad! I could swear that I saw a heavenly beauty standing before me. That just shows how much apprehension can affect the senses. But that delirium hasn't ended with her appearance and departure; for I could swear that I see my father with Benjamin, searching for me in a thicket in Canaan. I'll pay attention in order to find out whether this mirage can also speak.

The cart opens. A stage appears, suspended above, and Jacob enters as a venerable old man, and Benjamin, as a boy.

JACOB. Love's worries have kept me awake, my handsome Benjamin! I sent Joseph to see how the flocks were thriving and what his brothers were up to, and he hasn't come back, even though he's always very prompt. Even if they've taken the flocks from Shechem to Dothan in search of pasture, he should have returned by now. My love for him is troubled by this tardiness.

BENJAMIN. The lover is always impatient for the beloved's return.

JACOB. Benjamin, are you jealous?

BENJAMIN. Me jealous of Joseph? What an unjust suspicion! Joseph and I are like two bodies with a single soul, or one soul in two bodies. After all, we two are sons of Rachel, so a close bond unites us.

JACOB. I'm glad you love each other so. Since you and I share this same love, it's up to us to look for him. Help me climb up this little hill, whence I can see the road better. Perhaps I'll have the joy of seeing him coming from afar.

BENJAMIN. You needn't take that trouble, for here come Reuben, Judah, Issachar, and Manasseh. They'll bring us news of him.

Enter the brothers mentioned, talking to each other. They are carrying a
red tunic wrapped up in a piece of taffeta. They are dressed as
shepherds.

REUBEN. What a dreadful pain! You want me to be the one to tell him such
sad news?

JUDAH. It's up to you. As the eldest of us, Reuben, you'll know better how to
break it to him gently.

JACOB. What's going on? You come before me without greeting me? You seem
to be planning some excuse for not speaking to me. Why isn't my Joseph
with you? Oh, unjust pain! Doesn't my question deserve a better answer
than just tears? Will all of you keep silent? Can you do nothing but weep?

REUBEN. Your words only increase our pain, making it impossible for our
lips to articulate a sound, but since you demand an answer, let this speak
for us with mute rhetoric. *He unwraps the tunic.* Do you recognize . . .

JACOB. Oh, woe is me!

REUBEN. . . . this long dress you gave Joseph?

JACOB. No, it is a dark mystery! I gave it to him white, and you return it
stained with purple. What has occurred?

REUBEN. A beast—the fiercest, most ferocious miscarriage of the mountain, horrible offspring of its grottoes—as we passed the valley of Dothan,
emerged from its rude caves to feast its fangs on his young blood and
stain its claws. We found his lifeless body torn in pieces, his tunic in a
thousand tiny shreds, and . . .

JACOB. Silence! Be quiet! Your sharp tongue is a poisoned arrow that pierces
my heart in a thousand different places with each word that you speak.
Alas, my beloved Joseph! *He takes the tunic.*

BENJAMIN. How can I hear this and not die of a broken heart?

JACOB. Oh, gloomy, sad, and impure remnants, discovered to my sorrow![24]
What has this old man done to deserve to see the face of my best mirror
eclipsed? He was the light of my eyes. Why do you leave me in darkness, seeing the flower of his years turned to a withered springtime? He
was the crystal goblet in which I drank the liquor of his sweetness. Must
I now drink this bitter potion mixed with blood? Alas, dear Joseph! The
worst of beasts has killed you. Who can doubt it? It must have been the
worst of beasts. Oh Lord, that worst of beasts is envy, as a thousand
pens have written. Before I reflect on that, let this pain carry me away to
those dark mansions where so many of my ancestors lie buried.

Exit Jacob.

BENJAMIN. Oh, woe is me! My father's pain, though great, is only one. In me
it is two pains, for I feel both Joseph's pain and his.

Exit Benjamin.

REUBEN. You wouldn't let me pull him out of that cistern! You were determined to make us witness this lamentable scene.

ISSACHAR. Judah sold him so quickly!

JUDAH. That is irrelevant.

THE FOUR BROTHERS. Why accuse us? If he hadn't had those dreams, his good fortune would never have been spoiled.

Exeunt. The cart closes.

JOSEPH. Wait, stop, don't go away! Illusion, don't escape me until my father knows I am alive, and . . .

Enter the Cupbearer.

CUPBEARER. Where are you rushing off to?

JOSEPH. I don't know.

CUPBEARER. You can't say that my good fortune has made me forget you.

JOSEPH. No, I can see what a kindly man you are.

CUPBEARER. I have not just come to see you. I've come to take you with me. Don't you believe me?

JOSEPH. If this is good news, how can I believe it?

CUPBEARER. It's even better than you think. This is the king's own ring with which he guarantees your freedom. It is the king who has sent me for you.

JOSEPH. The king has sent you for me?

CUPBEARER. Yes.

JOSEPH. How can that be?

CUPBEARER. It is like this. The king had a dream . . . But I'd better tell you all this on the way. We can't waste time. Come, he's awaiting you.

JOSEPH. Oh, fortune! Please let this not be another illusion! If you're just teasing me, it's too little, too late; while if it's true, it is too much, too soon!

Exeunt. Enter Aseneth, as a lady, from one side, accompanied by musicians, men, and women. As she begins singing, the king enters from the other side, pacing as if worried.

ASENETH. *[Sings:]* Who is it that, though imprisoned
in a narrow, burning sphere,
would like to contain in himself
the whole wide stratosphere;

ALL WITH MUSICIANS. yet still can accommodate
complaints about his sad fate?

LADY 1. It is the heart of man
that lives in a narrow cell,
yet the greatest kingdom on earth
can't fill it, though there it may dwell;

he still can accommodate
complaints about his sad fate.

LADY 2.   As is proven by Egypt's great Pharaoh,
for even though he rules
all the land the river Nile
bathes with its fertile pools,

MUSICIANS.   he still can accommodate
complaints about his sad fate.

PHARAOH. Please stop that singing, for though your sweet song fills the air
with its metric harmony, it is no remedy for my sadness.

ASENETH. I'm sorry, sire. I've seen how all your servants sought to banish
your stubborn sadness. My father was priest at the Temple of Heliopolis,
where I was his high priestess. I've brought this choir and orchestra
from there, hoping perchance their sweet sounds might distract you.

KING. Alas, lovely Aseneth, your efforts have been in vain. I appreciate
your kindness, but my suffering is so great that, instead of relieving it,
you've only made it worse. I can have no comfort until I know what
heaven meant to tell me in my dreams; and there's no more hope of that.
I've consulted the infinite number of wise men and magicians of Egypt,
and none can satisfy me.

Enter the Cupbearer with Joseph.

CUPBEARER. This is Joseph, that Hebrew slave I told you about, who interpreted our dreams . . .

JOSEPH. . . . and who could wish nothing better than to lie prostrate at your
royal feet!

KING. Arise.

JOSEPH. *[Aside:]* Good heavens! What am I seeing? Isn't that the divine
beauty who appeared in my vision?

KING. Where are you from?

JOSEPH. From the land of Canaan.

KING. But there's been no war between the Hebrews and Egyptians in your
lifetime. How then were you taken captive?

JOSEPH. *(Aside:)* My story is so terrible, I'd die of shame to tell it, for I can't
bear to defame those whom I love most. *[To the King:]* It was the
Ishmaelites, sire, who bought me and sold me here.

KING. That explains how you came to be a slave, but why were you in jail?

JOSEPH. Even less can I speak of that. I'd rather die with the comfort of
knowing I'm innocent than sacrifice the honor of a woman. I will not
defend my own honor at the cost of another's honor. It would be of no
use to you to ruin another so as to honor me. Just let me serve you as

well as I can, which will depend on the extent to which God wills to enlighten me.

ASENETH.. How cleverly he protected the guilty party, yet still said what's on his mind!

KING. Though I'm sure you know why I've brought you here, I'll tell you all the same, in case there was some mistake in what you've heard. I dreamed that seven lovely cows came up from the river to its banks, and as they grazed on its springtime emeralds, I saw another seven emerge from those waves, so skinny that they looked like skeletons, and come towards them. They devoured all the fatness of those cows in their prime. Then I saw seven fertile ears of grain—each grain sparkling like a teardrop of the dew—and another seven parched by summer's heat before April could prosper them. They struggled, the dry ears won, and the river carried them all away.

JOSEPH. It's obvious that the river was a hieroglyphic meaning time, Great Lord, for it always flows and always moves forward, never turning back in its course. Therefore it is time that has produced this abundance of cows and ears of grain, and it is also time that in its fickleness has reduced all to nothingness. Your dream is seven fertile years in grain and cows, but their delight will end in seven sterile years. Since you have been warned of the damage that is to come, now store up plenty against want, and happiness against woe.

KING. Allow me to embrace you, for you are the first one I have spoken to who has been able to give me peace of mind. Again I say, let me embrace you. I can tell by the great peace your words have given me that your God speaks through you, and I can see how the wisdom He gives you exceeds that of all Egypt's wise men. Since you have foreseen the damage, you must be the one to prepare the remedy. Therefore, I order all to obey you, from my most noble vassal to the humblest of them all. You will bring luster to this post, for you have earned their respect. I hereby make you viceroy of Egypt. Put on my royal purple, take my ring, and with my chain around your neck, go out in public in the most triumphal chariot. All who encounter you will kneel before you. Come sit at my right hand, and all of you, applaud him in unison.

SOME. Long live Joseph!

OTHERS. May God grant him long life!

KING. Now listen: that name sounds foreign in our language, but its meaning in Syrian is Savior. Therefore, let everyone say: "Long live the Savior," since he has come to save us from the ruin to which we would otherwise have been condemned.

ALL. Long live Egypt's savior!

JOSEPH. Merciful stars, who would believe that it is others who now are sleeping, while I am the one who is dreaming!

KING. And you, fair Aseneth, now those choirs you brought truly have something worth singing about.

ASENETH. They do, indeed! Until today no man has ever pleased me; I've always frowned upon them all. But there's something about this young man that overcomes my natural modesty and makes me want to please him. Of all the miracles I've seen today, that is the most beautiful of all!

KING. Then what are you waiting for? Everyone join with me in singing.
    [He sings:]

	Since Joseph has now become
MUSICIANS.	Since Joseph has now become
KING.	Egypt's Savior by all adored,
MUSICIANS.	Egypt's Savior by all adored,
KING.	let the people cry out in accord,
MUSICIANS.	let the people cry out in accord,
KING.	Blessed be he who comes
	in the holy name of the Lord!
MUSICIANS.	Blessed be he who comes
	in the holy name of the Lord!
KING.	For his sake God chose to spare
	Egypt from sore distress.
	Let his praises fill the air;
	acclaim him with joyfulness.
	Crown him with laurel fair
	and olive for peacefulness.
	Let all join in this prayer
	and sing out with one accord:
ALL AND MUSICIANS.	Blessed be he who comes
	in the holy name of the Lord!

Exeunt, with the king leading Joseph and Aseneth by the hand. All cast their cloaks on the floor before the procession. Enter Dream from the other side of the stage.

DREAM. Blessed be he who comes in the holy name of the Lord? It was not in vain that that lovely divine virtue who shows him so much favor advised me to watch him for signs of faraway lights, of matters that must remain veiled in shadows until their destined time shall come. And it's not in vain that I have obeyed her. But what good has it done me? For no matter how much I look for signs and glimpses of that high sacrament she mentioned, which will be the fulfillment of all that's happened, I'm still utterly dumbfounded. Now I'd like to see if I can resolve this doubt. Oh, lovely new deity, who exceeds the whitest snow in purity, since I obeyed your command, now do my bidding. Return to that sovereign semblance that your love rendered visible to the theater of the world so that I could make amends.

Enter Chastity.

CHASTITY. What do you want of me?

DREAM. Just to show you how different my summons is from yours.

CHASTITY. How so?

DREAM. Your cries led me to a dungeon, while mine have brought you to a palace. You took me to see suffering, pain, and travail, while I have brought you to see rejoicing and celebration.

Offstage music of flageolets and kettledrums.

OFFSTAGE VOICE. Long live Egypt's great savior!

DREAM. See how, as he rides his triumphal chariot, the people acclaim him as their Savior! I have more than made up for all the troubles those dreams caused him. His present happiness outweighs those troubles as much as applause is greater than insult, triumph exceeds misery, and the crown of laurel exceeds total ruin. I have obeyed you as much as a second cause can do, for naturally the First Cause gives the orders. To reward my obedience, I'd like you to clarify something for me. You told me that all these visible signs foreshadow a mystery, which is Miracle of Miracles. Now I humbly beg you at least to give me a hint, if not altogether to solve this riddle.

CHASTITY. I will be glad to do so, on one condition.

DREAM. What's that?

CHASTITY. We'll have to behave like what we are: allegories, not real people. As such, we two know neither time nor place, so we can simply let interpolation—as if one act had ended, and another already begun—fill up the gap of years. So let's suppose the seven fertile years are over, and the years of famine have begun. You will see him at the granary that he has filled to overflowing during those good years. You'll see how he distributes bread to rich and poor alike, with no respect for persons.

DREAM. That's what I want!

CHASTITY. Then come with me to the top of the Mount of Vision, Joseph's hereditary patrimony. Since Joseph is the living image of his grandfather Isaac, it's only right that both of them should behold from that summit how the fields fill up with rational ants. Prudently, following the trail of straw the Nile has brought them,[25] they look for grain. You'll see him distribute it even to his brothers, without recalling how unkind they were to him. They're going up to Egypt from Canaan. But let's not waste time; just come along with me.

DREAM. It's as if I could see them now, as they go looking for him, saying . . .

Exeunt Dream and Chastity. Enter Reuben, Judah, Issachar, Zebulun, Gad, Asher, Naphtali, Manasseh, Simeon, and Levi, dressed as shepherds.

REUBEN. From here we can see the high towers of the sumptuous palace of Egypt's governor. We must go to him right now, trusting that his great providence will not fail to aid us because we are foreigners, since he helps everyone.

JUDAH. They say he is so generous, compassionate, gentle, and mild, I'm sure he'll be kind to us.

ISSACHAR. It seems we've come at the right time.

ZEBULUN. How so?

NAPHTALI. Judging by the splendor of that retinue, that must be he coming this way now.

MANASSEH. You're not mistaken, for all are kneeling to him.

SIMEON. We'd better do the same.

LEVI. Let's use the song our beggars use to move him to listen to us.

GAD. Since we've come here to seek alms, there's no harm in behaving like the beggars we truly are.

ASHER. Let's await him on our knees.

REUBEN. Tune up your voices, mixing music with laments.

       Enter Joseph, the Cupbearer, and others.

SOME BROTHERS. *[They sing:]*
       Since Heaven has shown favor
       to comfort our dismay
       and sent you as our savior,

OTHER BROTHERS.   give unto us this day
       our daily Bread, kind sir!

JOSEPH. That language and tune sound like Hebrew. Good heavens, the Hebrew language and melody here? But what I see now is even more shocking than what I heard! Aren't those my brothers? I'm utterly amazed to see them and shocked to hear them. But I'll use my eyes and ears to find out more.

SOME OF THEM.   Relieve our agony
       with your gracious favor.

Singing: Give unto us this day
       our daily Bread, kind sir!

JOSEPH. *[Aside:]* Yes, it is really they. So Heaven has now fulfilled that first dream I had, when their sheaves bowed down to mine. What an inscrutable omen! Wheat in both cases, and it's all bewildering! But they haven't recognized me. That's hardly surprising in my present happy state! I'll hide my feelings. But how can I, when my soul and very life long to embrace them, especially now that I have heard their affliction in the miserable cries with which they've sought to move me and obtain my favor?

THE BROTHERS AND MUSICIANS. Give unto us this day
our daily Bread, kind sir!

JOSEPH. *[Aside:]*Though my heart is in my throat and is beating like a drum, I must conceal my feelings until I learn more from them—without their knowing that it's me they speak to—about my father and my beloved Benjamin. I hope he hasn't inherited my misfortune, for hatred is a dreadful heritage that can hardly be escaped. *[To his brothers:]* Arise, get up from the ground, and tell me who you are, where you have come from, and what it is you want.

REUBEN. Oh, Sovereign Prince of Egypt, whom Heaven has made redeemer not only of your own but of all the neighboring kingdoms that come seeking your benevolence: we are of the Hebrew nation, though now we live in the land of Canaan, since God in His wisdom commanded our grandfather Abraham to leave his home and country and wander as a pilgrim, fleeing the false idols of Chaldea. But that is beside the point. The great famine these eastern climes have been enduring for the past seven years has reached such an extreme in Canaan that no leaf, no flower, no grass, no plants at all remain, but only thorns and stubble. Our streams and creeks have ceased to flow. Even the rivers are perishing from thirst, and the cattle are dying of hunger. Our most fertile grazing lands and our purest ponds—after seven years of sad, futile, sterile, aborted harvests—find fourteen feverish Februaries.[26] Whether in stream or meadow, there is nothing but pebbles to drink, nothing but dirt clods to eat. As the people perish from the inclement crop failures, their only consolation is seeing the earth crack open, yawning with horror. It has been said that it is a blessing for the field to provide open graves when the people are only cadavers. We are young. We could easily have gone to other lands, but our hands and feet are tied, for we are ten brothers kept at home by an ancient, venerable father who cannot follow us, for the years weigh heavy upon him. It is for his sake that we have come, more than for ourselves, seeking whatever bread, kind sir, you may wish to grant us. We have brought money to pay for it. Therefore, though heaven has closed its gates with heavy locks, God has entrusted the key to you. Not for us, but for the sake of our old father . . .

Joseph turns his back on them.

But, alas! Just when I thought my words were having some effect, you
turn your back to show you are not interested?

SOME BROTHERS. My lord?

OTHERS. My lord?

JOSEPH. *[Aside:]* They think I'm being cold when I'm overcome with pity.
They think I am hard-hearted, when I can't refrain from weeping. But I
must control myself to find out whether this affection is real or feigned.
I'll do so by showing my displeasure.

[To his brothers:] You say that you are brothers?

ALL. Yes, my lord.

JOSEPH. You are quite a band of brothers! Were there more of you besides?

REUBEN. Two more.

JOSEPH. Then why did they stay there instead of coming with you?

REUBEN. One of them was killed by a beast.

JOSEPH. All right then. And the other one?

REUBEN. He is too young to travel.

JOSEPH. *[Aside:]* I pray they have not killed him!

[To his brothers:] Now I realize that you are spies. You have deceived us with this story about wanting wheat, when in fact you have
come to spy out the defenses of this state because of the eternal enmity
between Hebrews and Egyptians. You plan to make war on us.

Aside: Since Benjamin is Rachel's son like me, I'm afraid they've
treated him the way they treated me.

ALL. My lord, please don't think that . . .

JOSEPH. That's enough. You'll never convince me that you are not traitors,
and I shall not believe you until you bring me that youngest brother, and
I see that he's alive. If not—*[aside:]* Who has ever experienced such an
inner conflict? How can love be so severe? How can outrage be so tender?—though I have shown pity to all others, I'll reserve a just punishment for your behavior!

ALL. What is this?

REUBEN. What do you think? Now we must pay for the hatred we bore one
brother with the love we feel for another.

JUDAH. That is true.

GAD. Heaven is meting out just punishment.

JOSEPH. What are you talking about? Do you admit your guilt?

REUBEN. Sir, we were only saying that if we go for Benjamin—for that is
the boy's name—it will be like tearing out a piece of that good old
man's very heart.

JUDAH. He loves him so much, he may refuse to entrust him to us.

JOSEPH. And why would he do that? After all, you are his brothers. Does he think you might cast him in a well? Or sell him to foreigners? Or feed him to wild beasts?

REUBEN. What sort of man is this, who can penetrate our thoughts?

ALL. Since we acknowledge our guilt, our suffering is just.

JOSEPH. *(Aside:)* Their attempts to get out of bringing him have made me even more suspicious.

[*To his brothers:*] There is nothing more to be said. Either you bring that lad before my eyes, or else I will put all ten of you to death as spies. And so that you may see that I temper my justice with mercy, I'm going to give you the wheat you asked for. However, as security that you'll come back with him, one of you must remain here bound and in prison.

REUBEN. We cannot but obey you. Which one of us do you want?

JOSEPH. *(Aside:)* Simeon behaved most cruelly toward me when they sold me. This is not revenge. I am doing him a favor, so that the one whose sin was greatest may be purged of that sin and win pardon.

ALL. He's looking at all of us.

JOSEPH. *(Pointing at Simeon:)* I choose him.

SIMEON. Woe is me!

REUBEN. As we sinned, we are punished. Simeon was the first to lay hands on him, so he is the first to suffer.

JOSEPH. Shechem.

CUPBEARER. Sir?

JOSEPH. Go with them, and say that I have ordered that they be given all the wheat they want. And take that one you saw me single out to prison as a hostage.

REUBEN. My lord, we are prostrate at your feet! You will see that we will obey you so enthusiastically that some may criticize our speed in going there and coming back, though in this case speed is warranted, and tardiness would be wrong.

CUPBEARER. Then come with me.

Exeunt the brothers.

JOSEPH. Shechem.

CUPBEARER. Sir?

JOSEPH. When they have paid for the wheat, have each one's money put in the mouth of his sack. And when you take that man I chose to jail, see that they don't treat him as an ordinary prisoner. They shouldn't pamper him; but I want him treated with respect.

CUPBEARER. Your wish is my command.

Exit the Cupbearer.

JOSEPH. Oh, love! How did I manage to control myself and refrain from embracing them? But until I know it's true that their anger hasn't harmed

Benjamin . . . But I'll think about that later, for if desire has not deceived me, I think I see entering the palace Aseneth, that lovely goddess
to whom I owe the kindness—though I still can't understand it—of that
delirium, ecstasy, or rapture, and I still haven't had a chance to thank
her.

Enter Aseneth.

ASENETH. *[To offstage companions:]* All of you, stay behind, for this time I
intend to speak clearly to the king, to find out if my father . . . but who
is this here?

JOSEPH. One who on seeing you, divine dawn of that sun whom you seek,
fears that you'll vanish again, as you have done on other occasions.
Please, my lady, this time don't hasten away as is your custom. You've
done me a wonderful favor; don't undo that kindness by leaving.

ASENETH. I'm sure I'd be happy to grant your request, Joseph, if only I
understood what you are saying. But it's strange to hear the word "favor" on the lips of a man as intelligent and wise as you. Indeed, the
word shocks me. What do you mean by "favor," for it sounds offensive?

JOSEPH. Why will you let me see you when you refuse to let me thank you?
It's hardly noble of you to make me look ignoble. If you are angry because I've failed to show you due gratitude, I simply haven't had the
chance. Chalk it up to bad luck, but not ingratitude.

ASENETH. But when have I ever let you see me? And what favor have I ever
done for you that you have been unable to thank me for?

JOSEPH. Once you saw me tormented by a doubt. You told me to judge by
what I saw. I did just that, and what I saw . . .

ASENETH. All this just seems to me . . .

JOSEPH. What?

ASENETH. . . . . like some sort of illusion. Since you are such a master of
dreams that others tell you their dreams so that you will interpret them,
interpret your own dream now.

JOSEPH. You'll not put me off with your insults.

ASENETH. What do you mean by that?

JOSEPH. As my whole life has shown, though dreams may be but dreams,
sometimes dreams come true.

ASENETH. How could it possibly be true that I spoke to you, or saw you, or
did you any favor? My vanity is such that if the lovely goddess of Chastity decided to take on human form, she would appear as me, for there's
no one else more like her! She and I are so alike that when our pagan
folk seek to portray that goddess, she's the spitting image of me. You'll
hardly find a single statue of her that doesn't look just like me; so if

you've seen some fantasy, it must have been she, for it couldn't have been I.

JOSEPH. Well, you've taken me down a peg! I'll not dare be bold with you henceforth; yet I'm grateful to you anyhow.

ASENETH. For what?

JOSEPH. For showing me that I was right to love you, even if that was an illusion. In my religion I adore Chastity as a virtue, and since you are her living image, I was right to adore you too.

ASENETH. That's what you think! But I'll show you such disdain that your embarrassment will serve as a warning to anyone else who dares approach me!

(Aside:) How can I tell such lies when in fact I'm thrilled that he loves me!

JOSEPH. In that case I won't approach you.

ASENETH. Why not?

JOSEPH. How could I dare tell you that I love you? Since it was only an illusion or a statue that embodied the idea of my blind fantasy, it would be bold of me to say that I've adored you since that moment.

ASENETH. Well, then . . .

JOSEPH. Stop torturing me! By saying what I will not say, I've already said it.

ASENETH. I knew it even before you didn't say it.

JOSEPH. If you chose to understand me, then how am I to blame?

ASENETH. Isn't that the same as saying it?

JOSEPH. No.

ASENETH. But aren't you insinuating it?

JOSEPH. Do I have your permission?

ASENETH. Yes, you do.

JOSEPH. Then listen. Everyone knows . . . ; but here comes the king.

ASENETH. Hush! You can tell me later.

Enter the King.

KING. Aseneth? Joseph? I'm delighted to see the two of you. Both of you have been weighing heavily on my mind, and I'd like you to help me unburden myself.

ASENETH.. I am your humble servant.

JOSEPH. I kneel before you.

KING. Aseneth, I'm sure that you have come, as you have done before, to ask me to reward you for the services I admit I owe your father. *[To Joseph:]* And you deserve my affection as well, not only for having restored my kingdom, but I might well say the whole world, since your great providence extends throughout the world and has earned you titles in three different languages: Joseph, Savior, Increase. Faced with these two great debts, I dare not decide which of you deserves the greater prize. And therefore, to avoid choosing wrongly, I have decided to consult you, Joseph, first concerning Aseneth. And after that, dear Aseneth, I shall ask you about Joseph; and when I've heard your thoughts, I'm sure I'll make the right decision. So hear me, Joseph. *[He speaks privately to Joseph:]* I have such high esteem for your person that I would like to ensure that you are not just temporarily dwelling in Egypt as a foreigner. The best way to do this is to arrange a marriage for you: so here is Aseneth.

JOSEPH. I kiss your hand a thousand times for such an honor! But I fear that, though I may deserve such a favor from you, I do not deserve it from her.

KING. I will determine that. *[He speaks privately to Aseneth:]* Aseneth, everyone knows how I appreciate Joseph, so you must know that too. In offering him to you, I'm really giving you my other self, for I am spoken for.

ASENETH. Please don't go on. I really have no right to choose; I can but obey your command.

KING. Since you are both aware of the reward I'm offering you, discuss it with each other. In view of these two debts, I cannot pay more, nor can I be satisfied with less.

Exit the King.

JOSEPH. Dare I ask, divine portent, what the king said to you? For until I hear it from your own lips, I'll not believe it.

ASENETH. He said nothing to me.

JOSEPH. Then he must have said it all to me.

ASENETH. Then don't ask me, but tell it to yourself. I'm torn between affection and respect. It's better that I not say it, nor even know it.

Exit Aseneth.

JOSEPH. Modesty kept her from speaking. Oh, infinite, immense God of Abraham, Isaac, and Jacob: When has anyone so undeserving as I attained so rich a reward?

Enter the Cupbearer.

CUPBEARER. I have good news for you, sir.

JOSEPH. What is it?

CUPBEARER. Time has accelerated—for it flies faster on wings of desire— and the ten Hebrew brothers are at your doorstep.

JOSEPH. Tell them to come in, and go and have the prisoner brought to me. *[Aside:]* So here is my second love, or perhaps I should say, my first.

For since one is a love of blood, and the other a fiery love, I must fight my feelings for both with fire and blood together.

Exit the Cupbearer. Enter the brothers. Benjamin is with them, as well as the country bumpkin Bato.

ALL. Great Lord, we kneel before you!

JOSEPH. Arise, get up from the floor!

REUBEN. My lord, in spite of our father's grief and pain, we have brought Benjamin to you, as you commanded.

JUDAH. *[To Benjamin:]* What are you waiting for? Go kneel before him!

BENJAMIN. If I may kiss your hand, it will be the greatest pleasure I could wish for.

JOSEPH. I wanted to see you because of what your brothers told me about you; welcome.

   (Aside:) How can I keep from hugging him to my breast? But there is still one thing I need to find out.

   [To Benjamin:] I am delighted to see you! How is your father?

BENJAMIN. He's terribly unhappy to be without me.

JOSEPH. Does he love you that much?

BENJAMIN. I am his youngest child, and men who have children in old age always love them very much. He also feels great love for me—although I don't deserve it—because I am Rachel's son, and I had another brother who was also her son, but he was lost; and therefore he has invested all that love that we two shared in me alone.

JOSEPH. How did your brother die?

BENJAMIN. I beg you not to ask me that.

JOSEPH. Why not?

BENJAMIN. Because when I think of Joseph, I get so upset that I can't speak. I can't bear to tell you the whole sad story. *Weeping:* Suffice it to say that he was killed by a beast.

JOSEPH. *[Aside:]* Heavens, how can his tears and mine not proclaim who he is, and who I am?

BENJAMIN. Anyhow, that's all beside the point. My lord, my aged father, who is extremely grateful for your generosity, has asked me to give you a small gift. He wishes it were more, but it's all that he could send due to the drought. Some suckling lambs, some honeycombs, butter, cheese— the poor gift of a poor shepherd; but the intent with which it's offered is richer than glittering gold or smoking incense.

Enter the Cupbearer with Simeon.

CUPBEARER. Here, sir, is the one who remained here as your hostage.

SIMEON. Everyone, let me hug you!

JUDAH. You can't say we didn't hurry back for you, Simeon!

SIMEON. I appreciate it.

REUBEN. *[To Benjamin:]* Since he seems to like you, tell him we're in a hurry.

BENJAMIN. My lord, since we have done as you commanded, and our father will be sick with worry till he sees us, we beg you to give us wheat and your permission to leave.

REUBEN. We have brought back double the price of the wheat you ordered sold us, for your clerks, by oversight or error, left the money we brought then in our bags.

JOSEPH. That's fine; but before you go away, in gratitude for Jacob's gift, I'd like you to dine with me.

(Aside to the Cupbearer:) Go have the tables set, and pay attention to what I say. Have them serve Benjamin a double portion of everything, for thus I must show preference to the son of the lovely Rachel. Then, when you give them the wheat, put back their money as you did before; but this time put my golden goblet in Benjamin's bag.

CUPBEARER. I shall do exactly as you say.

(Aside:) What mysteries are these, for I don't understand a thing?

JOSEPH. Come in, come in with me. This is my private chamber, where I want all of you to join me at my table. What's holding you back?

ALL. Our respect for you.

REUBEN. My lord, you want humble shepherds to sit down to eat with so lofty, so supreme a governor, whose person is second only to the king? Would you lower yourself to the status of a mere man?

JOSEPH. When you speak of my being the second person, becoming man, and giving sustenance to all the pilgrims who come to me, perhaps Heaven is hinting at the mystery of another sort of bread.

Exeunt. Bato remains onstage.

BATO. The whole time they were talking, I've just stood here like a bump on a log, and nobody paid me any mind. The old man sent me on this trip to wait on Benjamin, so he wouldn't have to care for his donkey. He sure paid attention to his dad! He hasn't cared for his donkey or for me either! I might as well be a donkey, as far as he's concerned. While he's sitting at that fancy table, would he ever think of saying: "Could someone take a plate to that dummy out there?" How many masters sit down to eat without even knowing whether their servants are eating or not! But I guess I should forgive him. He's nothing but a kid, and now he's rested his head on the viceroy's chest and fallen fast asleep! Maybe he's dumbfounded to be in such a grand place. What pretty sideboards! What quantities of meat! What drinks! What dapper squires! What greedy little pages! But they're no fools! Every time they manage to hide in a corner with a plate, they pick the bones in nothing flat! But now they're clearing the tables and saying their good-byes. They'll be setting out for the granary. I'd better follow them to load up the sacks. Nobody could say I don't have plenty of masters to wait on, especially at this hour, when they're all full and I'm still hungry. This palace is enormous! I don't know which way is out and which way's in; I can't tell whether I'm coming or going. Oh, here comes the governor!

Enter Joseph.

JOSEPH. Who are you?

BATO. Just give me a minute to think about it.

JOSEPH. You can't remember who you are?

BATO. What's so strange about that? People are always forgetting who they are.

JOSEPH. How did you get in here?

BATO. *(Walking.)* Like this.

JOSEPH. Who are you?

BATO. Now I remember. I'm Benjamin's donquerry.

JOSEPH. What is that supposed to mean?

BATO. Isn't the servant who cares for his master's horse his equerry?

JOSEPH. That's right.

BATO. Well then, the one who cares for his donkey must be his donquerry.

JOSEPH. You are Benjamin's servant?

BATO. Yes, sir.

JOSEPH. I'm sorry I got angry. Here, take this diamond.

BATO. But my lord, what good is this piece of a mirror stuck in a hunk of brass?

The Cupbearer is heard shouting offstage; then they all enter.

CUPBEARER. You'll all pay for your crime!

ALL. But please consider . . .

BENJAMIN. Oh, woe is me!

ALL. . . . that, though we are but shepherds . . .

Enter Benjamin in chains, carrying a golden chalice in his hand.

JOSEPH. What's going on?

CUPBEARER. My lord, these men have been so vile, so wretchedly ungrateful, that after you showed them such excessive honor and I gave them all the wheat they wanted, they stole this golden goblet, which is the lovely chalice of your most precious wine. When I missed it, I went after them, and I found it in the youngest brother's bag. I haven't even taken it back, so that you could see it in his hand when he confesses his crime.

JOSEPH. How very rude of you! Is this how you repay my hospitality?

ALL. My lord!

JOSEPH. Be quiet.

BENJAMIN. I beg you to listen to me.

BATO. Just look at that sly little Benjamin; they've caught him now!

BENJAMIN. You remember how my brothers brought you back the money they had taken away unawares, not knowing who had put it in their sacks? Wouldn't it make more sense to suppose the same thing happened to me, instead of taking me for a thief? For that would be a sacrilege unworthy of our noble blood. Though we may not be descended from kings, kings will be our descendants.

JOSEPH. A little less arrogance, Sir Thief! How dare you talk like that when your crime is clear for all to see? The rest of you are equally to blame, for you are his accomplices. Still, I'll just punish this one. In this kingdom it is the law that anyone who steals another's property must become that man's slave. Hence you can go on home, but Benjamin must stay here as my slave.

BENJAMIN. I don't mind being your slave, my lord. That's really more of a reward than punishment. What bothers me is my dear old father's grief. If he could not be comforted for the loss of one son who died tragically, how will he survive the loss of another who died in infamy? There is as great a difference between tragedy and crime as there is between an honorable death and a dishonorable life. Please pity him, not me! For I . . .

JOSEPH. I'll hear no more! You men, get out of here! Go home without him, for he is now my slave.

ALL. Put us to death, my lord, but don't send us back to our venerable father without Benjamin!

REUBEN. Yes, please do us that kindness, for death is a joyful release to one who is wretched! But if you won't, I'd be more useful to you as a slave. Please take me in his place!

MANASSEH. I'd be happy to replace him too.

SIMEON. Just take me back to jail!

JUDAH. Brand my face with your irons!

LEVI. Let me drag your chains!

ISSACHAR. Put me in your stocks!

NAPHTALI. Put a yoke on my neck so that I can draw your chariot!

REUBEN. We are all ready to drink . . . ,

GAD. . . . confessing that this is just punishment for a crime we committed. . . ,

REUBEN. . . . our death in that chalice full of bitterness . . .

ALL. . . . rather than go home without Benjamin.

JOSEPH. What more do I want, what am I waiting for? They have confessed their crime and drunk repentance in tears from my chalice of bitterness. Benjamin, let me embrace you! This broken heart of mine is bursting from my breast. And you too, Reuben, come here to my waiting arms!

REUBEN. I've never told you my name, so how do you know it?

JOSEPH. Don't be alarmed. Come here, Judah, Simeon, Levi, Gad . . .

ALL FOUR. What's going on?

JOSEPH. . . . and Issachar, Zebulun, Manasseh, and Asher. I await you with open arms, now that you have repented. Why does it surprise you that I know your names, for I am Joseph, your brother? Don't be frightened to see me in this post. You have confessed your crimes, and I have forgotten them.

SOME. We're so confused . . .

OTHERS. We're so upset . . .

OTHERS. We're so amazed . . .

OTHERS. We're so dumbfounded . . .

ALL. . . . that we don't know what to tell you.

JOSEPH. And I don't know what to answer. As I emerge from darkness, the brilliant light brings tears to my eyes.

BATO. Why am I standing here? I must take this news to the old man. What do you bet that, even though weighed down by his old age, he'll run right here to see him? This may be rushing things a bit, but what's the difference? It's in the script.

Exit Bato. Enter the King, Aseneth, and Musicians.

KING. What is the matter, Joseph? I have come to your chamber with Aseneth in order personally to give you your greatest reward. Why are you weeping?

JOSEPH. This time I'm weeping for joy. These men you see are my brothers, and I'm seized with rapture, not only to see them, but to think that what has happened to us is the sign of a mystery.

KING. How so?

JOSEPH. Heaven was tightly shut, and earth was needy. My brothers came here anxiously seeking bread, and they found it in the granary I prepared, stored up in that tabernacle.[27] They sat with me at table, and the youngest of the twelve held my chalice in his hands and fell asleep on my chest.[28] When he bore the burden of their crime, they wept for him aloud, saying it was the penalty for their sin. These are all glimpses, shadows, hints of the messiah promised to our fathers and grandfathers. They foresaw in bread and wine the loftiest sacrament.

KING. How can bread and wine be a sacrament?

A curtain opens, revealing a mountain. On top of it is Dream in a triumphal chariot.

DREAM. My ideas will explain it. From this lofty mountaintop where Chastity left me to enter Aseneth's breast, I've been observing how heaven crowned with a chaste love that man who formerly was vanquished by a twisted lust. At the same time, I've seen how four of my dreams foreshadow this mystery.

KING. Four dreams, you say?

DREAM. That's right.

KING. And what four dreams are those?

DREAM. The first was Jacob's dream, when he came to see Joseph, saying:

Enter Jacob and Bato.

JACOB. Let me embrace you, Joseph! Can I really be seeing you alive, after so many days of mourning for your death?

JOSEPH. You should speak to the king and Aseneth before you speak to me.

JACOB. Excuse me, my lord, for I am not myself. This all seems like a dream. It reminds me of a dream I had before, in which I saw heaven opened, and a ladder connecting heaven to the earth. Beautiful angels ascending represented man, while those descending stood for the Word.

DREAM. This was the first of my four dreams, about the Incarnate Word. The second and the third were those of the bread and the grapevine that give both death and life. Now let us rehearse them:

The two Shades reappear on a platform suspended in midair with a backdrop that opens like a fan.

SHADE 1: The bread which the birds devoured so that the guilty man could eat his judgment in it . . .

SHADE 2: The wine squeezed from a beautiful cluster of grapes to give life . . .

On another cart a curtain opens, revealing another altar with a sacrifice of wine.

SHADE 1: . . . is now become bread from heaven, which will serve as divine flesh in that bloodless sacrifice.

SHADE 2: . . . is now become blood of the Lamb sacrificed on the altar of the cross. The chalice caught it as it flowed from his breast.

ASENETH. But how can we be sure that all of this is true?

In one of the carts a curtain is drawn, revealing an altar with a sacrifice of bread; as they recite the verses above, a hinged platform opens toward center stage, revealing a large Host; and in another cart, a sacrifice of wine; and as the other hinged platform opens, it reveals a chalice, and Faith suspended in air, between the two Shades.

FAITH. I, who am Faith, can give you that assurance, for I have inner sight, and my intellect is held captive by my hearing.

KING. But we still haven't heard your fourth dream. What is it?

DREAM. Your own dream. In the first age of the world nature with great plenty enjoyed restful peace and calm; but then, because of sin, a great famine occurred; but Providence saved the day by giving the church a great barn full of bread, which as common nourishment for Christ's brothers made them the heirs of grace, represented by Aseneth, who exemplifies chastity.

KING. And when will all this happen?

DREAM. When a descendant of one of these twelve tribes, both God and man in body and soul, will give himself to man in so lofty a sacrament.

KING. Though I am a gentile, this miracle has converted me!

JOSEPH. That means that the gentiles will inherit the vineyard.

ASENETH.. And I, struck dumb with wonder, want only to be yours.

JOSEPH. Which means that Christ will celebrate his marriage with every virtue.

SOME. *[They sing:]*
      These wonders we behold,

OTHERS.   these miracles so great,
      have led us to the true fold,

DREAM.   so let us celebrate!

MUSICIANS. We're happy to have learned
      that dreams may be but dreams
      but *Sometimes Dreams Come True.*

ALL.   Please forgive our many faults!

Music of flageolets as the curtains close on the carts, and the play ends.

5

Sor Juana Inés de la Cruz:
Joseph's Scepter

Juana Inés de Asbaje y Ramírez was born on the ranch of San Miguel Nepantla, near Mexico City, either in 1648 or 1651, the illegitimate daughter of a Creole mother—born of Spanish parents in Mexico—and a Spanish military officer. Her father apparently abandoned the family when Juana was about two years old. A child prodigy, she is said to have learned to read at the age of three and to have composed her first religious poem at the age of eight. In 1659 she was sent to Mexico City, where she lived with relatives, to further her studies. In 1664 she moved into the viceregal palace, where she experienced the glamorous social life of the court as a protegée of the vicereine. Moved by a desire for the intellectual life and by a "great aversion to marriage," she entered the Discalced Carmelite convent of San José in Mexico City. Apparently she did not find the austere life of the Carmelites to her liking, however, and a few months later she withdrew from the convent and returned to the court. After a brief interval, she entered the Jeronymite convent of St. Paula, where on 24 February 1669, she took her vows as Sor Juana Inés de la Cruz. Though cloistered, the Jeronymite nuns led a life of comfort and leisure. As Luis Harss has noted,

> Sor Juana's cell was actually a spacious apartment with sitting room and kitchen. She had been endowed by a wealthy benefactor and, throughout her career, received countless gifts, including her famous collection of musical and scientific instruments and her library of up to four thousand books. The convent had a visiting room, her salon: among her admirers was the illustrious Carlos de Sigüenza y Góngora, Mexico's leading man of letters; and she corresponded with many other intellectual figures in Spanish America and Spain. She also retained court protection through

186

the tenures of four Viceroys, who favored her with commissions. And Mexico, then known as New Spain, was a grand court, ostentatiously aware of itself as the richest in the Spanish world.[1]

In this pleasant environment Sor Juana embarked on a rigorous program of self-education, intensively studying literature, music, and the sciences. She made herself useful by serving as the convent's accountant, and before long was receiving numerous commissions to write poems for both religious celebrations and special events at court. She soon became a prolific writer, producing a large body of work including satire, philosophy, theology, humorous poetry (some of it "fairly raunchy," to use Harss's term), courtly love poetry, a number of skits, and a delightful full-length comedy, *Pawns of a House (Los empeños de una casa)*. During the early 1680s, she developed a particularly close friendship with the vicereine María Luisa Manrique de Lara. When her husband's term as viceroy ended in 1686, María Luisa returned to Spain, where she made arrangements to publish the first volume of Sor Juana's poetry in Madrid in 1689, on the title page of which Sor Juana was flatteringly described as "the Tenth Muse."

However, her increasing fame was soon marred by controversy. Her Jesuit confessor sternly reprimanded her for writing and publishing work on topics highly unsuitable to a cloistered nun and ordered her to give up writing. She indignantly refused this demand. Further problems arose in 1690 when her erstwhile friend the bishop of Puebla without her consent published her critique of a sermon given by the prominent Jesuit Antonio de Vieira (1608–97). In an introductory letter, which he signed with the pseudonym Sor Filotea de la Cruz, the bishop urged Sor Juana to devote herself thenceforth exclusively to religious writing. She responded by publishing her autobiography, *Reply to Sister Filotea de la Cruz,* in 1691. The *Reply* "includes a spirited defense of the right of women to study in both secular and theological matters."[2] She argues that secular studies, far from being incompatible with the religious life, can actually be of great assistance in demonstrating the truths of theology. For Sor Juana, all knowledge is a seamless whole.

These arguments fell on deaf ears. As Mexico entered a period of crisis—marked by Indian uprisings against the viceroy, attacks by English and French pirates, disastrous floods, and famine—a stern new archbishop of Mexico who opposed all frivolous pursuits and had strong traditionalist views about women's place in society brought heavy pressure to bear on Sor Juana. This time no powerful friends came to her defense. There is considerable evidence that she was also tormented by inner doubts. In 1692 she gave up writing, sold all her books and scientific instruments, and gave the money to the poor. While devotedly caring for her fellow nuns during an epidemic of plague, she fell ill herself and died on 17 April 1695.

We do not know exactly when Sor Juana wrote the *auto sacramental* entitled *Joseph's Scepter (El cetro de José)*. Ezequiel Chávez has argued that the preoccupation with human sacrifice and polygamy in the *auto*'s prologue suggests a date in the 1680s, when one of the most massive Indian rebellions of the colonial period took place, threatening to restore those practices.[3] The rebellion was provoked by the excesses of some Spanish missionaries who sought to convert the Indians to Christianity by force. The Jesuit father Alegre described their conduct as follows: "One of them wanted to become the apostle of the Tubaris. He entered their lands by surprise with five or six armed Spaniards. He and his companions lived off the Indians for some days. Willy-nilly, he baptized the infants he found at their mothers' breasts. His zeal to make the adults submit was so extreme that, when some refused baptism, he tied them up and loaded them down with chains until they begged to be baptized. . . . His imprudence lighted a fire that would not be extinguished for many years, and placed all those new Christian communities in danger of perishing."[4] Beginning in 1684 in the northwestern coastal region of Sinaloa and in the western Sierra Madre, the revolt quickly spread as far east as Casas Grandes. Many different tribes united under the leadership of the Tarahumara chief Corosia, and began to attack Spanish missions and villages at the onset of winter in 1684. Fighting would continue sporadically until 1690, resulting in many casualties on both sides and great destruction of property.

In the play's prologue Sor Juana condemns attempts to convert the Indians to Christianity by force, which are not only contrary to Christian doctrine but, as recent events have shown, counterproductive: "Oh, insane human ambition, heedless even of yourself, whom you destroy just when you think you are triumphing!" She argues instead for the use of reason and persuasion. She acknowledges that the custom of human sacrifice is deeply rooted in Indian culture and possesses a certain inner logic of its own, which Christianity must refute convincingly if it is to succeed in abolishing it. The allegorical character Idolatry is willing to accept that there is one God, but insists that this God still deserves the best of sacrifices—human beings—and further argues that human meat is the best of all and lengthens the life of those who eat it. Faith replies that the play *Joseph's Scepter* will demonstrate how Christ in the Eucharist is not only a human but a divine sacrifice—the only one capable of fully placating God—and that eating Christ's body not only lengthens life but actually makes it eternal.

The principal inspiration for *Joseph's Scepter* came from Calderón's *Sometimes Dreams Come True*. What Sor Juana seems to have found espe-

cially attractive about Calderón's *auto* was the device of having an allegorical character (Chastity) explain the hidden meaning of Joseph's life to a
bewildered onlooker (Dream)—in other words, the attempt to decipher the
true meaning underlying the apparent fortuitousness of the events of a human life. In *Joseph's Scepter* she adopts that device but tries to outdo
Calderón. Not content with merely presenting the story of Joseph, she tries
to include the whole drama of salvation history, from the Fall through God's
covenant with Abraham, the renewal of that covenant to Jacob, and a series
of other episodes in the Hebrew Bible foreshadowing the redemption. Boldly
overturning the conventions of the genre, Sor Juana reduces the ostensible
plot of her *auto* (the story of Joseph) to the merest pretext, and transfers the
dramatic interest and conflict to the chorus. Furthermore, her choice of
allegorical characters is much more astute than Calderón's. Who, she must
have asked herself, had greater reason to be troubled by the signs and por-
tents veiled in Joseph's story than Satan?

Interestingly, Calderón's chorus had consisted of a wise, virtuous, *en-
lightened* female (Chastity), who provided instruction to a dark and ambivalent male character (Dream). Sor Juana substitutes a bright male figure
(Lucifer), accompanied by four sinister females—his wife Intelligence, his
mistress Knowledge, and their illegitimate daughters Envy and Conjecture. As Descartes had done some thirty or forty years earlier, she thus
presents a model of instrumental subjectivity at the epistemological level.
That is, she distances the subject, Lucifer, not only from the natural world
but even from his own mental operations. Her characterization of those
operations is also extremely interesting. The figure at the summit of the
hierarchy is Intelligence, Lucifer's legitimate wife—yet, significantly, Intelligence is sterile. It is her inferior, Knowledge, who bears Lucifer his
illegitimate daughters, Envy and Conjecture. Lucifer's desire for knowledge is motivated principally by Envy, his envy of humankind and of the
God-man Christ. The fact that the two daughters are illegitimate is also
noteworthy, since Sor Juana herself suffered from the stigma of illegiti-
macy. Octavio Paz has pointed out that Phaethon, a major character in Sor
Juana's *Dream,* was also a bastard, and comments that "the figure fasci-
nated her because it was a transposition, in the mythic world, of her childhood situation and, indeed, her entire life. Knowledge is daring, violence. . . .
The figure of Phaethon, falling from the heights . . . is a metaphor of the
original situation: the daring that attracts the admonitions of the elders."[5]

Glimpsing the beginning of Joseph's story, Lucifer worries that it contains hints of some divine plan to redeem humanity, and he calls upon his
female companions to help him understand its meaning. Even as he does
so, however, he has little hope that Intelligence will be able to console him,

for he suspects that God allowed her to remain with him after his banishment from paradise "perhaps...just so that having such a keen understanding might heighten my suffering. When I see that man is deprived of you, even though his sin was no greater than mine, I can only assume that this was no kindness towards me." Knowledge admits that she is his "severest torment," but tries to comfort Lucifer by revealing the scene of the Fall. Rather than being reassured by this momentary triumph, Lucifer is troubled by God's reference to bread when He condemns man to earn his bread by the sweat of his brow, and even more so by God's promise to establish enmity between the serpent and the woman, and His statement that she will break his head and he will lie in wait for her heel. Like a true scholar, Lucifer ponders the different symbolic meanings associated with the heel: innocence (philosophy), freedom (Egyptian hieroglyphics), and victory (other nations); none of this augurs well, yet he is unable to decipher its true meaning. Hoping to shed some light on the subject, Intelligence then shows him the scene where God promises Abraham that in his descendants all nations will be blessed. This only exacerbates Lucifer's confusion. How could this promise come true, since the world is contaminated by sin? Undaunted, Intelligence goes on to reveal God's promise to Jacob to give him the land where he is sleeping, and Jacob's promise in return that he will serve God if God will give him "Bread for my sustenance." This new mention of bread further distresses Lucifer, as does the appearance in Jacob's dream of a ladder joining earth and heaven, which leads him to suspect that somehow God means to descend to man, or to allow man to ascend to Him. However, he cannot interpret its meaning "until [he has] had a chance to see all the premises on which it's based," so he asks Conjecture to take him back to the story of Joseph. Before doing so, however, Conjecture calls Lucifer's attention to the fact that the meaning of Joseph's name in Hebrew is "Increase of God." The name is paradoxical: if God is infinite, how can He admit of any increase? Conjecture speculates that perhaps this may refer to the addition of another nature to the Divine Essence.

Intelligence then recalls Joseph's initial dreams of superiority, which Envy used to arouse his brothers' envy, hoping they would murder him. They ultimately decided instead to sell him into slavery, and he was taken to Egypt. This may be even more effective than death in preventing God from making use of Joseph, however. Deprived of good examples, and living among idolaters, Joseph is likely to be corrupted. Knowledge then transports Lucifer to Egypt, where he witnesses Putiphar's wife's temptation of Joseph. When Joseph flees from her, Lucifer, Intelligence, and Envy intervene in the action, posing as the woman's servants. They persuade her to inform her husband that Joseph has attempted to rape her, again hoping that this will result in his death. The action is then interrupted by a brief vignette in which Jacob is shown lamenting Joseph's death. Then Pharaoh appears, complaining of a disturbing dream that his wise men have been unable to interpret. His cupbearer tells him how Joseph correctly interpreted his dream and that of Pharaoh's baker when they were in prison. Intelligence complains that the very means she had employed to bring about Joseph's death have instead brought him to good fortune. She recounts Pharaoh's dreams but says that even she doesn't understand their meaning. They then return to Pharaoh's court to hear Joseph's interpretation. A new allegorical figure, Prophecy, appears and advises Joseph: "May your mind be filled with light, may you soar on my own wings, for Heaven has come to your aid. Understanding and wisdom I bring." Though lacking Lucifer's intelligence, Joseph effortlessly gives the correct interpretation by means of infused knowledge. Lucifer hopes to discredit Joseph's interpretation by demonstrating that he could have arrived at it through some natural means, such as the famous Nilometers mentioned by Herodotus; but Intelligence points out that such natural predictions never extend more than a year into the future, while Joseph's prophecy embraces fourteen years. Joseph then appears in a triumphal chariot, acclaimed as "Savior of the World." Lucifer is horrified by this title, but Intelligence consoles him by pointing out that, after all, Joseph is only a man.

Jacob then appears, complaining to his sons of the famine, and he sends them to Egypt to buy wheat. Prophecy proclaims that Joseph is "a figure of the one who in the age to come will be the true Redeemer and will atone for Adam's sin." When his brothers arrive, Joseph tests them by accusing them of spying. Now Intelligence is sure she has trapped Joseph. Since his brothers are not really spies, he must be ignorant (in which case he is no true prophet) or lying (in which case he is unjust). Prophecy, however, points out that Intelligence has failed to understand that Joseph's words were meant figuratively, not literally, and Conjecture is forced to admit Prophecy's superiority. Lucifer then spies on the banquet Joseph offers his brothers, as Prophecy explains how every detail of the banquet foreshadows some aspect of Christ's Last Supper. Lucifer has to admit that, though knowledge is natural to him, God diminishes it or obscures it when He doesn't want him to understand a celestial mystery. Though he can attain knowledge, he can never possess true wisdom, because God "won't let a wicked soul enter there, much less [Lucifer's] rebellious spirit!"

Intelligence then informs him of how Joseph had his cup planted in Benjamin's sack and, after a final test, revealed himself to his brothers and ordered them to bring their father to him. Jacob has now come to Egypt with all his family. Intelligence argues that this is the fulfillment of Jacob's dream, when God told him not to fear going down into Egypt, for He would make of him a great people, and Joseph would close his eyes. Since neither Lucifer nor his companions can comprehend the meaning of these mysterious words, they decide to observe Jacob's deathbed blessing of his sons in the hope of obtaining some clue. That clue, though still obscure, at last appears when Jacob bows to kiss Joseph's scepter, which, according to the stage directions, "has a roll of bread on its tip."

This culminating scene, from which the *auto* derives its title, is fraught with symbolism. I believe it embodies the *auto*'s overt message: true understanding and spiritual sustenance can be won only by abject submission to the divinely instituted patriarchal order (represented by the bread extended on the tip of the phallic scepter). Despairing, Intelligence exclaims to Lucifer: "I know when I'm defeated. After all that I've seen, though the abyss may be my prison, I can only take refuge there. I'll never rest easy again. If I stay here, what I see will torture me, but if I go back there, I'll suffer the torments of imagination."

Surely this *I,* like the one that appears at the end of Sor Juana's *Dream,* expresses her own inner torment as what Stephanie Merrim has termed "the creative woman, the monster heroine."[6] Merrim has detected a similar pattern and meaning in Sor Juana's *auto El divino Narciso* (The divine Narcissus): "Eco incarnates the same powers and sins attributed to Lucero in *El cetro de José*'s conventional presentation of the Devil: Eco's helpmeets and reflectors, Soberbia (Pride) and Amor Propio (Self-Love), accompany her every move; presumptuous, she sets herself up as a false god, and considering herself Narciso's [i.e., Christ's] equal, she employs her considerable intelligence to outwit Him; this ultimately limited intelligence fails her when faced with the drama of the Eucharist."[7]

Nevertheless, I cannot altogether agree with Merrim that the "personal script" that Sor Juana "enunciates from behind the mask of theatrical conventions" is not "the overtly 'feminist' message that Sor Juana's pronouncements in the *Respuesta* regarding women would lead us to expect. . . . Hardly subversive, indeed almost self-punishing, the script militates against the [dark heroine] who displays attributes of the woman writer."[8] That is indeed the surface meaning of *Joseph's Scepter.* Nevertheless, throughout the *auto* one senses a stubborn undercurrent of resistance to the play's myopic assurance that there is a single correct answer to every question, to its smug denial of the possibility of genuine mystery and complexity in the universe. Perversely, as in Milton's *Paradise Lost,* the most interesting character in the *auto*—in fact the *only* interesting character—turns out to be Lucifer, burdened like Sor Juana herself with an intelligence that brings more pain than pleasure, and like Sor Juana doomed to constant frustration in a world where the cards were stacked against him, where his best efforts turn out always to have been in vain. It is significant that Lucifer has more than three times as many lines in the *auto* than Joseph, its ostensible protagonist. Indeed, the *auto* might more appropriately have been entitled *The Tragedy of Lucifer.* I do not believe that either Milton or Sor Juana consciously intended readers to sympathize with the fallen angel; yet clearly both were drawn to that character's courageous refusal to submit in spite of all odds, and they were unable to hide their sympathy for the devil. Again a comparison with the character Phaethon in the *Dream* is instructive. As Octavio Paz has noted, "[F]or the majority of Spanish poets of her time, Phaethon is an example of imprudence and its punishment. For Sor Juana that punishment is a consecration."[9] Georgina Sabat-Rivers concurs with Paz and observes that another character in the *Dream*, Night, appears at the end of that poem, paralleling Phaethon's appearance at its beginning, and "reinforces what she had said apropos of Phaethon." Night is (temporarily) defeated by Day, but, like Phaethon, she represents "an urge to succeed and to rebel, even though in vain, to strive to comprehend the universe, which was Sor Juana's own major aim in life."[10]

Like the proverbial Freudian slip, this same subversive message manages to insinuate itself into *Joseph's Scepter.* I believe this reflects Sor Juana's own deeply conflicted subjectivity. If, however, one wanted to argue for a more consciously subversive intention in the *auto,* a case could be made that its title and climactic episode contain the key to its own deconstruction. As is well known, the scriptural texts most often cited in condemnation of Sor Juana's intellectual activity were two verses from Paul's epistles: "Let your women keep silence in the churches: for it is not permitted unto them to speak; but they are commanded to be under obedience *[subditas],* as also saith the law" (1 Cor. 14:34), and "Let women learn in silence with all subjection" (1 Tim. 2:11). Curiously, Sor Juana adapted the title of her *auto* from a passage in the same apostle's Epistle to the Hebrews: "By faith Jacob, when he was dying, blessed both the sons of Joseph; and worshipped the tip of his scepter *[adoravit fastigium virgae ejus]*" (Heb. 11:21). This verse is based on the Septuagint's mistranslation of the Hebrew *hmmtth* in Gen. 47:31, which it vocalized as *hammatteh* (the scepter) rather than *hammittah* (the bed). The Vulgate, aware of the mistake, correctly translates the verse in Genesis as: "adoravit Israel Deum, conversus ad lectuli caput" [Israel worshipped God, turning {or bowing} toward the head of the bed]. Since she surely consulted Genesis while writing *Joseph's Scepter,* Sor Juana must have been aware of this discrepancy. Medieval and Renaissance Bible commentators, scandalized by the statement that "Israel worshipped the tip of his scepter," sought to explain it away by saying that of course the real object of Jacob's worship was God, since the scepter must have represented the reign of Christ or some such thing.[11] Sor Juana was well aware that educated spectators (Inquisitors?) might be alarmed by her literal use of the controversial verse from Hebrews, and she supports it by a reference to a commentary that spuriously attributed to Maimonides a mention of this scepter. Note, however, that she is also acutely aware that the Jewish reference may get her into even deeper water: "But just in case some curious person wants to investigate further, I'll explain that Rabbi Moses himself wrote what we said about adoring the tip of the scepter, citing Paul's words 'adoring the tip.' And even though one shouldn't fully credit the words of the rabbis, in this case, since it goes against no dogma, but rather serves to aid devotion, I've employed it."

One could argue that by basing her entire *auto* on Paul's misinterpretation of the verse from Genesis, she might be implying that the apostle could be mistaken in other areas—such as his views about the proper role of women—as well. I hesitate to aver that this was her conscious intention, yet some inner compulsion surely led her to emphasize this very unusual, decentered aspect of the story of Joseph. It is a poignant example of the struggle of the female subject *(subjecta)* to liberate herself from her status of subjection *(subdita)* to internalized models of masculine authority.

The present translation is based on the edition by Adolfo Méndez Plancarte in volume 3 *(Autos y loas)* of the *Obras completas de Sor Juana Inés de la Cruz* (Mexico City: Fondo de Cultura Económica, 1976). I have, however, deleted the scene divisions he introduced. Although the original text is entirely in verse, I have translated it in prose except for passages intended to be sung.

PROLOGUE

Characters:

Faith	Nature
The Law of Grace	Idolatry
The Natural Law	Musicians

Singing offstage. Enter, by way of four hinged platforms, Faith and the Law of Grace, Nature and Natural Law.

MUSICIANS. *(Sing:)*   The Natural Law extends greetings,
                    as the Sun greets the break of day,

to the new Sun of our Faith
who gilds the hilltops with His rays,
a salutation
joyous, festive, happy, and gay.

CHORUS. And because she brings with her
the divine Law of Grace,
Nature gladly welcomes
what she has lacked till today
devoutly and humbly prostrate.

*Now Faith and the Law of Grace enter from one side, and Natural Law
and Nature from the other.*

NATURAL LAW. Welcome, divine Grace, who have come with your divine precepts to give me the perfection I lack! Without you I have been in such ignorant darkness that even my perfections have lacked their proper luster. And thus, as a sign of the joy with which my soul celebrates your fortunate arrival,

MUSICIANS. *(Sing:)* I greet you today,
joyous, festive, happy and gay.

NATURE. Welcome, beautiful Faith, to my humble abode, unworthy of your presence; but in keeping with your words, I hope to be forgiven for my defects and errors, and thus my salutation

MUSICIANS. *(Sing:)* at your feet I lay,
devoutly and humbly prostrate.

THE LAW OF GRACE. Natural Law, you are right to celebrate my love so joyfully, for the Supreme Power has decreed that we be sisters, or, to put it better, that we be so united that there should be no distance between us, for you are a part, and I am the whole that contains it, since Natural Law is part of the Law of Grace.

FAITH. Nature, I esteem the homage you offer to my love. And since the cause for this celebration is the recent conversion of the conquered Indies, where for so many long ages you have been deprived of me in every individual who populates the vast provinces of fertile America; while you, Natural Law, have not only been separated from the Law of Grace, which is what gilds your precepts and perfects your being, but at the same time have been undeservedly trodden underfoot by blind Idolatry, whose sacrilegious altars—stained with human blood in spite of your precepts—showed that men are more barbaric than the cruelest animals (for among them there is none who turns his ferocious claws against his own kind; and among men not only is there hatred, but animosity has become an art, and rage is cultivated, for why else are swords sharpened, guns loaded with powder, lances armed with iron . . . ? Oh, insane human ambition, heedless even of yourself, whom you destroy just when you think you are triumphing!) But, to get back to the point, I was saying that the cause for this celebration was your *(to the Natural Law:)* acknowledgment that the Law of Grace has come to give you that complement you have so desired for long ages; and your *(to Nature:)* recognition that the American people, through the mouths of my ministers, have given me a happy reception. Hence I think it's only fitting that we take some action to commemorate such a glorious event.

NATURE. What I would like best is for you to demolish the altars where my blood has so often been shed.

NATURAL LAW. I agree; but I would add that, since it is repugnant to the Natural Contract for men to have so many wives, thus untying that knot that binds them together in love, I urge you to order that marriages be celebrated publicly, and decree that anyone who had several wives while he was still a gentile, now live with his first wife, provided that she is a Christian. This would be a fitting monument.

LAW OF GRACE. Both of you have spoken within the natural limitations of your discourse. You, Nature, naturally feel torn apart by the tyrannical blindness of bloody sacrifices. And you, Natural Law, have limited yourself to regretting only what violates your precepts. I, however, as the Divine Law whose primary concern is the First Cause, consider it most important to remove those sacrilegious statues of false gods from the altar, and, after purifying the altars, to place there the sacred image of Christ, which is the sovereign banner in the battles of the church that follows the Law of Grace.

FAITH. *(To the Law of Grace:)* Although all of you have spoken well, you, as highest among them, have spoken best, for he who raises an altar erects the proper monument in which deeds will endure. I too would like to contribute something to this discussion. Although I am Faith and, as such, embrace all mysteries, the Holy Eucharist is particularly designated "the Mystery of Faith." Indeed, when a single emblem is chosen to represent me, it is a Chalice with a Host. Hence, I think the best thing to do would be to place the consecrated Host on the altar, because it is the very substance rather than a mere image. Furthermore, my proposal includes all of yours; for you, Nature, aim to remove the altars, and by placing the sacrament there, they will be purified; and if you, Natural Law, seek to make the conjugal bond eternal, when people see such great majesty and realize that it is God alone who ties that knot, they will be unable to dissolve it; and if you want images of Christ to be placed on the altars, I place Christ himself there, so that my intention accomplishes all your purposes.

Law of Grace. Well said!

Natural Law. So what are we waiting for?

Faith. Only for winged squadrons to descend from the spheres.

Nature. In that case, you invoke them, Faith, for celestial cherubs will come down in response to your call.

Faith. All of you, help me, so that our invocation may be more pleasing to God; for you, Law of Grace, are my superior in that I am a single virtue, while you include them all. Thus in divided choirs repeat in your several voices:

Each one moves to one side of the stage, and they sing:

Faith. Come from the heavenly sphere!

Law of Grace. Come from the crystalline palace!

Natural Law. Come from the throne on high!

Nature. Come from the eternal abode,

Faith. subtle intelligences,

Law of Grace. spiritual substances,

Natural Law. uncircumscribed essences,

Nature. sovereign entities,

Faith. who are divided into three hierarchies,

Law of Grace. . . . and include nine choirs,

Natural Law. . . . citizens of the Empyrean,

Nature. . . . dwellers in its homeland!

ALL.   Descend at our request,
                      to measure with your wings
                      the intensity of fire
                      and the wind's traveling.

Faith sings:

FAITH.   Come, run, and fly here now,
                      and with your flames so bright
                      these altars purify
                      for such a sacrifice.

The Law of Grace sings:

Law of Grace.   Fly, run, and come here now,
                      and in sweet harmony
                      of that eternal *Sanctus*[12]
                      teach us the melody.

The Natural Law sings:

Natural Law.   Come, run, and fly here now,
                      and in your shining hues,
                      provide your divine King
                      a proper retinue.

Nature sings:

NATURE.   Come down, ye mighty hosts
and stand upon the steps
to guard the marriage bed
of Solomon the Best.[13]

Faith sings:

FAITH.   Run, fly, and come here now!

Enter Idolatry, dressed as an Indian woman.

IDOLATRY. No, Faith, you'll not get your way as long as my rage endures! In
spite of my resistance you've managed to strip me of the crown I held
so peacefully for centuries, introducing your dictatorial rule in my empires and preaching the Christian Law, but you couldn't have done it if
your weapons hadn't first violently cleared a path for you. Even the
Natural Law, which in these kingdoms seemed at odds with me, has
taken your side. And yes, it's true that almost all my people, worn down
by your aggressive propaganda, have embraced your dogmas. You may
be powerful, but I repeat that you will not succeed in obliterating my
customs—they are too deeply rooted for that! So you may see me prostrate right now, but that doesn't mean I won't be able to keep you from
demolishing the altars where human victims are sacrificed.

FAITH. Who are you? How dare you sacrilegiously interfere with our plans?

IDOLATRY. Insult me all you like! You can't keep me from defending rights I
have held for so long. I am an allegorical idea, an abstract consideration, and as such I embrace practically the entire kingdom. Therefore,
speaking on everyone's behalf, as plenipotentiary of the Indians, I'm
here to tell you that it's fine for you to brag about how many converts
now follow your holy banners, but you'd better not try to force them to
give up their ancient custom of offering sacrifices. For your purposes it
is surely sufficient that they worship only one God, destroying the statues of their former gods. Since you command them to worship the Deity, surely there is nothing wrong with their offering that Deity the best
sacrifices, which are those of human blood. In fact, it makes more sense
than ever, for if He is a higher deity, He certainly deserves the best
possible offering, so why would you deprive Him of this worship? The
error lay not in the sacrifice but rather in its object, since it was offered
to false deities. Hence all that is needed is to change that object, sacri-
ficing to the true God.

NATURE. It wasn't just the object, it was the inhumane offering. How could
anyone believe that the God Who loves us so that He gave us life and
being would enjoy seeing our suffering and death?

LAW OF GRACE. That's right, His Sovereign Majesty does not want the sinner to die but to live,[14] and live in His grace.

NATURAL LAW. Furthermore, it is very repugnant to Natural Law for men to kill men. Thereby they break the rule that says: What you do not wish for yourself, do not unto another.

IDOLATRY. Such fine discussions are beyond me. I am a barbarian. I don't have the education to answer you on your own terms. All I'm saying is that, since you've won so many victories, you should be satisfied and grant my nation this one little concession. At least let us sacrifice the captives Tlaxcala[15] sends to the Mexican empire.

NATURAL LAW. Killing even one of them would violate the Natural Law, for they are all human beings.

NATURE. And it would hurt me to see any of them die, for they all came from my womb.

LAW OF GRACE. Killing any of them would suffice to offend the Law of Grace, for he who breaks a single precept attacks the Law in its entirety.[16]

IDOLATRY. Well, you'll just have to work this out somehow, because my nation is up in arms, and I tell you on their behalf that if you won't let us offer human sacrifices, don't think you can count on our obedience.

FAITH. Why is it that you're more stubborn about that point than about other things?

IDOLATRY. For two reasons: first, we believe that only the noblest victim can placate the deities; second, there is no tastier meat than flesh that has been sacrificed. My people believe that not only is it the best food, but it lengthens the life of all who eat it. This shouldn't surprise anybody, for this is what our Indian traditions have always said.

FAITH. All right, then tell me this: if I were to show you another way you could obtain those same benefits, but in an infinitely higher degree, would you be satisfied?

IDOLATRY. Why would you want to do that, since your whole aim has been to abolish my sacrifices?

FAITH. We'll show you.

All sing:
Come, run, and fly here now,
ye substances on high,
these altars purify
for such a sacrifice!

IDOLATRY. That's just lovely, but no amount of sweet singing will get you off the hook. You promised to give me a sacrifice containing the benefits I outlined, but instead you just sing hymns I can't understand.

FAITH. It's because you don't understand them that you fail to see that in fact they contain the answer to your request.

IDOLATRY. All right, explain it to me.

FAITH. Am I right that you said what you wanted was a human sacrifice, because only that would placate the Deity and at the same time, as food, not only give pleasure but lengthen the life of those who eat it?

IDOLATRY. Yes.

FAITH. I shall place on the altars a holocaust so pure, a victim so rare, an offering so supreme that He will be not just human but divine as well. This sacrifice won't just placate the Deity; it will entirely satisfy Him. It won't just offer the momentary pleasure of a good meal, but infinite pleasure; and it won't just make your life long, it will actually make it eternal.[17]

IDOLATRY. What sacrifice could possibly do such things?

FAITH. The Holy Eucharist, in which Christ transubstantiates the bread and wine into His own body.[18]

IDOLATRY. Well, I've had some instruction from your ministers in the mysteries you order us to believe, but still I find this notion of Christ becoming meat hard to accept. If you want me to understand it, you'll have to give me a better explanation of how bread could turn into flesh and blood and produce the astonishing effects you mentioned.

FAITH. It's going to take a while, so come along with me to where you can get the instruction you need.

IDOLATRY. How? Where?

FAITH. In the sacred story of a sacramental and allegorical play, where I'll do my best to show you the prophecies that speak of this holy mystery.

IDOLATRY. What's this play called?

FAITH. *Joseph's Scepter.* His life is full of mysteries concerning bread and wheat.

IDOLATRY. Well, what are you waiting for? Come on! If you can prove to me that He is a human sacrifice that placates God, that I can eat Him, and that He will give me eternal life, as you say, then the argument is over, and you win!

LAW OF GRACE. The sooner, the better!

NATURE. Hold on! Have you forgotten that we were discussing erecting a monument?

FAITH. What better monument, what greater benefit to Faith could there be than for a soul to surrender, for on that soul is engraved the eternal laurel wreath it will attain? So all of you join your voices to mine and repeat:

Sings:	When the Holy Eucharist	
	is worshiped and praised,	
	true monuments of Faith	
	in souls are firmly raised!	
ALL.	When the Holy Eucharist	
	is worshiped and praised,	
	true monuments of Faith	
	in souls are firmly raised!	

Characters:

Jacob	Gad	[Eve]
Joseph	Asher	[Abraham]
Reuben	Naphtali	Prophecy
Simeon	Benjamin	Putiphar's Wife
Levi	Lucifer	Pharaoh
Judah	Intelligence	Cupbearer
Zebulun	Knowledge	A Crowd
Issachar	Envy	Majordomo
Dan	Conjecture	Musician
	[Adam]	

Offstage voice: Throw the dreamer in the pit! If we decide to kill him, we'll see what good his dreams do him.

Enter Joseph's brothers.

JUDAH. Now that he's down in that cistern, and we've stripped him of his fancy tunic, which was what made us mad in the first place, what's the point of killing him? We'd only have his blood on our hands. You know, Ishmaelite merchants with camels laden with fragrances and resins from Gilead are also passing by here on their way to Egypt. Why not sell him to them as a slave? That way we wouldn't have to dirty our hands, and we'd accomplish our goal of getting him out of our father's sight. *(Aside:)* I'm trying to prevent the greater evil of his death.

REUBEN. Judah, we all accept your advice, so let's go and sell him.

Exeunt.

Enter Intelligence, Knowledge, Lucifer, Envy, and Conjecture.

LUCIFER. Lovely Intelligence, my wife, ever since that first happy day when I came into being in that happy sphere, you and Envy have been my constant companions through all my ups and downs. You've been so kind, so faithful, and so loving that you were not ashamed to stay with me at that terrible moment when Beauty and Grace abandoned me to stay by the Supreme Throne. You alone, always constant, went down with me to the abyss. Perhaps it was just so that having such a keen understanding might heighten my suffering. When I see that man is deprived of you, even though his sin was no greater than mine, I can only assume that this was no kindness towards me.[19]

CONJECTURE. Your own Conjecture could have told you that, for I'm the daughter you had by your mistress Knowledge. I'll help you draw your own conclusions.

ENVY. And I'll make you wish you hadn't, for I am Envy. I'm your daughter too, even if I am an asp that slithers around your burning breast eating up your guts. I've been your favorite ever since your perverted Knowledge aborted once too often. Yes, I'm your favorite of all the vices you employ for different purposes in your ceaseless war with heaven.

LUCIFER. Yes, yes, that's right. Could we drop this pointless argument and get to the matter I wanted to discuss with you? I think we've established that it was no act of kindness or mercy on God's part to leave me with Knowledge, nor was being deprived of it a major punishment for man. I'll continue now, and you will see how in the cases to follow—which also foreshadow things that are yet to be—in different ways God has given man obscure hints that there may be some hope for his redemption; and as the ages have gone by, God has indeed given him possibilities of appeal, whereas my own sentence was irrevocable. Even though it seems hard to believe, I can't escape the conclusion that God intends to save man, while I am eternally damned to suffer for one sin. I'm especially troubled by the strange new sign represented by this handsome young man whose brothers just cruelly sold him. I'm not sure what it is I see in him. I don't know what to think. What is it that he stands for or mysteriously prefigures? I'm like someone squinting to try to figure out what a faraway painting is supposed to represent. Since I can't ignore him, I've decided to call on you, Knowledge, to see whether between the two of us we may be able to figure something out. Since distance and time have no bearing on your idea, let's turn back the clock and return to an earlier age where we may be able to pick up some hint that Conjecture can then use to help me decide whether my gloomy forecast is correct.

KNOWLEDGE. Lucifer, you were right when you said that I'm your severest torment. What better proof could there be than that now you're ordering me to renew your pains by examining the times and signs that presage good for man and bad for you? Anyhow, since you've asked me to do it, and your wish is my command, I'll start with the part that may give you some comfort, for it would be silly of me not to offer you what little comfort I can. And since Knowledge has the rhetorical license to fabricate and form visible representations of invisible objects, turn now your eyes towards Paradise, and you will see how God Himself spoke to fragile clay in its tragic sinfulness, saying. . . . But let God speak for Himself.

The cart representing Paradise opens, revealing Adam and Eve, and an offstage voice sings:

MUSICIAN. *(Voice of God):*

> Foolish, blind, and mad,
> you chose to honor Eve,
> ignoring my command,
> preferring her caprice.
> You chose to eat the fruit
> of that forbidden tree—
> the only one I banned
> to test your loyalty.
> From now on you will eat
> herbs that are hard to grow,
> seasoned with your fatigue,
> with hard work and with woe.
> Cursed will be the land:
> instead of tasty fruit,
> it will give your weary arms
> thorns as its produce.
> Your bread will cost you dear.
> Sweat will run down your brow
> until to dust you go,
> as dust you are even now.[20]

LUCIFER. Hold on, for I'm not sure why this mention of bread disturbs me, nor exactly what it foreshadows. What bread is this that will require so much sweat? For if man is sentenced to eat grass, which the earth will produce without the exertion of the plow, what purpose is there in assigning him another form of nourishment? But never mind; if you will, Knowledge, tell me my sentence, though I may weep to hear it.

KNOWLEDGE. You will hear it better represented in the idea that has already taken shape.

MUSICIAN. *(Voice of God:)*

> For causing so much evil,
> you will certainly be cursed

> among brutes and animals;
> and, to make matters worse,
> with shame your very breast
> will serve you in place of feet:
> you'll slither without rest.
> Dirt alone will serve you
> as unappetizing food,
> and between you and woman,
> eternal hate will brood.
> Victorious, she will break
> your stiff neck and your pride,
> while, always at her heel,
> to trip her you will strive.[21]

ENVY. It's easy to see that God's sole intent is to do you an eternal wrong; for, although He is angry on account of man's sin, He doesn't curse him, but the earth and you, unfairly calling you cursed among all beasts.

CONJECTURE. Hence I can conjecture that He means to provide him with a remedy in the future. This is obvious from His plan to provoke hatred between you and woman, so that she and her offspring will break your head. Oh, what a delicious irony! Consider it if you can, for this is a point that calls for Intelligence.

INTELLIGENCE. I am Intelligence, but it does me little good, for all my discourse falters when I try to figure out what hidden mystery that clause contains. It seems to me illogical that woman, who has already entered my domain through sin, could then be able to vanquish me. She is a slave; so how could she make me grovel under her heel? What offspring of hers could dare oppose me, since they are all doomed to slavery? For the son of a slave must be a slave himself by irrevocable decree. So how can this be? Heaven help me! With what confused veil has God covered this stupendous secret, so that I glimpse its meaning but can't fully understand it?

LUCIFER. Not only that, but you don't explain how I would lie in wait for her foot or heel, which your light informs me symbolizes many different things: for philosophy in its wisdom considers it a symbol of innocence; while in Egypt it has been a fearful hieroglyphic thought to represent freedom; and other nations have considered it an emblem of victory. Oh, memory! How it pains me for my Intelligence to see it signify freedom, victory, and innocence. Conjecture, what can you infer?

CONJECTURE. Much and little.

ENVY. I've seen enough to suspect that it is for man's good; so we must hasten to do him harm.

LUCIFER. That's just what I'm trying to do. But, so that I can proceed with all due caution, Intelligence, show me another figure, and let's see what your discourse makes of it.

The cart of Adam closes; and that of Abraham opens, revealing a starry sky.

ABRAHAM. Lord, if I die without sons, what good can You do me? For only a son could be my heir. You have given me no offspring, so, luckless as I am, I'll have to leave my house to my servant.

> *A voice sings offstage (Voice of God):*
> Have no more fear of that;
> your son shall be your heir.
> If you could only count
> the stars in heaven so fair,
> so great will be your offspring,
> too numerous to guess!
> In your distinguished lineage
> all nations will be blessed.[22]

LUCIFER. Enough, Intelligence! Take it away! What lineage can be blessed, since the world is already contaminated by sin?

INTELLIGENCE. Let's see another figure, and hear what you infer from it, Conjecture.

Another cart opens; in it appears Jacob asleep at the foot of the ladder, and at the top of the ladder, the Lord; an offstage voice sings.

MUSICIAN. *(Voice of God:)*
> The God of Abraham
> and your father Isaac lives.
> This land whereon you sleep
> to you I will surely give.
> Your offspring will exceed
> the sands that are in the sea,
> and in your seed and you
> all nations blessed shall be.

> *Jacob awakens and gets up.*

JACOB. Surely God is in this place, but in my ignorance I was unaware of it. This is no doubt the house of God and gate of heaven. Therefore, if God will protect me on the journey I must make, and give me bread for my sustenance, the Lord will be my God. And the rock I have set up as an altar will be called the Lord's house; and of all that His kindness gives me, I shall sacrifice a tithe.[23]

> *Exit Jacob.*

LUCIFER. Intelligence, what is this?

INTELLIGENCE. Why are you upset?

LUCIFER. Because God has repeated that blessing, and once again that reference to bread fills me with horror and sad foreboding. What can be the meaning of that mysterious ladder that joins high heaven and earth, so that anyone who wishes can go up there; for that gate was firmly locked by original sin? And not only—be still, my heart!—does it provide a passageway from earth to heaven, but from man to God, which is what I fear most! For if you take a good look at both ends of the ladder, you can see (oh, how shocking!) that God is at one end, and man is at the other. Hence, if man goes up or God comes down, that can only mean . . . No, I just don't understand it, and I don't want to ponder it now until I've had a chance to see all the premises on which it's based. But all these figures concern what is past. In order for you to draw your inferences and reach the conclusion we already suspect, let's put aside these noteworthy events of the past, while keeping them in mind for future reference, and get back to the present. This boy Joseph . . .

CONJECTURE. Hold on! You need to pay attention to that name.

LUCIFER. What's so special about the name of Joseph that causes you so much alarm?

KNOWLEDGE. The fact that it means "increase of God."

LUCIFER. That is indeed a mystery. However, since the infinite cannot increase or decrease, I can't accept it. Even if Joseph does mean "increase of God," it must be an increase that He gives, not one that He receives.

INTELLIGENCE. Fine, but I still suspect . . .

KNOWLEDGE. What could you possibly suspect?

CONJECTURE. Why is it that, though heaven puts mysteries everywhere, this one particularly attracts my attention? I wish I could explain it, but I can't, for it's a very subtle point that even your intelligence can't comprehend. What I mean is that I can't help fearing that, even though the divine essence is infinite, it admits of another nature, which—although it would not in any way increase its greatness—because it didn't have it before, could be termed an "increase." Who can doubt it? And without ceasing to be what it always has been, it could receive a being that it didn't have before.

ENVY. Hush! Don't go on, for you're only increasing my fury!

INTELLIGENCE. Then let's go back to Joseph. You've already seen the mysterious dreams he had, that in one he saw the stars, sun, and moon with their glorious lights bow down to him; and in the other he saw how all the sheaves bowed down and gladly humbled themselves before him. And on account of that, his envious brothers . . .

ENVY. . . . incited inhumanely by my rage, decided to murder him. But Judah, opposing such a bloody plan, commuted the sentence of death to that of being sold, which will be even worse for him. For not only will he suffer the vile treatment of a slave, but once he's there, all manner of vices will be able to overtake him. For who can doubt that even the most righteous man will change his customs when he lives among idolaters? Surrounded daily by so many infidels, some of their ways will surely stick to him. Thus, at least we've managed to separate him from good examples, and it's been my experience that few men can do good without a model. But let's just go there, since distance cannot daunt us.

KNOWLEDGE. That's right, for when we see him, it will be all the easier for us to vanquish him.

CONJECTURE. What are we waiting for? Let's go to Egypt!

INTELLIGENCE. Let's go!

Exeunt.
Enter Putiphar's Wife and Joseph.

WIFE. Wait, you handsome Hebrew! If my beauty and grace are not enough to attract you, if the treasures of Arabia in my golden curls won't hold you captive—after all, I realize they're but soft chains; if the rays from my eyes, the silver of my forehead, the rubies in my mouth, or my pearly cheeks don't move you or excite you or make you fall in love, I realize they are ephemeral beauties that must render tribute to time. Still, you should be moved by the surrender of my soul, for the soul's treasures are immortal. Don't run away, Joseph! Wait! At least turn your face to me. Look at me, for you won't sully your chastity by looking. Turn your eyes to me!

JOSEPH. No, I won't, for he who doesn't control his eyes won't be able to control his heart, since he's flinging the door wide open! I must not permit my eyes to look at what I am not permitted to desire. Even though the commandment doesn't include looking, since sight provides species to the soul that arouse its desire and stir up its flames, if I ever take them in, I'll never be able to erase them, and it will be hard to resist them. It would be foolhardy for me to let my enemy into my own house.

WIFE. All right then, you ingrate! If sweetness and affection can't win over your ungrateful nature, I'll just take you by force, like this . . . !

JOSEPH. Get away! Let go of me!

WIFE. Let go of you? Not until I . . .

JOSEPH. Heaven help me!

Enter Prophecy, who separates them; Joseph runs away, leaving
Putiphar's Wife alone.

PROPHECY. Here I am, for Heaven never fails those who call upon it. Run, Joseph! For God only defends those who defend themselves.

Joseph runs away.

WIFE. The ungrateful boy ran away, but he left his cape here in my hands. What new madness incites me? All my love has turned to rage. Help, servants, family!

Enter Lucifer, Intelligence, and Envy.

LUCIFER. We have been waiting on Putiphar disguised as servants of his household, so that we could more conveniently watch this woman, who has been chasing him with my encouragement. Since she's calling us, let's go and see what's happened.

WIFE. Help! Is there no one else at home? Help! Is there no one to help me?

They all come in.

INTELLIGENCE. Here we are. What do you want?

WIFE. What do you think? Do you recognize this cape?

ALL. Of course; it belongs to the slave.

WIFE. Well (I'm out of breath!), that circumcised traitor tried (I'm so upset!) to rape and dishonor me! He tried to destroy my reputation with flattery, but I resisted nobly, and the cowardly traitor left his cape in my hands when he heard me crying for help. This cape is evidence that I'm telling the truth.

SERVANT 1: What are you saying? What impudence!

SERVANT 2: What ignoble boldness!

INTELLIGENCE. A servant tried to rape you?

ENVY. A peasant dared offend you?

LUCIFER. *(Aside, to his companions:)* Let's push this fraud to the limit, to see if by doing so we can bring an end to this Hebrew's life and the fears he's inspired in me.

INTELLIGENCE. An excellent idea. Since this foolish woman thinks we are her servants (when in fact we were the very ones who incited her to tempt Joseph to sin), and since he chastely fled from her, spoiling all our plans, now let's use this as a pretext to kill him, and thereby remedy all our worries. Go to it, Lucifer!

LUCIFER. Yes, indeed. *(To Putiphar's Wife:)* Madam, this disloyalty, which brought such a base person to violate the decorum due to your person and proper respect for your house, is such a weighty crime that not even his life could pay for it.

WIFE. Then what shall I do?

INTELLIGENCE. Tell your husband, so that he can avenge this crime by taking his life.

WIFE. That's a very good suggestion.

INTELLIGENCE. All your servants will take up this cause. Let's go to see that this traitor quickly pays for his infamy by public execution!

(Each one aside.)

WIFE. Thus I'll pay him back for the insult of rejecting me.

LUCIFER. Thus, when he dies, I'll put an end to the signs that are killing me.

INTELLIGENCE. Thus, by his death I'll defend myself against the fears he causes me.

ENVY. Thus, I'll relieve my rage by doing him this outrage. Let's go then, and let the traitor die!

WIFE. Let him die, since he's killing me!

Exeunt. Enter Jacob and the brothers.

JACOB. There can be no comfort for me, since I lost my son; and even all my grief is not equal to what I've lost. His mother—alas, my love! Alas, my dearest Rachel!—called his brother Ben-oni (which means "son of my sorrow"), a name that doesn't suit him and would have been more appropriate for Joseph. You died in that agony that Heaven destined for you, but at least you had the comfort of knowing that in dying, you gave life to Benjamin. But I am fated to cope with a greater pain, which I can't exchange for one I would have chosen. Even if I die, it won't bring Joseph back.

JUDAH. Father, don't grieve so much! If a wild beast killed him, and it's already done, what good will all your grieving do?

REUBEN. It frightens me to see your pain.

ZEBULUN. You've wept enough; now stop!

JACOB. I will not! As long as I live, I will carry this pain in my soul, and I will go down to the abyss weeping for my son Joseph!

Exeunt; and enter Pharaoh and his cupbearer and retinue.

MUSICIANS. *(They sing:)*

> Long may great Pharaoh live!
> May his inherited glory
> be o'ershadowed by his deeds,
> and let all recount his story,
> for he is the living emblem
> of the honor and the glory
> that Egypt so admires.
> Hurrah, hurrah for Pharaoh!

PHARAOH. What good is all this glory and honor if a dream can ruin it and an apprehension can take it all away?

CUPBEARER. Great Lord, what trouble could there be in all the world worth your lofty soul's concern? What could oppress your august heart? Your strength is so sublime, your nature so invincible; could any pain suffice to bring you down? Enjoy yourself!

PHARAOH. How can I? In all the Egyptian science of my soothsayers, there is none who can decipher the obscure enigma of my two dreams. Mysteriously, they hint at both misfortune and prosperity. At once they offer severe admonitions and compassionate advice, and I don't know whether this concerns me or my kingdom. Does it affect my grandeur or my very life? I infer from this that heaven wants me to avoid the damage—for sometimes, when bad things are foreseen, one can limit the harm they do—or else to prepare a remedy—for some misfortunes can actually be avoided by preventive measures. But either way I look at this misfortune—whether it be contingent or necessary—there is no way I can take such measures, since I don't know the form the misfortune will take. One who doesn't know the misfortune, no matter how much it disturbs him, can hardly take steps to prevent it or even have the necessary patience to endure it.

CUPBEARER. My lord, let me give you a piece of advice (and in it I confess a sin of ingratitude on my part, for I should certainly have remembered a youth who gave me the good news that I would survive). Know that, when I and another member of your household were in jail, a Hebrew lad was imprisoned there with us. Each of us dreamed two dreams, and when we told them to each other in the morning, the Hebrew gave different interpretations of them, which have actually come true. As he predicted, the other man was executed; while I, as he announced, returned to my former dignity. Hence, Great Lord, you may be sure that he will tell you the mysteries in your dreams if you inform him of them, for I have seen no truer spirit of prophecy.

PHARAOH. So what are you waiting for? Go get him, and we'll see if he predicts the truth for me, as he did for you.

CUPBEARER. Your wish is my command.

PHARAOH. Be off then, and I'll await him here.

CUPBEARER. In the meantime, let the musicians play.

MUSICIANS.: Long may great Pharaoh live!, *etc.*

Exeunt to the sound of music.
Enter Intelligence, Knowledge, and Lucifer.

INTELLIGENCE. Lucifer, can you believe my bad luck? The very means I so cleverly chose to end this Hebrew's hateful life have brought him to greater exaltation! Since God assists him and gives him knowledge of the future, can there be any doubt that now He will also tell him the meaning of Pharaoh's dreams? In his dreams Pharaoh saw seven shining cows—fat, healthy, and beautiful ones—grazing on the green banks of the Nile. These were followed by another seven, which were so hungry, skinny, and ill favored that, emptying that field, they gobbled up the first ones voraciously. But what was even stranger was that, after all that food, they ended up just as jaundiced, pale, and skinny as before. His other dream, which was very similar to the first one, was of a fertile branch on which sprouted seven green and gorgeous ears of wheat; and after them another seven, so parched and withered that one could hardly recognize in them even the beard of an ear of grain. And the same thing happened with the ears of grain as with the cows; all dried up, so that no trace of the previous abundance remained. Among all the soothsayers of Egypt, none has been found who can understand what event the mysterious order and number in this enigma foretell. It's obvious that it's not just a product of his fantasy, because it is so orderly and consistent; for two different hieroglyphics portray two different misfortunes, each one confirming the other and proving that it is not a natural dream. Of course the wise men will be unable to divine its meaning, since even I, who am the only one who could provide it, don't understand.

LUCIFER. Then we must pay close attention to his reply. And since, as I've already pointed out, no distance can daunt me, no obstacle can hinder me, let's see in this perspective what he answers Pharaoh.

INTELLIGENCE. Let's hear his prophecy.

Pharaoh appears on a throne; Joseph is standing before him; and Prophecy, on a balcony, sings.

PROPHECY. *(Sings:)*

> Oh Joseph, hearken and hear
> how enlightenment comes from me.
> Sacred Prophecy seizes your soul,
> so hearken, and listen, and see!
> Open the eyes of your mind
> and see what is yet to be.
> The dream I will help you explain
> in all of its mystery,
> so hearken, and listen, and see!
> May your mind be filled with light,
> may you soar on my own wings,
> for heaven has come to your aid.
> Understanding and wisdom I bring,
> so hearken, and listen, and see!

JOSEPH. *(To Pharaoh:)* It is not I who answers you, my lord, but God who advises you that this dream is one and the same, for it has only one meaning. The cows and the ears of grain stand for the same thing, which is that seven years are to come in Egypt so plentiful, so rich in crops, that your barns and granaries won't be able to hold the seeds. But after that, the good times will change to bad, and fortune into misfortune. There will come another seven years so sterile that there can be no sowing or reaping in all these provinces. Therefore, Great Lord, you would be wise to provide a remedy by storing up the surplus fruits of the seven plentiful years in barns so that, when the shortage comes, your kingdom will have sustenance.

LUCIFER. Intelligence, that's enough! Take it away! Draw that mortal curtain, for I can't bear this torture any longer!

The curtain closes on the scene.

Now tell me: Though God clarifies for this man the obscure lines of the future, could he have deduced what's to come by the use of unaided reason?

INTELLIGENCE. No, for if there were any indications in the aspects of the heavens, or the prevailing winds, or the temperatures that differentiate climates, or other such hidden causes, men would be able to figure out the event they foretell, although they wouldn't fully understand. For example, the Egyptians can tell by the rising and falling of the Nile what kind of crops they will have. They can determine this by examining some wells into which the Nile flows. When the Nile is at high tide, if the wells rise no higher than twelve cubits, it is an indication of sterility; but if it exceeds seventeen cubits, it indicates a bumper crop.[24] If any of these natural signs had occurred, they would have been able to figure it out, either through their acquired knowledge or natural reason or skill in astrology, which is a human conjecture, not divine revelation. In that case I would have understood it better than he, and would have informed the soothsayers. Furthermore, it is impossible to predict events so far in the future on the basis of the Nile's currents. At best, that would enable one to predict a single year. But what do you care about that, for it's beside the point?

LUCIFER. Just to see whether in the future I might be able to use such reasoning to discredit his truth with my lies, and make him look like a false prophet. For surely someone will say that it was just natural science.

KNOWLEDGE. In his reply he already foresaw and frustrated your intent, because he affirmed that it was God who replied. But listen, for the people are joyfully acclaiming him, crying out with a single voice.

Offstage voice: May he rule and enjoy, triumph and live happily!

Enter Joseph in a triumphal chariot, with a retinue and musicians.

MUSICIANS. *(Singing:)*
>The Savior of the World
>in his kindness and compassion
>has redeemed all Egypt
>from a great misfortune.
>Therefore, let all acclaim him
>in this most joyous fashion:

ALL. may he rule and enjoy, triumph and live happily!

MUSICIANS. Because he dressed so humbly,
>appearances deceived us.
>If we had called him prophet,
>who would have believed us?
>The wicked sought to hurt him,
>but their arrows ricocheted,
>and now, to their annoyance,
>his virtue is repaid.
>So come bow down to him
>and while on bended knee,
>his scepter's ears of grain,
>acclaim triumphantly,
>repeating joyfully:

ALL. may he rule and enjoy, triumph and live happily!
>*The chariot turns around and leaves the stage.*

LUCIFER. Intelligence, what is this? I'm running out of life and patience. Let the depths now hide me! I can't bear to hear those words: "Savior of the World."

INTELLIGENCE. Calm down. Remember, he's only a man.

LUCIFER. Oh, woe is me! What difference does that make? How many signs must you see before you come to the conclusion that God means to redeem the world?

INTELLIGENCE. Let's follow the parade to have a closer look.
>*Enter Jacob and his sons.*

Offstage voice: All you who live in Canaan, beg Heaven for relief! We've eaten all the food, and now we're perishing of hunger!

Offstage voice 1: Heaven, have pity!

Offstage voice 2: Ye gods, look kindly on us!

Offstage voice 3: Help us, we're perishing!

JACOB. What is this, sons? Don't you hear the wretched laments of our poor family, who cry out so woefully while being hacked to pieces by this terrible drought? Then why are you so negligent? Since you know they're selling wheat in Egypt, why don't you go there and use our money to redeem the misfortune of lack of sustenance? Besides having heard this, we have seen proof, for the river's currents are full of straw.[25]

JUDAH. We were only awaiting your command, sir.

JACOB. Well, now you have it. Go prepare your camels to bring back wheat. You can all go except my dear Benjamin. Since he's the smallest, I'm afraid some accident might happen on the road, and I don't want to put him at risk.

REUBEN. Let him stay then, and the rest of us will go and obey you.

JACOB. Go, and I will stay here praying to the God of Abraham and Isaac to prosper your journey.

Exeunt. Enter Prophecy.

PROPHECY. See how from His throne on high, God's infinite majesty has sent me to the world, for I am His spirit of prophecy. I have come to help Joseph, for God wants to make of him a sort of foreshadowing or figure of the one who in the age to come will be the true redeemer and will atone for Adam's sin, paying God's justice an infinite price. He will release man from the chains of original sin by serving at once as priest and sacrifice. He will nourish humankind on sovereign wheat. This man prefigures him, for God wills to leave a testament of the former age in His scripture, so that later they'll be able to compare the figure to the one he prefigured, and will understand the mystery contained in this. Also, until that happy day comes, this figure will give them hope. Furthermore, as I can see from here—for neither distance nor the darkness of the whole wide future can resist my keen view—that disobedient people will one day seek to deny His son made man, and thus they will be condemned by the testimony stored up against them. For I, as God's clear trumpet, will always be crying out in the mouth of one prophet or another, and confirming one event by another, so that their fierce rage will be unable to deny me, no matter how much they want to. But, to get back to Joseph, I've come to help him, so that the world will see in him the living idea of the savior. Invisibly I shall enter his spirit, so that as a true prophet, he can diffuse his predictions through the world. But here he comes! I'll hide here. He won't be able to see me, though I am right beside him.

Enter Joseph and a number of commoners.

JOSEPH. Open the barns, open those abundant granaries that my prudence has provided for the people's nourishment.

FIRST MAN. Great savior of Egypt!

SECOND MAN. Great governor of the kingdom!

FIRST MAN. The king has sent us to you . . .

SECOND MAN. . . . that you may give us food.

FIRST MAN. Sell us wheat, for you can see . . .

SECOND MAN. . . . that we are dying of hunger.

ALL. You are the father of our land, and as such, our father. Give us our daily bread![26]

PROPHECY. Other, nobler impulses will give voice to these same words in another, happier time, when bread will be elevated to serve as nourishment for both body and soul.

JOSEPH. That's just what I've saved it for. Take it, and pay the overseers for the wheat, so they can put the money in the royal treasury.

FIRST MAN. Heaven grant that you live eternal ages!

SECOND MAN. May your good fortune never wane!

      The commoners leave. Enter Joseph's brothers.

JUDAH. We kneel before you, Great Viceroy!

LEVI. We kneel to offer our homage, Lofty Prince! We are ten wretched foreigners who beg for your assistance.

JOSEPH. *(Aside:)* Heaven help me! What is this I see? These are my brothers! But I must hide my feelings, though my heart wants to jump out of my breast.

      (To his brothers:) Tell me: Where are you from?

JUDAH. My lord, our homeland is Canaan, and we have come from there to buy food, for we have nothing to eat.

JOSEPH. *(Aside:)* My dreams are coming true!

      (To his brothers:) I'm certain you are spies, and you have come here to discover the weak points in our defenses.

LEVI. No, Great Lord! We have not come for any such evil purpose, but only to buy provisions. Don't judge your servants thus, for we are all sons of one father, and we are doing nothing dishonest.

JOSEPH. That is not true. I know you've come to find the places that are ill guarded, and see what offensive and defensive weapons we have here.

REUBEN. No, my lord! You see here twelve brothers of an aged father. The smallest one stayed behind as companion to our father in his old age, and the other one who is missing is dead.

JOSEPH. I'm certain that you are spies. To catch you with your own words, you will all be imprisoned here. And, by Pharaoh, whom I venerate, you will not leave until that brother you mentioned comes here. Therefore, let one of you go at once for him; and the others will be my prisoners until I find out whether what you told me is true. Guards, imprison them at once!

LEVI. *(Aside, to his brothers:)* We deserve to suffer like this, for we cruelly failed to heed our brother Joseph's laments, and that's why heaven chose to put us through this pain.

REUBEN. Didn't I tell you you were doing wrong? But you refused to listen to me, and now we will pay for his blood.

JOSEPH. Take them away while I find out the truth.

Exeunt. Enter Conjecture.

CONJECTURE. I'm looking for Lucifer, for I can never be away from him for even a second. But, since I have permission to make myself visible, I function as a necessary substance of his being, using indispensable human speech as a character in a play. If the words are rightly understood, they don't hinder the intelligent, and the ignorant need them badly. I said I was looking for Lucifer, because for once I have some good news for him. But here he comes with Intelligence. Because she is so wise, she always precedes me in order of operation, for she is the first to discern causes and effects and circumstances. I follow right behind, drawing inferences from the propositions I've understood. Doubtless, she's already told him what's going on, but I'll join them anyway just in case there's any need for inference.

Enter Lucifer and Intelligence.

INTELLIGENCE. It seems to me that Joseph has either lied or else he's mistaken, for he called his brothers spies and ordered them imprisoned until they tell the truth. But here is Conjecture, just the one you were looking for!

LUCIFER. Well, let's see what she thinks.

CONJECTURE. You needn't take the trouble to repeat what I've seen for myself; for there's nothing more annoying than having to hear someone repeat what you already know. You have proposed that Joseph is lying, or he's mistaken, for he must either know or not know that they are his brothers. If he knows who they are, he's falsely treating them as enemies, saying that they are spies, and he has repeated that lie no less than three times. If he doesn't know who they are, then he must be mistaken. These two premises lead me to infer that he is either guilty or ignorant. If he doesn't know who they are, then he's no prophet; and if he does, then he's unjust.

INTELLIGENCE. You make a strong case there, for it's a dilemma containing both affirmation and negation. But my knowledge won't be satisfied, nor will I have any rest, until I can see where his fault lies.

Enter Prophecy.

PROPHECY. There is no fault in him.

LUCIFER. Who are you, sovereign beauty? Your face and your words are terrifying. How can I be frightened by such beauty?

PROPHECY. I am God's spirit of prophecy, Joseph's companion. To show you that you're the one who's wrong when you accuse him of being guilty or ignorant, I say that you are both guilty and ignorant yourself. Joseph knows perfectly well that they are his brothers, and when he calls them spies, he doesn't mean it literally but figuratively.

CONJECTURE. Then explain how you can defend him when he tells them that if they don't bring Benjamin, by Pharaoh's life, he swears that they are spies. In that case he's not merely affirming, but actually swearing!

PROPHECY. It's all the same. If they don't keep the bargain, he will treat them as spies, and he will punish them as such for violating his command.

CONJECTURE. Yes, but . . .

PROPHECY. Go ahead.

CONJECTURE. There's a noose around my neck!

PROPHECY. Why don't you go on?

CONJECTURE. Because you're stifling my voice. Lucifer, let's get out of here, for your Conjecture is no match for Prophecy!

Exeunt.

PROPHECY. Ungrateful creature, how vain is your pride and arrogance! Your conjecture can never match my high judgments.

Enter the Majordomo and Joseph's brothers.

MAJORDOMO. Come on in. Don't be afraid, for you've kept your promise to bring your brother here. My master appreciates that so much that he's given orders that you should dine at his table today.

REUBEN. Sir, the reason we're afraid is that we found all the money we paid you for the wheat in our sacks while we were on our way home, and we have no idea how it got there. We're returning it to you now, so that you won't suspect we could have been so wicked as to rob you. We've also brought more money so you will sell us another load of wheat.

MAJORDOMO. This must be some miracle your God has done; for I still have the money you gave me on account. Come on inside. My master is waiting for you to wash your feet, so that you can be clean when you eat.

Exeunt. Enter Lucifer.

LUCIFER. No matter how much Prophecy threatens me, my pride will not surrender! I'll keep an eye on this supper from here. I don't know what it is that's bothering me. Now I see them all sitting down at the table. Damn! What sort of supper is this? They're all eating, but Benjamin has a bigger portion. But I hear Prophecy singing, and even though I understand only the letter and not the meaning, I'd better listen anyway.

The curtain opens, revealing a table. Joseph and all his brothers are sitting there. Prophecy is on the balcony.

PROPHECY. *(Sings:)*

> This table of another table,
> these twelve men of another twelve
> are symbols by which God has chosen
> His true promise to foretell.
> Come to the table, come to the table!
> Prophecy has set this table
> to foretell that other one,
> which for mankind God will set
> in His unfathomable wisdom.
> This bread, fruit of human striving,
> sustains, and with it man is fed,
> but that other bread of life is
> when it ceases to be bread.
> Here Benjamin, beloved brother,
> receives a meal by far the best.
> Another Benjamin in future
> will be preferred to all the rest.[27]
> While here they wash their feet with care,
> it cleanses but their bodies mean,
> but baptism will wash their souls,
> and then from sin they will be clean.
> Come to the table, come to the table!

The curtain closes on the table, and Lucifer alone remains onstage.

LUCIFER. Heavens, what are these enigmas? What other table? What other twelve men is she talking about? And if divine wisdom is planning a dinner, why did she mention no food but bread? Wouldn't royal magnificence want to show off by serving the most exquisite, royal, and costly delicacies? Yet she mentioned only the most common food. And even if it were so fortunate as to be considered the best of foods, wouldn't He make it of the richest and most substantial wheat and protect it from humidity? If so, then why—oh, I'm so confused!—did she say it would cease to be bread? If it decays and takes some other form, having repudiated the first one, then after its transformation, it won't any longer be bread. In that case, why did she call it "bread of life"? It's easy to understand how bread can cease to be bread and turn into something else when it decays, for that is consistent with nature's order of successive mutations of matter. But how can it be bread, yet not bread? Who can resolve these contradictions? But I hear singing far away. Let's see what it's saying.

Offstage, Prophecy sings:

PROPHECY.   Joseph's brothers are one thing,
             and yet they seem to be another,
             though they are in fact his brothers,
             that they are spies it is apparent.
             God Almighty can distinguish
             substance from mere accident.

LUCIFER. Heavens, now you're offering me still another dark enigma? I'm
still reeling from the first one, and now you oppress me with another.
I'm so confused, so dumbfounded to hear this that I seem to be missing
my Intelligence, and my Knowledge isn't working. But who could doubt
it? For whenever God wills, He darkens my knowledge and confounds
my reasoning. Although knowledge is a natural gift in me, which I can
never lose, it can at least be diminished and darkened, when God doesn't
want me to know something, especially when it has to do with His celestial secrets, which are called wisdom. He won't let a wicked soul
enter there, much less my rebellious spirit! I'm utterly amazed! This is
all so confusing! What cruel darkness clouds the keen light of my angelic mind!

Enter Intelligence.

INTELLIGENCE. What's going on, Lucifer? Where have you been? It seems
I've been separated from you, and you don't seem to be yourself. What
has distracted you? What's the matter? What are you worrying about?

LUCIFER. Why are you asking me if you don't know yourself? Oh, damn my
knowledge or my ignorance, for both of them offend me—one with
what it knows, and the other with what it can't understand!

INTELLIGENCE. Well, Lucifer, you may already know this, but listen to me
anyway. After Joseph prepared that famous banquet, whose circumstances puzzled you so much that they deprived you of me—maybe
someone understands all that!—he kindly made himself known to his
brothers by means of a trick. When they were leaving, he ordered his
servants to put the goblet he uses to drink and prophesy in Benjamin's
sack in such a way that they would not see what was happening. They
went off, knowing nothing, and right then he sent his ministers after
them to accuse them of robbery. They were amazed to hear that; and
just like an innocent man who is accused of something he knows he
didn't do, they told him that if the goblet was found with them, they
would all be slaves, and the one who stole it would justly be put to
death. The diligent minister accepted their sentence, and when the goblet was found in Benjamin's sack, he made them return to Joseph. They
were so ashamed to see him that they knelt down in dismay; but he
could not longer contain his pity, and in tears he told them who he was,

and ordered them to go back and bring their father to Egypt, where everyone obeys him. Pharaoh agreed to this, and Jacob came to Egypt with all his offspring. He was happily welcomed and given all the land of Goshen for his sons and his family, which is multiplying every day. Now you're probably wondering why I'm telling you all these things you already know, especially because they don't seem to have anything to do with the problem that's bothering you. You're afraid of Joseph, and it really doesn't matter to you whether Jacob came or not. Joseph, however, decided to bring him to Egypt to support him. Well, there's no mystery there; that's nothing but the kindness a good son should show his father. Nevertheless, I would urge you to recall the solemn vision Jacob had at the Well of the Oath, when God told him: "Fear not, Jacob; go down to Egypt, for there I will make you the head of many peoples. I will go down with you; and when you return from there, I will also lead you out. And your son Joseph"—listen carefully, for this is the important part—"will put his hands on your eyes." Now you might say this just means that Joseph will still be alive when Jacob dies, and will close his eyes; and that's certainly a minor circumstance to be concerned about, particularly because Jacob has so many sons, so who cares whether Joseph should be the one to close his eyes? And that's why I've come to consult you, to see what you infer from that.

LUCIFER. What am I supposed to infer, if you're so puzzled? Why ask me what you should rightfully be the one to tell me?

INTELLIGENCE. Well, what do you think, Conjecture?

LUCIFER. Why are you asking Conjecture, since she has only the being that you confer on her? If you're so mixed up, you won't give her any basis for conjecture. When she has no premises to form a judgment, Conjecture is worthless!

INTELLIGENCE. How about Envy then?

LUCIFER. Though I have her in a general way, and also in particular, I don't know where I've put her. It's hardly surprising that I can't tell you where she is, since I'm so confused. I certainly have Envy, but I don't know of whom.

INTELLIGENCE. Well, isn't Joseph the object of our cruel anxiety?

LUCIFER. He is, and he isn't. Insofar as he practices virtue, he is the one who offends me; but my pride has no fear that Joseph will redeem the world's ancient loss. So it is Joseph, and it isn't; for though he too offends me, it's not really him that I fear but the one that he represents.

INTELLIGENCE. Let's go spy on him, Lucifer. Maybe when we see him, simple apprehension will succeed where knowledge has failed.

LUCIFER. I have no choice but to follow you, so take me where you will!

A cart opens, and Jacob appears in bed; Joseph and all his sons are at his side. Prophecy, on the balcony, sings.

PROPHECY.   Come, come, all ye mortals
at the sound of my song.
Come hear the mysteries
that to the future belong.
Pray heed, and hear the wonders!
In Jacob's old mouth
I shall now prophesy
the redemption of the world
and the future of the tribes.
Pray heed, and hear the wonders!

Lucifer, Intelligence, Conjecture, and Envy come out to eavesdrop.

CONJECTURE. Since we've come back to see Joseph, let's see what's going on.

INTELLIGENCE. I hear voices here. It is the voice of Prophecy, saying in sonorous hymns:

PROPHECY. *(Sings:)*
Pray heed and hear the wonders!

LUCIFER. What could be the wonder that she's summoning people to hear?

CONJECTURE. Let's listen and see whether we can understand its meaning.

PROPHECY. *(Sings:)*
Come, come, all ye mortals
at the sound of my song.
Come hear the mysteries
that to the future belong.

LUCIFER. Intelligence.

INTELLIGENCE. Be quiet until we've heard the whole thing, and then we can discuss what it means.

LUCIFER. You're right.

JACOB. Since my death is drawing near, all of you, listen to me together, as I tell you the things that will befall you later. Hear, oh sons of Jacob, and lend attentive ears! Hear the prophecy of Israel, your father.

PROPHECY. *(Sings:)*
Hear the wonders!

JACOB. Reuben, you are my firstborn, beginning of my sorrow. All your brothers will surpass you in power and good fortune. May you never increase! May you be like water poured out, for you dared violate the bed of your respected father.

PROPHECY. *(Sings:)*
Hear the wonders!

JACOB. Levi and Simeon, you have been vessels of iniquity. Let my glory not be joined to them, nor my soul enter into their counsel, for they killed with anger. Cursed be their anger! In Jacob and in Israel may they be separated and divided.

PROPHECY. *(Sings:)*
> Hear the wonders!

JACOB. Judah, a strong lion, you will be applauded by all, and the sons of your father will bow down to you. You will not lack the scepter nor a victorious captain until the hope of peoples has come into the world.

PROPHECY. *(Sings:)*
> Hear the wonders!

JACOB. Zebulun, your dwelling will be on the beach by the sea. Issachar, strong ass, will lie down in excellent borders.

PROPHECY. *(Sings:)*
> Hear the wonders!

JACOB. Dan, a coiling snake, will be on the roads, biting the horse's foot so the horseman will fall unawares.

PROPHECY. *(Sings:)*
> Hear the wonders!

JACOB. Gad, a warrior, will soon go to martial exercise; and Asher, substantial bread, will give delight to royal appetites.

PROPHECY. *(Sings:)*
> Hear the wonders!

JACOB. Naphtali, a deer let loose, will speak in an elegant style; and my son Joseph will be increase and beauty.

PROPHECY. *(Sings:)*
> Hear the wonders!

JACOB. Benjamin, a voracious wolf, will eat the prey at dawn, and will divide the spoil in the evening.

PROPHECY. *(Sings:)*
> Hear the wonders!

INTELLIGENCE. Lucifer, have you heard these confusing prophecies?

LUCIFER. They all come down to that same first principle: that God means to redeem man from sin—especially the prophecy about Judah, for you heard him say that his brothers would bow down to him. Let's listen, for he's starting to prophesy again.

JACOB. Joseph, my dear son, if I have found grace in your eyes; if, as I trust, you will fulfill my request and obey my commandment, do not deny me the last consolation I ask. I sense that the exact time of my death is approaching. However, I am comforted by knowing that I'm leaving you alive. I don't want my body to be buried in Egypt, but where my elders and yours are buried, which is in the double cave that is in Canaan, in the field that my grandfather Abraham bought from Ephron the Hittite to be his burial place. There he and Sarah lie together, and Rebekah with Isaac, and in that same sepulcher is Leah. Therefore, I beg you to carry me there to be buried with my elders. Will you do so?

JOSEPH. It will be done as you have said.

JACOB. Then apply that hand which has liberated Egypt to my thigh—for this is the most solemn rite in our oaths—and swear that you will do so.

JOSEPH. I swear it by the living God of Abraham, Isaac, and Jacob, whom God promised that in their offspring all men would be blessed, when the clouds rain down in his flesh the sacred dew of the just one, and when the divine Savior sprouts from the earth.

PROPHECY. *(Sings:)*
> Hear the wonders!

Jacob kisses Joseph's scepter, which has a roll of bread on
its point.

JACOB. I adore him, and I see him in spirit prefigured in your rod, not only joined to my flesh in hypostatic union,[28] but hidden behind the veil of that insignia which on your scepter has been a sign of your providence. For it has always been customary in Egypt and elsewhere for the hero to bear a sculptured hieroglyphic of his greatest deed. Since in your case that was having saved Egypt with wheat, they put that emblem of wheat at the top of your scepter, which I adore as a sacred symbol of the loftiest sacrament that coming ages will adore, on account of whom the Vessel of Choice[29] will say of me that, dying in the faith, I worshiped the tip of your staff,[30] where I see this great mystery hidden.

PROPHECY. *(Sings:)* Hear the wonders!

LUCIFER. Intelligence, I don't know what to make of this—except that from this day on I'll never be able to see wheat or ears of grain without feeling the most abject terror! If this is the beginning, I can already see how dreadful the end will be for me. I can't take any more of this. Let's get out of here!

INTELLIGENCE. I know when I'm defeated! After all that I've seen, though the abyss may be my prison, I can only take refuge there. I'll never rest easy again. If I stay here, what I see will torture me, but if I go back there, I'll suffer the torments of imagination.

CONJECTURE. I'm no good either place. There's no need for Conjecture when the facts are crystal clear.

A curtain is drawn, covering all this, and Prophecy alone remains
onstage. Another cart opens, revealing a Chalice and Host,
and two Choirs.

PROPHECY. Be off then, for where light appears, darkness cannot remain! And you out there—no longer sons of Jacob who saw only dim glimpses of the sacrament, but sons of light, since the shadows have flown away and the figures contained in the sacred prophecies I spoke through so many prophets are now fulfilled—transcending the ages, I, who formerly was Prophecy, speak now with the voice of faith. This is no contradiction, for it is an act of faith to believe in what is yet to be without having seen it. Believing in God means believing what He said, believing against time, or in this case, against the evidence of the senses. But just in case some curious person wants to investigate further, I'll explain that Rabbi Moses himself wrote what we said about adoring the tip of the scepter, citing Paul's words "adoring the tip."[31] And even though one shouldn't fully credit the words of the rabbis, in this case, since it goes against no dogma, but rather serves to aid devotion, I've employed it. To get back to my point, you who are happy sons of light, and enjoy full possession of what the ancients could only hope for, bow down and worship this divine mystery, this high sacrament. And with tenderness and weeping, join me in saying that if indeed God showed His benefits, His wonders and mysteries to the Hebrews, He has done much more for us.

Prophecy sings, and the Choirs join in the chorus.

PROPHECY. *(Sings:)*
Mystery of mysteries,
wonder of all wonders!
The manna in the desert
had many different flavors.
This bread has but one,
of infinity it savors.[32]

CHOIRS. Mystery of mysteries,
wonder of all wonders!

PROPHECY. God sustained Elijah
with bread on hot stones baked,[33]
but whoever eats this bread
of eternal life partakes.

CHOIRS. Mystery of mysteries,
wonder of all wonders!

PROPHECY. The bread of God's sweet presence
kept David strong and whole.[34]
Now God Himself is food
for every human soul.

CHOIRS. Mystery of mysteries,
wonder of all wonders!

PROPHECY.   Through seven hungry years
Joseph's wheat fed mankind,
but this bread will endure
until the end of time.

CHOIRS.   Mystery of mysteries,
wonder of all wonders!

Exeunt, singing.

6

Isaac de Matatia Aboab:
Harassed But Happy

Around the time when Sor Juana was writing *Joseph's Scepter* in Mexico, the Jewish writer Isaac de Matatia Aboab composed his remarkable three-part play *Harassed But Happy (El perseguido dichoso)* in Amsterdam. It is fitting that we conclude this anthology with that play, which is at once the last version of the story written during the classical period of Spanish literature known as the Golden Age, the fullest dramatic version of the story ever written, and the only one written by a professing Jew.

At the time of their expulsion from Spain, most of the Castilian Jews—about 120,000—sought refuge in nearby Portugal, where King João II initially admitted them for a period of eight months in return for payment of a substantial fee. When the eight-month grace period expired, six hundred wealthy families were allowed to remain as Jews in Portugal, while the others were given the choice of conversion to Catholicism or slavery.[1] The illustrious Aboab family, who had settled in Oporto, were among the fortunate few. However, when João's successor, Manoel I, sought the hand of Ferdinand and Isabella's daughter in marriage, they agreed to the marriage only on condition that Manoel expel the remaining Jews from Portugal. In order to remain in Portugal the Aboab family converted to Catholicism in 1497, changing their name to Dias. Some members of the family later achieved great distinction there as physicians, attorneys, writers, and businessmen. Though outwardly Catholic, many of them continued to practice Judaism in secret.

Toward the end of the sixteenth century, the Inquisition began to persecute these Judaizers in Portugal even more savagely than in Spain. Some of them then chose to return to Spain; others sought refuge in the Americas, while still others began to establish a community in Amsterdam, which would eventually achieve such wealth and intellectual and artistic distinc-

226

tion that in the seventeenth century Amsterdam came to be known as "the new Jerusalem." As Herbert I. Bloom has observed, "Amsterdam with its growing prominence in the galaxy of commercial cities, welcomed the persecuted Jews, especially since they were traders, and traders who by long experience and wide international connections could bring wealth and influence to the city on the Amstel. The Jews realized the relative tolerance of the developing commercial city, and the advantages accruing from settlement in the northern metropolis. They went there because Amsterdam was the enemy of Spain and because its star was in the ascendant."[2] By 1630 it is estimated that the Sephardic community in Amsterdam, consisting mostly of Portuguese immigrants, numbered a thousand.[3]

Manoel Dias Henriques (1594–1667) left Oporto to seek his fortune in Mexico, but hunted down by the Inquisition there, he made his escape to Amsterdam in 1626. Upon arriving in Amsterdam, he began to practice Judaism openly, adopting the name of Matatia Aboab. That same year he married a fellow Portuguese immigrant, Esther Naar (born in Tomar in 1599 and formerly known as Isabel de Pina). The couple would eventually have ten children. The fourth of these, Isaac de Matatia Aboab,[4] was born in Amsterdam on 6 September 1631.

Little is known about the life of Isaac de Matatia Aboab. Attempts to research his activities have been complicated by the fact that he has often been confused with his better-known namesake and contemporary Rabbi Isaac Aboab da Fonseca (1605–93); it is often impossible to ascertain which man contemporary references to "Isaac Aboab" refer to. Isaac de Matatia Aboab seems to have been a prosperous merchant and a relatively prominent member of Amsterdam's Jewish community. On 3 April 1669, when he was thirty-seven, he married his sixteen-year-old niece[5] Sarah Curiel. The couple had four sons: Matatia, David, Moshe, and Emanuel. In 1687 an *Order of Blessings* published in Amsterdam was dedicated to Aboab. In 1688, and again in 1697, he was elected one of the *parnassim* (trustees) of the Talmud Torah, or Jewish school, of Amsterdam.

According to H. P. Salomon, Aboab served as a sort of librarian or "living repository of all literary memorabilia of and concerning the Portuguese Jews of Amsterdam."[6] Aboab's only published work was a volume of moral exhortations in Hebrew, with a Dutch translation, addressed to his eldest son and dated 10 June 1677. A Portuguese translation of this work, entitled *Doutrina Particular,* was published in 1687 and reprinted in 1691.[7] In February 1676 he completed a genealogy and history tracing the Aboab family back to the year 1497.[8] In 1682 he commissioned Benjamin Senior Godines to compile a miscellaneous manuscript in Portuguese, containing such items as Maimonides' Thirteen Articles of the Faith, the seven Noahide laws, the formula of confession *(Vidduy),* and several polemical texts against Christianity. Aboab compiled a collection entitled *Stories, Canticles, Riddles, and Other Curiosities*[9] in 1683. In 1685 he penned a twenty-eight page manuscript of moral exhortations addressed to his nephews. In 1687 he commissioned Shelomo Oliveira to write a bilingual book called *Peraḥ Shushan* in Hebrew and *Ramelhete de flores* in Portuguese, which claimed to define each of the sciences and to summarize its essential contents. In 1690 he compiled a treatise on the medicinal uses of precious stones, and in the same year he commissioned Benjamin Senior Godines to edit and copy Abraham Zacuto's treatise on medicine for him. His wife Sarah died on 30 August 1691. In 1693 Aboab commissioned a Spanish translation of Isaac Abravanel's commentary on the Passover Haggadah, *Zevaḥ Pesaḥ.* He commissioned Benjamin Senior Godines to paint three morality pictures for him—a memento mori (1694), a series of scenes from the life of the patriarch Isaac (1695), and a painting exhorting humility and charity to the poor (1696)—all of which are now in the Jewish Museum in London.[10] Isaac de Matatia Aboab died in Amsterdam on 19 March 1707, at the age of seventy-five.

The play *Harassed But Happy* has come down to us in two manuscripts— one in the author's own hand, signed and dated "Amsterdam 5446" (= 1685–86), and the other, an eighteenth-century copy. Both are the property of the Portugees Israelitisch Seminarium Ets Haim of Amsterdam but are now on permanent loan to the Jewish National and University Library, Jerusalem.[11] It is difficult to determine the exact date of composition of the play, however, because a sonnet on the second page of the manuscript bears the date 1652, and the back cover of the binding of the autograph manuscript is stamped with the date "anno 5454" (= 1693–94).

It is equally difficult to ascertain Aboab's purpose in writing the play. Perhaps it was intended for performance in conjunction with the celebration of Purim or another Jewish holiday. We know that *Dialogo dos montes,* an allegorical play in Portuguese by Rehuel Yeshurun (alias Paul de Piña) was performed in Amsterdam's Beth Jacob synagogue during Shevuot of 1624; later, however, the community's bylaws forbade such performances there.[12] The Jewish community continued to sponsor play performances, sometimes even bringing theater companies from Spain, a practice that was forbidden by Amsterdam's Board of Aldermen in 1683.[13] The length of *Harassed But Happy* made performance in a single sitting all but impossible; it might, however, have been performed on successive days. Alternatively, it may have been intended merely for reading rather than performance; in that case it might be considered a "novel in dialogue" like Fernando de Rojas's very influential *La Celestina* (1499) rather than a drama proper. This suspicion is reinforced by the fact that at the conclusion of part 1, Aboab addresses the "reader" *(lector)*. We should bear in mind, however, that the conclusion of part 2 pointedly states: "si gustare el discreto / oír la tersera parte . . ." [If our learned audience / still wants to *hear* the rest . . .]; but those words could refer to a public reading as well as to a performance. A passage at the end of part 2 suggests that the actor playing the role of Joseph would have been exhausted by that point: "Since long hours on the stage / you have spent up to now / as the hero of this play, / it's time for you to rest." Professor Harm den Boer has recently suggested that the play was probably written for performance during the holiday of Purim, like two other anonymous plays—one on Haman and Mordecai, and the other on Jacob and Esau—that were published with the official approval of the leaders of Amsterdam's Jewish community in 1699.[14]

The play is written in an eloquent Spanish that is, however, heavily contaminated by Aboab's native Portuguese. Though most of Amsterdam's Jews were native speakers of Portuguese, they tended to compose their literary works in Spanish because of the greater prestige of the latter language. They also eagerly kept abreast of the latest literary fashions in Spain and imitated them in their own works. *Harassed But Happy* reveals the author's familiarity with some of Spain's classic writers, such as Garcilaso de la Vega and Luis de Góngora. The play's principal model seems to have been Carvajal's *Josephine Tragedy;* many speeches in *Harassed But Happy* closely paraphrase passages from that play, though Aboab has deleted all references to Christianity. Though the harm done by envy remains the play's central theme, Aboab eliminates the use of the allegorical character Envy. He also transcribes the original Hebrew names of the characters and places mentioned in the text as accurately as possible, eschewing the conventional Spanish forms of those names. Aboab may also have known Lope de Vega's play *The Trials of Jacob*. One poetic phrase frequently used in Lope's play— the notion that Jacob loved to see himself reflected in Benjamin's face as in a mirror—also occurs several times in *Harassed But Happy*. Some passages in the play also suggest that he was familiar with the *Sefer ha-Yashar,* perhaps in a Ladino version such as the mid-seventeenth-century one recently published by Moshe Lazar.[15]

Superficially, parts 1 and 2 of *Harassed But Happy* appear to adhere to the conventions of the Spanish Golden Age *comedia:* they are three-act, polymetric[16] tragicomedies. On closer examination, however, the structure of the play turns out to be very peculiar indeed. Golden Age *comedias* are usually about three thousand verses long, approximately equally divided among the three acts. Acts 1 and 2 of the first two parts of *Harassed But Happy* are unusually short,[17] while in each case the third act is unusually long.[18] Hence, in spite of the division into three acts, each of the parts seems in fact to consist of two symmetrical halves. The playwright's use of scenes is also highly unusual. I use the term "scene" to indicate a section of the play that occurs when all actors momentarily vacate the stage. Conventionally in the Spanish theater, when a character appears in one such scene, she or he does not immediately reappear in the following one. There are occasional exceptions to this rule of course; but in *Harassed But Happy* the exceptions far outnumber cases in which Aboab follows the rule. In performance this could lead to considerable confusion. Aboab's use of verse is also unconventional; he often changes the verse form—or, in the case of *romance,* the assonance—in mid-scene for no apparent reason. He shows a marked preference for *silvas* in lyrical passages and even in some narrative passages *(relaciones),* which would normally have been cast in *romance*; fully 8.5 percent of parts 1 and 2 are written in this meter. Such a preference is easy to understand, for the *silva,* with its irregular combination of heptasyllables and hendecasyllables and its lack of restrictions with regard to rhyme[19]—even permitting an occasional unrhymed verse—was most suitable for an author whose skills in versification were very limited. The play in fact contains numerous defects in both meter and rhyme.

But if parts 1 and 2 are somewhat peculiar, part 3 is altogether anomalous. Unlike the other two parts, it contains only two brief scenes, and is only 431 verses long. Furthermore, except for a sixteen-line passage of *silva* introducing Ya'akob's prophecies, its versification is highly irregular, consisting of stanzas ranging from four to six verses in length, each stanza having two rhymes (the most common rhyme scheme is aABAB). The first line of each stanza is usually a tetrasyllable, and the others are octosyllables, so that the meter could be described as a type of *copla de pie quebrado.* Further complicating matters is the fact that the language of part 3 is much more archaic than that of the other two parts. Part 3 is also the only part of the play that contains Ladino and Hebrew words.[20] This suggests to me that part 3 (and perhaps the clumsy sonnet that introduces the play) was written by someone else at an earlier date, and that Aboab then decided to write parts 1 and 2 to provide the background leading up to the climactic concluding scene of Ya'akob's prophecies.

Although the structure and versification of *Harassed But Happy* are awkward and amateurish by comparison with the Spanish *comedias* of the period, its development of the plot is highly original and admirable. The biblical story of Joseph is inherently dramatic, containing an unusual number of passages in dialogue and speeches quoted at length,[21] and it lends itself particularly well to the three-act *comedia* format, since it seems to fall naturally into three parts. Nevertheless, it poses serious problems for the dramatist. The first of these is the story's very familiarity. How can a playwright manage to create any real suspense when the audience already knows how the story will end? As we have seen, Lope de Vega sought to "defamiliarize" the material by introducing a pastoral subplot dealing with the shepherd Bato's love for the shepherdess Lida, who in turn loved Benjamin, as well as a few other novel twists. Similarly, Calderón complicated matters by having the allegorical character Chastity appear to Joseph in the form of his future wife Asenath. When Joseph thanks the real Asenath for the favor she has shown him, she is offended by the suggestion that she might formerly have allowed him any undue familiarity, and this for a while seems to spoil his chances of marrying her. One wonders whether Aboab might have known Calderón's play or some other version of the story of Joseph and Asenath—perhaps Mira de Amescua's *El más feliz cautiverio*—for the complications he introduces in the story are also based on Joseph's relationship with his future wife.

A second problem confronting any would-be dramatist of the Joseph story is how to avoid portraying the chaste Joseph as a sanctimonious prig. This difficulty posed a much greater challenge in macho seventeenth-century Hispanic culture, which generally viewed chastity as a feminine virtue, while men were expected to display sexual prowess. Aboab skillfully solved this problem by having Yoseph meet and fall in love with Asenath on the very day of his arrival in Egypt. His subsequent stern rejection of Zenobia could then be attributed not so much to his innate aversion to sex as to the fact that he was already in love with someone else. Further complications could then be introduced when a jealous Asenath suspected that Zenobia's charge that Yoseph had attempted to rape her might be true, and therefore unjustly reprimanded Yoseph. Offended by her lack of trust in him, Yoseph's ardor for Asenath temporarily cooled, and he considered having an affair with the jailer's daughter Cumena. The two lovers were of course finally reconciled, but not before overcoming a serious of interesting hurdles.

The fact that every single woman who encounters Yoseph in the play—Asenath and her maid Rezinda, Zenobia and her maid Matilde, the jailer's daughter Cumena, and Potiphar's daughter Semiramis—is instantly smitten with love for him makes for several scenes of high comedy, culminating in a veritable catfight when three of those women vie for Joseph's hand. As the title *Harassed But Happy*[22] indicates, much of the play's attraction for its original audience or readers lay in the fact that it is above all what Freud would have called a male wish-fulfillment fantasy.

The play also makes very effective use of dramatic irony. One could cite many examples, but perhaps the most noteworthy one is the shepherd's song in part 1, act 1, which recalls the story of Cain and Abel and warns Yoseph to turn back and return home before it is too late. This may have been inspired by Lope de Vega's use of a similar song in his *Knight from Olmedo (El caballero de Olmedo)* warning the character Alonso that death awaits him if he persists in his dangerous journey to Olmedo. As in the case of Alonso, the otherwise highly idealized Yoseph of *Harassed But Happy* seems guilty of hubris for disregarding the warning. Another possible echo of *El caballero de Olmedo* is the play's frequent references to the beauty of spring and its promise of new life (e.g., the poems spoken by Shimʿon and Yehudah, which frame the scene in which Yoseph is cast into the well); the references add poignancy to Yoseph's sufferings. The play's poetic unity is enhanced by the constant use of animal imagery (especially the crocodile, emblematic of hypocrisy) and maritime imagery (references to fragile boats cast adrift at the mercy of the sea); the latter emphasize the characters' sense of helplessness, of being the playthings of forces more powerful than themselves.

Approximately 75 percent of parts 1 and 2 are written in *romance* or *redondillas,* both of which meters closely approximate the rhythms of normal Spanish prose. As I have done with the other plays in this anthology, I have translated those parts of the play in prose, reserving the use of verse for songs and particularly lyrical, or obtrusively poetic, passages. The latter are usually virtuoso set-pieces (such as Rezinda's description of Joseph's triumphal parade) in which the author sought to showcase his skill as a poet, and might well be compared to arias in an opera. I have added some stage directions enclosed in square brackets.

On the story's theme[23]

When Yoseph went to Egypt as a slave,
the tunic that had brought him so much woe,
now stained with a kid's blood, they cruelly throw
before his father, causing him to rave.
With horror gazing on those remnants grave
of his lost son, Yaʿakob would fain borrow
complaints from all past mourners for his sorrow;
both past and present trials he would engrave.
"Oh, son," he cried, "my dearest love so true!
What animal, what savage beast perverse
could steal my very soul by killing you?"
Yet in his heart he knew and then did curse
the wicked harpy who his Yoseph slew:
'twas Envy, for not even death is worse.

PART 1

Characters:

Ya'akob	[Other servants of Potiphar]
Re'uven	Asenath, Potiphar's daughter
Shim'on	Rezinda, her maid
Levi	Zenobia, Potiphar's wife
Yoseph	Potiphar
Gad	[Yehudah]
[Asher]	[Two] Ishmaelites
[Yissaskhar]	Matilde, Zenobia's maid
A shepherd	

ACT 1

Enter Shim'on and Levi.

SHIM'ON. Who could put up with this? I'll tear him in a thousand pieces—and I don't mean just his tunic, which is only cloth, but its wearer as well!

LEVI. The lad is his father's pride and joy, and he prefers him to all our nobility.

SHIM'ON. Since he is Rachel's son, he means to give him the birthright. Our mother is no slave, and we were not born bastards.

LEVI. I know where all this love comes from, brother. It's all because with that smooth tongue of his, he tells him tales of everything we do, making up a thousand lies and falsehoods about us.

SHIM'ON. But I'm worried that things will get even worse. What if he sends us to live among barbarians, as our grandfather did with his bastards, and arranges for everything that God has promised him to go only to the boy, for all the ages to come?

LEVI. He'll not live to see that day! Before that happens, he'll give up his life in these strong arms of mine. I've heard that he is shameless . . . But hold on, here comes Mr. Smarty-pants now. Let's see what new flattery he comes up with, what falsehoods come from his lips.

Enter Yoseph.

What's up?

YOSEPH. Great things! I'm troubled by a dream I've had.

SHIM'ON. Oh, so now you've had a dream. How nice!

YOSEPH. Many dreams are miraculous.

SHIM'ON. Well, you shouldn't believe in dreams, for dreams are deceptive.

YOSEPH. That's just what I think, so I haven't paid much attention to this one. Still, it's upset me, and I'd feel better if you'd let me tell it to you.

SHIM'ON. Then cut out the nonsense, and get to the point.

YOSEPH. It was that flowery season,[24] the most fertile part of summer, when the sun weighs the days of the year in his scales; when the painted birds sing of their love from the loftiest branches in the groves and meadows; and finally, when the farmer takes his sickle in hand to gather up the fruit of his sowing and take it home. I dreamed that we were all spread out through the fields tying up the stalks of wheat that had already been reaped. I looked upon my sheaf and saw it miraculously stand up, without any hand touching it. Your sheaves stood up too, but then they gathered around mine and bowed down to it, as if it were the god of the countryside. I awoke from that vision and realized that dreams are but chimeras, to which I attach little importance.

SHIM'ON. I know very well that your deliriums and your vain thoughts make you dream at night what you've thought about during the day. If you think you will rule over all your brothers and be our absolute master, or that we would let you get away with such a thing, you are badly mistaken. Before that happens, these fields will produce stars, and the sky will be full of roses and flowers, the sea will grow grass, and fish will swim in the meadows. Your madness drives you to these insane dreams, for these dreams of yours are just as nonsensical as they are false. If the favor the old man has shown you has made you dream such dreams, that madness serves your own self-interest and would do me harm. Just remember that I have the power to turn all that paternal affection and coddling into sad laments.

YOSEPH. My brother, I am shocked that you take dreams seriously, and that you dare say I am proud, for that is false. If my father loves me, I thank holy heaven; but that doesn't make me presume that I am anything more than a tiny worm. You are my older brothers, and I am obliged by law to serve you and obey you; and my humility knows better than to give you any cause for offense. Don't take offense, then. Why should you hate me, when I esteem and love you? I'm sorry if the dreams I've told you have offended you. You know that only men dream, not insensate brutes.

LEVI. How humble you act, and how cleverly you lower yourself, you lion in sheep's clothing, you tiger posing as a meek little lamb! Don't think you can fool us, for we know all your tricks, and how you always carry tales to the old man, telling him of wickedness we've never even thought of. Get out of here, and remember that your life . . .

YOSEPH. Oh, brother, what have I done to offend you?

LEVI. You know just as well as we do.

Exeunt Shim'on and Levi.

YOSEPH.   Oh cruel Envy, monster, oh fierce beast,
              oh basilisk, who wounds with a mere look,
              oh crocodile who slithers from the brook,
              shedding sad tears o'er the corpse on which you feast!
              If you continue thus to harass me,
              and time does not undo the harm you've done,
              there'll be no cure, or I can think of none,
              for life's own blood you suck with ghoulish glee.
              Oh wretched tunic, this is all your fault!
              You were the cause of all my suffering.
              I should have torn it to a thousand shreds to halt
              the harm that wearing it to me did bring.
              But what can I do? Such terrors now assault
              me, for Envy, my brothers' eyes blinding,
              o'erpowers them, and they long with bated breath
              to hound me to a cruel, bitter death.

[Enter Ya'akob.]

YA'AKOB.   What ails you, son? My love, my darling boy,
              what troubles you, and thereby troubles me?

YOSEPH.   That colored tunic has brought me no joy,
              but rather has engendered a harpy,
              a hydra to relentlessly annoy,
              with its ten heads, insatiable, bloodthirsty.
              Those mouths would feed on me, but my poor flesh
              will not suffice their hunger to refresh.
              My brothers, sir, are envious of that gift.
              Your love has pushed them to insanity,
              creating between them and me a rift.
              They threaten me in their audacity,
              speak harshly to me, to hate me are swift.
              It's my bad luck, a real calamity!
              but with the help of God Whom I hold dear,
              and your support, nothing indeed I fear.

YA'AKOB. My dear son, apple of my eye, your brothers were very wrong to
    trouble me with this insane jealousy. After all, I am their father, and I
    would never treat them unjustly. If I gave you a tunic, they should know
    that I didn't mean thereby to displease them. It is your virtue that in-
    spires this love in me; but even if you weren't so good, the very fact that

you are the son of Rachel, who meant everything to me, would make me love you. If she were alive, I'd surely love all of you equally; but since you are the living reminder of her beautiful face, how can they blame me for loving you, and all the more so, given your rare virtue? Don't be distressed, my son. I will solve this problem, and I will show you how to calm their anger. I'll pretend to love you less for a while, and perhaps this will distract them and keep them from getting any angrier.

YOSEPH. It's vital that you do so, father. It's the only way to save my life, which you love so. Should you forget and fail to crush this evil in the bud, and should their envy and mortal hate continue, it will surely cut me down before my time, in spite of the fact that I've always been a loyal brother.

Exeunt. Enter Levi and Yehudah.

LEVI. What do you think of the dreamer? What hypocrisies he tries to get away with!

YEHUDAH. I think he means to be master of us all. At least, that's what I fear; but what bothers me the most is to see how much his father loves the boy. The old man must see something in him, for he cares about nothing else. Maybe heaven has revealed to him just what we fear. If so, his father is badly mistaken, for if he means to do anything to spite us, we'll send the boy straight off to rest with his mother.

LEVI. If this goes any further, and we go along with it, in one way or another he will become master of this house.

YEHUDAH. In that case, it's up to us to prevent any further harm, even if it means taking his life. I'll murder him as if he were a stranger. If someone has to weep, better it should be him than us!

LEVI. I agree with you, even if it means I have to act cruelly.

Exeunt. Enter Ya'akob, Yehudah, and Shim'on.

YA'AKOB. I know very well that you hate him because I show him love, and that you always speak harshly to him. It never occurred to me that such wicked tendencies could occur among brothers, especially sons of Ya'akob; for almighty God, Who redeemed me from so much misfortune, promised and swore that He would propagate my seed. All of you are already a living emblem of that divine promise, for I see that all of you are saints. Hence, my sons, I hope that if you follow virtue, the people of God will emerge from your multitude. So that the divine plan may be fulfilled, be brotherly, be kind, for that is for your own good. Please be friends, as I beseech you. Let there be no ill will among you, for you are all equal, and I have not shown preference to any one. I wish God's favor for all of you equally, and I love you just as much as I love Yoseph.

YEHUDAH. Our lord and father, why are you saying these things? What suspicions has he told you now? No doubt the lad has gone to you with lying complaints about us. What have we done to him? Or how have we ever offended him? As for me, may God abandon me if I have ever offended him with these lips! If he has complained to you about me, his complaints are unfounded.

YA'AKOB. I know that they're just the complaints of an inexperienced lad, because it would make no sense for you to act tough with him. Gentleness is what's called for in dealing with someone so innocent.

SHIM'ON. If the boy was talking about me, father, you are absolutely right; but he gave me good reason to say much more to him than I did. He came and told us a dream in such an offhand way that it's a wonder we didn't do something crazy. He told us, as if it were some wonderful thing, how he saw all our sheaves bow down before his sheaf. What do you think of that? Would anyone have the patience to put up with such nonsense if it weren't coming from such an innocent lad?

YA'AKOB. Pay no attention to dreams, for they are usually vain.

SHIM'ON. Yes, but he means to be king and lord over his brothers.

YA'AKOB. Well, that will never happen, for you are all equal in honor, and you will all be lords, as God has promised.

Enter Yoseph.

YEHUDAH. Yoseph, just what did you think you were doing, complaining to my father? What's more, to make matters worse, you insisted that he let you come with us.

YOSEPH. I have no complaints about you, but the person I complained about knows very well whether he gave me just cause.

SHIM'ON. It's true that I scolded you, but you were to blame. Who would have thought you'd tell us such a dream?

YOSEPH. Am I to blame for a dream? Men have dreams because they're rational, and God made me a man. I'd tell you still another one, which has upset me even more, but I'm afraid you'd take offense, since I am so unlucky, and you all think the worst of me, considering my virtue a crime and a grave sin.

SHIM'ON. Well, go ahead and tell it. I'll bet anything that it is in your favor.

YOSEPH. God knows best, for He is the author of it, but I will tell you the truth. Last night I saw the sky adorned with stars, whose eternal torches made that night seem day. As I considered the beauty of their images, the eminence of their lights, the greatness of their globes, and how there were twelve signs, though only seven planets, with Titan[25] in their midst as king of the spheres; gazing on all those lights, with which the author of the heavens beautified them so as to increase our wonderment, and praising Him Who made them and rendered them eternal, I fell asleep. Then my senses formed new phantasms. I saw the sun and moon and eleven of the stars in the sky bow down in reverence unto the ground. That is what I dreamed. Nevertheless, I'm only recounting it as a chimera, for dreams are vanity, and no one should pay attention to them.

LEVI.　　How right I was about his foolish dream!
　　　　How well I prophesied that it would seem
　　　　insulting to us all, that it would be
　　　　more nonsense. A fine prophecy!
　　　　What do you think of his intentions now,
　　　　oh father? Does he think we'll scrape and bow
　　　　unto him? Don't you see that we were right
　　　　to resent the dream he had the other night?

YA'AKOB.　Yoseph, what dream is this? Do you now crave
　　　　that your mother, who lies moldering in her grave,
　　　　should bow to you? Would it not be bizarre
　　　　for us, as if we were the sun and moon,
　　　　and all your brothers, each one like a star,
　　　　to bow to you? Oh, how inopportune
　　　　is this your vision! Son, please be aware
　　　　that just to hear you does your father scare!
　　　　Control yourself, no more such dreams review,
　　　　for you will drive your brothers to hate you,
　　　　conceiving envy and malevolence.
　　　　Though I know well your innocence,
　　　　and dreams are but the merest vanity,
　　　　one should not speak with such inanity.
　　　　It makes one doubt that you are truly wise.
　　　　Give up such thoughts, for thus do I advise.
　　　　No more chimeras, for they will cause strife!
　　　　Do not embitter your poor father's life.

YOSEPH. If I have spoken out of turn, forgive me, for I have sinned; but it never occurred to me that my words might offend anyone, or that my vain dreams could give rise to envy. Those dreams never made me think that I was greater than my brothers. Since they are older than I, I owe them respect, and I subject myself to their wishes out of fraternal obligation.

YA'AKOB. That's just what I'd advise you to do, son, for it is an excellent law that the younger should obey the older. *[To the brothers:]* And none of you should pay attention to that dream, for God blessed all of you, from the oldest to the youngest. Don't let it worry you, for it's nothing but vanity. Now, son, take the sheep to the meadows, for they are renewed with green grass. The little lambs are jumping, and the sheep are dancing to get out of their sheepfolds.

YEHUDAH. We've already taken care of that, father. The shepherds are already leading the flocks to the flowery fields, and we will follow them there. It's getting late; we should be off now.

YA'AKOB. That's what I say. Yoseph will stay here with me, and may heaven keep all of you.

Exeunt Ya'akob and Yoseph.

LEVI. Well, that second dream was just fine! No doubt, he thinks that by God's will he will be king of everyone. Well, he may be a king among barbarous pagans, but he'll not live to see the day when he rules over his own brothers. The best thing for us to do is kill him before this goes any further. We'll see whether fortune will give him a scepter then. Letting him live, if that means we must be slaves, would clearly offend our high honor.

SHIM'ON. Well, then, the boy must die! That will stop him from dreaming anymore. Let's go, for the flock is already on its way to Shechem. Anyone who doesn't agree with this cannot be held in honor.

Exeunt. Enter Ya'akob.

YA'AKOB. If I am not mistaken, Yoseph's dreams are true. The fact that he dreamed the same thing twice means they are not dreams but an oracle of heaven,[26] revealing that he will hold some eminent post of power and greatness over all his brothers. If this is God's will, no human can prevent it, for God has many different ways to make His sovereign intentions take effect, since He is absolute Lord of the world, which He created.

[Enter Yoseph.]

YOSEPH. I have come looking for you, father, for I was lonely without you.

YA'AKOB. I am glad that you've come, son. I love you as you love me; just seeing you is a comfort in my trials. Great was the love I bore your mother, but now that she is gone, since you are her living portrait, I love that image that I see in you, and hence I always long to have you by my side. Still, it's been many days since your brothers departed. Now I would like to send you, though your absence will cost me dearly, to find out how they and their flocks are faring.

YOSEPH. Here I am, sir. Send me, for I'll gladly bear the trials of the road, knowing that I am pleasing you.

YA'AKOB. Then go to Shechem, my son. Take them these gifts, and come back with their reply. Don't tarry, for I am anxious lest some misfortune or danger befall you. May He Who has saved me from a thousand anxieties return you to my eyes.

YOSEPH. Father, I'm going. Give me your blessing.

YA'AKOB. Go on, then, my dear son, and may God send His holy angels to keep watch over you.

Exeunt. Enter a shepherd from one side, and Yoseph from the other.

YOSEPH. Without light or company, I am passing through this rough terrain with no one to tell me the way. If I am not confused, these lofty peaks are the mountains of Shechem, which is my destination, but neither in valley nor meadow do I see any sign of the flocks—not a single sheep or lamb.

The shepherd sings:

SHEPHERD.   It was just at the beginning
of that happy Golden Age,
ere Envy had begun
to fill men's hearts with rage.

YOSEPH. I hear a voice. There is someone here who may be able to give me news of the brothers I'm looking for, for I am lost. He's still far away, but he's coming this way. While I wait, I'll try to figure out what it is he's singing in that uncouth style.

He resumes his singing:

SHEPHERD.   After the first man,
that disobedient brute,
damaged all mankind,
eating forbidden fruit;
after Mother Earth,
which had been Paradise,
began to bring forth thorns,
of Adam's curse the price,
the patriarch begat
two sons in days of old.
One did till the earth,
the other, sheep did hold.
Both brought unto the Lord
of the world a sacrifice.
Hevel's He accepted,
but Kayin's did He despise.
Rejected by his Lord,
Kayin did sorely sin
by envying Hevel;
thus Envy did begin.
Finding him alone,
his doom did he pronounce.

He covered up his blood,
but his crime it did denounce.
Now do not trust your brothers,
for even if they're good,
if Envy goads them on,
they'll surely drink your blood.
Oh shepherds, run away
from this fierce crocodile,
for after killing you,
it will shed tears with guile!

YOSEPH. A bad omen! I don't like the sound of these echoes produced by an ignorant country lad, though I scarcely understand what they mean. Some angel has come from heaven to warn me of suffering I've been suspecting, of misfortunes I can't seem to resist. He speaks of the effects of envy, a yawning abyss where my good fortune will be buried if God doesn't lend His help. I should turn back rather than subject myself to the danger of desperate whims or envious caprice. I could go back home and excuse myself to my father by saying I lost my way, and I would seem no less manly for that. But it would be cowardly not to go on with my plan, taking the voice of a little bird for a bad omen. Yes, I'll continue my journey, for such presages are false, and only ignorant gentiles give credence to them.

SHEPHERD. Hello, young traveler! Where are you going so boldly through this wild mountain range? Don't you know you could fall off a cliff? You have lost your way. Turn back while you can, for there are wild animals here, just like those treacherous men who prey on the innocent when they least expect it, tearing them in a thousand pieces. That shouldn't surprise you, for there are plenty of lawless men who would kill their own brothers for the slightest reason.

YOSEPH. This is a second warning. What are you saying, good man, for I'm not sure I understand you?

SHEPHERD. I think my words speak for themselves. I am telling you that you are headed straight for a dangerous cliff, and that there are beasts in these mountains that kill without provocation. Turn back, turn back, son! Go back to the level road, for you've gone astray from the path.

YOSEPH. Then show me the way.

SHEPHERD. I've already told you very well. It is vital that you turn back at once.

YOSEPH. But which way?

SHEPHERD. Go back the way you came if you want to escape from the beasts.

YOSEPH. What do you mean? Can there be beasts on such well-traveled roads?

SHEPHERD. Yes, there are beasts that are ravenous and hell-bent on their prey.

YOSEPH. No doubt, this man is an angel, since he is giving me such clear warnings. Heaven means to remedy my misfortunes and trials. These are not the chance sayings of an ignorant country man; divine intelligence must be moving his lips. But I'll test him one more time, just to be certain. Friend, do you know perchance where the flocks of Ya'akob's sons are grazing?

SHEPHERD. I am very familiar with those meek little lambs. They are fair lads who boast of their bravery and are very arrogant. Like ruffians, on the slightest suspicion—if they suspect that someone has slighted them—they took the life of their nearest kin. They are extremely envious when it comes to matters of rank, and they'll not allow another to have power or be esteemed. They are the height of pride, they are envy incarnate, braggadocio and presumption raised to the very stars! If anyone should be so foolish as to try to strut around like a rooster in their midst, they'll put a stop to that show of manliness by giving him a bitter burial.

YOSEPH. Not so fast, little shepherd. Guard your tongue. You should know that those shepherds are my very own brothers, and I'll not allow you to talk that way behind their backs. When you insult them, you insult me too.

SHEPHERD. Your brothers, you say? A fine lot of brothers you have! Time will show you just what sort of brothers you have. I can see you are going after them.

YOSEPH. That I am, but I can't find them. Can you tell me which green fields they occupy?

SHEPHERD. They were here for a while, but finding the pasture meager, they drove their flocks to Dothan. You will find them in Dothan for sure. Get a move on; that's where they are; but you'd be smarter to return to your father to save yourself the trouble and the danger of the road, for there are fierce lions there.

YOSEPH. I really must talk to them, for I have a message to give them. God keep you, for I'm leaving.

SHEPHERD. God guide you, son! But I'm very worried about the ferocious animals that prowl the meadows.

Exeunt. Enter Re'uven and Gad.

RE'UVEN. Gad, round up those lambs that are climbing up the crags. We don't want the wolf to come and eat them.

GAD. You're right, there are a great many of them in these mountains.

RE'UVEN. And the meadow is full of basilisks[27] with poisonous eyes and malignant thoughts. God preserve you from falling into their sharp fangs,

for their rage would not spare the purest, whitest ermine. If they catch
an innocent yearling, so tender and young that it's still at its mother's
breast, they'll strip it of its skin, like the golden fleece that so many
envied with insane obsession.

GAD. Just what are you getting at?

RE'UVEN. I'm talking about envy, that very semblance of hell, most merciless of passions the world has ever seen. I cannot mollify it, no matter
how I try. His innocence won't suffice any more than all my words to
persuade you to give up your barbarous designs.

GAD. You needn't worry about that as long as my father is alive; but as soon
as he closes his eyes, the boy is in great danger.

RE'UVEN. I don't consider him safe even in his father's lifetime, for they
keep howling like a she-wolf whose cubs have been taken from her.

GAD. He is safe with his father.

RE'UVEN. He is not safe, I tell you. They'll snatch him from his embrace,
dead or alive. I insist that that innocent child is at great risk of being
harmed by them.

ACT 2

*Enter Yehudah, Shim‘on, Re’uven, [Levi, Asher, Dan, Gad, Naphtali,]
and Yissaskhar.*

SHIM‘ON.   Now the flowery spring
has painted all these bowers,
and opening gay flowers,
new life to all will bring.
Dawn rises, inviting
the sweet birds to disclose
their songs in verse or prose
to the sun that gilds the day,
spreading joy in its way,
giving fragrance to the rose.
          With eyes of wonderment
on this beauty do I gaze,
but what does most amaze
is that proud adolescent.
Like a peacock content
he spreads his lyrelike plumes,
but sadness then consumes

his joy and his conceit:
seeing his hideous feet,
he ceases to presume.[28]
    When I think of Yoseph's dreams,
I am like that peacock.
I feel the same dire shock
and sense of loss, it seems,
for if fate truly deems
that he will have fortune,
and be raised up to the moon,
as slaves we are doomed to cower,
for, faced with God's great power,
our own strength can but swoon.

We'd better just finish him off and put an end to all our worries. Surely heaven does not intend for him to be king and lord.

RE'UVEN. This is grave wickedness, fierce rigor, a strange determination, a cruel envy and passion against your brother. You are all blinded by hatred, and you haven't considered what you are doing. Would you slay your brother in cold blood on account of an impious suspicion, a crazy, vain dream? Don't you realize that one day you must give an account to God, and that I and all of us will be stained with his blood and guilty before God? I am the eldest. As such, I can never agree to be a traitor or a murderer. Rather, I'll give my own life in defense of that ignorant lad. That is the only thing a God-fearing man can do.

LEVI. You are the very one who should kill him. As the eldest, you should realize that he is depriving you of your honor and status.

RE'UVEN. I disagree, and I refuse to do such a dreadful thing. I care nothing about dreams, for they are nothing but dreams;[29] but I do attach great value to a human soul.

SHIM'ON. Well, you're certainly fond of the boy, but he'll give you what you deserve. You may be the firstborn today, but tomorrow you'll be a slave.

YISSASKHAR. There comes our dreamer, eagerly coming down the mountainside.

SHIM'ON. That's him alright.

YISSASKHAR. Yes, it's him.

SHIM'ON. I don't see him.

YISSASKHAR. You don't? I can see him very clearly.

SHIM'ON. He certainly picked the right moment to show up, just when we were plotting his death. His misfortune and bad luck must have sent him here. Now is our chance to kill him.

RE'UVEN. Oh brothers! Don't stain your hands with blood! That's going too far! We are doing terrible violence to God, to the boy, and to the loving father who sends us gifts by his hand. It would be cruel to kill him. Instead, throw him in a well, and let his life end there, for he won't be able to escape. That would be better for you than committing an outright murder.

YEHUDAH. Your mercy makes us all merciful. Your will be done.

RE'UVEN. Then do as I say, brothers. Don't behave like tyrants, for killing him would be very cruel.

Enter Yoseph.

YOSEPH. Thanks be to heaven, at last I am out of danger! I have traveled many roads to get here, and I am so glad to see you! Come, let me hug you, brothers. That will comfort me for all the trials I've been through, though now I count them as naught, since I have found you well.

SHIM'ON. You dare ask for a hug? I'll hug that stiff neck of yours so tight that you'll soon join Pluto as ruler of Hades, for that's the only place where the puffed up and the proud deserve to rule.

YOSEPH. How has my innocence sinned against you, brothers? I've come with such humility unto your feet, so loyally unto your breasts, with such longing to find you and such joy to see you. I have been traveling night and day with heartfelt desire to come before your eyes, to know how you are faring, to bring news of my father, who is already bewailing my absence. Are these your tender hugs? Is this the sort of reception I deserve after coming from so far away to visit you? Was it only for this that my poor, sad father sent me to see how you were faring in this wilderness? Look at me, brothers, for I am your true brother. If you cruelly kill me, you will regret it and will weep tenderly for me once I am gone. I am just a boy. My whole life is before me, so please take pity. If I don't deserve it, at least respect an aged father. Don't extinguish this bright light that has come back to the world. Preserve it, for one day you may need it.

SHIM'ON. What goodness could shine forth from one so full of haughty presumption, insane thoughts, vain hopes, and infamous desires, one who aspires to be king, and who dreams such dreams as yours? Give up that tunic that first made us jealous; just looking at it gives me pain and torment. *[Strips him of the tunic.]* You can say good-bye to all your finery, for the honorable old man will give you no more frills to cause us spite. Get moving, for your grave will be a well full of snakes and scorpions, the vermin of the desert. You can thank Re'uven for your life. We have spared it out of respect for him until we decide just what to do with you.

RE'UVEN. Don't be upset. Accept all these troubles with patience, for heaven will come to your aid when you least expect it. Place all your hope in

God, for He is the help of the good, and He will find a way to set you free. Your brothers have gone mad. They are doing these dreadful things because they are enraged by your dreams of power; but, since you are innocent, Yoseph, hope in heaven, which will protect your innocence and soon restore you to your father.

YOSEPH. How have I sinned, Re'uven? What crimes have I done, what wickedness have I committed? Am I to blame for my dreams? Haven't I always been obedient? Haven't I done as I was told? Haven't I respected my brothers, both young and old? If my father loves me well, if he finds me pleasing, if he shows me greater love, surely that's not my fault. I am truly unfortunate, born under an unlucky star, for strangers love me while my own people hate me. You are the eldest of all, you are in charge; they all obey you and respect you. Defend my innocence, plead my cause, excuse my error and guilt, though truly I have done no wrong. They have stripped me naked here, but still I am clothed in innocence and justice. 'Tis justice I implore from all of you and from eternal God.

LEVI. You talk too much. You always did know how to lay on fancy rhetoric, but now you can go converse with the desert snakes. Get moving, follow me, for I can't bear to listen to your impertinence any longer.

YOSEPH. Where am I going?

LEVI. Straight to hell, where you'll make your abode, if you survive, with mortal basilisks and slimy snakes.

YOSEPH. Then, brothers, if that's your decision, please kill me now, for I will die happier if you are the ones who kill me. I forgive you, brother, if I can forgive, but I fear that my blood, like that of Hevel, will cry out to heaven. How well that shepherd in the mountains warned me when he sang of that very story; and how foolish, ignorant, and stupid I was to close my eyes to his veiled advice, failing to give credence to his predictions! Clearly, he was an angel, as now I know and see, and heaven was warning me of this misfortune I am suffering, which I then hardly suspected. I didn't believe it. I was wrong, but who could guess that brothers would do such an ugly deed as this?

SHIM'ON. Get him out of my sight. It upsets me just to see him. Let Levi and Asher take him away. The rest of us can stay here, for it's time to eat. Summon the shepherds and tell them to take whatever food they've prepared out of their bags.

Exeunt Levi and Asher with Yoseph.

YEHUDAH.　　　　　In this verdant field,
　　　　　embroidered with flowers colorful or pale,
　　　　　now to sheer pleasure yield,
　　　　　and hearken to the sweet-voiced nightingale.

Let's sit down and be still,
as of this sumptuous food we eat our fill.
        Since that ingrate
we've now consigned to a narrow prison cell,
we all should celebrate.
Let him on his misfortune sadly dwell,
while we rejoice
and toast our victory with gladsome voice.

RE'UVEN.   I am downcast;
if you don't mind, unto my hut I'll go.
Today I'll fast;
perhaps I'll dine with you on the morrow.
No longer sad,
I'll join your party and with you be glad.
                [He walks away from them.]
[Aside:]   With heaven's aid,
I'll free the lad, for I am sore afraid
those ravenous wolves
will soon devour that innocent dove.
I'll set him free
if heaven wills he be at liberty.
                Exeunt. Enter Levi and Asher.

LEVI. Weeping and wailing, restless and impatient, Yoseph is in the well among venomous snakes. Those tears he sheds, those sighs he sighs, those laments he pronounces could soften the very rocks. He's weeping pitifully, complaining of his fate, raising his voice to the heavens, shedding tears on the earth for the sore pain that he feels. I know it was weak of me, but even I couldn't help weeping. Only a brute could have done otherwise. Don't be so cruel, brothers! Take him out of that torment into the sunlight. Let him live in heavy chains. Left there, he will surely die, for he doesn't have the strength to resist such suffering.

SHIM'ON. Yes, that's an excellent idea. He should not die at the hands of his own brothers. We only did that so we wouldn't have to witness his pitiful tragedy.

YISSASKHAR. I see some foreigners on that mountainside. They must be merchants, for they are loaded down with goods.

YEHUDAH. This happenstance is just the opportunity we were hoping for. We can solve our problem and be the richer for it. Since our brother is suffering miserably in the well, and his sin wasn't really so great, he's not very guilty, and his error was unintentional, we can save ourselves trouble, avoid shedding innocent blood, and at the same time be rid of his constant rivalry by selling him as a slave. Let him rule somewhere where we won't have to see him. These businessmen will be happy to purchase him. They'll consider him worth more than diamonds, for his good looks will make him more marketable.

LEVI. I think you are right. Let's wait for them to get here, and then we'll find out if they're interested in him. We won't drive too hard a bargain, for our main goal is that he should rule far away, since he aspires to rule.

Enter [two] Ishmaelite merchants.

ISHMAELITES. Heaven keep you, shepherds!

YEHUDAH. And heaven prosper you! Where are you coming from this fine day?

ISHMAELITES. From Gil'ad, where we have bought some perfumes. We are merchants by trade, as you can see. If you have anything to sell, let us see it, as long as it's cheap.

YEHUDAH. We have a slave who is as good as gold. I am sure that if you buy him, you can sell him for a fortune.

ISHMAELITE [1]. May we see him?

YEHUDAH. Wait here. They will bring him right away. Asher, Levi, Dan: go get him quickly, and take plenty of rope to draw him out of the well. Gentlemen, he's a handsome lad with many fine qualities. He's a fine astrologer, always studying the winds. When he dreams, he'll tell you wonderful things, though his dreams have gotten him into trouble up to now, for some of them are so pretentious that they defy competition, and he's very touchy about them. He has other fine qualities. He can see the sun at night, and the moon in its chariot, and stars that kneel down. When you see him, you'll be wild about him. He aspires to a crown (but that doesn't concern you, for it is neither here nor there). However, you'll have to give us forty silver coins for him.

ISHMAELITE [2]. Well, you've certainly put a high price on him.

YEHUDAH. That's not much, for, though he has little experience in your business, time, which tests everything, will make him a great merchant. He will make you rich if you are lucky.

ISHMAELITE [1]. You've got that right, for without luck a merchant is like the waning moon and will never get ahead. But how much did you say I'll have to pay for the lad?

YEHUDAH. I told you, but if it bothers you so much, you can deduct five or ten.

ISHMAELITE [2]. It seems to me that twenty pieces of silver would be a fair price.

YEHUDAH. Don't take me for a fool! I know he's worth more than that. If you want to buy the lad and take him away with you, I won't insist on forty, but you will have to pay thirty.

ISHMAELITE [2]. Be satisfied with the twenty, for I am reluctant to pay you even that much for the lad. If not, I'll just bid you farewell.

YEHUDAH. He's yours; but he deserves to be treated with respect. Here comes the little wretch. Isn't he good-looking? What do you think?

Enter Yoseph.

ISHMAELITE [1]. Yes, he's shapely, and he carries himself well.

YOSEPH. Oh my brothers! What are you doing? Would you sell me as a slave? My luck is bad indeed! Have you forgotten that I am the son of your own father, who is pious, just, and saintly? Didn't he give you honor and even your very being? What sort of excuse will you give him to make him stop weeping? I am to be a slave? And where am I to go?

SHIM'ON. You're going straight to Egypt.

YOSEPH. How could you be capable of selling me? Brothers, I can't believe it! A slave? How cruel! Death itself would be better, and by killing me you would be sure I'd never be a king or master over you.

SHIM'ON. No, it's better that you not die, for that would be unjust. You'll go to Egypt to be king for the dreams that you dreamed.

YOSEPH. How can you be so harsh? Take pity on my youth. Don't you see that it's very cruel to sell your own flesh and blood? Brothers, kill me with your own hands, for that would be less wicked. Put an end to my life; thereby you'll end my weeping. This tyranny is just as bad as murder. But I know that just because I ask you, you will refuse to do it, for what you like best is to see me weep, and sob, and suffer. An unlucky man like me would have been better off unborn. But I will bear this affliction, stifling my anger with the tears of my eyes and the anxiety of my heart; for a slave must surely suffer a thousand pains weighed down with irons and chains, living in constant weeping; and now I must go through all this hardship as a slave in a foreign land.

LEVI. I'm sure you'll find a fine silk tunic made to measure for you over there.

ISHMAELITE [2]. Do you want to count the money? We are wasting our precious time here.

YEHUDAH. Give it to me.

ISHMAELITE [2]. I have already counted it out. Count it again for yourself if you like, but give us the lad, for we must be on our way. Farewell.

YEHUDAH. Here is the boy; please treat him well.

YOSEPH. So I have really been sold, though I am a son of Israel! Since the grim reaper has cut me down before my time, brothers, at least give me the consolation of one last embrace. Let me kiss your hands and feet, since I shall not see you again. Farewell, Asher; farewell, Gad; farewell, Dan and Naphtali! I bid you all farewell, for our companionship is done. Truly, you will never see me again, since I am being led into slavery. Tell my father to grieve for me with my mother, for now he has good reason to grieve.

GAD. We're awfully sorry to see you so unhappy.

ISHMAELITE [2]. Come on, we must get out of here. We can't delay any longer.

YOSEPH. Sir, these are my brothers, and I will miss them very much.

ISHMAELITE [2]. They've certainly acted very brotherly toward you, Yoseph. Now tell them good-bye once and for all.

YOSEPH. Good-bye, and may God give me patience!

Exeunt. Enter Re'uven [holding Yoseph's torn tunic in his hand].

RE'UVEN.　　Oh cruel envy, who could ever chart
　　　　　　the harm done by blind wrath, your poison dart?
　　　　　　Yoseph they must have slain,
　　　　　　and buried him while I was gone; 'tis plain.
　　　　　　What a strange tale of woe!
　　　　　　That his own flesh could kill him and not know
　　　　　　his childish innocence!
　　　　　　How wicked is this dreadful violence!
　　　　　　I thought that I could save you. I was wrong.
　　　　　　I stayed away too long,
　　　　　　for these ravenous wolves on violence bent
　　　　　　must have suspected that was my intent;
　　　　　　guessing that their actions I'd oppose,
　　　　　　your life and mine they've brought unto its close.
　　　　　　You have found rest in heaven's heights azure
　　　　　　amid the shining lights and souls so pure,
　　　　　　but I am cast adrift on stormy sea,
　　　　　　with no rudder I can hold.
　　　　　　What excuse can I offer, how be free
　　　　　　of the accusations of my father old?
　　　　　　What can I do? How can I expurgate
　　　　　　this guilt? Oh father so unfortunate!
　　　　　　You'll no more see the son whom you loved so;
　　　　　　your life henceforth will be but endless woe.

YISSASKHAR.　There comes Re'uven with that tunic torn,
　　　　　　and he is forlorn.
　　　　　　He has surely concluded, or at least does dread,
　　　　　　since Yoseph is missing, he must be dead.

YEHUDAH.　　Re'uven, please tell us: why are you so sad?

RE'UVEN.   What do you think? You have slain that lad,
though he was innocent,
and by that act your father's blood you've spent,
so sad and old, alas,
for Yoseph was his very looking glass!
Such cruelty you've nurtured in your breast!
How could you thus the closest bonds detest
of blood paternal?
Its cry will be eternal,
unto the God Who does all truth attain,
seeking revenge for that most heinous stain.

YEHUDAH.   Calm down, if Yoseph's life you long to save,
for we have only sold him as a slave.
'Tis better thus, it may be a good thing,
for now in Egypt he can be a king.

RE'UVEN.   Oh, woe is me! How dare you be so bold!
Poor Yoseph as a slave you've sold?
What shall we say to that old grieving man?

YEHUDAH.   We have already thought of a good plan.
That tunic that caused all of us such pain
with the blood of a kid we now will sorely stain.
We'll say the cause
of Yoseph's death was a wild beast's savage claws.
We'll tear it up
and say that beast on Yoseph's flesh did sup.

RE'UVEN.   Oh, yes, that all sounds very good to you,
but have you considered what this news will do
to our poor sire? His grief you'll not allay
unless him too you now propose to slay.

ACT 3

Enter Ya'akob.

YA'AKOB. How long and how drawn out the hours seem to one who waits! Waiting is an endless torment. I am awaiting Yoseph, but my hope is turning to despair, for this long delay makes me fear some danger. After all, the fields of Shechem are not so very far away. He should have been back by now if things had gone well. Oh my son, your absence costs me dear, for I fear the disasters of the road, which are so common! May heaven keep you from harm and soon bring you back to my eyes, so that this sad and afflicted old man may have some peace.

Enter Re'uven, Shim'on, Levi, Yehudah, and the other brothers.

RE'UVEN. I haven't the heart to break such bad news to him. You do it, since you have been the cause of this harm. Yehudah is the one who should do it, for he is the better speaker. He will never hear such a great wickedness from my mouth.

YA'AKOB. Welcome home, my sons! Do you bring good tidings? What, no answer? What's wrong? Why don't you come up to me? Where is Yoseph? Re'uven, why are you all so silent? Where have you left my son? Speak to me. I am already distressed, and I feel that my soul is departing.

YEHUDAH. What can we tell you of Yoseph, since we haven't seen him? Still, we presume from the evidence we've seen that you must have sent him there.

YA'AKOB. What evidence? Out with it!

YEHUDAH. I'm afraid you'll be offended, and I dare not say, for the news is bad, father.

YA'AKOB. The blood in my veins has turned to ice just from hearing you! Speak up, Yehudah, but be careful what you say, for I am as good as dead!

YEHUDAH. And rightly so, for the news I bring is more cruel than death itself. I regret to have to tell you, but I must. We found this garment; see if it is your son's.

YA'AKOB.   Alas, sweet token of my boy![30]
Alas, my Yoseph! Light of these old eyes!
My happiness, my joy,
sole comfort in my pain and in my sighs,
my choicest company,
my son, my Yoseph, you were all to me!
        What vengeful Fate
has cut your thread of life in tender years
and spared this hoary pate
alive such bitterness to contemplate?
Why didn't you take me,
oh cruel one, and not leave me to see
        with these reluctant eyes
this coat of colors that for him I made,
a wretched sacrifice?
I meant this gift to be an accolade,
but it brought only scorn,
and now by a fierce lion it is torn.

Yoseph, my North Star,
my sweet love, in my darkness brightest light,
companion without par,
your brilliance and your conduct so upright
to mourn I shall not cease;
with each new day my grief will yet increase.
    Oh Rachel, weep and wail
in Ramah[31] for the dear son you have lost.
This outrage now assail;
but though you mourn this bitter holocaust,
his father's grief
will outstrip yours and never find relief.
    Now you with souls so pure
find rest, for as a star in heaven you rise,
while I this pain endure,
knowing I am the cause of your demise,
until that happy day
when I join you and shed this mortal clay.
    Your woeful tragedy,
your tale, son torn from my fond embrace,
will live in memory;
to the sun's own sphere your saga I will raise,
as grieving I lament
your short life, those few years so quickly spent.
    I alone am to blame;
I know it was my fault, my darling boy.
I must now bear that shame,
for if your company was my sole joy,
why did I send you there?
Knowing the danger, why did I not beware?
    I was the instrument
of this misfortune, oh my dearest son.
I was the monster insolent
that preyed upon you with malice wanton.
I failed to cherish
your life enough, and thus caused you to perish.
    Thus in unending strife
I'll mourn for you, and will not cease to rave.
I took your innocent life,
and thereby madly carved out my own grave.

I long now for your sight,
though I can see you still, oh brightest light!

RE'UVEN.   Oh father good,
be still, for this excess of grief severe,
won't bring back his cold blood,
e'en though you shed for him so many a tear.
Rest, father, for a while;
by grieving so, your own life you defile.

YA'AKOB.   What good is life?
My life was Yoseph; he is no longer here.
Death's keen-edged knife
has severed us, for I was Yoseph's sphere,
for his bright sun
gave light unto my eyes. I am undone.
      This misery is mine;
'tis I who must eternally lament
and for him pine.
Till death I'll live in sorrow and torment.
Now let me weep
until at last with Yoseph I can sleep.

Exeunt. Enter the Ishmaelites with Yoseph.

ISHMAELITE [1]. This country seat on the banks of the fertile Nile is the property of a noble Egyptian, a grandee of the kingdom. His name is Potiphar. He is fabulously rich, lord and absolute prince of On, among his other titles. It is just two leagues from the city of Memphis, first in all Africa for its excellent situation and antiquities. There our wearisome journey at last will end, and there too you will acquire an estimable master. However, our animals are running out of fodder. We will go down to that nearby village to buy some. You stay here with the camels, and beware, for this region is full of lions and other wild animals. Watch out, don't fall asleep, for a disaster could easily occur. Take this javelin and stand guard. God keep you till we return!

Exeunt. Enter Asenath and her maid Rezinda, singing.

ASENATH AND REZINDA.
      Now that the lovely dawn
      precedes the rising sun,
      as he lifts his gilded locks
      above the proud mountain,
      the little birds with glee,
      both nightingale and lark,
      salute him as he comes,

banishing the dark.
To the green fields the sheep
follow the shepherd boy,
as to the merry flute
he sings of mirth and joy.
Now all the withered plants
are happily blooming,
as the sun enters Aries,[32]
and earth greets returning spring.

REZINDA. Oh, madam, we are done for! A terrible crocodile is crawling out of the Nile. May God preserve our lives!

ASENATH. We are as good as dead, for there's no one here to help us.

YOSEPH. Ladies, don't be afraid! My courage will defend you.

ASENATH. You are an angel, who has come down from heaven to help us. But you are lovely as a flower, and I don't want you to wilt. That animal is ferocious, and I fear for your life.

YOSEPH. I would gladly die for you. But both of you, take shelter over there where the camels are, and leave this to me.

ASENATH. May heaven preserve you, and me too! Your beauty should be sheltered, not put at risk like this.

YOSEPH. Take shelter while I attack.

ASENATH. Yes, sir, I'm doing so.

YOSEPH. I'll kill it with a single shot if I am my father's son.

ASENATH. He's going straight up to it. May heaven protect him from harm!

YOSEPH. Come here, you savage beast, for I will skin you alive!

ASENATH. It is poised to attack! But now he's shot it and nailed it to the ground with the point of his javelin. Brave deed! Great courage! Who would have guessed that such a tender lad would do a deed like that! I am obliged to him.

He cuts off its head and brings it to the lady.

YOSEPH. Madam, accept this token from your humble slave.

ASENATH. Sir, I feel just as stricken as that beast. But you should know who I am, who it is that owes you such a debt: I am a noble and honorable woman and much obliged to you. I am the daughter of an illustrious man whose name is Poti-phera. As time goes on, his reputation will inform you of his great nobility. I came to this country seat for recreation, along with my ladies and my mother. My bad luck brought me to this meadow—but no, it was good luck, for I saw you here. You have risked your life on my behalf. I was as good as dead, but you saved my life by killing that beast. Hence I dare ask that you tell me who you are, so that my honor can repay one to whom I owe so much.

YOSEPH. Madam, my misfortune—though now I think it fortune, since it gave me this chance to see you and oblige you—has brought me from my homeland to be a slave in this land of yours; but if I am to be your slave, I'll be free with your protection. I was born of noble parents and brought up in the greatest luxury the world has ever known. I was my noble father's delight, his love, his closest confidant; but envy, like a lightning bolt, struck down all that glory, for then my brothers, jealous of my good fortune, harassed me like strangers on account of certain dreams I saw. There's no point in recounting them now; suffice it to say that because they presaged greatness, my brothers envied me. One day I went out to the fields where their flocks were grazing, and when they saw me alone there, instead of killing me—which others might have done—they sold me as a slave to get me out of their sight. Fortunately, I was purchased—for that's how I met you here—by some men who have gone to the village to buy food. I don't know where they are taking me, but I know I am more the slave of your rare loveliness than of the men who bought me.

ASENATH. You were not born to be a slave, and so indeed you shall not be a slave, even if my wealth is not enough and I must sell myself. Those "gentlemen" you refer to must have stolen you. I'd like to have a word with them.

YOSEPH. Here they come. If I am not mistaken, that is them.

Enter the Ishmaelites.

ISHMAELITE [1]. Yoseph, what beasts have you encountered? If these are the beasts that attack you, you should stay in the wild forever.

ASENATH. Whence have you brought this lad?

ISHMAELITE [1]. I haven't brought him from anywhere; he has come here on his own two feet.

ASENATH. Yes, I can see that; but I'm certain you are thieves who have stolen him, and because he is so young, you have tricked him with your deceit. If that is the case, I shall have you both hanged.

ISHMAELITE [2]. Upon my life, that is not so! We paid good money for him.

ASENATH. Do you mean to sell him?

ISHMAELITE [2]. Yes, we do, but we can only sell him to one master.

ASENATH. What do you mean by that? I do not understand.

ISHMAELITE [2]. Madam, I mean that he is already sold; for I am obliged to Potiphar, since he supplies all the money I need to do my business, and I promised to bring him such a slave. This one is fit for a king, and he needs him in his palace. Hence, I will not sell him for any price, for if Potiphar found out, it would cost me very dear.

ASENATH. Is there nothing to be done?

ISHMAELITE [2]. No, there is not, for I've brought him specially for him; but next time I'll bring you a handsome slave.

ASENATH. *[Aside:]* A fine consolation that is, when I'm on fire with a thousand flames!

[To Yoseph:] What is your name?

YOSEPH. Madam, my name is Yoseph.

ASENATH. Well, Yoseph, as a down payment on your ransom, accept this ring from my hand. *[To the Ishmaelites:]* Don't you dare take it from him on the pretense that he's your slave, for if you do, you will surely die!

ISHMAELITE [1]. You can rest assured of that, madam. And now, please excuse us, for it is late, and we must go.

YOSEPH. Farewell, madam, though I wish I could remain here to gaze on your lovely eyes, which I idolize, and to make you understand how grateful I am for the favor I have received from your generous hand.

ASENATH. Don't be upset, Yoseph. Know that I carry you in this honored breast, and that I shan't forget you. I'll say no more.

Exeunt the Ishmaelites with Yoseph.

ASENATH. Rezinda, I am lost. I am enslaved to that slave. If I can't live with him, what good is life? His face captivated me, his brightness blinded me, my heart beat so I thought that I should faint. His deeds obliged me, seeing his excellent qualities, to surrender my will to love. I am so changed from what I was before that I feel like the sun itself, while I am consumed by fire.

REZINDA. Not so fast, my lady! You are very much in love; but if you think you are on fire, I too am burning up.

ASENATH. What? Did you like his looks?

REZINDA. Would I should find such favor in God's eyes as he has found in mine!

ASENATH. Rezinda, there's not enough of him to go around. I demand that you cease loving him. It's only right that my love should come first. He did that deed for me; it was for my sake that he slew that monster. I inspired his courage and his bravery. I am obliged to him. He likes my looks, and he is in love with me too; I am sure of it. If you continue to sigh for him, you will be doing wrong; so I forbid you to cast eyes upon him again.

REZINDA. Love entered through my eyes, and it is a passion that is born from the heart and is uncontrollable. What you would have me do?

ASENATH. Don't make me mad, Rezinda. All right, you can look at him with your eyes, but just don't speak to him with your lips. I, with heaven's help, hope to attain his hand. If you love him, it's obvious that I'll have to be jealous of you. You know that jealousy is hell. If you persist, I will make sure he never sees you, much less loves you.

REZINDA. Madam, God forbid that my love should anger you. I'll close both mouth and eyes, though my heart will still adore him.

ASENATH. Let's go then, for I have to think up some lie to tell my mother, for I want to see my father so that I can arrange to see my slave.

Exeunt. Enter Potiphar and Yoseph.

POTIPHAR. I think it was very harsh and even tyrannical for your brothers to have sold you on account of a mere fantasy. Your youth and your good looks deserved better treatment. Your brothers have treated you with a rigor unworthy of human beings, much less brothers, who should treat each other kindly. But if you have found only deceit, betrayal, and ill will among your own, you will find greater kindness and mercy among strangers. I will look with kindly eyes upon your tender youth, your innocent age, for your suffering has moved me. I shall treat you as my own son so that you can forget past hardships. If a monstrous envy banished you from your homeland, in this foreign land you will turn out to have been harassed but happy.

YOSEPH. With a loyal soul and a sincere heart I hope with heaven's help, though I may be a foreigner, to accomplish deeds that will make me worthy to be called your true son.

Enter Zenobia, Potiphar's wife.

ZENOBIA. I have been told that you have acquired a very handsome slave, whose gorgeous body is as rare as a diamond. Please don't think me foolish, or consider it frivolous of me to have come here so early in the morning just to see him. Is this he? His beauty is unequaled, superhuman.

POTIPHAR. Madam, that is he, and I am so content with him that I don't think I would part with him for any price.

YOSEPH. *[Kneels before her.]* My lady, allow this slave to kiss your feet, for if you are as kind as my master, truly I can thank God for having set me free.

ZENOBIA. Get up. I can't allow the sun to bow before the moon. Fortunate are you, and lucky was your birth, for though it be a torment to be a slave in a foreign land, let that not pain you, for if your master loves you, your mistress too will strip you of those chains.

YOSEPH. If I have found favor in your eyes and therefore dare speak so boldly, I shall say that I am no slave but a free man. Yet I'll gladly be enslaved to your every wish. It is only right that I should obey one who shows me such kindness, when I have found only unjust harshness among my own brothers.

POTIPHAR. As a first installment on the favors I mean to do you, I shall give you an honorable post. You will be in charge of all my farmhands. When they harvest fair Pomona's[33] fruit and flowers, you will store them up and afterwards distribute them. Following my instructions, you will give the servants their rations and supply my table. Come with me now, for since you are such a novice, I want to explain everything to you.

YOSEPH. I kiss your feet. Serving you will be my greatest pleasure, my lord. For this high honor that you've done me, in spite of my unworthiness, may merciful heaven permit that you live as long as Nestor.[34]

Exeunt Potiphar and Yoseph.

ZENOBIA. He is indeed a pearl most excellent.
A royal jewel set in purest gold,
a truly priceless pendant
that round my throat I would rejoice to hold
is this young slave, whose beauty does contrive
of freedom e'en his masters to deprive.
How can this have happened so apace,
how could such deadly poison flood my eyes?
His beauteous body caught me by surprise,
the radiant light of his refulgent face.
If honor can't displace
this love, if shame it does o'erwhelm,
how can this fragile boat without a helm,
adrift on stormy sea,
with no anchor to save,
from this captive be free,
or yet escape this slave,
so heavily armed, setting the soul afire
with these assaults of deadly cannon fire?
Oh cruel husband! How could you behave
this way! To your own house you've brought
a fire in which I'm caught,
temptation from this sweetest of all slaves,
whose slave I am, though he's my property.
I mean no disrespect.
What can I do, since he means all to me,
and my own eyes reflect
his beauty, and his features love to trace,
his virtues and his all-surpassing grace?
Enough of this! My soul has now decided
to love him in your spite,

for it could not be right
to lose him and therefore by love be chided.
In this war I have sided
with love, though conjugal decorum I offend,
with every breath
I know that to lose him would be my death.
I'll love him without end.
His beauty means the world to me.
I hope that love will give me victory.

Exit Zenobia. Enter Asenath and Rezinda.

ASENATH. Pretending I've come calling—a good disguise for love—I'll better camouflage my true intention. We'll find out if there's any hope of ransoming my slave. Rezinda, knock on that door.

REZINDA. Your wish is my command.

She knocks. [Zenobia answers. She is accompanied by her servant Matilde.]

ZENOBIA. Yoseph, is that you knocking? Who's there?

ASENATH. Your humble servant.

ZENOBIA. What? Is it you, my lady?

ASENATH. I was just passing by, and I thought it would be rude to pass up this opportunity to ask you how you are.

ZENOBIA. May God preserve you! I am at your disposal. I deem it great good fortune and an inestimable favor that your loveliness has come to call on me today.

ASENATH. Your beauty dazzles like the noonday sun. Thus outshone, what light could I possibly have?

ZENOBIA. You're just saying that to please. You know very well that your eyes would suffice to blind the brightest lights.

ASENATH. Truly you embarrass me. But please tell me what's new, for you have someone in your house who must have brought you news.

ZENOBIA. Are you referring to my slave?

ASENATH. Indeed I am. Since he has come here from the desert, he must have a thing or two to tell.

ZENOBIA. Have you already heard all about him?

ASENATH. Not all, but someone who saw him told me that he's as sweet as sugar and honey.

ZENOBIA. That's the truth.

ASENATH. Can't we have a look at him?

ZENOBIA. Just to give you pleasure, I'll bring him right away. Wait here. *[To Matilde:]* Call Yoseph, and tell him to come to my room.

MATILDE. No sooner said than done. I'll fly like the wind. *[Aside:]* This is the chance I've been waiting for. Now no one can stop me from telling him about myself and letting him know my feelings. I'm sure that he desires me. I can tell by the way he acts; and it's no wonder, for they say I'm not bad-looking.

She meets Yoseph [in the wings].

Yoseph, I was just going to get you, for my lady wants to see you. First, though, I have to tell you that I am burning up with love for you. Don't think I'm exaggerating; for if love is blind, I am blinded by your fire.

YOSEPH. Stop it, Matilde.

MATILDE. What? Can't you be even a little bit nice to poor Matilde? That's awfully rude of you.

ZENOBIA. Here he comes. What do you think of him?

ASENATH. He's not so bad-looking.

ZENOBIA. That's an awfully cold answer. You may think it strange, but I think he is unequaled.

ASENATH. *[Aside:]* She's burning with love for Yoseph. Upon my life, I'm afraid she'll conquer him, for there's nothing like an inside job.

Enter Yoseph.

YOSEPH. Madam, I was told that you wanted me to come here. Is there anything I can do for you?

ZENOBIA. Just look at his elegant manliness! Relax, pull up a chair. We're among friends.

YOSEPH. I left my master at the palace, and I wouldn't be surprised if he needs me there.

ZENOBIA. This lady came to see me—very likely because she's heard about you—and I want to entertain her.

YOSEPH. Heard about me? I can't believe it! After all, I'm nothing but a worm, and who bothers to look at a worm?

ASENATH. That may be so, but if there were a fierce crocodile around here, one of us—or maybe even two—would be certainly be glad to see you.

YOSEPH. That's a different story. If a crocodile were to come out of the Nile to prey upon passers-by, surely anyone would come to the aid of a damsel in distress. It would be his chance to win honor and fame by cruelly killing the monster, and besides, the lady would surely show him sweet love, and he too would be inflamed with love.

ASENATH. You seem to know a great deal about love. But you are right; if he saved the lady, it would be only right for her to show him favor. However, she was born under a contrary star, for since the man she loves is absent, he'll forget her soon enough.

YOSEPH. How can you say such a thing? Love is constant, and no one can keep a true lover from his love, when it has taken root in both their souls. No matter what torment he endures, he will not forget her. Your aspersions on loyalty and love are insulting to an honorable man.

ZENOBIA. Your analysis of love is eloquent, but I have a thing or two to say as well. When a woman is in love, even if she loves an inferior and knows it will do her harm and stain her honor, she will not desist from her pursuit until she entirely possesses the man she loves. Love is irrational, not ruled by intellect. It takes outrageous risks, endures all danger, and single-mindedly pursues the loved one, even if he is a foreigner.

YOSEPH. You two can discuss these matters at greater length. I'm off to the palace. You already know my opinion. I stand by what I have said, and you may rest assured that I have chosen my words very carefully.

ASENATH. So have I, and I too must be going, for I have things to do.

ZENOBIA. Why hurry off, my lady?

ASENATH. Please excuse me for now. I hope to come back soon.

Exeunt. Enter Potiphar and Yoseph.

POTIPHAR. Have you measured out the grain?

YOSEPH. Yes, sir.

POTIPHAR. What did it come to?

YOSEPH. Three hundred bushels of the early wheat. I estimate that what remains to reap will come to double that, for it is very fertile.

POTIPHAR. And have they sheared the sheep?

YOSEPH. Yes, sir, and by my reckoning we have three thousand hundredweight of wool.

POTIPHAR. Ever since you came to my house, holy heaven has blessed me. I owe you all this profit you have brought me. It is because of you that I am now so prosperous, and therefore I've decided to put you in charge of all my income and estates. Make whatever arrangements you like, and order what seems right and just to you. I entrust everything I have to you. It is all yours to do with as you choose. I expect no accounting. You will be like a sovereign lord.

YOSEPH. I shall give you an exact account of everything that you entrust to me.

POTIPHAR. I am already amply convinced of your virtue and acumen. Farewell; I have to go to the palace now.

YOSEPH. May heaven make you happy! I am your slave. I owe everything I am to you.

Exit Potiphar. Enter Zenobia.

ZENOBIA. I see that Potiphar has left. He must be going to the palace. Yoseph must be here, for I saw him come in with him. What shall I do? My slippery fate has placed me in a quandary. Love urges me to follow my desire, but rigorous honor demands that I renounce this happiness and trample love underfoot. Love is blind and whimsical, insisting that I close my eyes to honor, which is another kind of fire. This is my dilemma: I don't know which way to go. Should I follow honor and remain loyal as I ought, or should I go with love's sweet desire? If I speak to him, I'm lost. If I don't, it's even worse. Both honor and love are endangering my life. Since either choice means death, and I really have to choose, I'll cast my lot with love. Yes, I shall speak to him. Be patient, honor. You'll just have to forgive me, for I must follow my destiny. Are you here, Yoseph?

YOSEPH. Yes, ma'am.

ZENOBIA. Where is your master?

YOSEPH. He went to the palace.

ZENOBIA. How long ago?

YOSEPH. Just now.

ZENOBIA. And what are you doing now?

YOSEPH. I was just working on the accounts of a landholder to whom I pay the income from the sheep.

ZENOBIA. I have a more urgent account to settle with you. If we can work things out, I shall be satisfied.

YOSEPH. I am at your service.

ZENOBIA. What I have to tell you is that a certain lady who is intelligent, beautiful, and of good repute—in fact she is a relative of mine—is in love with you. On your account she is suffering greatly and despairs of life. Since she is rather bashful, she's asked me to speak to you on her behalf. We are so close that I agreed to do her this great favor, for it's as much in my own interest as in hers.

YOSEPH. I can't believe any woman would want to bother with me.

ZENOBIA. Your sweet body is worth a king's ransom.

YOSEPH. All I can say is that that lady chose a poor object for her affection.

ZENOBIA. What if it were I who loved you and desired you? Then what would you say?

YOSEPH. I would tell you to uphold the honor and loyalty you owe your husband. Marriage is indeed a very high estate and permits no mixture of another love.

ZENOBIA. Can't you see that I'm dying for you? You're the only thing I live for. You may have been a slave, but I am your slave now.

YOSEPH. Madam, it is wrong for you act so foolishly. I am going now, and when I'm gone, please forget this ever happened.

Exit Yoseph.

ZENOBIA. He's gone! How could he leave me here like this? How could he so rudely ignore my pleas? I shall put out this fire with your blood and

with your life! Oh no, not that! Surely love will find some way to win
him over. I'll have to harass him relentlessly. If at first you don't succeed . . .

Exit Zenobia. Enter Asenath, veiled; she comes upon Yoseph.

ASENATH. Oh, sir!

YOSEPH. Are you calling me, ma'am?

ASENATH. Yes.

YOSEPH. What do you want from me?

ASENATH. Just two ounces of love.

YOSEPH. You're out of luck, for I've sold all I had.

ASENATH. I picked a fine time to show up!

YOSEPH. You are too late. Forgive me. My love must be very tasty, since so
many of you are hungry for it.

ASENATH. I think you are harassed but happy.

YOSEPH. Unhappy would be more like it.

ASENATH. How can you call this unhappiness?

YOSEPH. How could I call it happiness, since I was born unhappy?

ASENATH. What is the matter?

YOSEPH. What do you think? Everywhere I turn—forgive me!—some woman
molests and harasses me, and they all think they should win. I only have
one soul, and I have already given that to the woman I love.

ASENATH. Well, if you've already given it away, and there's nothing left for
me, farewell, kind sir.

YOSEPH. Farewell.

ASENATH. Farewell, it's my bad luck.

She lifts her veil.

YOSEPH. Is it you, my love? Forgive me. I didn't know you.

ASENATH. You'd better save such words for that woman or person to whom
you've surrendered your soul. I can only bewail my fate, for I was so
unlucky as to have trusted you.

YOSEPH. By those two bright eyes that enlighten all I see, you're the only
one I long for, you are my only love! Be careful what you say. You are
offending my honor.

ASENATH. Don't be upset, sweet love. I was just testing you. Are you surprised that I'd be jealous with so many harpies around to embitter my
life and drive me mad?

YOSEPH. What have I done to deserve this happiness? What are you doing
here?

ASENATH. I came looking for you, and I've found the day itself, for when
you are absent, it is darkest night.

YOSEPH. Oh light of my eyes, when I gaze upon your beauty, the sun rises in the east. Seeing you makes me happy and banishes my suffering, but I have no lack of troubles everywhere I go.

ASENATH. What's wrong, my love?

YOSEPH. I have a problem that I must keep secret. A powerful woman wrongly loves me and wants me all for herself. She doesn't know that you are the only love my heart can cherish. My dear, I'll say no more; but I must warn you that this enemy is very powerful, and her love is like a thorn in my flesh.

ASENATH. It's not hard to figure out who is the source of your troubles, but I'd better keep that to myself. Farewell, my love. My maid is waiting for me, and I don't want her or anyone else to see us talking to each other.

Exeunt. Enter Zenobia [removing her jewelry and outer garments].

ZENOBIA. What good is all this finery—gold, diamonds, pearls, the ornaments befitting my rank, my noble blood—if a slave's eyes, like a basilisk, can wound me with poisoned arrows and cruelly murder me? I cannot resist him. How could I fend off so many lightning bolts, such cruel pains? I know that I am just like a moth rushing headlong into the candle of his sun, and that my wings will be consumed if I go there. Yet it would be cowardly to abandon this heroic enterprise. Though he is a slave and I am his mistress, love makes all equal. Here comes my enemy. If Occasion[35] offers me the hair of her brow, I shall not fail to seize it.

Enter Yoseph [wearing a loincloth and a cape].

Yoseph, if you are kind—and surely you must be, for heaven made you a monster of nature in virtues—take pity on me. Unlock the chain with which your rare beauty has imprisoned me. Don't let me perish at your hands, which must be kind. If you refuse this request, you might as well just kill me with your own hands.

YOSEPH. Madam, if your requests were just and chaste, I would accept them as your son; I would obey as your slave; but the love you've shown me and this unchaste affliction is no love but rather cruelty, not fondness but offense. You are behaving tyrannically towards me, for you use your power to force me to love you, though it would be wrong to love another man's wife. Since my master has entrusted all his property to me, I am obliged to him, and conscience forbids that I should spoil or steal anything that is his. You are placing his honor at risk, and I am obliged to defend him. Remember, he is a noble man, and you are staining his nobility.

ZENOBIA. Don't meddle with my honor. That concerns me alone.

YOSEPH. But that's just what I was saying.

ZENOBIA. Don't presume to advise me, for I don't need your exhortations.

YOSEPH. Your Excellency, remember . . .

ZENOBIA. How can you call me Excellency when I humble myself as your slave? Don't address me that way; call me your slave or blackamoor, for your tyrannical love has overturned my status.

YOSEPH. You are right about that. This love, which would trample your honor and my loyalty and purity underfoot, is tyrannical indeed. But I am like the touchstone; I'll never trade the pure gold of my loyalty for some base metal. I am a rock, a craggy reef proof against all the crashing waves and storms of the sea of your desires.

ZENOBIA. You ingrate! How can you scorn a woman who loves you and begs you, who casts her honor at your lowborn feet! Have you forgotten you're a slave and poor, and that I can take revenge for your tyrannical offenses? Don't you know that I could submerge you in the center of the earth or in the abyss itself with the slightest hint from my tongue?

YOSEPH. I know I am a slave subject to all kinds of misery, yet I am free to remain loyal to my nobility.

ZENOBIA. Is there nothing to be done?

YOSEPH. No, your complaints are all in vain.

ZENOBIA. You are nothing but a mad peasant, so insane that I am sorry I ever cast eyes on you!

YOSEPH. How much better it would be if you had cast them on my master!

ZENOBIA. Silence that cursed tongue before I tear it out so that you'll never be able to boast that once I loved you.

YOSEPH. Gladly. With your permission I will go now.

ZENOBIA. Oh no you won't! Since you refuse my love and won't consent, I shall just have to rape you. *[She grabs him by his cape.]*

YOSEPH. Let go, madam! I warn you that you are offending your honor, God, me, and your husband all at once.

ZENOBIA. What do I care? You are most impertinent!

YOSEPH. And you are mad and blind. Let go of my cape at once, or else just keep it.

He runs away, leaving the cape behind.

ZENOBIA. Oh cruel enemy, how dare you run away? Come back, listen, hold on, wait! He's gone. He left here naked, abandoning his cape just like an animal. Well, that cape will be a witness, a piece of evidence to sentence him to death, for in my rage I'll get revenge for this affront. When a scorned woman seeks revenge, she won't rest until she tastes the blood of the offender. I shall cry out to heaven. Help, maids, boys, servants, lackeys! Where are you? Is there no one to take pity on an aggrieved woman, an unfortunate female? Justice, justice, heavens, since there is no justice on earth!

Enter the servants.

MATILDE. What's wrong, my lady? What sad cries are these?

ZENOBIA. They are not cries but mournful laments that I pronounce at my own funeral. What lewdness have you ever seen in me, oh infamous man, that emboldened you to attack my chaste honor! Who could believe it?

MATILDE. What is wrong with you?

ZENOBIA. Misfortunes, and more than misfortunes: pain to see that a slave, or rather a wild beast, would dare to look at me! How dare he put my honor to the test, lasciviously seducing me, first with his pleas and then attempting rape. I was all alone, but my purity was here to defend me, refusing to let him stain my chastity. I cried out for him to let me go, and when he saw that his madness and violence could not overpower me, he left his cape behind and ran away, fearing the punishment his crime deserves and I will see he gets.

MATILDE. Is this the sorry end of so much trust and haughtiness, such finery here at home, such confusion at the court, where those lovely eyes of his attracted both married ladies and maidens, sparing none who did not pay him tribute? Wouldn't he have been better off to have addressed those compliments to me? For after all, I am his equal, and I would gladly have remedied his sweet complaints. He deserves to be cast into a narrow prison cell.

ZENOBIA. Where is your master? Is there no one to tell him about this?

MATILDE. Calm down, for I hear his voice now. Madam, rest assured that he will avenge this offense and punish the man who aggrieved you.

Enter Potiphar.

POTIPHAR. What is wrong, my lady? Who has caused you this torment?

ZENOBIA. I am ashamed to tell you, though it is clear as day, but the injury I've suffered, since it affects your honor, requires me to speak up, trusting that you will take just revenge for such a mad attempt. The slave that you brought to this house for my misfortune, and thinking him loyal, conferred such high responsibilities on him, was emboldened by that treatment to dally with me. He came here tenderly with that face that's like a flower to seduce me with his love, and his madness went so far that, disregarding your honor, he tried to take me by force. But I, forever pure, remained faithful as I ought and resisted his attack. Seeing that matters had come to such an atrocious pass, I cried out to save my honor and my life. Fearing the servants, who were already headed here, he ran away, leaving his cape behind as evidence of his crime. Sir, if you allow a vile, obscure slave to get away with this, whose honor will be safe? Should this occur, what woman will feel free in her own home, even if closed in by strong walls?

POTIPHAR. What you have said is sufficient proof for me. I believe all you've said. I shall see that the Hebrew ends his days in prison. Why couldn't he have been content with the esteem I showed him, though he was but a slave? He deserves to die. If he escaped from one well, I have another from which he'll not come out alive. Go to your room. If I catch him, I'll take the revenge his wickedness deserves. Hold on! I can't believe my eyes! Isn't that the shameless man himself? Either he is not guilty or he holds me in utter contempt. More likely, he is insane and has come back to sin again.

Enter Yoseph.

How dare you come here, infamous traitor? Have you so little shame that you come into my presence to provoke my wrath? Get out of here, you wretch!

YOSEPH. Sir, my innocence makes me bold.

POTIPHAR. Has anyone ever seen such madness? This man is insane. Do you think my honor such a worthless thing? Do you dare offend my wife, thereby offending me, leaving behind your cape—which shall now serve as your shroud—and after behaving like that, so ungrateful for all the good I have done you, to come here now? Oh madman, vain and impertinent! You have surely lost your mind.

YOSEPH. Sir, she is deceived; this is nothing but a vain caprice. I would never cast my eyes on an honorable woman. I have always shown respect even to the lowest of your maids, and therefore I'd be even more punctilious when your honor is involved. She is deceived, my lord; Yoseph is innocent.

POTIPHAR. *[Aside:]* His persuasive words have convinced me that the boy is innocent, and that this is just her imagination. But since she has caused a scandal by loudly voicing her complaints, I cannot pardon him. As a public example, Yoseph will have to go to jail for now.*[To the servants:]* Remove him from my sight and take him to prison.

YOSEPH. I am a slave. It is only right that I should not open my mouth here. My lord, God alone knows if I have offended you. Since I am innocent, He will set me free, and then my loyalty will shine like the sun rising in the east.

ZENOBIA. You and I both know whether or not you are innocent, but I am the one who will be believed. Your pride provoked this harshness against you.

YOSEPH. Since I refused to do your bidding, it's not surprising that you are angry. But you know very well that you are wrong. I'll say no more. You are sending me to prison, so to prison I must go. Since you know the truth, however, you may regret this later. Since seeing me offends you,

I thank God that I am to be taken from your sight, for thus neither of us
will henceforth be able to offend the other

[A SERVANT.] *[To the audience:]* "Harassed but happy" he's called,
though thus far unfortunate.
For this charge importunate
in jail he must be walled.
I am sure you are appalled,
dear reader, but my art
has more things to impart,
for I shall you regale
with the best part of his tale
in this play's Second Part.

Finis.

PART 2

Characters:

Ya'akob	Binyamin
Yoseph	Dan
Par'oh	Chamberlain
Butler	Menasheh
Baker	Asenath, Poti-phera's daughter
Jailer	Rezinda, her maid
Secretary	Semiramis, Potiphar's daughter
Re'uven	Cumena, the jailer's daughter
Shim'on	A lackey
Levi	Potiphar
Yehudah	[Poti-phera]

ACT 1

Enter the Butler and Baker with Yoseph.

YOSEPH. I know you can't help suffering from all this pain and hardship, but
such trials always befall noble men. Aristocratic gentlemen like you can
give us all a lesson in how to confront the greatest hardships with courage.

BUTLER. Such helpful advice proceeds from your rare intelligence. You are the very model of patience in suffering. I have been told by those who know about these matters that you were brought innocent to this terrible place.

YOSEPH. God knows that that is true; but since patience attains all things, I trust that God will avenge this wrong, for He is the Judge of innocence.

BUTLER. Are you a free man?

YOSEPH. No, sir. I was indeed born free but taken as a slave from my native soil. My envious brothers, whom I never harmed by word or deed, sold me.

BUTLER. That wasn't a very fraternal way to act; but if your own people could thus deceive and betray, what wonder is it that foreigners have treated you so harshly? I am sure that a person who is used to being free and holding an honorable position must suffer all the more when he finds himself in these straits. Being here without cause can only increase your pain, seeing your feet in chains and your body imprisoned.

YOSEPH. Sir, merciful heaven will defend my innocence and punish the malice of those impious, envious men. But I hear the jailer opening the door.

BAKER. That's a bad sign.

YOSEPH. No, it is good, for he's probably bringing some gift. I am sure of it, because he is a virtuous man and that is his custom.

Enter the Jailer.

JAILER. Gentlemen, I can't tell you how much I regret your suffering. Still, here you will lack for nothing. As long as Yoseph is here, you will have little need of me. Yoseph, take these gifts for these gentlemen and yourself. I wish they could be better.

YOSEPH. They are not bad at all. They will help us get through this day, for every day spent in prison seems very long.

JAILER. Your pleasant conversation is a joy to listen to and helps the time pass quickly. Yoseph, I entrust these gentlemen to your diligence.

YOSEPH. I gladly accept that task; indeed, I consider it an honor.

JAILER. You have a special place in my heart, Yoseph, and therefore I put you in charge of the whole prison. Here are the keys; open and close as you wish, for I trust you with everything.

YOSEPH. I am your humble slave. Since you have such confidence in me, I shall serve you loyally.

JAILER. Yoseph, I love you well. Your rare virtue, which shines just like the stars, makes me want to free you from slavery.

BUTLER. The comradeship of a man like him lessens our suffering.

JAILER. Yes, you'll get through these trials more easily with him, for he is divine. Please treat him with respect.

BAKER. You need not even ask, for he commands respect.

YOSEPH. I am very happy to have won such favor from you, though I do not deserve it. Thank you, sir, for the gift and the favors you have done me and these gentlemen.

JAILER. You needn't thank me, for I am your friend.

Exeunt. Enter Asenath, Rezinda, and Yoseph.

ASENATH. You may go now, Rezinda. Even at the risk of my own life, I mean to speak to him, for I can't bear such misfortune.

REZINDA. I will do as you say, but I warn you that if someone recognizes you, you are lost. There are a thousand spies around here.

ASENATH. I don't care anymore. This anguish has driven me crazy. Knock, or else I will knock.

REZINDA. I'll knock, my lady.

YOSEPH. Who is that knocking?

REZINDA. A lady who would like to speak to a prisoner.

YOSEPH. Which one?

REZINDA. Yoseph, who entered this prison a few days ago. I'd like very much to see him.

YOSEPH. Well, here he is. Who has come to visit me?

ASENATH. Since you ask, I am the maid of a lady who is as unfortunate and distressed as she is intelligent and beautiful. In the first bloom of youth, just when her happy dawn was waiting to greet the sun of which she was the precursor; just when she hoped to enjoy happy hours of love and with hymeneal bliss to celebrate her wedding; when she thought her longing was coming to an end and cherished the hope of achieving true happiness, the haughty sea was stirred and lashed her fragile bark with its waves, casting it upon a rock or a craggy reef. All her hopes of a prosperous journey came to naught; her life, her love, her happiness were dashed to pieces.

YOSEPH. Those complaints are confusing. I'm just an ignorant man, and I can't understand what your mistress means to say.

ASENATH. She means that you've forgotten her and all that you owe her, for she gave you the only soul she had, hoping to set you free and make you master of her person and her wealth. Instead, with illicit love and odious affections, with dishonor, infamy, and insane presumption, you have soiled her decorum, despised her honor, abandoned her love, and cast a pall over her happiness. Now that she knows of your unfaithfulness, your false love and deceiving words, she admonishes you never again to dare to speak her name, to wipe out all the love she felt for you from your mind and memory, to forget those eyes with which she adored you, the services she did you, the jewels that she gave you. She wants nothing more to do with a man who weeps false tears in her presence, and then dishonors her behind her back, attempting, ungrateful to God, his master, and his master's wife, to make illicit, adulterous love to his mistress.

YOSEPH. Tell me, my lady, if you are perchance the goddess whom I adore, idolizing her beauty, so that I may speak clearly to you.

ASENATH. I know not if I am she, for your ingratitude has changed me. I am another person now, and I shall not listen, or permit, or give heed to your flattery; and so, farewell.

[She walks away from Yoseph toward the wings.]

YOSEPH. Let me just say one thing . . . She's gone away and left me burning up with the fire from her mouth, for the lips of a jealous woman always emit such flames.

Yoseph goes back inside.

REZINDA. Ma'am, I just don't understand you. You spend all your time weeping over your lover's misfortunes, and you claim to be furious about the unfair way he's been treated, and then you come here and insult him, when he has done nothing to offend you or make you jealous. You are just increasing the suffering of a poor prisoner.

ASENATH. Rezinda, you are right. I love him and adore him, for our two souls are one. But now I am quite sure that the charges brought against him were all the unjust lies of a woman he had scorned.

REZINDA. None of this makes any sense to me.

ASENATH. You idiot! You're the one who makes no sense. Let's get out of here. You don't know what you're talking about.

Exeunt. Enter Cumena, the Jailer's daughter.

CUMENA. I wonder who that veiled lady was who just left here. If I am not mistaken, she is in love with Yoseph and was courting him. If she comes back again, as she probably will, I'll give her something she won't soon forget! I've only seen my prisoner once, but he has been my only reason for living ever since I met him. I'm taking him these gifts, even though it is not ladylike. I shall tell him they are from my father, or maybe I'll dare tell him the truth. Open the door, Yoseph.

YOSEPH. Who's there?

CUMENA. It's me. Are you alone?

YOSEPH. Yes, I am.

CUMENA. This is my chance!

YOSEPH. What are your orders, madam?

CUMENA. I have come not to order but to obey. I'm bringing you this gift, which my father just brought me from the palace. I thought it would be better for you to have it.

YOSEPH. Thank you for your kindness.

CUMENA. No, thank me for my love. This gift deserves no thanks, but you should be grateful that I'm offering you my very soul. It has been yours since the first day that I saw you. If you are honorable, Yoseph, you will treat it well, for it is mine.

YOSEPH. Madam, I accept your intentions with all my heart, but since I am the slave of the person who put me in this prison, and as a prisoner, I cannot even dispose freely of my affections . . . What more can I say? A prisoner is not master even of his own will.

CUMENA. That may be so, but I am glad to know that you would accept my love if you could. That will keep my hope alive.

YOSEPH. While there is life, there's hope; but there is little hope for me.

CUMENA. Your kind words are enough for me. I am obliged to you.

YOSEPH. You shouldn't be, for I am far beyond your reach.

CUMENA. Let me know if there is anything I can do for you, for I know you are confined here in those chains.

YOSEPH. It pains me just to see you and hear your words, since I cannot repay your love as I would wish. You had better forget all this. Don't think me harsh for disillusioning you. If God should set me free from this prison, I will fulfill my obligation.

CUMENA. That's all I ask and hope. Farewell! My mother is waiting for me, and I don't want to anger her.

[Exit Cumena.]

YOSEPH. You have exhausted me! I wish you were a thousand leagues away!

Exit Yoseph; he reenters with the Butler and Cupbearer.

YOSEPH. All the other prisoners weighed down with chains and irons in this prison seem happy, though they suffer a thousand affronts, yet you two are so sad that it pains me to look at you. Some secret distress must be tormenting you.

BUTLER. You are right. Last night, among other fantasies, I had a dream that is bothering me, and I wish I knew what it meant.

YOSEPH. Cheer up, and tell me your dream. Though I am ignorant, I may be able to come up with a favorable interpretation and save you from this torment.

BUTLER. All right then, hear my dream: I was gazing on a lovely grapevine full of leaves and flowers. All at once, it put forth three ripe clusters, as beautiful as the sun, for it was the sun that nourished and gilded them. I was holding in my hand the cup with which I served my lord the king

when I was his cupbearer; and with the other hand I squeezed those
clusters into my cup, and then handed it to the king.

YOSEPH. Sir, this dream was meant to comfort you. Heaven intends to restore your honor. The three ripe clusters that you squeezed are three
days. In three days you will return to your post and once again serve
Par'oh as you did before, handing him his cup just as you used to do.
This is the meaning of your dream. Don't disregard it, for it is true, and
what I have said will happen without fail. But when you find yourself
before Par'oh, since I have done you this kindness, remember my innocence, for you know that I was kidnapped and brought here from my
land, and that the man who has put me here is blind and deceived. I have
done nothing wrong. The vain whim of a Circe has done me all this
harm to placate her rage.

BUTLER. I promise you, Yoseph, that if this prophecy should one day come
true, I will do you a thousand favors. I will inform the king both of your
innocence and of your rare intelligence, for Par'oh has great need of a
person so erudite and knowledgeable.

BAKER. Since you have interpreted the butler's obscure dream with your
knowledge, which is like that of an angel, I am certain you can also give
a favorable interpretation to my dream. If so, I shall free you from slavery and take you out of prison. Now to escape this anxiety, I shall tell
you of my dream without adding the slightest thing. Since I am His
Majesty's baker, I saw three baskets, and in each one was a large amount
of many kinds of food. I was carrying all of them on my head, and the
topmost one containing the best food was attacked by a flock of birds,
which devoured all the food. I tried my best to protect it from them, but
I couldn't do so.

YOSEPH. I wish it were not you who had that dream, for it foretells misfortune and a very sad event. Those three baskets you saw are three days.
Those harpies are your enemies. They will take you out of prison, putting a sad end to all your woes, for he who rules all Egypt will hang you
from a tree in punishment of your crime. Thus all alone, with no one to
come to your assistance, your flesh will be eaten by birds instead of
worms, and you will be unable to defend yourself.

BAKER. You are just an insane troublemaker! All that you say is senseless,
for no one under the sun can foretell the future. No one can ever be
certain what is going to happen, and even when people try to guess the
future by studying the stars and planets, there is no truth in what they
say.

YOSEPH. May God have mercy on your soul.

Exeunt. Enter a secretary with the Jailer.

SECRETARY. I have come on behalf of the king to pronounce the sentences of some of the men who are imprisoned here for different crimes. Open the prison door so that I can read the king's decision for them to hear.

JAILER. The door is already open.

SECRETARY. Summon the two eunuchs who are chained up here, the butler and the baker.

SECRETARY. They'll be here right away.

[Enter the Butler and the Baker.]

Greetings, gentlemen. Your trials have been held in the king's own presence, for today he celebrates his birthday. Listen, and you will hear what he has commanded concerning both of you—honor and life for one, and bad news for the other. Sir Butler, since the king has found you guiltless of any crime against His Majesty, he commands you to return to your former post, performing your usual duties in his house and at his table. The baker, since there is proof that he committed treason against the king, has been condemned to death by hanging. Both of you, come with me now. The ill-fated man should be patient, for it was his own sin that has led him to die suspended between heaven and earth.

Exeunt. Enter Rezinda.

REZINDA. I'll just knock on the door, and he will answer if I'm not mistaken, for he has all the keys to the jail in his hands.

YOSEPH. Who's knocking? Answer me.

REZINDA. One who wants to serve you and talk to you.

[Yoseph opens the door.]

YOSEPH. Who are you?

REZINDA. Don't you recognize me? I am Rezinda, and I am bringing news of your lady. She begs you to forgive her for everything that's happened, for her complaints and jealousy. She knows she was mistaken, and she is painfully aware that she has offended you, though you were innocent and guiltless. She would not have you think that only those blessed by good fortune can know love, or that love requires prosperity. Now that you have sunk to the lowest point and are heavily weighed down by those chains, she loves you even more than before and longs for your embrace. She worships the sight of you, and your great courtesy has only refined her love.

YOSEPH. Please inform your mistress that I am very much surprised and shocked that a woman as noble as she could be so fickle. She has disappointed me, and I have a disappointment in store for her as well. I can't accept so changeable a love. If it was my imprisonment that made her despise me so ungratefully, please tell her that I never betrayed my master, that my loyalty shines like the sun, and that its rays will burn the witnesses who falsely testified against me. If she had really loved me as she now claims, she would never have come here to add to my afflictions. Before doing such a thing, she should have investigated to find out whether I had really done anything to deserve such harsh treatment. So now she is convinced that I am honorable. That's nice to know, but her apology cannot undo the wrong she's done me—her cruelty, the pain her words have caused me by soiling such a pure love, such sincere faithfulness, such a grateful breast, a soul so disabused, a heart she set on fire! Please give her back this ring she gave me. It would be wrong for an unfaithful man, an ingrate to accept such a noble token from a lady who has abandoned a chaste and sincere love on account of false suspicions.

REZINDA. Forgive me, but I could not so insult my mistress. Besides, that token is too sacred for my hands to touch. You will have to give it back to her with your own hand if love can find no remedy for your harshness. But I trust it will, for love performs miracles.

YOSEPH. In that case just tell her what I said.

REZINDA. Indeed I will, if I can manage to remember all of it.

Exeunt. Enter Asenath and Rezinda.

ASENATH. Rezinda, what news do you bring me of my love?

REZINDA. I don't know what to say, considering how my visit went.

ASENATH. What do you mean? Has the jail collapsed?

REZINDA. No, your love has collapsed, which is even worse.

ASENATH. What are you saying? Alas, poor me! Is he sick? Is he in danger?

REZINDA. He is not the one who collapsed; it's you.

ASENATH. How so?

REZINDA. He is deeply offended by your disdain. He wants no more to do with a love that has caused him such pain. He says that if your love were constant, you would be constant too, but he sees that love is unreliable, and you are fickle. If you were really offended when you heard what had happened and how he had been imprisoned, you should have taken pains to find out whether he was guilty; for he was innocent. It was imprudent of you to go there and further torment an unfortunate man. Whatever love he formerly held for you is dead. The soul that once adored you is now consigned to oblivion. He asked me to return that ring you gave him, but I refused to take it.

ASENATH. You were right to do so. How could this have happened? I am lost; but I admit that I caused all of this. But what's the use of talking? I must go and see him.

REZINDA. Where are you going?

ASENATH. To seek my death if I can't find my life.

REZINDA. Hold on, you are befuddled. You should first give some thought to whether going there is a good idea.

ASENATH. What have I got to lose?

REZINDA. Your reputation.

ASENATH. Love is irrational and can't be bothered with such details.

REZINDA. You're giving him just what he wants. Can't you see that if you humiliate yourself like this, he will have all the more reason to despise you?

ASENATH. I'm sorry; I can't bluff any longer. I'm dying for him!

REZINDA. You should never have been so cruel in the first place. What was the point of scolding him like that?

ASENATH. What can I do? What's done is done. I admit I was ill advised.

REZINDA. Then you'll just have to be patient now.

ASENATH. How can I do that? The more he plays hard to get, the more I love and adore him.

REZINDA. You are forgetting your dignity.

ASENATH. Perseverance will prevail.

REZINDA. All right then, we might as well go talk to him, since you stubbornly refuse to take advice.

ASENATH. If he gives me the cold shoulder . . .

REZINDA. You will just have to suffer in silence. Since you don't have the patience to wait for an opportunity when you wouldn't have to risk your reputation, go ahead and talk to him, but just remember that your life hangs in the balance. If he will speak to you, you'll live; if not, you'll die.

ASENATH. Even so, I am determined to hear what he thinks from his own mouth.

REZINDA. Are you crazy, or am I the crazy one?

ASENATH. Don't worry, I'll watch out.

REZINDA. No, you won't. How can you watch out, since you're blinded with love? How can you watch without eyes? Love wears a blindfold with a double knot.

ASENATH. That may be so, but the fire of love makes the lover's mind more keen.

REZINDA. Then please make up that keen mind of yours.

ASENATH. What would you have me do? I want to go, but I don't want to go. Just when I think my mind is made up to go, I turn around. It seems I can neither go nor stay. My soul tries to go, but my body refuses to move. The best way to win him over would be to ransom him and get him out of prison. If he were my slave, he'd be grateful for that favor and would be obliged to do as I wish. I'll go and see his mistress. I'll find out from her own lips whether she loves or hates him.

Someone knocks on the door.

REZINDA. Yes.

ASENATH. Go see who's knocking. Who could be coming here at this hour?

[Rezinda goes to the door.]

REZINDA. Speak of the devil! It's our prisoner's mistress.

Enter Zenobia.

ASENATH. To what do I owe this pleasure, madam?

ZENOBIA. I am grateful for your kindness, and as a token of my esteem I have come to kiss your hands.

ASENATH. I consider that a signal honor; but such excessive courtesy will make me more your slave than your good friend. You are indeed welcome; I think God has brought you here. Won't you please tell me what's happened to that man who was so ungrateful for the confidence and favor you and your husband showed him?

ZENOBIA. Madam, don't mention him to me. I cannot bear to think of him.

ASENATH. Why not?

ZENOBIA. Do you think I could ever forgive his presumption and audacity in daring to cast his eyes on me?

ASENATH. Love is the cause of such errors. I'd certainly never hate someone who loved and desired me. Hatred inspires more hatred, and love inspires love.

ZENOBIA. But that's just why I hate him with all my heart.

ASENATH. You hate him for loving you?

ZENOBIA. How could a man who damages my honor and tries to destroy my reputation love me? By merely doing so he has defamed me.

ASENATH. Ah, now I understand you, madam. Now I know the reason and the cause for your complaints, and they are perfectly justified. In fact he hated you, and you have paid him back with hatred. Of course you were right to hate a man who first had hated you.

ZENOBIA. What are you getting at? It's true that I despise him, but it's obvious that he is in love with me.

ASENATH. But didn't you say he sought to do you harm?

ZENOBIA. I said that he damaged my honor. Otherwise, his rare courtesy would not deserve such harshness. But it was his misfortune to be a fool. If he had humbled himself at my feet, I would gladly have pardoned his errors and many faults; but instead he arrogantly defended his cause and tried to make me look guilty, when I was the injured party.

ASENATH. Well, now he is in jail, and he is certainly of no use to you there. Would you like to sell him?

ZENOBIA. I would rather sell myself as a slave; for, although he disobeyed his mistress, I still hope to pardon him and return him to my favor and bring him back to serve me. After all, he did love me, and I am not altogether unappreciative of his flirtation. As you yourself pointed out, it is easy to forgive errors and faults committed out of love. Once I have broken the madness of his arrogance, he will come crawling back to me and try to win me over.

ASENATH. *[Aside:]* Well, at least she hasn't minced her words. There's no need to investigate further, for she has given away the whole plot of this farce without my even coaxing her. Now I know she loves him, and she still intends to enjoy him—oh impious, impure, unjust, unchaste woman! *[To Zenobia:]* Well, my lady, it's a relief to know that his crime wasn't so terrible after all. They say that even the devil isn't as ugly as they paint him.

ZENOBIA. I must take into account the excellent service he has rendered us, increasing the prosperity of our house.

ASENATH. Then why not just set him free and put an end to his misfortunes?

ZENOBIA. You certainly have a lot to say in his defense. I think you're in love with him.

ASENATH. I've never seen him in my life, except for that day when I called on you, and he spoke with such eloquence. That's why I felt especially sorry for him when I found out that he was innocently suffering the misery of prison, and all because of a cruel, lying woman.

ZENOBIA. Watch your tongue, madam! I really ought to slap you in the face for such ignorant words. But I am a guest in your house, so I'll let it pass for now. Anyway, they say that one should not take offense at the words of an ignorant madwoman.

ASENATH. That is hardly the way an honest woman talks. But never mind, your notoriety is revenge enough for me. Even the children in the city streets and in the public squares are singing popular songs about your "virtues."

ZENOBIA. No one has anything on me. I am an honest married woman; but word of your lewdness is sure to get around, since you are so ardently pursuing an infamous slave, and even begging me on his behalf, which is a sure sign of a bad woman. But I will get revenge on both of you. Tomorrow I shall see that he's impaled, and along with him, your hope.

ASENATH. What a good idea! That will surely publicize your infamy. But you'll not get away with it, for I will defend his cause and see that he gets justice. His innocence is reason enough for me to save him. That's all I have to say. Get out of here, you cursed hag!

Asenath leaves the room.

ZENOBIA. I've never seen debauchery like this! Infamous, shameless bitch! By the immortal gods, since you love and desire him, to get revenge on you I'll take revenge on him, thus burying at once your joy and his misfortune!

ACT 2

Enter Par'oh and his butler.

PAR'OH. Why do I maintain so many sophists, so-called sages; why do I always heed their stupid lies? When I really need them, they are so foolish, ignorant, and coarse they can't even manage to interpret my dreams! They are no sages, no soothsayers at all, when I am worried to death. Now save me from this pain, or else I'll hang you all from the highest tower!

BUTLER. Though I hesitate to bring up a mistake I made so long ago, and which you have by now forgotten, I have no choice, for it entails another memory I should have borne in mind. If you will listen, perhaps I can relieve your torment and your rage. I dare not question that it's justified, for I am obliged to obey your every wish. When you cast me and your baker in prison, sire, we met a Hebrew boy there who could have been a king. We heard that he was a slave of your servant Potiphar. Send for him now, for he possesses the spirit of prophecy.

PAR'OH. Then have him come at once. Send Captain Luzartes for him.

BUTLER. While he goes for him, I will recount his divine qualities if my rude tongue can manage to describe them properly. He is a genteel young man, gallant, learned, eloquent, well versed in everything, especially the sciences. His mind is brilliant, and his wit is both agile and subtle. One night just before the morning star appeared in the gates of the east, the baker and I each had a dream with profound implications. The day dawned bright, but our hearts were dark and sad with a melancholy that enshrouded our very souls. We could not rest without knowing what our dreams revealed. He came to us, and seeing our faces pale and troubled, asked why we were so worried. We told him our dreams, and he interpreted them for us. With his brilliant mind, the clear and subtle wit of his divine genius, he told us exactly what our dreams meant; and everything he said came true exactly as he had predicted. I was returned to my post, and today you see me here serving you; but the baker, sad and bitter, was hanged for his crime; and all of this was just as the lad had said. I am certain that he will be able to give a clear interpretation of your dreams with the spirit of God. He possesses a knowledge surpassing that of any other mortal, indeed like that of the immortal gods.

PAR'OH. I can hardly wait to meet him, for these dreams are tormenting me. If he can interpret them, I will declare him unique in all of Egypt; he will be the North Star by which this court is guided.

BUTLER. Sire, here he comes. Just look at his noble bearing and the beauty of his form; you will find that his appearance reflects his inward grace.

Enter Yoseph.

YOSEPH. I present myself at your command and bow before your royal feet.

PAR'OH. Yoseph, I already know all about your prudence, your knowledge, and your clear intelligence. I know you interpret dreams, for you are endowed with rare abilities. I am troubled by a dream that is very obscure and puzzling. I have found no one who could interpret it. Those who have tried have only angered me, for I can tell that their futile attempts are nothing but a shot in the dark. If in your wisdom you can give me a straightforward explanation, which bears no signs of falsehood or deceit, to repay you for that miracle at that very moment I shall adopt you as my son.

YOSEPH. My only prayer is that heaven permit me to give you an answer promising health and blessing. But if, as a mere human, I should fail, and God reserves the meaning for Himself, please excuse me.

PAR'OH. Give heed then, since you are so intelligent and well advised. I will tell you briefly the dream that troubles me. I dreamed that by the shore of our fertile river, in a meadow made cool and pleasant by the flooding of the Nile, were seven beauteous cows. I had never seen their like in fatness throughout the land of Egypt. After them came seven more to the same meadow, but these were so lean and dried up that they were a veritable prodigy of ugliness to the eyes, offending all the senses. Those lean ones consumed the fat ones as if they were mere mosquitoes, but afterwards gave not the slightest sign that they were in their bellies, for they remained just as lean and ugly as they had been before. I awoke; but then I dreamed another wondrous dream. This time I saw a field as delightful as the Elysian fields themselves, and there seven beauteous stalks of wheat that stood out from all the rest, filled to bursting with grain that was wonderful to see and gave delight. But then in the very same place I saw others, foul and dry, all straw and no grain, beaten by the winds and blasted by tornadoes. There was no substance in them that could nourish a living thing. All at once the thin stalks ate the fat ones, but afterwards remained exactly as I had first seen them. Then I awoke, so tormented and afflicted that I can have no rest until I know what all this means.

YOSEPH. Sire, those first lovely and beauteous cows that you saw coming up on the river bank with solemn pomp, and the lean ones that followed them, causing wonder and dismay; and likewise, the seven stalks that were bursting with grain, and the frightful dry ones—both mean seven years, and then another seven. My lord's dreams are both one and the same. God has revealed what He has decreed in His divine tribunal to Par'oh in miraculous visions. Seven years are to come when the earth will brightly shine and overflow with beauty for the abundance of its fruit, especially wheat, which is what is most needful for human sustenance, for the rest is only dross. But after those years will come the piteous afflictions of seven more, whose cruel famine, all embracing, will completely wipe out all memory of the former abundance, for its ravenous mouth will devour everything. If you would be merciful, sire, to so many souls that depend on you, give them life with your mighty hand. Cause wheat and grain to be gathered up in copious abundance during the years of plenty. Choose a wise and prudent man to govern, one whom you can respect and trust, to go throughout all Egypt and diligently gather up the wheat, storing it in your villages with care. This is most important, for the fact that your dreams were repeated is a sign that heaven means to bring this about very soon. Let this man choose deputies who will diligently go to the remotest regions, storing up food which your merciful hand will later distribute during the years of famine, which will be very harsh, for the whole earth will be scorched by the sun. Thus you will give Egypt life and exalt your crown by giving bread to the hungry and winning eternal glory for yourself.

PAR'OH. Your interpretation pleases me. I am sure that it is absolutely correct, for my soul welcomes it and my senses approve it. I knew that the interpretations my sorcerers had given me were fallacious, and I dismissed them as chimeras. No matter how hard we tried, how could we possibly find a man like this, to whom the gods reveal these occult secrets and secret visions? No doubt he is a light from the highest of all spheres! Since heaven favors you, revealing secret things, there is no man on earth who can equal you in wisdom and understanding. Hence, you shall be that man that you have advised me to choose to carry out this rarest providence. Therefore I choose you to be supreme, second only to me among all my governors. You alone shall command, none will have greater power than you, for I intend you to be unique in Egypt. Take this ring which I confer upon you as a royal token that you may use it to seal the decrees of my kingdom. Go out and take possession of the government of my lands, making whatever provisions you desire. *[To his servants:]* And you, prepare my chariot, for I want him to go out in triumph so that he may be known to all, and all may know that Egypt owes its very life and existence, and our kingdom owes all its might, to his lofty intelligence. Honor him as your master, for that is what he is, since he surpasses all others.

YOSEPH. Sire, I owe all I am to you. I hope that this choice of yours will prove useful to the kingdom and your crown.

Exeunt. Enter Asenath and Rezinda.

ASENATH. Did you see the governor?

REZINDA. Did I ever! If you had been there, you'd be even more in love with him.

ASENATH. Tell me all about it, and may heaven bring you good luck!

REZINDA. If your ladyship would give me something, I could tell you wonders.

ASENATH. You picked the right moment to ask. Since I am to be the vicereine, I'll give you this diamond for the good news that you've brought.

REZINDA. Since you've repaid my love so well, may heaven grant that you win him soon. His Lordship the Governor . . .

But listen: the new day
through gates of dawn began to make its way.
Your lover at that hour
was sowing pearls and dew on every flower.
His chariot of gold,
though like a star, seemed pale and cold,
when that sun did appear,
bringing down the day from his fourth sphere.[36]
He was all clad in flaming rays of light—
I mean those diamonds so bright,
whose brilliance crystalline
blinded even eagles' eyes so keen.
Such pomp and circumstance,
surrounded his advance!
Timbrels and drums did play,
in a consummate warlike display,
for then on every side
fierce warriors saluted him with pride.
Leading the gay parade,
of noblemen a brilliant cavalcade—
their litters, horses, coaches were a sight—

but seemed like darkest night
in contrast with the day
of gallant Yoseph in his glad array.
Next came a very elegant brigade:[37]
grave archers, all their arrows tipped with gold,
to guard his person fair.
Then music filled the air,
sweet verses, candid, terse, and bold
in lovely harmony,
echoing heaven's angelic hierarchy;
truly it did entice
a vision here on earth of paradise.
Fame went before that throng,
with sonorous trumpet echoing the song,
loudly proclaiming the great excellence
of his magnificence.
With reverence heartfelt
the multitude of onlookers then knelt,
showing profound respect
to Yoseph's God Who made him so perfect.
Down twisting roads,
whose citizens had adorned all their abodes
with royal finery,
passed that parade, and with it the beauty
of that great governor whom you'd embrace,
whose happy face
in brightness did eclipse the stars that shine.
In every window maids and ladies fine
with longing groaned,
and countless blessings on his head intoned.
Each longed to stand
beside him and to win his noble hand;
each longed to wed
that handsome man and share his marriage bed.
At last, though all eyes yet to see him yearned,
to the palace he returned.
The king himself was waiting at that place
with a loving embrace
for that man he loved so much:
of Yoseph's triumph that was the final touch.

Today he reigns supreme,
for only he deserves the king's esteem.
He rules alone;
all patronage and honor does he own.
He's the North Star,
the court's sole guide, its master without par.
Who would have thought
that one who only yesterday was brought
here as a slave could overcome that fate,
rising so quickly to such high estate
that now he sits upon a golden throne,
and all of Egypt bows to him alone?

ASENATH. Your description deserves an even nobler diamond; but the time will come when I can repay you as I ought. Still, that grandeur which heaven has conferred on him troubles me, for now I am less noble than he. To tell the truth, I'd gladly see him somewhat more lowly, for then my own rank would ensure that he'd love me.

REZINDA. No, you are wrong about that. Now that he is so exalted, you are certain to win him.

ASENATH. How so?

REZINDA. Because now you are equals. You are a noblewoman, and he is the viceroy. Now you are well matched, and it's only right that you should be joined in marriage. But before that can happen, you must take the measures that your honor dictates.

ASENATH. What must I do?

REZINDA. Tell your father of your love, and he will arrange everything.

ASENATH. You are right. I shall go and talk to him, for any further delay would be dangerous.

REZINDA. May God grant you your wish!

ASENATH. If He does, I shall be a queen.

Exeunt. Enter Par'oh and Yoseph, [accompanied by servants].

YOSEPH. Your sovereign dreams have now begun to take effect, for the wheat crop is most fertile and abundant.

PAR'OH. My subjects owe you their life for interpreting those dreams.

YOSEPH. Nay, my lord, we owe it all to you, for God gave you that revelation.

PAR'OH. It is our ancient custom to hold public audience. I would like you to attend today so that I may draw on your great intelligence. This will also give me an opportunity to publicize my confidence in you, for I intend for you to preside over today's audience.

YOSEPH. Lovingly I kneel before your feet.

PAR'OH. Come, draw up a chair, for people are beginning to arrive.

Enter Poti-phera[38] and his daughter Asenath.

POTI-PHERA. This noble maiden kneels at your royal feet to ask for justice. As king, it is your duty to do her justice.

PAR'OH. I have never refused justice to anyone, much less to a shining star like this young lady. But what is her complaint?

ASENATH. My lord and king, I complain of a young man to whom I gave a token that I esteem more than life itself, because it means my life. I asked him to keep it for me, trusting in his nobility, for though he was then a commoner, I already thought him noble. Now times have changed, and I am afraid he will refuse to return it, since he has become the sun of your own sphere. I come to ask for justice, or if not justice, clemency, for my womanly estate requires both.

PAR'OH. Who is he? You must speak plainly, for I cannot pronounce sentence without hearing the other side. I must hear all the evidence before deciding.

ASENATH. He is not very far from you.

PAR'OH. Well, he can't be very near, for the only one who is here is Yoseph, and he would never commit such an offense.

ASENATH. He is the very man I'm complaining about, my lord, for he is the depository of that inestimable token. Command him to give it to me, sire, for he promised to return it. Now he may say that he was only teasing, but I assure you he was very serious then.

PAR'OH. Yoseph, what is your reply?

YOSEPH. I admit that this young lady is correct. She did indeed give me a diamond in gratitude for a service I rendered her. That gift was truly excessive as a reward for someone of my lowly and humble status. I don't deny that I still have it here and will give it to her if I must. I have guarded it with all my heart, as a reminder of the one who gave it to me. Here it is, madam. God forbid that I should keep another's property! You are no longer mine. Now I know your fickleness very well and realize how wrong I was to trust you, since you have come today to ask for what I thought was truly mine.

ASENATH. That is not my diamond. The diamond that I gave you had far more carats and was lovelier, more excellent than this one. I want that other diamond back; the one you offer me is not the one I've come to seek. Don't try to trick me. That is unworthy of you, since now you possess such vast estates and income.

YOSEPH. If this is merely greed, I shall gladly place all my jewels at your disposal. Feel free to choose the richest of them all if that will satisfy you. *[To a servant:]* Boy, take this key and bring me my jewelry box.

ASENATH. No, that would be a waste of time. The rich jewel that I gave you is in your very heart: for it was my own soul with all its potencies,[39] a firm and constant love, sincere affection. I gave you that soul, as noble as it is perfect, not now, in your present kingly state, but when you were still a slave—as humble as could be and at your lowest point, in irons and chains, despised by all. That soul is all I want. If you are honorable, now give it back to me, for I cannot live without it. Take pity on my misfortune! Please give it to me, though it is your own; for the first day that I saw you on the dry sands of the fertile Nile, overcome by your grace and beauty, I gladly surrendered it, holding nothing back. The time has come for you to return it to one who has waited so long.

YOSEPH. Madam, I confess that crime. It would be wrong to deny the debt I owe you or to hide my true desire, but although by nature I am endowed with free will, I will do nothing without His Majesty's consent. Therefore please bide your time. Be patient, for this is a tribunal whose purpose is to administer strict justice.

Enter Potiphar with his daughter Semiramis.

POTIPHAR. Word has reached me that a woman has come here to ask for Yoseph's hand in marriage, though she is unworthy of him. You are well aware that he was once my slave, though of illustrious birth and distinguished for his virtue, more estimable even than his noble blood. That fact entitles me to special preference, for I have invested more in him than anyone. Furthermore, I deserve to hold first place, both because I am a noble, honored knight and because I have my daughter here beside me. She was brought up with him, and he knows her sterling reputation, and also that she loves him and adores him. Therefore strict justice demands that you do me this honor. I offer all my property as her dowry.

YOSEPH. Sire, you have given me more than I want or need. I shall therefore gladly reimburse my lord Potiphar, whom I esteem, for the price that he paid for me. In fact I'll double it, thus settling any debt that I may owe him. But I leave it up to you to say what's right.

Enter the Jailer and his daughter.

JAILER. Sire, I have come here in full confidence that your heroic clemency will grant my petition and the plea of this young lady. She is my daughter, highborn, and as intelligent as she is lovely. Humbly prostrate at your royal feet, she begs for justice or at least for alms. Please intercede for her with Yoseph, whom she tenderly loves and adores, and with whom she would be joined in hymeneal troth. Yoseph has long been well aware of her intentions, for when he was in prison, she was all his delight, and they were already one in word and soul. He can attest that the many gifts she gave him were tokens of a chaste love that he should now repay. And though she is no longer his equal, since the crown has raised him to the spheres, and he is now the sun of your own dawn, love, which can equal all, will make them equal, and thus they will be proof against all murmuring tongues.

Par῾oh. Well, this was all you lacked! You must have been born under a lucky star, for everyone is smitten with love for you. All men would be your friends, all women adore you. You have bewitched them with the graces that adorn you. I am not surprised that all these women have come to seek your hand, for if I had a daughter, I would give her to you alone. The one you choose will know that she is fortunate indeed, for winning you, she will have won a jewel beyond all price. Now choose which one you want. It is true that all are beautiful, but you must weigh their merits and choose accordingly.

Cumena. My lord, if your choice is to be based on merit, I hope to be so fortunate that your love will choose me.

Asenath. What merit makes you think that you deserve my spouse?

Cumena. Your spouse? By God, that's very funny! Just who gave him to you?

Asenath. Heaven, which showed its preference in the graces that it gave me.

Cumena. You are no competition.

Semiramis. Well, you can't compete with me, for I am prettier than you, and I am nobler than either one of you.

Asenath. You'd better change your tune. Remember, I know you well, and I could say a thing or two about your noble ancestry.

Semiramis. Just what do you claim to know, madam?

Asenath. That I am my father's daughter, and you are your mother's. I'll just leave it at that for now.

Semiramis. My parents are as highborn as yours.

Asenath. That may well be, but I'm the one that's getting married here.

Cumena. [To Par῾oh:] If Your Majesty weren't here, I'd give her a piece of my mind.

Asenath. You should stick to your prisoners. Don't you see that you can't compare with either one of us? You are really out of place.

Cumena. I deserve him just as much as you do.

Asenath. Enough of your impertinence! Come back some other time, for this is not your day. The stars have ruled against you.

Semiramis. And against you as well. I alone am worthy on account of my rare beauty.

ASENATH. You think you're lily-white when you are as red as a poppy. Your snobbishness is unbearable, your glaring eyes could kill, your mouth is a harpoon with which you'd soon slay love. Any man who saw your temper and that "rare beauty" of yours might indeed smart from your heat, but your frigidity would soon cool him off.

SEMIRAMIS. I can't believe you dare make fun of me, for I am grace itself.

ASENATH. You may be well endowed, but you don't have a man to call your own. You are crazy to persist in this pursuit. You might as well go home, for you are out of luck. Can't you see that it's absurd to court a man who already loves me, indeed who burns with love for me? For I am his and he is mine. He has given me his word; he has long favored me, and our love is eternal.

SEMIRAMIS. Have you forgotten that he was my father's slave?

ASENATH. I remember very well how your mother treated him. Maybe when she was chasing him, she intended to give him to you. Well, she may have put him in prison, but now he's free from such tyrannous violence, because his innocence has been proven.

YOSEPH. Dear ladies, please leave off this quarreling, for here is the judge who will decide which of you three is right.

CUMENA. Sire, since you must judge, please do me justice!

ASENATH. He will do justice all right, but it will be as I have said.

SEMIRAMIS. How dare you presume?

ASENATH. If you can, so can I. Besides, I know that I am the chosen one.

SEMIRAMIS. Don't count your chickens before they hatch!

ASENATH. You can put those words where the sun never shines!

SEMIRAMIS. I don't know what you mean, for my sun shines everywhere.

ASENATH. I think it's setting now; its light has grown quite dim. It's going to sleep in Neptune's fond embrace. Sweet dreams, for that is all you'll ever get! If Paris is the judge of love, then I am Venus, and this golden apple will ensure my victory.

YOSEPH. Please say no more, or I'll have none of you. Such spiteful words have never won a lover. Sire, if you leave it up to me, I promise I shall choose a bride appropriate to the honor I have acquired. My lord Potiphar, pray excuse me. I may indeed have eaten your bread, but I repaid you well. Your daughter is truly worthy of a crown, but I would not want a wife who might turn out like her mother. The jailer's daughter is a true Egyptian goddess, as beauteous as Venus, worthy to compete with Pallas. If indeed she loved me once, she is not the only one. Many have sought my hand. This kingdom has no shortage of madwomen! Still, I am duty-bound to defend her honor, for I would not be ungrateful to one who has shown me kindness. Since heaven has raised me to this place, I promise

generously to repay all your good deeds in due time. But the only woman
I can choose to be my spouse is she to whom I gave my word and soul.
She will be my loving consort if your majesty agrees. Asenath, my beloved, since the moment I first saw her on those sandy banks and sacrificed a crocodile to her glory, is the one who dwells in my heart and
possesses my soul with all its potencies. If you would give me a bride,
please grant me her. I wish to live with her while this brief life endures,
to serve her as I serve Your Majesty. Her dear companionship will
strengthen me the better to serve you.

PAR'OH. Well have you chosen, Yoseph! I gladly second your choice, for I
see that it is excellent.

YOSEPH. Now, my dearest one, give me your hand in marriage.

ASENATH. I give you my hand and my soul, though both were already yours.
Now that I have won this victory, I can truly say that I was born under a
lucky star.

POTI-PHERA. My son, you bring me honor with your illustrious person.

YOSEPH. Hearing you call me son is honor enough for me.

PAR'OH. Let us go. *[To the servants:]* Now prepare the most sumptuous of
feasts, for I mean to celebrate this wedding as if it were my own.

ACT 3

Enter Ya'akob and his sons.

YA'AKOB.   With every moment our hunger grows worse.
    Now food runs out,
    and all our children pout
    and, weeping, our necessity rehearse.
    Yet you neglect
    to seek some remedy this hunger could deflect;
    for I am told
    that silver or e'en gold
    in this land won't suffice to buy us bread,
    but down in Egypt, I have heard it said,
    wheat does abound;
    people go there to buy from all around.
    Ere things grow worse for us, my sons, I plead,
    ere all of us have perished of starvation,
    that we may feed

> our wives and children, all this holy nation,
> no more behold
> the misery that now does them enfold,
> no longer brood;
> prepare your animals and cleverly contrive
> to buy us food,
> and then this famine we shall all survive.
> If you stay here,
> this hunger will slay all of us, I fear.

YEHUDAH. Indeed, sir, we have heard from travelers that such provisions are available in Egypt, and are for sale at a high price to all, both natives and foreigners, who can pay. It is said that their king dreamed that for seven years the earth would not produce enough to sustain life, and thus warned in advance, they stored up wheat to sell to their own people and to foreigners. Therefore, sir, we shall be on our way if first you will give us your blessing to protect us from all danger.

YA'AKOB. Binyamin will stay here with me, and you will buy enough food for his children. I dare not be without him. I couldn't bear to have you all away, and besides, I am afraid some disaster or danger may befall him. He is the only son I have left of his mother, since I lost his brother, and he is my only consolation for that loss.

YEHUDAH. Although your words offend us, as an indication of how little you trust his own brothers, for your sake and for that of his many little children, just this once we will agree that he stay here with you and play with the children. Farewell, sir; we must go to prepare our things.

YA'AKOB. May God guide you, my sons.

Exeunt. Enter Yoseph and his chamberlain [and other servants].

YOSEPH. Take wheat from the granaries of Ra'amses to provide for the court.

CHAMBERLAIN. Sir, our citizens are crying out to the king for bread, and he has sent them to you.

YOSEPH. If that is the king's command, supply all of them with grain. Sell it to them on a first-come, first-served basis, provided they pay cash.

CHAMBERLAIN. What would you have me charge them?

YOSEPH. Two silver *reales* per bushel.

CHAMBERLAIN. That's not expensive.

YOSEPH. No, it is very cheap. But in such times of famine I wish to be kind.

CHAMBERLAIN. You are the light of Egypt, for that is truly great virtue toward an afflicted people.

YOSEPH. Be sure to maintain the proper order in your distribution, attending first to the first one who gets here. If any foreigners come from other nations, don't give them provisions until you have first consulted me, for they might be our enemies who would take advantage of these circumstances to betray us.

CHAMBERLAIN. Sir, I shall obey your command.

YOSEPH. Go then, and courteously see to the people's needs.

Exit the Chamberlain; enter Menasheh.

MENASHEH. Sir, my mother sent me here to ask for your blessing, for I have finished my lessons.

YOSEPH. Come here, dear child. How are you? Are your studies going well?

MENASHEH. Yes, sir, I have learned to write the consonants and point them well, and also to conjugate the verbs. My brother Ephraim has not come, my lord and father. He is always in his mother's arms.

YOSEPH. He is still a child; he has plenty of time yet. May heaven make you both worthy of the goods and favors that it promised your grandfather.

MENASHEH. Oh, father, won't you tell me where my grandfather is?

YOSEPH. He is far away, my dear. One day you will see him.

MENASHEH. Please send me there, sir, so that I can see him.

YOSEPH. You are still a child.

MENASHEH. Yes, but I have your courage, which inspires me to attempt great things for my age.

YOSEPH. My son, I am very happy to see such manly qualities in you.

Enter the Chamberlain.

CHAMBERLAIN. Sir, in keeping with your orders that I should let you know for your own private reasons if anyone came here from afar, I have come to tell you that ten men have just arrived. They are all as tall as pine trees, of wondrous stature, for the shortest of them is a giant. They say they have come for bread, for there is famine in their land. It is up to you to decide whether they come in peace or war.

YOSEPH. Bring them here. We will test them and find out who they are.

CHAMBERLAIN. I'm going.

YOSEPH. My heart beats faster with this news.

Enter Yoseph's brothers; they kneel before him.

YEHUDAH. Sir, the harshness of these cruel times brings us unto your mercy to save our lives. The famine has now spread throughout the world. We have heard that you provide bread for all, sustaining many a wretched soul.

YOSEPH. Where are you from?

YEHUDAH. My lord, we have come from Kinaʿan to buy bread from you. We trust you will sell it to us, for the land is needy, and famine is consuming all we have.

YOSEPH. So you say that's why you've come? Still, I suspect that all of you are spies, come to scout out the weakness of the land and to attack us. *[Aside:]* These are my brothers, but they don't recognize me. Now I can easily see what is in their hearts.

RE'UVEN. Sir, please don't think such dreadful things of us, for we are well known.

YOSEPH. But I know you still better. You have come in this disguise to examine our walls and towers.

RE'UVEN. You are very much mistaken. We are all brothers, and sons of an honorable man, and we have all come at his behest to buy grain.

YOSEPH. You are all brothers? That's very hard to believe.

RE'UVEN. Well, sir, I would have you know that there were two more besides us.

YOSEPH. Two of you are still coming?

RE'UVEN. One of them is lost, sir, and the other has stayed at home with his father.

YOSEPH. Those very words convince me you are lying. So you don't want to tell me the truth; you'd rather die. Still, you will speak the truth, or I shall hang all of you.

RE'UVEN. Sir, what do you want from us?

YOSEPH. Admit that you are lying and that you have made up all you've said about that other brother, or those other two.

RE'UVEN. I swear by my very life that it is true! One of our brothers died, and the other is at home with our father now.

YOSEPH. Anyone could see that's all a lie. First you said he was lost, and now you say he's dead.

SHIM'ON. That's just a manner of speaking in our land. The word can mean either thing.

YOSEPH. You are lying. This is all false, by God! I'm no fool, and I can see very well that you are a bully.

SHIM'ON. Sir, please don't be so rude!

YOSEPH. How can I be polite to you, since you killed an innocent man, and now you are trying to fool me by denying it?

RE'UVEN. Someone must have lied to you about us.

YOSEPH. You seem like an honest man. I wish I could forgive the others for your sake; but unfortunately, your pleas, though so well spoken, can't make up for the deeds of these mad, arrogant men. You'll just have to suffer along with the others, since your authority somehow failed to tame all these wild colts.

YEHUDAH. Sir, please don't be angry with us or think us spies.

YOSEPH. Since your hypocrisy was capable of selling a just man, aren't you just trying to pull the wool over my eyes now?

YEHUDAH. I don't understand what you are referring to.

YOSEPH. Well, I understand you very well, and I know that it was all your idea.

LEVI. Please rest assured that no harm will come to you on our account.

YOSEPH. You are very good at making up such lies to deceive an innocent man, and just when he least suspects it, you will pounce upon him and take his very life.

LEVI. You are wrong about all of this; there is no malice in us.

YOSEPH. God knows the truth, and so does some unfortunate man. I think you are envious of the success and confidence another man enjoys. Deceived by envy, you will commit a thousand wicked deeds. But you should know that God will punish both your former and present sins. I shall treat you just as you treated that man. You will pay for your insane ideas in prison. After suffering torture, you shall all be slaves, since you refuse to tell the truth about why you have come here, though I can see it clearly. Take them away from me! Carry them off to jail.

They lead them away.

YOSEPH. *[To the Chamberlain:]* I may have scolded those men, but make sure that they are well cared for and given plenty to eat in prison. I would not be so merciless as to hold them prisoners and deny them nourishment.

CHAMBERLAIN. I understand, and I shall do as you say.

Exeunt. The Chamberlain returns with a lackey.

CHAMBERLAIN. Did you take the prisoners' asses to the stables?

LACKEY. Yes, sir, but I think our master should have tortured all of them.

CHAMBERLAIN. What business is that of yours, you idiot?

LACKEY. I wish my lord had hanged them and let me inherit their asses.

CHAMBERLAIN. What impertinence! And just why would he give them to you?

LACKEY. Because I know how to get along with asses such as those. I understand their language, and they understand me.

CHAMBERLAIN. I've never seen you act so foolishly! You are an ignorant savage; but, since you understand them, go and give straw and barley to their asses.

LACKEY. One of my new buddies has such white hair that I would gladly trade one of my own for him, if that's okay with you.

CHAMBERLAIN. Enough of your nonsense! Go and do as I say.

LACKEY. All right.

CHAMBERLAIN. That's better.

LACKEY. I'll do as you say, but if you hang those friends of mine, don't forget to give me the white ass.

Enter Yoseph.

YOSEPH. Release the prisoners. It is not right for us to treat poor foreigners so cruelly for so long. Bring them here with your own hands.

CHAMBERLAIN. I shall bring them right away.

LACKEY. If you would just torture them, I'm sure they'd all sing like canaries.

YOSEPH. Who asked for your advice? What do you have to do with those men?

LACKEY. I can see in their faces that they are nothing but thieves.

YOSEPH. Too much wine has made you bold.

LACKEY. If you'd give me a little more, I could tell you as many bad things about them as the Jew said about bacon.

Enter the Chamberlain with the prisoners.

YOSEPH. I have not meant to treat you harshly, though your stubbornness deserves a dreadful punishment. However, I too fear God. You can prove that you are telling the truth by bringing me that younger brother of whom you have spoken. I shall give you plenty of food to provide for your households and for the journey back, and you shall return here, bringing me that lad. As I have said, in that way you can prove that you deserve to be believed and allowed into our land as if you were our greatest friends. One of you must remain here as hostage. If you deal righteously with me, he will be fine; but if you stay there and fail to bring the lad here, I'll see that you regret it. I warn you not to return without him.

YEHUDAH. We shall do exactly as you say; but you should know that that lad is the only remaining child of his mother, and that his father cannot live without him. He will not want to give him up, for his love for him is supreme. Therefore I am very worried that it will be difficult to bring the lad here without causing his father great pain.

YOSEPH. If you return here without him, you shall not see my face.

YEHUDAH. Have you no mercy? Can't you see that this is cruel?

YOSEPH. If you deal honestly with me, you need not worry about bringing him here, for I promise to look after him.

YEHUDAH. Yes, but this will cause that old man great suffering and torment.

YOSEPH. There is nothing more to say. I have already told you my intention at least two or three times over.

YEHUDAH. It would be easier to dry up the sea or measure the broad heavens than to argue with you. Still, I am sure that your insistence will cause that old man great sadness, and we can't help being concerned about him.

YOSEPH. Set out with your provisions, which are already prepared for you, and go home without delay. Just remember what I have told you, and farewell.

YEHUDAH. Farewell, sir, and may heaven, which has made you the protector of so many people, prosper you with its divine favor.

Exeunt the brothers.

YOSEPH. *[To the Chamberlain:]* Fill their saddlebags with all the wheat they can carry. Don't worry if they don't have enough money. Put all their money in the mouth of each of their bags, but don't let any of them see you. In due time you will understand why this must be done secretly. Also take very good care of the prisoner who is remaining here, so that he will have no reason to complain he has been mistreated.

CHAMBERLAIN. I have carefully noted all that you have said and will do just as you wish, my lord.

YOSEPH. I have full confidence in your ability.

CHAMBERLAIN. Sir, it is only right that I obey. In everything my will is subject to your command.

Exeunt. Enter Shim'on and the Chamberlain.

CHAMBERLAIN. Brother, don't be upset. You'll have to stay in jail today, but I promise to do everything I can to alleviate your suffering. This spacious drawing room, furnished with every comfort, will be your prison cell; you can see that it is no dungeon. You can go out in the garden and take your pleasure there. The one who orders you waited on like this is surely no cruel man.

SHIM'ON. Sir, I thank you for this kindness with all my heart. I know I don't deserve such goodness and such favors. What pains me most is that your master has chosen me alone of all my brothers to stay here in this prison. I must be very unlucky to be the chosen one.

CHAMBERLAIN. Now don't complain! Imprisonment is not death, especially since this room affords you every comfort.

SHIM'ON. Sir, no comfort can compare with freedom.

CHAMBERLAIN. It would truly show ingratitude both to God and men for you to complain of the good treatment you have received here.

SHIM'ON. I really didn't mean to complain. Rather, I give you a thousand thanks, for I do not deserve such affability.

CHAMBERLAIN. You are welcome. Is there anything you want?

SHIM'ON. No, sir. I should serve you.

CHAMBERLAIN. Do you need any money?

SHIM'ON. May you live a thousand years!

CHAMBERLAIN. I shall be going, then; and I'll give orders that you be treated well.

SHIM'ON. The highest virtue shines in your rare prudence.

Exeunt. Enter Ya'akob and Binyamin.

YA'AKOB. Binyamin, this long delay has worried me and caused me pain.

BINYAMIN. It's probably just because such a multitude had gone there to buy, and they had to wait their turn. Don't be upset, sir, for heaven will watch over them.

YA'AKOB. I can't help worrying, for I am their father, and I love them. My
son, I'll have no peace until I see them.

BINYAMIN. Father, I trust in God they are all well.

YA'AKOB. That's what I'd like to know. If I knew that, their absence wouldn't
bother me, and I wouldn't fret over this delay. But on the one hand we
are running out of food, and the famine is increasing, and the children
weep; and on the other, all these months and days of waiting have increased my anxiety and decreased my hope.

BINYAMIN. That very anxiety makes each day like a year, and thus you only
aggravate your suffering.

Enter the sons.

But here they are now!

RE'UVEN. Give us your feet to kiss, my lord.

YA'AKOB. Oh, sons! How I have suffered from your absence. Welcome! Are
you all well?

RE'UVEN. We are all in good health, father; but distressed and afflicted with
worry.

YA'AKOB. Did you have trouble getting the bread? Did they refuse to give it
to you? Tell me, set my mind at ease.

YEHUDAH. I'll do so, sir, if you will listen.

> Telling you our story
> will just refresh that painful memory,
> which now is blurred,
> a long succession of events unheard,
> at first like magic,
> but too soon turning tragic.
> God smiled on us as we set out that day,
> and in prosperity we made our way,
> amidst a motley crew,
> for famine all the world did then imbue.
> We reached the court,
> and to the viceroy we had resort,
> whose mere presence
> in majesty and beauty, eminence,
> the glorious splendor of his handsome face,
> his grave aspect, his bearing, and his grace,
> his rare goodness,
> seemed more than mortal, truly limitless,
> for in him did inhere,
> yea, in that Egyptian man, the sun's own sphere.
> But then that famous prince

behaved toward us with rude belligerence,
so cruel and so base
that if he had not had an angel's face,
I would have been quite sure
he was a Fury come from hell[40]
or some monster all impure.
His first sally—
for after sighing, forces he did rally—
was to try on for size
the notion that we, all of us, were spies;
if that were not enough,
that we were public thieves and bandits rough,
who had come there
with falsehood and disguise, and that we'd dare
spy out their nudity
and then attack them with impunity.
His fiery tongue
answered with many an insult, many a wrong
when humbly we did try
those unreasonable charges to deny.
The words we spoke were just as clear as day,
attempting our nobility to display,
our high birth stating,
but he did torture us, interrogating,
and then at last
he locked us up. Three days in jail we passed
in irons and chains,
where we endured the most horrendous pains.
His fearsome rage at last he did abate,
perhaps to compensate
our guiltless innocence.
Freed from that jail and into his presence
we came, though still morose,
and this is what that man did then propose:
"For coming to this land
its fortresses to spy,
you all deserve a thousand times to die,
or that I should remand
you to prison, where in chains you'll stand,
sustaining life
on bread and water, suffering great strife;

yet God I fear,
and would not show myself with you severe.
No, I would pity you,
and would believe that what you say is true,
on one condition:
that younger brother whose present position
is at your father's side, who loves him dear,
you must bring here,
for only by that deed
will I be satisfied, and you be freed.
Your beasts now load
with sustenance to take to your abode,
while one of you as hostage remains here
so that no treason from you I shall fear."
He chose Shim'on from all of us that day,
and in a kindly way
bade us farewell, and then from us withdrew.
These are the trials that we have been through.

YA'AKOB. You have left Shim'on in Egypt, Yoseph was devoured by a wild beast, and now you would take Binyamin, who is all that I have left, and leave me here to mourn him. No, you will not live to see that day! I shall not let him out of my sight! I have already endured trials enough. Why did you have to tell him that you had another brother, knowing full well that he was a tyrant? You were insane to do that!

YEHUDAH. Sir, he had inside information, and he made the most detailed inquiries about our family. His demands were so insistent that it was impossible to keep anything from him, even if I had wanted to lie. Who could have guessed that he would ask such strange questions? I had no choice but to give him a straight answer.

YA'AKOB. You were not thinking, and you acted most unwisely. But what can I do? A poor old man must suffer such slings! Indeed I am the only one to suffer, and this is the worst of all.

RE'UVEN. You must give us Binyamin. It is important.

YA'AKOB. Never! I will not risk him as I did his brother.

RE'UVEN. If you will just entrust him to me, I promise you . . .

YA'AKOB. You might as well talk to the wind. You're wasting your breath. Don't wear me out; I can't take any more.

RE'UVEN. I will give you one of my own sons, or all of them. If I should be so unfortunate as to fail to bring him back to you, you can take revenge on them.

YA'AKOB. Your words are senseless, for your sons are mine as well. I know that you mean well, but to argue with an old man like this is terrible.

RE'UVEN. In that case there is no way that we can go back to Egypt.

YA'AKOB. What you are asking is impossible.

RE'UVEN. Very well; but hunger will soon make you forget that love of yours.

Enter Dan.

DAN. I have come to tell you all a very strange thing. When I was going to take our wheat to the mill, I opened up my sack and found my money just inside, those very same silver *reales* I had taken there! Amazed, I went through all your sacks to check, and I found all your money there; there was all the money that we had taken with us!

YA'AKOB. Maybe this was some mistake, and it was left there by accident.

YEHUDAH. My lord and father, don't be upset or angry. I beg you by your life to give heed to two things I have to tell you. I am well aware that a virile heart like yours expects few words and has little patience with excuses. The famine has now grown very severe. The duties and obligations of each of us are clear, for our families have doubled in size. Without Binyamin we cannot return for more provisions, for without him we will not be admitted at court. Confide him to me alone; trust in my noble heart, for I will give my life and my very soul for him if necessary, and I will return him to your embrace, father, though I be cast into a bonfire on burning bulls of bronze. You may consider me eternally guilty and a criminal—as heaven watches over you with its two lights—and never forgive me if I don't bring him back to you, if I fail to bring him here to the very spot where you handed him over to me with this condition. Father, you will just have to be content with these exhortations. If you let yourself be blinded with love, you will regret it later.

YA'AKOB. You press me very hard, but trusting in your noble and honorable behavior and sure that you will do just as you say, I give him to you. I do so with those conditions so that fulfilling this task will bring you heroic renown. To persuade that prince to show mercy, you will take him some fruits of our land, of the very best we have, and also double the money for the grain, for if this was some mistake, it's only right that they should be paid their due. May the God Who has redeemed me from so many vexations grant you His help and grace in the eyes of that man.

Exeunt. Enter Yoseph and the Chamberlain.

CHAMBERLAIN. Many foreigners are coming to seek bread, and the grain in the city is running out.

YOSEPH. You may open the granaries in the nearest villages. Provide all of them with grain, as long as they have money. Let no one go away unsatisfied; there will be enough for all, for God provides for all and is merciful to all.

CHAMBERLAIN. Many have run out of money and are bringing gold and silver jewelry.

YOSEPH. I am sorry to hear that, but we have no choice but to take it. It is the king's treasury, and I must administer it. To do otherwise would be unjust.

[Enter a lackey.]

LACKEY. Sir, those giants who were in prison here have just now returned.

YOSEPH. Is there one more than before?

LACKEY. I counted them by their asses, which are what I like best, and if I counted right, there are ten of them in all.

YOSEPH. Yes, there must be ten of them. Stable their asses, assign them rooms, and prepare a meal, for they are to dine with me tonight.

CHAMBERLAIN. I shall do so.

YOSEPH. Bring me that other brother, for I mean to honor all of them.

Exeunt. Enter the ten brothers with the Chamberlain.

CHAMBERLAIN. Have you all come this time?

RE'UVEN. Yes, sir.

CHAMBERLAIN. The youngest one as well?

RE'UVEN. Here he is.

CHAMBERLAIN. Very well. Wait for me in this room. I am going to get your brother, so that you can see each other, and then you'll know how fond I am of you.

Exit the Chamberlain.

LEVI. This kind reception and this exaggerated courtesy must be meant to camouflage some perverse plan. He must intend to catch us here on account of that money that was returned to us. He must have meant to do that all along. Yes, that must be his plan, and I think it's all an excuse to enslave us and seize our asses.

Enter the Chamberlain with Shim'on.

Sir, when we came down here before, we had no intention of deceiving you, for we have always been honest men. We brought money to pay for our purchases, but when we emptied our sacks and saddlebags, we found those very same *reales* inside them. Perhaps that was a mistake of the man who tied up the bags, and he accidentally put the money back inside. Your servants, noticing this oversight or inadvertence, so as not to have this on our conscience—for we have noble hearts—have brought back double the money, trusting in your mercy.

CHAMBERLAIN. Don't be afraid, for your God and the God of your forefathers, Who has shown you greater favor than He has shown to us, has

dealt kindly with you. Since you are His friends, He hid that money in
your saddlebags, for His hand has never failed to do such favors. I have
your money here. You needn't worry that I'd ask you for it again, for I
have been well paid. Since you have brought your other brother, don't
be afraid, for my master, God preserve him, longs to see him. Tonight
you will dine with him.

RE'UVEN. If you would be so kind, please give us some vessels, for we have
brought some gifts for His Lordship and would like to give them to him.

CHAMBERLAIN. I shall be glad to do so; but you really needn't have bothered,
for your host values your lives more than you do yourselves. Take those
dishes that are on the table and make your preparations right away, for
he will be here soon.

RE'UVEN. We appreciate your kindness. Dan, take out the gifts.

DAN. Here they are, brothers.

RE'UVEN. Put some on every plate, for that way they will be more attractive.
Enter Yoseph.

YOSEPH. Welcome!

RE'UVEN. Sir, your servant our father humbly sends you this gift. Though it
is unworthy of a prince, he sends it with love, begging that you kindly
accept it from our hands. Although the gifts are humble, they are the
produce of our land, and he sends them by my brothers as first fruits and
tribute.

YOSEPH. That father you just mentioned—is he still alive?

RE'UVEN. Yes, sir, and he commends himself to your grace and love.

YOSEPH. Have you brought the lad, as you promised?

RE'UVEN. Although his father sorely misses him, we have brought him here.
He is yours to command, but please show him mercy!

YOSEPH. *[Embracing him.]* May God keep you, my son! *[Aside:]* How can
I control myself?
[He goes inside to weep, and then returns, wiping his eyes.]
Bring bread, and seat each of these men in his proper place according to his
rank, for I intend to honor all of them.
[They lead them to their seats in the order of their age.]

YEHUDAH. How can this be? Who told him our ages or birth dates? They are
seating all of us from the eldest to the youngest in the order of our age.
This is no accident; surely there is some mystery in this.

YOSEPH. Give this gift to the youngest. I want to honor him, for he came
here only at my command, to give me pleasure.

BINYAMIN. I accept this honor from your hand, though I regret that I am all
unworthy of it.

YOSEPH. A toast to your health!

BINYAMIN. Thank you, sir. May heaven protect your life!

YOSEPH. All of you, drink with me, for I consider you my brothers.

YEHUDAH. Indeed, sir, you have treated us like a true brother.

YOSEPH. If you only knew how much I love you, you would say even more. No son of your own father, no matter how good a brother, could love you as I do.

RE'UVEN. We appreciate your kindness.

YOSEPH. Yes, I have indeed decided to treat you like my brothers, though once you were ungrateful to my love.

YEHUDAH. But sir, now you know that we were telling you the truth, for we have brought this lad, and we told you that our other brother was dead.

YOSEPH. Yes, that's the truth. I must acknowledge that you are truthful men. What is the lad's name?

BINYAMIN. Binyamin, your servant.

YOSEPH. Well, Binyamin, accept this plate I offer you, and rest assured that I am as fond of you as if you were my own mother's son. That's no exaggeration, for my lips speak only truth.

BINYAMIN. Sir, how can I ever repay such love, for I owe you my very life?

YOSEPH. Nature commonly performs such miracles among men, uniting two souls that dwell in different bodies, for they come from the same source, and joining their affections in secret ways . . .

CHAMBERLAIN. My lord . . .

YOSEPH. Please serve these gentlemen. They must be noblemen, for otherwise why would they have come from so far away to keep their word to me?

CHAMBERLAIN. Sir, I think they have had enough of the god Bacchus and now would rather rest in the arms of the god Morpheus.

YOSEPH. Then let them go and take a nap. I'll do so too, for it is time. I feel the wine weighing me down, for it is a heavy element.

Exeunt. Enter Yoseph and the Chamberlain.

YOSEPH. Have you attended to those men?

CHAMBERLAIN. Yes, I have sent them on their way.

YOSEPH. Did you do as I advised?

CHAMBERLAIN. Each sack is labeled with their names, so there can be no mistake. The cup is in Binyamin's sack.

YOSEPH. Very well. What you must do now is go after them, taking plenty of people, and catch them by surprise. Insult them, accuse them of insane behavior. Then open their sacks, from the first one to the last, which is where you will find the cup. Arrest Binyamin as a thief and bring him here.

CHAMBERLAIN. Sir, I shall do as you say.

YOSEPH. Then do so without delay.

    Exeunt. Enter the eleven brothers dressed for the road.

YEHUDAH. That governor of Egypt didn't treat us so badly.

RE'UVEN. His image is inscribed on my very soul.

YEHUDAH. There is none equal to him in all the universe for prudence and intelligence, for politeness and kindliness in everything he says.

    Enter the Chamberlain with a crowd of soldiers.

CHAMBERLAIN. Here are the thieves!

YEHUDAH. What is this, sir?

CHAMBERLAIN. What do you think? Your wicked behavior and your clever treason. What horrible ingrates you have been to my master! After he treated you with love and unheard of kindness, who would have thought that you would steal the finest object in his house and table, his own divining cup? I know you have that goblet here with you. You have been ungrateful both to him and to God! This is no laughing matter.

RE'UVEN. Watch what you're saying! Such insults are very cruel to men who have been so loyal both in word and deed. We didn't hide those coins that we found. We brought them back to you, so how could you think we'd steal from one who treated us so well? Now search our sacks. If you find that cup, if we have done such wickedness, don't pardon whomever it may be. If one of us sinned against you and God as a thief, that man shall die, and all the rest of us will be slaves to you and your master forever, as payment for that error. We will serve you from now on as slaves, which is like hell on earth.

CHAMBERLAIN. No, only the thief will be my master's slave to pay for his malice. The rest of you may go on home with God's blessing. Unload the saddlebags, and we will search them carefully, whether you like it or not.

RE'UVEN. These are mortal insults!

CHAMBERLAIN. Let each one open his own bag, and we will look inside.

RE'UVEN. We shall do as you say, though it is a waste of time.

    They search the sacks and find the cup in that of Binyamin.

CHAMBERLAIN. Here it is. Now you cannot claim that you are not guilty.

RE'UVEN. Sir, we are not guilty, though you think you know otherwise.

CHAMBERLAIN. What I know is that the thief must come with me. The rest of you, go home with your provisions.

YEHUDAH. No, sir, we will go back with you.

CHAMBERLAIN. You can do as you like.

YEHUDAH. That we shall, for it wouldn't be right for us to leave our brother.

    Exeunt. Enter Yoseph and Menasheh.

YOSEPH. Those men, your uncles, will be here right away. The bravest of them all is Yehudah. Watch him carefully, and when I scold them, if you see him getting upset, go up beside him and stroke his hair.

Enter the eleven brothers.

YOSEPH. Is this how you repay me or reward me for such signal acts of love and friendship? You were foolish and ungrateful to steal my cup. Yes, you were ill advised. Didn't you realize that I know how to divine and could easily find out who stole my cup? You thought you'd get away with stealing the cup I drink from? I am well aware of all your wickedness and treachery.

RE'UVEN. Sir, please don't wound us with insulting words, for every word that comes out of your mouth is like a lightning bolt. We were born honorable men, and we have upheld the honor of our ancestors, the like of which the world has never seen.

YOSEPH. Shall I tell you who you really are, to show you that I can divine and that I know the wickedness that mars you? Two of you, offended by a certain courtship, destroyed a whole city,[41] seizing the booty and jewels, with no consideration for the innocent people who had changed their religion in order to live with you.[42] And you committed still another ugly deed, another tragic act of wickedness, when you sold one of your own brothers to a barbarous troop of Ishmaelites. Thus betraying your own blood and nature itself, you stained your honor.

SHIM'ON. *[To his brothers:]* How can we defend ourselves against such notorious truths? No doubt, this has befallen us and heaven is now repaying us for the cruelty with which we treated poor Yoseph, when we coldly beheld his misery and suffering.

RE'UVEN. How many times I begged you to give up your insane designs, but you refused to listen, and now his blood cries out for vengeance. Heaven remembers him and will avenge the innocence of his glorious soul.

Yoseph withdraws to his room to weep, and then returns.

YEHUDAH.   I shall make bold
              to speak to you, my inward thoughts unfold.
              No longer be enraged by that foul deed;
              nobly forget all that, and my words heed,
              for you are kind.
              In eminence with Par'oh you're aligned.
              The first request
              that formerly to us you have addressed,
              the very first—
              perhaps the worst—
              was asking us with no apparent guile

if we had other brothers. With a smile
we told the truth;
we did indeed have one, we said; forsooth,
he was at home,
with his father, who would not let him roam,
for of his mother only he was left.
His father was bereft
when his poor brother died,
and, grieving for that son, his father cried.
This youngest was his father's pride and joy;
he idolized, adored, the handsome boy.
Yet your command
was that here in your presence he should stand.
We begged you that cruel notion to discard,
but you were stubborn as a diamond's hard.
We knew that if this thing should come to pass—
for he was his looking glass,
his image and the apple of his eye—
if he left him, our father soon would die.
But back unto our father did we tread
and asked him for the boy, as you had said.
Then all unwillingly he let us take
the boy from him; 'twas only for my sake.
And so, to please you,
we brought you Binyamin, although we knew
our father's pain;
without that sun his moon would surely wane.
And now with this incredible falsehood,
though he is good,
our brother you accuse.
Though guiltless, punishment he'll not refuse,
nor yet shall we,
for we are subject to your rule, not free.
Let mercy now pervade
your heart, and please accept this trade:
set free the lad, for he is all the pleasure
of his poor father, and his only treasure.
Gladly will I remain here as your slave;
indeed, your every wish to do I crave
and serve you always and without reprieve,

for I know well that this lad's soul does cleave
unto his father's, and that he exists
for him; in him consists
his life, his health. On him does he rely,
and he will surely die
if his eyes see
the lad left here enslaved, in misery.
I cannot bear
to see my father die of grief and care,
for I know well that his only desire,
his only goal,
was soon to see his son. I can't control
my grief. With shame I am on fire.
My solemn word I gave;
I can't go back and leave him here a slave.
Now please observe
if my words your attention do deserve.
Think well on them, and act in such a way
my father you'll not slay,
for he is all my comfort, my sole care.
If not, by heaven on high I swear . . . !

YOSEPH. Swear what? How dare you in my presence shout?
YEHUDAH. You may be sure you'd rather not find out.
YOSEPH. What makes you bold and brash?
YEHUDAH. Be careful or I shall do something rash,
in spite of danger.
Menasheh approaches him and strokes his hair.
But what is this? This fellow is no stranger.
But I don't care, for what have I to fear?
I think some sorcery he's working here.
YOSEPH. My statecraft
can't manage now to pilot my own craft;
if I'm not careful, this ship will be wrecked.
Servants, get out of here! My wish respect.

I shall conceal myself no longer; to do so would surely offend heaven.
Who do you think it is that speaks to you and causes you such distress?
I am Yoseph, your brother, whom your envy and jealousy sold to those
barbarous merchants in Dothan as a slave. Give me news of my father.
Is he still alive? He must be very old. Come close to me, my brothers; I
would not have you stay so far away. Don't be astonished, speak to me.

Don't be afraid because you sold me here, for you have only been the instrument of that action. Heaven's Creator sent me here for your good, to save you. That famine which God secretly revealed to Par'oh, when I interpreted his dreams, has lasted two years now, and it will yet last five more, during which the fertile earth will not produce a sprout. Its cruelty will bring such extremes of misery that mothers will eat their own children; but God, Who is always merciful, regarding the merits of many—particularly our father and grandfathers—has sent me ahead of you, giving me knowledge and secret understanding to anticipate these times and prepare bread for you. I have stored it up for you and for your children, for my father and his household. Thus it was not you, my brothers, who sent me here; it was the mercy of Him Who reigns forever that put me on this throne and gave me power over Egypt. I am like Par'oh's father; I govern in his place. Now go quickly to my father, whom I await. Tell him of the honors I have acquired here, and tell him to come to me, for with all my soul I long to see him and to supply the needs of these rigorous times. He will dwell in the land of Goshen, which is not far from the court. There it will be easier for him to survive these years, and for me to provide sustenance for him and your families, your servants, and your slaves. Your own eyes have witnessed this honor and this power. My brother Binyamin, who now stands here before me, will tell my father of the love I have for all of you, and how I hold you all within my heart as brothers. I now consider everything that has happened fortunate, because it was all ordained by heaven. Now that you have heard these explanations, come here, for my arms are open to embrace you and to clutch you to my heart and breast.

He embraces his brothers one by one. When Binyamin's turn comes, he weeps and says:

My brother dear, my mother's younger child,
who down on us from heaven now has smiled,
her face in you I see,
putting an end to all my misery,
all my regret,
for now at last I'll manage to forget
the trials, and the pain, and the disgrace
that I have suffered in this foreign place.

BINYAMIN. Brother, I never believed
I'd see you, for I have grieved
too long for you, certain that you were dead,
but now that I see your glory round me spread,

I dare but crave
to stay here with you as your humble slave.

RE'UVEN. Sir, all your brothers in humility[43]
are here prostrate
to beg forgiveness, our sins expurgate.
You we've oppressed.

SHIM'ON. But from your noble breast
forgive us now.

YEHUDAH. Before you we bow,
imploring you to forget all that great wrong,
for you are strong
to forget wickedness
that must be seen as childish foolishness.

YOSEPH. Beloved brothers, all that guilt restrain.
Those pleas so vain
offend my graciousness,
or rather, would ignore my tenderness
of heart, my temperance.
You should have confidence,
brothers, in you no evil do I scan,
for that was all just part of God's own plan
by heaven directed
for your good, that you all might be protected
by me here in this place.
Let no one for what's past now feel disgrace,
but with all diligence,
and all your energy and competence,
bring me my father,[44]
for the famine grows worse with every passing day.
It will be better for him here to stay.

Enter Parʿoh.

PARʿOH. Because I love you well and view your happiness as my own, I have
come here, for I have been told that your brothers have come, and I
wanted to congratulate you on this happy event. Your love has brought
me here. Are these your brothers?

YOSEPH. Yes my lord, they are at your service. Please give them your royal
feet to kiss, and then I shall be all the more indebted to you.

PARʿOH. I shall do no such thing. Instead let me embrace these honored
men, these noble knights, for their nobility is inscribed upon their dig-
nified faces. How is your father?

YEHUDAH. Your servant our father is well but very old.

PAR'OH. Yoseph, send for him, for I swear and promise you to treat him as my own father, since you are like my brother. Send some of my coaches and wagons for him and his family with plenty of provisions. Tell him that here he will lack for nothing, for I offer him the fields of my kingdom for his cattle, and my cities for commerce.

YOSEPH. Bowing before your royal feet, I promise to serve you with all my heart in payment of such supreme kindness.

PAR'OH. Stay here with your brothers. I shall leave it up to you to attend to them.

YOSEPH. My lord, may you reign forever!

Exit Par'oh.

Well have you seen, my brothers, the honor heaven has done me. Now go and tell my father so that he will come here right away. Now I want to give each one of you two changes of clothing, and five for my brother Binyamin. I shall also give him three hundred pesos for the expenses of the trip. Take my father ten well-equipped coaches for his baggage and twenty she-asses for the journey, besides your own asses, which will be loaded up with wheat. I shall await you here with open arms.

YEHUDAH. At last we recognize that your noble breast far exceeds our own. Your divine dreams were sacred prophecies whose effects we now behold, and our envy was a divine mystery through which the Lord did His work, for His secrets are great. Though once we harassed you for our advantage, today, sir, we must call you "harassed but happy," since you have achieved such bliss after such suffering. Egypt will make statues of you for the eternal ages, while we, to whom you give life—for we owe our lives to God and to you—now beg for your embrace to strengthen us as we set out to take news of you back to your father. This will restore him to life, for he has been as good as dead.

YOSEPH. I give you my arms and my clean, pure, true heart, along with my very soul. Hasten to bring my father. Be friendly to each other; may no altercations mar your journey.

YEHUDAH.   Oh harassed but happy man,
                    we give you our solemn vow.
                    Since long hours on the stage
                    you have spent up to now
                    as the hero of this play,
                    it's time for you to rest.
                    If our learned audience
                    still wants to hear the rest,
                    the Third Part is still to come,
                    and I promise it's the best.

PART 3

Characters:

Re'uven	Levi
Ya'akob	Dan
Yehudah	Yoseph
Shim'on	Par'oh

Enter Re'uven, Yehudah, Shim'on, Levi, and Dan.

RE'UVEN. Slow down, brothers! There's no need to hurry, since this time we
are going home in triumph. As we cross these plains, let's discuss what
has occurred. What do you think of all these wonders? A meek and
gentle man at last receives all he deserves and is raised up to the summit. Can you believe this amazing twist of Fortune's wheel? Even when
we think we understand God's secrets, we should not presume or boast
but always remain humble. You have seen very well how you tried to
prevent the fulfillment of his dreams, and yet you all fell at his feet.
Shim'on, now lead us in a song, and we'll all join in. Let's sing about the
wonders we've beheld.

They sing:

> Our sorrow is now over
> and no more we'll sing of sadness,
> no longer weep and wail
> but celebrate our gladness;
> for now our weary hearts
> at last will find surcease.
> Our former suffering
> this pleasure will increase.
> Now let us all sing out,
> for this tale has ended well
> and the very pains of hell
> we will forget tomorrow,
> for now ended is our sorrow.

Enter Ya'akob.

YA'AKOB. What a celebration! What beautiful music! Here come my sons,
and my heart tells me that my suffering is now over. Let it be so! God
grant that all my hellish pains today come to an end! What gorgeous
clothing! So many carriages! What can this be? It looks like a great
caravan of camels and wagons.

YEHUDAH. Father, now banish and dismiss all your anxiety and cares. Announce to all the world that your misfortunes are over. We have good
news for you that will surely make you rejoice. I don't know how to tell
you our good fortune.

YAʿAKOB. For pity's sake, tell me that news. What is the meaning of your
happy song? Please tell me, for I am hanging on your every word. May
I triumphantly enjoy this happiness, since I have suffered so!

YEHUDAH. Father, words will not suffice to tell the wonders. Have you heard?
Yoseph, your dear son for whom you have wept so much, is alive and
well and prosperous in Egypt. No one could properly recount his greatness, for such nobility and goodness exceeds the power of speech.

YAʿAKOB. If only I could see him! I know not whether to believe this news
I've heard. What's more, I don't know how to cope with such great joy.
I am so used to suffering that I have forgotten how to rejoice.

SHIMʿON. Forget all those troubles now, for I bear witness that I have seen
Yoseph safe and sound with these very eyes.

YAʿAKOB. You must be mad! Did you really see him, or was that just a dream?

SHIMʿON. I swear that I have seen him, just as I told you.

LEVI. Father, what will it take to convince you? Lift up your heart, for he is
as mighty as the king. Arouse your senses and proclaim throughout the
town that no one now alive has ever seen such wonders.

YAʿAKOB. I still can't quite believe it. Can such a marvelous thing be true?
Eyes, tell me whether I'm awake or sleeping. Now hurry up and help
me take off this mournful sackcloth. I must be gaily dressed to celebrate
this unalloyed delight.

YEHUDAH. Yoseph implores you to come there right away with your wives
and children and grandchildren. There you can live in peace. He says
that you should sell your bakeries and mills, your vineyards and houses.
Don't be concerned about your property, for he will replace it all a hundred times over.

YAʿAKOB. From your mouth to God's ears! My sons, I long to go and see
him ere I die, that he may bury me if God will.

DAN. Enough of this! Start packing at once, for we must be on our way. *[To
Levi:]* I can't believe you are still standing around, for the others have
already set out.

LEVI. There's no need for further discussion. Let us go! Watch out for strag-
glers, and make sure that no one gets left behind.

[They pick up their bags and begin to move across the stage.]

YAʿAKOB. I am exhausted! My sons, do you want to stop and rest during the
journey? Even if it takes a thousand days, I don't want to pause for a

minute. No matter how hard the journey, it will be worth it. Are we getting close?

YEHUDAH. Father, do you see that fenced area in the distance? We will get to the oasis around noon. From there you can see the land. Oh look, father! Don't get too excited. Do you see the men who have come with him?

YA'AKOB. Yes, but where is my Yoseph? Oh my son! Where are you now, my joy and all my glory? Blessed be He who brought me to your house! All this traveling was well worthwhile. Now I am so blessed that I think it was easy indeed, since I have reached this happiness. Oh Lord God! When have I have ever deserved to find such peace? You are the cause of all of this, and now I can die content.

[Enter Yoseph.]

YOSEPH. My lord and father, crown of my head! Today I've found the greatest happiness that could ever be imagined.

YA'AKOB. Is this possible? Can I believe that I have lived to enjoy your triumph? Who would have thought that I would live to see you? I shall never grow weary of gazing upon your shining face. Now that all my wishes are fulfilled, what more do I want of life?

YOSEPH. Oh my brothers and nephews, I love you so! Oh my wonderful father, the king wants to see your gray head. Indeed, he says that he is dying to meet you.

YA'AKOB. What great nobility! May God protect his highness.

[Enter Par'oh.]

PAR'OH. Welcome, honored old man! May God keep you from all sadness henceforth. I am amazed that you are so old. Exactly how old are you?

YA'AKOB. A hundred and thirty, and I am still young, for I have lived less than my forefathers, but few of those years have been good.

PAR'OH. Oh what a well-lived life! What an admirable face! I consider it a high honor to have a man like you come here to live in my kingdom. Are you well? Though this is a foreign land, consider it your own and live here just as you wish. Time has amply shown how much I owe to Yoseph, for even his high estate is less than he deserves. Who are these men?

YOSEPH. They are my brothers, whose only desire is to serve your greatness.

PAR'OH. And what is their occupation?

YEHUDAH. All our lives we have been known as cattlemen. The famine has brought us here from our home in Kina'an.

PAR'OH. Are you listening, Yoseph? Please make arrangements to provide lodging for these people, assigning a house to every husband and wife, as is fitting. I would like to retain your honorable father by my side, so that he may help me rule my kingdom with his advice, for he is old and wise. In return for his assistance I will give him and your brothers the best things of the land in winter and summertime.

YOSEPH. My lord, I kiss your hands.

PAR'OH. Your family shall live here in this city and possess it as their own, for here I have my throne. Let no one refuse this gift. *[To Ya'akob:]* Now please give me your blessing and go and get some rest.

YA'AKOB. I gratefully accept your kindness. May you live as long as you could want, and may you be prosperous. May the river rise out of its banks at your command. May all obey and fear you from east to west. Sire, I commend myself to you.

PAR'OH. May God give you all that you desire. May you know peace in your old age and be well provided for so long as life endures.

[Exeunt.] Enter Ya'akob and his sons.

YA'AKOB. Now hear these words of prophecy and take them to heart. Fear the true God. That must always come first, even on this last of my days on earth. Keep His covenant, and always be swift to please Him. Wealth, money, and possessions have no importance, provided you do not sin against His Law. Then your soul will be rewarded for serving Him, and even if you be burned alive,[45] you should accept that gladly. Study both night and day without rest, even when you walk by the way.[46] This is what man must do until he dies. Before going to work, he should rejoice to contemplate and pray, praising God for all His benefits, and understanding that God exists, and He is one with absolute power, and there can be no other. He brings comfort to those who sleep in the dust.[47] Always be mindful of the Law that came down from heaven and never changes. He punishes all with a full hand and likewise rewards all good men and women, striking down the wicked without exception. Believe in prophecy and in all the prophets, the greatest of whom was Moses, who spoke precisely of the hidden things. None is like unto him in honor, for he was first among all creatures born in this world.[48] While yet I have possession of my faculties, I want to give you my blessing with the help of God and for your consolation.

> Re'uven,
> may God bless you among men
> with riches and plenty
> and as many daughters and sons
> as there is sand in the sea.
> Shim'on,
> may God to your prayers hearken,

and may your brother Levi,
offer the sacrifice;
before the Lord may he
forever be
His minister upright,
to serve him as is right,
and have no property
to distract him from that rite.
His brothers good
will fill his hands with food,
so that both young and old
his service may behold
and honor his priesthood.
Yehudah I endow
with the gift of sovereignty.
Let all his brothers bow
and obey him constantly.
May he have prosperity
and rule o'er all around,
for in my prophecy
he is a lion crowned.
Yissaskhar
has fortune without par:
to study is his duty.
What distress could mar
a portion of such beauty?
Your dwelling place
will be blessed with every grace—
honey, and bread, and wine—
and no disgrace
will make you from that joy and peace decline.
Zevulun, your portion
is an enviable fortune:
the riches of the sea will come to you,
and all your sons will be born two by two.
Dan, I foresee
that just as fierce will be your enemy
as a scorpion.
From him God set you free
and hear your orison.
Asher

from all will have obedience rare;
to none will he submit.
His land o'er there
will be blessed with oil infinite.
Gad, may you defeat
your enemies and win a victory.
When they are at your feet,
may your renown fill history.
Naphtali, you I greet!
Your land will earn you money
for barley and for wheat,
pomegranates, milk, and honey.
May all your enemies kneel
in terror at your feet;
may you cut them like sharp steel
at the harvest of the wheat!
Yoseph so resplendent,
may you be blessed forever
and have many a descendant.
May your tribes be
as numerous as the fishes in the sea,
which no eye can comprehend,
may they multiply without end.
May your territory
be fruitful, all necessities to supply,
and may its glory
provoke no evil eye.
Binyamin,
may God, with his *yamin*[49]
in our days all these gifts to you expand,
revealing His *yamin*
to all of you. With generous hand
I give to you
the blessing that God's Temple true
be built within your land;
and wealth and comfort may it bring to you.
May He take all of us, as would be best,
back to our holy land,
and there He'll test
who lives by His command.
Yea, very soon

may He grant us that supreme boon,
as His book states,
all of us with our mates,
that gift on us bestow,
but now 'tis time to go.

Finis. Laus Deo.[50]

APPENDIX

Vincent of Beauvais:
Speculum Historiale

CXVIII. From the Story of Asseneth. *Of Asseneth's arrogance.*

In the first of the seven years of plenty Pharaoh sent Joseph out to gather the grain. Joseph came to the region of Heliopolis, whose prince was the priest Putifar, Pharaoh's chief minister and counselor. Putifar's daughter Asseneth was the loveliest maiden in the world and was in every way similar to the daughters of the Hebrews. She was haughty and proud, despising all men, albeit she had never yet seen a man.

There was a great, high tower connected to Putifar's house, the top floor of which contained ten chambers. The first of these was large and handsome, paved with porphyry; the walls were covered with precious stones, and the ceilings were fretted with gold. Within this chamber were Egyptian gods of gold and silver that Asseneth worshiped and feared, and to which she offered daily sacrifices. The second chamber held Asseneth's finery of gold and silver and jewels and precious linens. In the third chamber were all kinds of good food, for it was Asseneth's pantry. The remaining seven chambers were occupied by seven exceedingly beautiful virgins, who waited upon her. No man had ever spoken to them, not even a male child.

There were three windows in Asseneth's chamber. The first one, which was very large, faced the east; the second faced south; and the third faced north. In the room was a golden bed spread with splendid purple cloths woven out of jacinth and purple and byssus and embroidered with gold. Asseneth slept in that bed by herself, and no man had ever sat upon it.

This translation is based on a facsimile of a 1634 edition (Graz, Austria: Akademische Druck-u. Velagsanstalt, 1965), 4:42–44.

A large courtyard encircled the house. Its walls were very high and were built of square stones. In them there were four iron gates, each of which was guarded by eighteen very strong young armed men. On the right side of the courtyard was a fountain of living water from which water flowed down into cisterns that watered all the trees that were planted in that courtyard, which were beautiful and fruitful. Asseneth was as great as Sarah, as lovely as Rebecca, as beautiful as Rachel.

CXIX. Of how Joseph dissuaded her from worshiping idols.

Joseph sent Putifar a message that he would like to stay in his house. Putifar was delighted, and he told his daughter that Joseph, the Strong Man of God, was coming, and that he wanted to give her to him in marriage. She indignantly replied that she wanted to marry the king's son, not some slave. As they were speaking, someone came and announced Joseph's arrival. Asseneth fled up to her penthouse, and Joseph arrived sitting in Pharaoh's own chariot, which was entirely of gold and was drawn by four horses white as snow wearing gilded bridles. Joseph was wearing a very splendid white tunic and a cloak woven of purple and gold. He had a golden crown on his head, and all around the crown were twelve choice stones adorned with twelve golden stars. He had a royal scepter in his hand and an olive branch heavy with fruit. Putifar and his wife went out to meet him, and bowed down to him, and brought him into the courtyard, and the doors of the courtyard were closed. Asseneth saw Joseph and was very upset about what she had said concerning him. She said: "Behold, the sun has come down to us from heaven in his chariot! I did not know that Joseph was the son of God; for what man could beget such beauty, or what woman's womb could bear such light?" Joseph went into Putifar's house, and they washed his feet. And Joseph asked: "Who is that woman who was at the upstairs window? Get her out of this house!" for he was afraid she would bother him as all the other women did, excitedly sending him messages with all sorts of gifts, which he threw away with indignation and insults. But Putifar said: "Lord, that is my daughter who is a virgin and despises all men, albeit she has never before seen a man but me and now you. If you please, let her come and greet you." Thinking that if she despised all men, surely she wouldn't force herself upon him, Joseph said to her father: "If your daughter is a virgin, I love her like my own sister. Have her mother go up and bring her here." When she stood before Joseph, her father said to her: "Greet your brother, who despises all foreign women just as you despise all men." Asseneth said: "Hail, you are blessed by God on high!" Joseph replied:

"May God, Who gives life to everything, bless you." Putifar told his daughter to kiss Joseph, but when she tried to do so, Joseph held out his hand and put it on her chest, saying: "It is not fitting for a man who worships the living God, and eats the bread of life, and drinks from the chalice of incorruption, to be kissed by an alien woman whose mouth kisses deaf and dumb idols, and who eats from their table bread of strangulation, and drinks from their sponges a chalice of insidiousness, concealing the chalice, and anoints herself with inscrutable oil."

CXX. Of Asseneth's penance and angelic consolation.

When Asseneth heard Joseph's words, she was greatly saddened and wept, and Joseph took pity on her and put his hand on her head and blessed her. Asseneth took to her bed and fell ill on account of the fear and joy she felt. She did penance and renounced the gods she had worshiped. Joseph ate and drank, and when he was ready to leave, Putifar asked him to stay for a day. Joseph couldn't, but he promised to return on the eighth day. Asseneth put on a black tunic, which had been her mourning robe when her younger brother had died, and closing the door upon herself, she wept and threw all her idols out the window that faced north. She also cast all her royal food to the dogs, and put ashes on her head and on the floor, and wept bitterly for seven days. At dawn on the eighth day the cocks crowed, and the dogs barked. Asseneth looked out the window that faced east and saw the morning star, and right beside her the heavens were split asunder, and a great light appeared. Seeing that, Asseneth fell upon her face in the ashes. Lo, a man came down from heaven and stood by Asseneth's head and called her by name, but she was too frightened to reply. He called out a second time: "Asseneth, Asseneth!" This time she answered: "Here I am. Tell me, my lord, who are you?" He replied: "I am a prince of the house of God, and the captain of the Lord's host. Arise and stand upon your feet, and I shall speak unto you." And Asseneth raised up her head and beheld a man who was in every way like Joseph, wearing a stole and a crown and holding a royal scepter. His face was like lightning, and his eyes were like the sun's rays, and the hair upon his head was like a flame of fire. Seeing that, Asseneth was struck by fear and fell upon her face, but the angel comforted her and raised her up, saying: "Take off that black hair shirt that you have put on, remove that sackcloth from your loins, put away all your sadness and shake off the ashes from your head, and wash your face and hands with living water, and put on your best clothes and jewelry, and I shall speak unto you." When she had done as he said, she hurried back to the angel, who said unto her: "Take that veil off your head, for you are a virgin. Be comforted and rejoice, virgin Asseneth, for your name is written in the Book of the Living and will never be erased. Behold, from today on you are renewed and given life, and you will eat the bread of blessing and drink the cup of incorruption, for you shall be anointed with holy chrism. Behold, today I have given you Joseph as your spouse, and your name will no more be called Asseneth but Many Refuges, for your penitence, which is the daughter of the Most High and an eternally joyful, laughing, modest virgin, has interceded with the Most High on your behalf. But when Asseneth asked the angel his name, he replied: "My name is written by the finger of God in the Book of the Most High, and everything written in that book is ineffable, and it is not fitting that mortal men should hear or say it."

CXXI.. Of the table and the honeycomb which she set before the angel.

Taking hold of the top of his cloak, Asseneth said: "If I have found grace in your eyes, sit now a little while upon this bed, on which no man has ever sat, and I will prepare a table for you," and the angel replied: "Bring it quickly." And she set bread and fragrant old wine and a new table before him. The angel said: "Bring me a honeycomb too." She was very sad, because she had no honeycomb, but the angel said unto her: "Go into your pantry and you will find a honeycomb on your table." And she found a honeycomb as white as snow and very pure, sweet-smelling honey. And Asseneth said: "Lord, I had no honeycomb, but your holy mouth spoke, and there it was, exuding this fragrance like the breath of your mouth." And the angel smiled at what Asseneth said, and extending his hand, he touched her head saying: "Blessed are you, for you have put away idols and believed in the one God, and blessed are those who come to the Lord in penitence, for they will eat of this honeycomb, which the bees of God's paradise made from the dew of the roses of paradise. All of God's angels eat this, and he who eats it will never die." And extending his hand, he broke off a little piece of the honeycomb and ate it himself, and put the rest in Asseneth's mouth, and he said: "Behold, you have eaten the bread of life and have been anointed with the holy chrism, and from today on your flesh will be renewed, and your bones will be healed, and your strength will never wane, and your youth will not see old age, and your beauty will never decay, and you will be like unto a city built for all those fleeing to the name of God the Almighty King of the ages." And he extended his hand and touched the honeycomb he had broken, and it was whole again as before. Extending his right hand, he touched the top of the honeycomb with his index finger pointing east, drew his finger back towards himself, and stuck it into the edge of the honeycomb that was facing west, and the path of his finger was traced in blood. Then he extended his hand again, and touched the honeycomb with his fingertip on the north side of it and drew his finger over to the south side, and the path of his finger was traced in blood while Asseneth looked on. Then he said: "Look at the honeycomb," and many bees white as snow came out of it, and their wings were as purple as hyacinths. They all flew around Asseneth and made a honeycomb in her hands and ate of it, and Asseneth said to the bees: "Go to your place," and they all flew east towards paradise. The angel said: "Thus will be all the words I have spoken to you today," and the angel held out his hand a third time and touched the honeycomb, and fire sprang up from the table and consumed the honeycomb, but did not touch the table, and the fragrance of the smoke from the honeycomb was exceedingly sweet.

CXXII. Of the blessing of the seven virgins and Asseneth's marriage.

And Asseneth said to the angel: "I have seven virgins who have been brought up with me since infancy, and were born on the same night as I. I will summon them, and you will bless them as you have blessed me." She ordered them summoned, and he blessed them, saying: "May the Lord God Most High bless you, and may you be like seven columns of the City of Refuge." Then he ordered Asseneth to clear the table, and when she had done so, the angel disappeared from her eyes. She turned around and saw what appeared to be a chariot with four horses flying eastward through the sky. Asseneth then begged him to forgive her for having spoken to him so boldly. Hardly had she said this when a young man of Putifar's household announced: "Behold, Joseph, the Strong Man of God, is coming; his servant is already at your door." Asseneth hastened out to meet Joseph, and stood by the stable. When Joseph entered the courtyard, Asseneth greeted him and told him the words the angel had said unto her, and she washed his feet. The very next day Joseph asked Pharaoh to give him Asseneth as his wife, and Pharaoh gave her to him, and put the best crowns he had on their heads, and made them kiss each other. And he gave them a wedding and a great banquet that lasted seven days, and he gave orders that no one do any work during the days of Joseph's nuptials, and he called Joseph the son of God, and Asseneth daughter of the Most High.

Notes

Preface

1. The *Encyclopaedia Judaica,* s.v. "Joseph," notes that by 1560 there were twelve English plays on the subject. Thiebolt Gart's allegorical play *Joseph* (1540) is considered the outstanding German drama of the sixteenth century. The Dutch Catholic playwright Joost van den Vondel wrote three plays on the subject: *Joseph* (1635), *Joseph in Dothan* (1640), and *Joseph in Egypten* (1640); and the eminent jurist and statesman Hugo de Groot (Grotius) devoted the verse tragedy *Sophompaneas* (Eng. trans. 1562) to it.

2. Philadelphia: Jewish Publication Society, 1997.

3. I quote from Rabbi Arragel's paraphrase in the *Biblia de Alba.*

Chapter 1. Miguel de Carvajal: *The Josephine Tragedy*

1. Trinity Sunday is the first Sunday after Pentecost, which is the fiftieth day after Easter (corresponding to the Jewish holiday of Shevuot, which falls forty-nine days after Passover). Corpus Christi is therefore almost nine weeks after Easter, and normally occurs in the month of June.

2. See Melveena McKendrick, *Theatre in Spain, 1490-1700* (Cambridge: Cambridge University Press, 1989), p. 8.

3. Miguel de Carvajal, *Tragedia Josephina,* ed. Joseph Gillet (Princeton: Princeton University Press, 1932).

4. Miguel Romera Navarro, *Historia de la literatura española* (Boston: Heath, 1928), p. 125.

5. McKendrick, *Theatre in Spain,* pp. 34, 40.

6. Carvajal adopts the spelling of this name used in the Vulgate.

7. As far as I have been able to determine, Carvajal was the first to apply this name—a latinized version of the originally Persian Zulaikha or Zaliqa—to Potiphar's wife. The choice was appropriate; the third-century Syrian queen Zenobia was famed for her beauty, intelligence, and ruthlessness. She was believed to have murdered her husband and son by a previous marriage, and she unsuccessfully attempted to conquer Egypt.

323

8. David Gitlitz, "*Conversos* and the Fusion of Worlds in Micael de Carvajal's *Tragedia Josephina*," *Hispanic Review* 40 (1972): 260–61.

9. B. Netanyahu, *Don Isaac Abravanel, Statesman and Philosopher* (Philadelphia: Jewish Publication Society, 1968), p. 33.

10. Yitzhak Baer, *A History of the Jews in Christian Spain* (Philadelphia: Jewish Publication Society, 1966), 2:485 n. 4.

11. Alfonso Toro, *La familia Carvajal* (Mexico City: Editorial Patria, 1944).

12. David Gitlitz, "La actitud cristiano-nueva en 'Las cortes de la muerte'," *Segismundo* 9 (1974): 141–64.

13. The *Sefer ha-Yashar* is a Hebrew epic written in Spain, probably in the second half of the twelfth century. The *Poema de Yosef* is a Judeo-Spanish narrative poem on the life of Joseph probably written around the middle of the fourteenth century. I have included critical studies and translations of both works in my book *Coat of Many Cultures*.

14. Translated from the Latin in Marcel Bataillon, *Erasmo y España,* trans. Antonio Alatorre (Mexico City: Fondo de Cultura Económica, 1966), p. 490.

15. *High Holiday Prayer Book,* ed. Rabbi Morris Silverman (Hartford, Conn.: Prayer Book Press, 1951), p. 383.

16. *Tragedia Josephina,* ed. Gillet, p. 171 n.

17. "Those who smell of garlic must have eaten it."

18. Gitlitz, "*Conversos* and the Fusion of Worlds," 269–70.

19. Significantly, theater was the literary genre most extensively banned in the Valdés *Index.* See Antonio Márquez, *Literatura e Inquisición en España, 1478–1834* (Madrid: Taurus, 1980), pp. 189–200.

20. In Roman mythology the Sibyls were believed to write their prophecies on leaves. Cf. Aeneas's words to the Cumaean Sibyl: "Only one thing I beg. / Do not commit your prophecies to leaves, / Lest they become the mock and sport of the whirl / Of the wind. Speak with your mouth, I beg you!" *Aeneid* 6.74–77. The translation is from Vergil, *The Aeneid,* trans. Patric Dickinson (New York: New American Library, 1961), p. 122. The hundred doors of the Sibyl's shrine are mentioned in verse 81.

21. Dangerous rocks off the coast of Sicily, often personified by poets as sea-monsters.

22. This clause imitates the opening of the Roman historian Sallust's *Catilina.*

23. Second-century Roman biographer of the twelve Caesars.

24. Wis. 1:4.

25. The prologues to each part of the play are spoken by a character known in Spanish as the *faraute* (from an Old German word meaning "herald" or "messenger"). I believe the text suggests that the actor who speaks the prologue should be dressed in a recognizably Jewish costume, and (in performance in English) should use Yiddish intonation and Jewish gestures.

26. "Inasmuch as the adornment of this holy celebration . . ."

27. This is Joseph Gillet's rendering of the garbled original: "Hasticoz hextingert tanque gut liber het lifex lancemann." The transcription is highly tentative, but the meaning might be something like: "You stinker, I'll thank God by His Passion to flay you [alive]. Sleep well then, my countryman."

28. Roughly: "By St. Nulla's [i.e., Nobody's] cunt, may cancer 'cure' you of the drinker's disease [Gillet speculates this is gout] you have now."

29. "By Holy God, go away, my friend, and give me some of that good wine."

30. The Spanish text has "Coco ni Madrigal," well-known wines, named for the cities in Spain where they were produced.

31. Immensely popular and influential romance of chivalry first published in Zaragoza in 1508 by Garci Ordóñez (or Rodríguez) de Montalvo, who claimed to have revised the first three books and authored the fourth book himself.

32. Modernization of a medieval romance of chivalry of the Breton cycle. The earliest known Spanish version dates from 1515.

33. The description of the iconography of Envy is adapted from Cesare Ripa's *Iconologia* (Rome, 1593).

34. David Gitlitz has pointed out that the brothers are immediately identified as Jews by their use of the form "Dio" for God, employed by Spanish Jews rather than the usual "Dios," which they mistakenly considered a plural. See Gitlitz, "*Conversos* and the Fusion of Worlds," p. 262.

35. Judah's words paraphrase the words of the high priest Caiaphas concerning Jesus: "that it was expedient that one man should die for the people" (John 18:14).

36. An obvious reference to Jesus. Unlike his brothers, Reuben uses the Christian form "Dios," thus identifying himself as a "proto-Christian" (Gitlitz, "*Conversos* and the Fusion of Worlds," p. 263).

37. Perhaps a reference to the Jewish laws of Kashruth, which require that the knife used to slaughter an animal be razor-sharp, so as to inflict as little pain as possible.

38. In this scene the wine is made to stand for Joseph's blood, thereby heightening the portrayal of Joseph as a Christ figure (the Communion wine is identified as Christ's blood).

39. The Spanish text attributes this dialogue with the merchants to Gad, but it is clear from the previous passage that it was *Zebulun* who went to fetch the merchants, while Gad stayed behind to pull Joseph out of the well.

40. One suspects that in the original production, the merchants would have been portrayed as Muslims.

41. The biblical account says that Joseph's brothers sold him for *twenty* pieces of silver (Gen. 37:28). Carvajal uses the figure thirty, and has Judah set the price, to establish a closer parallel with Christ's passion. Judas sold Jesus to the chief priests for thirty pieces of silver (Matt. 26:15).

42. Ps. 137:1: "By the rivers of Babylon, There we sat down, yea, we wept, When we remembered Zion."

43. In the original production a real animal was probably slaughtered onstage.

44. Reference to the Jewish custom that mourners sit on the ground.

45. The jackal-headed son of Osiris and Nephtis.

46. Charles V, who was crowned in Bologna on 24 February 1530, and opened the Diet of Augsburg on 20 June 1530.

47. Charles V's brother Ferdinand became King of Romans on 5 January 1531.

48. Suleiman I the Magnificent, who besieged Vienna in 1529 and again in 1532.

49. Sophy, as Gillet points out, was in fact a title used by the kings of Persia.

50. Carvajal dedicated the 1545 edition of the play to Alonso Dávalos y Aquino, marqués del Gasto (1502–46), governor of Milan and captain general of Italy.

51. The Spanish word here is *malsín,* from the Hebrew *malshin* (informer), a word used by the Spanish Jews for traitors who denounced their activities to the Christian authorities.

52. Psalm 117 plus the doxology: "O praise the Lord, all ye nations; Laud him, all ye peoples. For His mercy is great toward us; And the truth of the Lord endureth forever. Glory be to the Father, and to the Son, and to the Holy Ghost. As it was in the beginning, is now, and ever shall be, world without end. Amen."

53. Paraphrase of Ps. 115:17–18: "The dead praise not the Lord . . . , But we will bless the Lord . . . from this time forth and for ever."

54. "Thanks be to God."

55. Apparently a misprint for "Ito bonis habebis" [You will have more of these good {things}"], i.e., Carvajal's works.

56. "Praise be to God, peace to the living, and rest to the dead."

CHAPTER 2. ANONYMOUS: *JOSEPH'S WEDDING*

1. C. Burchard, introduction to his translation of *Joseph and Aseneth,* in *The Old Testament Pseudepigrapha,* ed. James H. Charlesworth (Garden City, N.Y.: Doubleday, 1985), 2:177.

2. Ibid., p. 183.

3. See his critical edition of *Joseph et Aséneth* (Leiden: E. J. Brill, 1968), pp. 117–23.

4. Burchard, introduction to *Joseph and Aseneth,* p. 198.

5. Cataloged as MS 273.

6. Eduardo González Pedroso, ed., *Autos sacramentales desde su origen hasta fines del Siglo XVII* (Madrid: Rivadeneyra, 1865); *Los desposorios de Josef* is on pp. 54–61.

7. Léo Rouanet, ed. *Colección de autos, farsas y coloquios del siglo XVI,* 4 vols. (Barcelona: L'Avenç, 1901). *Los desposorios de Joseph* is in volume 1, pp. 331–57; the notes to the play are in volume 4, pp. 179–82.

8. Melveena McKendrick, *Theatre in Spain, 1400–1700* (Cambridge: Cambridge University Press, 1989), p. 38.

9. J. Sánchez Arjona, ed., *Noticias referentes a los anales del teatro en Sevilla desde Lope de Rueda hasta finales del siglo XVII* (Seville, 1898), p. 55.

10. "Strictly speaking, each [of the two carts used in performance] was regarded as a half-cart *(medio carro),* the two together making up the *carro.* The reason for this is not known, but the most likely explanation is that the original, larger pageant floats were constructed in two sections for ease of storage and manoeuvring and that this subsequently inspired the two-cart performance." McKendrick, *Theatre in Spain,* p. 209 n. 4.

11. Published by Cristóbal Pérez Pastor in the *Revista española,* 15 June 1901, and reproduced in Rouanet, ed., *Colleción,* 4:180–81.

12. Rouanet, ed., *Colección,* 4:181–82.

13. The cast list in the MS has "Un villano" [a peasant], but his character is designated in the text as "bobo" [a fool].

14. This is the most common form of her name in the text; however, the form "Asenec," which is closer to the biblical Aseneth, also occurs several times.

CHAPTER 3. LOPE DE VEGA: *THE TRIALS OF JACOB; OR, SOMETIMES DREAMS COME TRUE*

1. See S. Griswold Morley and Courtney Bruerton, *Cronología de las comedias de Lope de Vega* (Madrid: Gredos, 1968), pp. 398–99.

2. An anonymous fifteenth- or sixteenth-century Morisco romance on the story of Joseph first published by Francisco Guillén Robles in the volume *Leyendas de José, hijo de*

Jacob, y de Alejandro Magno (Zaragoza: Imprenta del Hospicio Provincial, 1888). I have included a critical study and translation of this work in my *Coat of Many Cultures.*

3. Joseph's half-sister Dinah, daughter of Leah, was raped by Shechem, prince of the Hivites, who afterwards sought her hand in marriage (Genesis 34). The reference here establishes the connection between the present play and Lope's earlier *The Rape of Dinah* (1615–22).

4. The sun enters the zodiacal sign of Aries (i.e., the ram) around 21 March, signifying the beginning of spring.

5. The sun enters the sign of Virgo on 23 August, marking the beginning of the harvest time.

6. "Hermes thrice greatest" was the patron and teacher of the occult arts.

7. Mythical serpent slain by Apollo near Delphi.

8. The seven-headed Lernaean Hydra, which Hercules slew with the aid of Iolaus.

9. In his translation of Gen. 42:1 in the *Biblia de Alba,* Rabbi Moses Arragel of Guadalajara notes: "[T]here was a river that went from Egypt to Canaan, and Joseph, sensing that this brothers and father were looking for bread, sent straw with ears of grain, and they reached Canaan. When Jacob saw them, he said: 'By this I see that there is food in Egypt.'" I have included all of Arragel's translation and commentary on the story of Joseph in my book *Coat of Many Cultures.*

10. A pastoral pseudonym often used by Lope.

CHAPTER 4. PEDRO CALDERÓN DE LA BARCA: *SOMETIMES DREAMS COME TRUE*

1. Manuel Durán, "Towards a Psychological Profile of Pedro Calderón de la Barca," in *Approaches to the Theater of Calderón,* ed. Michael McGaha (Lanham, Md.: University Press of America), pp. 17–31.

2. Ibid., p. 25.

3. Gerald Brenan, *The Literature of the Spanish People* (Harmondsworth, U.K.: Penguin Books, 1963), p. 255.

4. Ángel del Río, *Historia de la literatura española* (New York: Holt, Rinehart, and Winston, 1963), 1:445.

5. The other is *Belshazzar's Feast (La cena de Baltasar)* of 1634.

6. Ángel Valbuena Prat, *Historia de la literatura española* (Barcelona: Gustavo Gili, 1964), 2:542.

7. Alexander Parker, *The Allegorical Drama of Calderón* (Oxford: Dolphin Book Company, 1943), p. 47.

8. The Spanish puns on the fact that the word *Di* (Speak) is also the first syllable of Diana's name. The reference to Ana here is to the Queen Mother, Mariana of Austria, widow of Philip IV, who was regent during the minority of her son Carlos II.

9. In Hebrew, Hannah.

10. Court mourning for the death of Philip IV in 1665 had only ended in January 1670 with the performance of Calderón's play *Fieras afemina amor* in honor of the Queen Mother's birthday.

11. The original Spanish has "Enter all."

12. Original: "All and Musicians."

13. Cf. Ps. 137:1–2: "By the rivers of Babylon, / There we sat down, yes, we wept / When we remembered Zion. / Upon the willows thereof / We hanged up our harps."

14. Another name for the aster (Sp. *siempreviva*).

15. S = Sunflower. E = Willow. G = Laurel. V = Violet. N = Narcissus. D = Diana. O = Olympus.

16. Born 11 November 1661, Carlos II was eight years old when this play was performed for the Corpus Christi holiday of 1670.

17. Calderón seems to have confused Dan (the only one of Jacob's twelve sons who doesn't appear in the play) with Manasseh, who was Joseph's firstborn son by Aseneth. This confusion suggests that he did not consult the biblical text while writing the *auto* but instead followed the earlier dramatic versions.

18. It was the custom in Spanish universities for a new student to treat his seniors to a dinner, known as *la patente* (initiation).

19. Genesis 28.

20. The Spanish puns on the double meaning of the homonym *hierros/yerros* (irons/ errors).

21. Reference to the manna with which God fed the Israelites during their wanderings in the desert.

22. Cf. Exod. 13:21: "The Lord went before them in a pillar of cloud by day, to guide them along the way, and in a pillar of fire by night, to give them light. . . ."

23. Reference to the two criminals who were crucified with Christ. Cf. Luke 24:39–43: "And one of the malefactors which were hanged railed on him, saying: If thou be Christ, save thyself and us. But the other answering rebuked him saying, Dost thou not fear God, seeing thou art in the same condemnation? And we indeed justly; for we receive the due reward of our deeds: but this man hath done nothing amiss. And he said unto Jesus: Lord, remember me when thou comest into thy kingdom. And Jesus said unto him, Verily I say unto thee, Today thou shalt be with me in paradise."

24. The lines "Funestas, tristes, impuras / prendas, por mi mal halladas" echo the first line of the famous Sonnet X of Garcilaso de la Vega (1503–36): "¡Oh, dulces prendas, por mi mal halladas . . . !"

25. See Rabbi Arragel's commentary on Gen. 42:1, cited above.

26. In Spanish folklore February was considered a dangerous, unlucky month. In his *Tesoro de la lengua Castellana o Española* Sebastián de Cobarrubias notes: "Colloquially, we call February 'mad,' because the weather is so intemperate and changeable then, for in a single day it rains and the sun shines, it snows, clears up, and the wind blows."

27. The Spanish puns on the word *custodia* ("custody," but also "monstrance"—the vessel in which the consecrated host was exposed for the veneration of the faithful). I have tried to achieve a similar effect with the word "tabernacle" ("a temporary structure" but also "the ornamental locked box in the middle of the altar where the consecrated host is stored").

28. The whole episode is presented as foreshadowing the Last Supper. Benjamin represents first the evangelist John, the "beloved disciple" (John 13:23: "Now there was leaning on Jesus' bosom one of his disciples, whom Jesus loved"), and then Jesus himself.

CHAPTER 5. SOR JUANA INÉS DE LA CRUZ: *JOSEPH'S SCEPTER*

1. Luis Harss, *Sor Juana's Dream* (New York: Lumen Books, 1986), p. 4.

2. George H. Tavard, *Juana Inés de la Cruz and the Theology of Beauty* (Notre Dame, Ind.: University of Notre Dame Press, 1991), p. 7.

3. Ezequiel Chávez, *Ensayo de psicología de Sor Juana Inés de la Cruz* (Barcelona: Araluce, 1931), p. 194.

4. Father Alegre, *Historia de la Compañía de Jesús en Nueva España,* 3:52; cited in Luis González Obregón, *Rebeliones indígenas y precursores de la independencia mexicana en los siglos XVI, XVII, y XVIII* (Mexico City: Ediciones Fuente Cultural, 1952).

5. Octavio Paz, *Sor Juana Inés de la Cruz, o las trampas de la fe* (Barcelona: Seix Barral, 1988), p. 122.

6. Stephanie Merrim, "*Mores Geometricae:* The 'Womanscript' in the Theater of Sor Juana Inés de la Cruz," in *Feminist Perspectives on Sor Juana Inés de la Cruz,* ed. Stephanie Merrim (Detroit: Wayne State University Press, 1991), p. 114.

7. Ibid., p. 113.

8. Ibid., p. 95.

9. Paz, *Sor Juana Inés de la Cruz,* p. 123.

10. Georgina Sabat-Rivers, "A Feminist Reading of Sor Juana's *Dream,*" in Merrim, ed., *Feminist Perspectives on Sor Juana Inés de la Cruz,* p. 157.

11. See Helmut W. Attridge, *The Epistle to the Hebrews: A Commentary on the Epistle to the Hebrews,* ed. Helmut Koester (Philadelphia: Fortress Press, 1989), p. 336.

12. "Above Him stood the seraphim; each one had six wings: with twain he covered his face, and with twain he covered his feet, and with twain he did fly. And one called unto another, and said: Holy, holy, holy is the Lord of hosts: The whole earth is full of His glory" (Isa. 6:2). This "angelic hymn" forms a part of the synagogue liturgy (the *Kedushah*), whence it was adopted as part of the Catholic Mass (the *Sanctus*).

13. "Behold, it is the litter of Solomon; Threescore mighty men are about it, / Of the mighty men of Israel" (Song of Sol. 3:7). By "Solomon the Best" [el mejor Salomón], Sor Juana means Christ; his "bed" is an image of the monstrance in which the Communion Host is venerated.

14. "Have I any pleasure at all that the wicked should die? saith the Lord God; and not rather that he should return from his ways and live?" (Ezek. 18:23).

15. An Indian republic founded in the thirteenth century by a branch of the Nahuatlan people, who probably migrated from the western shores of Lake Texcoco. The people of Tlaxcala were a major source of sacrificial victims, captured by the Aztecs in the so-called *guerras floridas* (flowery wars) for that purpose.

16. "For if a man breaks just one commandment and keeps all the others, he is guilty of breaking all of them" (James 2:10).

17. "I am the bread of life. Your ancestors ate manna in the wilderness, yet they are dead. I am speaking of the bread that comes down from heaven; whoever eats it will never die. I am the living bread that has come down from heaven; if anyone eats this bread, he will live for ever. The bread which I shall give is my own flesh, given for the life of the world" (John 6:48–51).

18. I.e., the outward appearance (accidents) of bread and wine remain, but the substance is transformed into that of Christ's body and blood.

19. Cf. Isa. 14:12–15: "How art thou fallen from heaven, / O day star, son of the morning! How art thou cut down to the ground, / That didst cast lots over the nations! And thou saidst in thy heart: 'I will ascend into heaven, / Above the stars of God / Will I exalt my throne; / And I will sit upon the mount of meeting, / In the uttermost parts of the north; I will ascend above the heights of the clouds; / I will be like the Most High.' Yet thou shalt be brought down to the nether-world, / To the uttermost parts of the pit."

20. Cf. Gen. 3:17–19: "To Adam He said, 'Because you did as your wife said and ate of the tree about which I commanded you, 'You shall not eat it,' Cursed be the ground

because of you; By toil shall you eat of it / All the days of your life: Thorns and thistles shall it sprout for you; / But your food shall be the grasses of the field; / By the sweat of your brow / Shall you get bread to eat, / Until you return to the ground— / For from it you were taken. / For dust you are, / And to dust you shall return."

21. Cf. Gen. 3:14–15: "Then the Lord God said to the serpent, 'Because you did this, / More cursed shall you be / Than all cattle / And all the wild beasts: / On your belly shall you crawl / And dirt shall you eat / All the days of your life. / I will put enmity / Between you and the woman, / And between your offspring and hers; / They shall strike at your head, / And you shall strike at their heel.'"

22. Cf. Gen. 15:1–5: "Some time later, the word of the Lord came to Abram in a vision, saying, 'Fear not, Abram, / I am a shield to you; / Your reward shall be very great.' But Abram said, 'O Lord God, what can You give me, seeing that I shall die childless, and the one in charge of my household is Dammasek Eliezer!' Abram said further, 'Since You have granted me no offspring, my steward will be my heir.' The word of the Lord came to him in reply, 'That one shall not be your heir; none but your very own issue shall be your heir.' He took him outside and said, 'Look toward heaven and count the stars, if you are able to count them.' And He added, 'So shall your offspring be.'" Later, God blessed Abraham again, telling him: "I will bestow My blessing upon you and make your descendants as numerous as the stars in heaven and the sands of the seashore; and your descendants shall seize the gates of their foes. All the nations of the earth shall bless themselves by your descendants . . ." (Gen. 22: 17–18).

23. Cf. Gen. 28:12–22: "[Jacob] had a dream; a stairway was set on the ground and its top reached the sky, and angels of God were going up and down on it. And the Lord was standing beside him and He said, 'I am the Lord, the God of your father Abraham and the God of Isaac: the ground on which you are lying I will give to you and your offspring. Your descendants shall be as the dust of the earth; you shall spread out to the west and to the east, to the north and to the south. All the families of the earth shall bless themselves by you and your descendants. Remember, I am with you: I will protect you wherever you go and will bring you back to this land. I will not leave you until I have done what I promised you.' Jacob awoke from his sleep and said, 'Surely the Lord is present in this place, and I did not know it!' Shaken, he said, 'How awesome is this place! This is none other than the abode of God, and that is the gateway to heaven.' Early in the morning, Jacob took the stone that he had put under his head and set it up as a pillar and poured oil on the top of it. He named that site Bethel; but previously the name of the city had been Luz. Jacob then made a vow, saying, 'If God remains with me, if He protects me on this journey that I am making, and gives me bread to eat and clothing to wear, and if I return safe to my father's house—the Lord shall be my God. And this stone, which I have set up as a pillar, shall be God's abode; and of all that You have given me, I will set aside a tithe for You.'"

24. Herodotus described these wells, which he called "Nilometers." Pliny remarked: "twelve cubits of water, famine . . . ; fourteen, joy . . . ; sixteen, plenty." Daniel-Rops, *Le Peuple de la Bible* (Paris, 1950), pp. 57–58; cited in Adolfo Méndez Plancarte, ed., *Obras completas de Sor Juana Inés de la Cruz* (Mexico City: Fondo de Cultura Económica, 1976), pp. 3:623–24.

25. See Rabbi Arragel's commentary on Gen. 42:1, cited above.

26. Cf. Luke 11:3–4: "Our Father . . . , Give us this day our daily bread."

27. Sor Juana presents Joseph's meal with his eleven brothers as foreshadowing the Last Supper. "Another Benjamin" refers to the evangelist John, known as the "beloved disciple" (cf. John 13:23).

28. I.e., the union of the divine and human natures in Christ.

29. Reference to the apostle Paul, described in Acts 9:15 as "a chosen vessel unto me, to bear my name before the Gentiles, and kings, and the children of Israel."

30. Heb. 11:21: "By faith Jacob, as he was dying, blessed each of Joseph's sons, and bowed in worship over the tip of his staff."

31. Rabbi Moses ben Maimon (1135–1204), better known as Maimonides, the greatest thinker of medieval Spanish Jewry; the reference here is spurious.

32. The apocryphal Wisdom of Solomon 16:21 says of manna that "In this substance you showed your sweetness to your children, and pleasing each one's desire, it changed into the taste he wanted."

33. "And [Elijah] lay down and slept under a broom-tree; and behold, an angel touched him, and said unto him: 'Arise and eat.' And he looked, and behold, there was at his head a cake baked on hot stones, and a cruse of water. And he did eat and drink, and laid him down again" (1 Kings 19:5–6).

34. "So the priest gave [David] holy bread; for there was no bread but the showbread, that was taken from before the Lord, to put hot bread in the day when it was taken away" (1 Sam. 21:7).

CHAPTER 6. ISAAC DE MATATIA ABOAB: *HARASSED BUT HAPPY*

1. See Jane S. Gerber, *The Jews of Spain: A History of the Sephardic Experience* (New York: Free Press, 1992), pp. 141–42.

2. Herbert I. Bloom, *The Economic Activities of the Jews of Amsterdam in the Seventeenth and Eighteenth Centuries* (Williamsport, Pa.: Bayard Press, 1937), p. xv.

3. Ibid., p. 11.

4. As was the custom among Portuguese Jews of his time, Aboab used the preposition *de* (or in Portuguese *do*) as a patronymic, equivalent to the Hebrew *Ben*. The name thus means: Isaac, Son of Matatia Aboab.

5. Daughter of his sister Rachel Aboab and of David Curiel, alias Lope Ramirez.

6. H. P. Salomon, *Portrait of a New Christian: Fernão Alvares Melo,* 1569–1632 (Paris: Fundação Calouste Gulbenkian, 1982), p. 132 n. 27.

7. A modern edition of this work was published by Moses Bensabat Amzalek in Lisbon in 1925.

8. Edited by I. S. Révah in "La relation génealogique d'I. de M. Aboab," *Boletim de bibliografia Luso-Brasileira* 2 (1961): 276–310.

9. The autograph manuscript is now in the Bibliothèque Royale, Brussels (MS II.93).

10. See Alfred Rubens, *A Jewish Iconography* (London: Jewish Museum, 1954), pp. 65–67.

11. Detailed descriptions of these manuscripts can be found in L. Fuks and R. G. Fuks-Mansfeld, *Hebrew and Judaic Manuscripts in Amsterdam Public Collections* (Leiden: E. J. Brill, 1975), p. 162.

12. See Henry V. Besso, *Dramatic Literature of the Sephardic Jews of Amsterdam in the Seventeenth and Eighteenth Centuries* (New York: Hispanic Institute, 1947), p. 32.

13. Ibid., p. 33.

14. Harm den Boer, *La literatura sefardí de Amsterdam* (Alcalá de Henares: Instituto Internacional de Estudios Sefardíes y Andalusíes, 1995), p. 165.

15. In Moshe Lazar, *Joseph and His Brethren: Three Ladino Versions* (Culver City, Calif.: Labyrinthos, 1990), pp. 265–315.

16. Aboab uses seven different metric forms in parts 1 and 2: *romance, octavas reales, décimas, redondillas, silva, lira,* and *quintillas,* all of which were standard in Spanish *comedias* of the period.

17. With only 559 verses, part 1, act 2 is about half the length of a normal act; the whole of part 1 is only 2,354 verses long, and therefore about 20 percent shorter than normal.

18. With 1,400 verses, part 2, act 3, is almost one-and-a-half times the normal length.

19. Aboab's *silvas* are usually arranged in rhyming couplets with an occasional quatrain rhyming ABBA to break up the monotony.

20. It consistently uses the Ladino form *el Dio* (God), while the remainder of the play employs the standard Spanish form *Dios;* the Ladino verb *meldar* (to study) appears, and the Hebrew word *yamin* (right hand) is used twice.

21. Notably Judah's eloquent defense of Benjamin.

22. Translating the title was problematic, since both words in the Spanish original—*perseguido* and *dichoso*—are ambiguous. *Perseguido* can mean both "chased, pursued" (as Joseph is pursued and "sexually harassed" by so many women) and "persecuted" (by his brothers); while *dichoso* can mean anything from "happy" or "fortunate" to "blessed." The title's charm thus lies in its double entendre.

23. Although the title page of the autograph manuscript bears the Jewish date 5446 (= 1686), this sonnet on the following page is dated 1652.

24. Yoseph begins to recount his dream with a slightly abbreviated version of the famous first line of Luis de Góngora's poem *Soledades:* "Era del año la estación florida. . . ."

25. The Sun personified.

26. Ya'akob's words anticipate what Yoseph will tell Par'oh: "As for Pharaoh having the same dream twice, it means that the matter has been determined by God, and that God will soon carry it out" (Gen. 41:32).

27. A mythical animal whose very sight was believed to kill.

28. The proud peacock's dismay on beholding its ugly feet was proverbial in Spanish. When Sancho sets out to assume his post as governor of Barataria, Don Quixote advises him not to be puffed up with pride: "Do this, and the memory of the fact that you once herded pigs in your own country will come to serve as the ugly feet to the tail of your folly" (*D.Q.* 2.42). The translation is from *The Ingenious Gentleman Don Quixote de la Mancha,* trans. Samuel Putnam (New York: Modern Library, 1949), p. 780.

29. This famous proverb ("Los sueños, sueños son") is quoted several times in Calderón's well-known play *La vida es sueño (Life Is a Dream)* and in his *auto sacramental* entitled *Sometimes Dreams Come True.*

30. The opening line of Ya'akob's lament echoes the first line of Garcilaso de la Vega's famous sonnet X: "Oh dulces prendas, por mi mal halladas . . ." ("Oh sweet souvenirs, discovered to my sorrow . . .").

31. Jer. 31:15: "Thus saith the Lord: A voice is heard in Ramah, / Lamentation and bitter weeping, / Rachel weeping for her children; / She refuseth to be comforted for her children, / Because they are not."

32. The sun enters the sign of Aries on 21 March, marking the beginning of spring.

33. Roman goddess who presided over fruit trees.

34. The oldest and wisest of the kings who took part in the Trojan War.

35. The Roman goddess Occasion, or Opportunity, was portrayed as a woman with a lock of hair hanging from her brow. To take advantage of an opportunity was, figuratively, to seize her by the hair.

36.   In the Ptolemaic system the heavens were divided into seven spheres, corresponding to the distance of the seven planets from the earth, which was viewed as the center of the universe: (1) the Moon; (2) Mercury; (3) Venus; (4) the Sun; (5) Mars; (6) Jupiter; (7) Saturn.

37.   This verse does not rhyme in the original Spanish.

38.   The Spanish text mistakenly lists Asenath's father as "Potifar" throughout this scene.

39.   In Scholastic philosophy the potencies of the soul are the intellect and will (some Scholastics include memory as well).

40.   This line does not rhyme in the original Spanish.

41.   Reference to Simeon and Levi's destruction of Shechem in revenge for the rape of their sister Dinah.

42.   This line could be interpreted as a veiled attack on Christian Spaniards, who persecuted and despoiled the Jews even after they had converted to Catholicism.

43.   This line does not rhyme in the original Spanish.

44.   This line does not rhyme in the original Spanish.

45.   Reference to the Inquisition's burning of Judaizers at the stake.

46.   Deut. 6:7: "Impress them upon your children. Recite them when you stay at home and when you are away, when you lie down and when you get up."

47.   Cf. the Amidah (or silent devotion) of the Jewish liturgy: "Thou . . . keepest faith to them that sleep in the dust."

48.   Cf. the Thirteen Principles of the Faith, as stated by Maimonides: "(6) I believe with perfect faith that all the words of the prophets are true; (7) I believe with perfect faith that the prophecy of Moses our teacher, peace be upon him, was true, and that he was the chief of the prophets, both of those that preceded and of those that followed him; (8) I believe with perfect faith that the Law will not be changed, and that there will never be another Law from the Creator, blessed be His name . . . ; (11) I believe with perfect faith that the Creator, blessed be His name, rewards those who keep His commandments and punishes those who transgress them."

49.   Hebrew: "right hand."

50.   Latin: "Praise be to God."

Bibliography

Attridge, Harold W. *The Epistle to the Hebrews: A Commentary on the Epistle to the Hebrews.* Edited by Helmut Koester. Philadelphia: Fortress Press, 1989.

Autos sacramentales desde su origen hasta fines del Siglo XVII. Edited by Eduardo González Pedroso. Biblioteca de Autores Españoles, vol. 58. Madrid: Rivadeneyra, 1865.

Baer, Yitzhak. *A History of the Jews in Christian Spain.* 2 vols. Philadelphia: Jewish Publication Society, 1966.

Bataillon, Marcel. *Erasmo y España.* Translated by Antonio Alatorre. Mexico City: Fondo de Cultura Económica, 1966.

Besso, Henry V. *Dramatic Literature of the Sephardic Jews of Amsterdam in the XVIIth and XVIIIth Centuries.* New York: Hispanic Institute, 1947.

Bloom, Herbert I. *The Economic Activities of the Jews of Amsterdam in the Seventeenth and Eighteenth Centuries.* Williamsport, Pa.: The Bayard Press, 1937.

Boer, Harm den. *La literatura sefardí de Amsterdam.* Alcalá de Henares: Instituto Internacional de Estudios Sefardíes y Andalusíes, 1995.

Brenan, Gerald. *The Literature of the Spanish People.* Harmondsworth, U.K.: Penguin Books, 1963.

Carvajal, Micael de. *Tragedia Josephina.* Edited by Joseph E. Gillet. Princeton: Princeton Univ. Press, 1932.

Cervantes, Miguel de. *The Ingenious Gentleman Don Quixote de la Mancha.* Translated by Samuel Putnam. New York: The Modern Library, 1949.

Chávez, Ezequiel. *Ensayo de psicología de Sor Juana Inés de la Cruz.* Barcelona: Araluce, 1931.

Cobarrubias, Sebastián de. *Tesoro de la lengua Castellana o Española.* Madrid: Ediciones Turner, 1977.

Colección de autos, farsas y coloquios del siglo XVI. Edited by Léo Rouanet. 4 vols. Barcelona: L'Avenç, 1901.

Durán, Manuel. "Towards a Psychological Profile of Pedro Calderón de la Barca." In *Approaches to the Theater of Calderón,* edited by Michael McGaha, 17–31. Lanham, Md.: University Press of America, 1982:

Fuks, L., and R. G. Fuks-Mansfeld. *Hebrew and Judaic Manuscripts in Amsterdam*. Leiden: E. J. Brill, 1975.

Gerber, Jane S. *The Jews of Spain: A History of the Sephardic Experience*. New York: The Free Press, 1992.

Gitlitz, David. "La actitud cristiano-nueva en 'Las cortes de la muerte'." *Segismundo* 9 (1974): 141–64.

———. "*Conversos* and the Fusion of Worlds in Micael de Carvajal's *Tragedia Josephina*." *Hispanic Review* 40 (1972): 260–70.

González Obregón, Luis. *Rebeliones indígenas y precursores de la independencia mexicana en los siglos XVI, XVII, y XVIII*. Mexico City: Ediciones Fuente Cultural, 1952.

High Holiday Prayer Book. Edited by Rabbi Morris Silverman. Hartford, Conn.: Prayer Book Press, 1951.

Joseph and His Brothers: Three Ladino Versions. Edited by Moshe Lazar. Culver City, Calif.: Labyrinthos, 1990.

Joseph et Aséneth. Edited by Marc Philonenko. Leiden: E. J. Brill, 1968.

Juana Inés de la Cruz, Sor. *Obras completas*. Edited by Adolfo Méndez Plancarte. 4 vols. Mexico City: Fondo de Cultura Económica, 1951–57.

———. *Sor Juana's Dream*. Translated by Luis Harss. New York: Lumen Books, 1986.

Leyendas de José, hijo de Jacob, y de Alejandro Magno. Edited by Francisco Guillén Robles. Zaragoza: Imprenta del Hospicio Provincial, 1888.

Márquez, Antonio. *Literatura e Inquisición en España, 1478–1834*. Madrid: Taurus, 1980.

McGaha, Michael. *Coat of Many Cultures: The Story of Joseph in Spanish Literature, 1200–1492*. Philadelphia: Jewish Publication Society, 1997.

McKendrick, Melveena. *Theatre in Spain, 1490–1700*. Cambridge: Cambridge Univ. Press, 1989.

Merrim, Stephanie. "*Mores Geometricae:* The 'Womanscript' in the Theater of Sor Juana Inés de la Cruz." In *Feminist Perspectives on Sor Juana Inés de la Cruz,* edited by Stephanie Merrim, 94–123. Detroit: Wayne State University Press, 1991.

Morley, S. Griswold, and Courtney Bruerton. *Cronología de las comedias de Lope de Vega*. Translated by María Rosa Cortes. Madrid: Gredos, 1968.

Netanyahu, Benzion. *Don Isaac Abravanel, Statesman and Philosopher*. Philadelphia: Jewish Publication Society, 1968.

The Old Testament Pseudepigrapha. Edited by James H. Charlesworth. 2 vols. Garden City, N.Y.: Doubleday, 1985.

Parker, Alexander A. *The Allegorical Drama of Calderón*. Oxford: Dolphin Book Company, 1943.

Paz, Octavio. *Sor Juana Inés de la Cruz, o las trampas de la fe*. Barcelona: Seix Barral, 1988.

Révah, Israel S. "La relation généalogique d'I. de M. Aboab." *Boletim de biliografia Luso-Brasileira* 2 (1961): 276–310.

Río, Ángel del. *Historia de la literatura española*. 2 vols. New York: Holt, Rinehart, and Winston, 1963.

Ripa, Cesare. *Baroque and Rococo Pictorial Imagery: The 1758–60 Hertel Edition of Ripa's "Iconologia."* Translated by Edward A. Maser. New York: Dover, 1971.

Romera Navarro, Miguel. *Historia de la literatura española.* Boston: Heath, 1928.

Rubens, Afred. *A Jewish Iconography.* London: The Jewish Museum, 1954.

Sabat-Rivers, Georgina. "A Feminist Reading of Sor Juana's *Dream.*" In *Feminist Perspectives on Sor Juana Inés de la Cruz,* edited by Stephanie Merrim, 142–61. Detroit: Wayne State University Press, 1991.

Salomon, H. P. *Portrait of a New Christian: Fernao Alvares Melo, 1569–1632.* Paris: Fundação Calouste Gulbenkian, 1982.

Sánchez Arjona, José. *Noticias referentes a los anales del teatro en Sevilla desde Lope de Rueda hasta finales del siglo XVII.* Seville, 1898.

Tavard, George H. *Juana Inés de la Cruz and the Theology of Beauty.* Notre Dame, Ind.: University of Notre Dame Press, 1991.

Toro, Alfonso. *La familia Carvajal.* Mexico City: Editorial Patria, 1944.

Valbuena Prat, Ángel. *Historia de la literatura española.* 3 vols. Barcelona: Gustavo Gili, 1964.

Vega, Lope de. *Obras.* Edited by Marcelino Menéndez Pelayo. 15 vols. Madrid: Real Academia Española, 1890–1913.

Vergil. *The Aeneid.* Translated by Patric Dickson. New York: New American Library, 1961.

Vincent of Beauvais. *Bibliotheca Mundi. Speculum Quadruplex, Naturale, Doctrinale, Morale, Historiale.* 4 vols. Graz, Austria: Akademische Druck-u. Verlagsanstalt, 1965.

Index

337